Norfolk
& Suffolk

timeout.com

Time Out Guides Ltd
Universal House
251 Tottenham Court Road
London W1T 7AB
United Kingdom
Tel: +44 (0)20 7813 3000
Fax: +44 (0)20 7813 6001
Email: guides@timeout.com
www.timeout.com

Published by Time Out Guides Ltd, a wholly owned subsidiary of Time Out Group Ltd.
Time Out and the Time Out logo are trademarks of Time Out Group Ltd.

© **Time Out Group Ltd 2010**

10 9 8 7 6 5 4 3 2

This edition first published in Great Britain in 2010 by Ebury Publishing.
A Random House Group Company
20 Vauxhall Bridge Road, London SW1V 2SA

Random House Australia Pty Ltd 20 Alfred Street, Milsons Point, Sydney, New South Wales 2061, Australia

Random House New Zealand Ltd 18 Poland Road, Glenfield, Auckland 10, New Zealand

Random House South Africa (Pty) Ltd Isle of Houghton, Corner Boundary Road & Carse O'Gowrie,
Houghton 2198, South Africa

Random House UK Limited Reg. No. 954009

Distributed in USA by Publishers Group West
1700 Fourth Street, Berkeley, California 94710

Distributed in Canada by Publishers Group Canada
250A Carlton Street, Toronto, Ontario M5A 2L1

For further distribution details, see www.timeout.com.

ISBN: 9-78184670-185-6

A CIP catalogue record for this book is available from the British Library.

Printed and bound by Firmengruppe APPL, aprinta druck, Wemding, Germany.

The Random House Group Limited supports The Forest Stewardship Council (FSC), the leading international
forest certification organisation. All our titles that are printed on Greenpeace approved FSC certified paper
carry the FSC logo. Our paper procurement policy can be found at www.randomhouse.co.uk/environment.

Time Out carbon-offsets its flights with Trees for Cities (www.treesforcities.org).

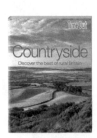

Published by

Time Out Guides Limited
Universal House
251 Tottenham Court Road
London W1T 7AB
Tel +44 (0)20 7813 3000
Fax +44 (0)20 7813 6001
email guides@timeout.com
www.timeout.com

Editorial

Authors *Norfolk* Yolanda Zappaterra, *Suffolk* Emma Perry
Editors Sarah Guy, Cath Phillips
Researchers Alex Brown, Gemma Pritchard, William Crow
Proofreader Mandy Martinez
Indexer Jackie Brind

Managing Director Peter Fiennes
Editorial Director Sarah Guy
Series Editor Cath Phillips
Business Manager Daniel Allen
Editorial Manager Holly Pick
Assistant Management Accountant Ija Krasnikova

Design

Art Director Scott Moore
Art Editor Pinelope Kourmouzoglou
Senior Designer Henry Elphick
Graphic Designers Kei Ishimaru, Nicola Wilson
Advertising Designer Jodi Sher

Picture Desk

Picture Editor Jael Marschner
Deputy Picture Editor Lynn Chambers
Picture Researcher Gemma Walters
Picture Desk Assistant Ben Rowe
Picture Librarian Christina Theisen

Advertising

Commercial Director Mark Phillips
Sales Manager Alison Wallen
Advertising Sales Ben Holt, Jason Trotman
Copy Controller Alison Bourke

Marketing

Sales & Marketing Director, North America & Latin America
Lisa Levinson
Senior Publishing Brand Manager Luthfa Begum
Art Director Anthony Huggins
Circulation & Distribution Manager Dan Collins
Marketing Intern Alana Benton

Production

Group Production Director Mark Lamond
Production Manager Brendan McKeown
Production Controller Damian Bennett

Time Out Group

Director & Founder Tony Elliott
Chief Executive Officer David King
Group Financial Director Paul Rakkar
Group General Manager/Director Nichola Coulthard
Time Out Communications Ltd MD David Pepper
Time Out International Ltd MD Cathy Runciman
Time Out Magazine Ltd Publisher/MD Mark Elliott
Group IT Director Simon Chappell
Marketing & Circulation Director Catherine Demajo

Thanks to Will Fulford-Jones, Anna Norman, Ros Sales, Elizabeth Winding; *Norfolk* Paul Dickson, David Marshall, Paul Murphy; *Suffolk* Liz and Matt Boulton, Alan Clayton, Joanna and Matthew Clayton, Nick Coleman, Henry Elphick, Jo and Adrian Evans, John Fothergill, Emma and Sam Jennings, Dominic, Flora and Polly Maxwell, Deirdre Maxwell Scott, Lara Moore, Tina Miller, Sue Muir, Fran Paffard, Jean and Gerry Parton, Jenny Perry, Brandon Robshaw, Susie Williams, Jo Willacy.

Maps pages 20, 162 Kei Ishimaru.

This product contains mapping from Ordnance Survey with permission of HMSO. © Crown Copyright, all rights reserved. Licence number: 100049681.

Cover photography Travel Library Limited/SuperStock.

Back cover photography Alys Tomlinson; English Heritage Photo Library.

Photography Alys Tomlinson, except: page 13 Malcolm Watson; page 17 Paul Wesley Griggs; pages 21, 24, 25 Leonard Smith; pages 30, 124, 241 English Heritage Photo Library; pages 37 (top), 55 Chris Herring; pages 37, 40, 41, 52, 53, 54, 61, 72 (top, bottom), 183, 184, 192, 195, 279 (bottom) Sam Robbins; page 45 Pamela Farrell; pages 46, 47 RSPB Images; page 59 Peter Brown; pages 72 (middle), 74, 248, 249 Chris Pierre; page 87 (left) James Austin; page 87 (right) Nigel Young; page 90 (top) Caledonian Air Surveys Ltd; page 90 (bottom) Action Images; pages 130, 131 RSPB Images; pages 188, 189 Stephen Wolfenden; page 191 Susie Williams; page 194 Brian Hoffman/Alamy; page 201 Suffolk Coastal District Council; pages 202, 203, 206 Jonathan Perugia; page 247 Daniel Nielson; page 262 Darren Chung; page 286 Douglas Atfield.

The following images were provided by the featured establishments: pages 12, 33, 36, 42, 48, 64, 65, 73, 84, 89, 99, 102, 136, 137, 138, 140, 141, 144, 170, 171, 175, 197, 207, 212, 227, 242, 250, 258, 259, 264, 265, 276, 279 (top), 281, 282, 283, 289, 296.

About the guide

Norfolk & Suffolk is one in a new series of Time Out guides covering Britain. We've used our local knowledge to reveal the best of the region, and while we've included all the big attractions, we've gone beneath the surface to uncover plenty of small or hidden treasures too.

Between them, the two East Anglian counties offer a breathtaking variety of countryside: from open heath to wild marshland, and miles of magnificent coastline, including shingle spits and dune-backed sands. There are walks and cycle trails galore, and a huge number of wildlife and nature reserves. Exploring the towns and villages – medieval Lavenham, smart Burnham Market, independent Woodbridge – brings rewards too. There's a vibrant cultural scene, from the world-renowned Aldeburgh Music Festival and Norwich's Foster-designed Sainsbury Centre to many smaller museums, galleries and arts events, and plenty of historic houses and landscaped gardens. And the pubs, cafés and restaurants just get better every year, with local produce increasingly celebrated.

TELEPHONE NUMBERS

All phone numbers listed in this guide assume that you're ringing from within Britain. If you're calling from elsewhere, dial your international access code, then 44 for the UK; follow that with the phone number, dropping the first zero of the area code.

OPENING TIMES

Part of the charm of the countryside is that it's not like the city. But this means beware opening times; places often close for the winter months, or open only at weekends, and some shops still shut for lunch. If you're eating out, many places still finish serving at 2pm sharp for lunch and at 9pm for dinner. So if you're making a journey, always phone to check. This goes for attractions too, especially outside the summer holiday season. While every effort has been made to ensure the accuracy of the information contained in this guide, the publisher cannot accept any responsibility for errors it may contain.

ADVERTISERS

The recommendations in *Norfolk & Suffolk* are based on the experiences of Time Out's reviewers. No payment or PR invitation has secured inclusion or influenced content. The editors choose which places to include. Advertisers have no influence over content; an advertiser may receive a bad review or no review at all.

FEEDBACK

We hope you enjoy the guide. We always welcome suggestions for places to include in future editions and take note of your criticism of our choices. You can email us at guides@timeout.com.

Contents

Discover the best of Britain's beaches

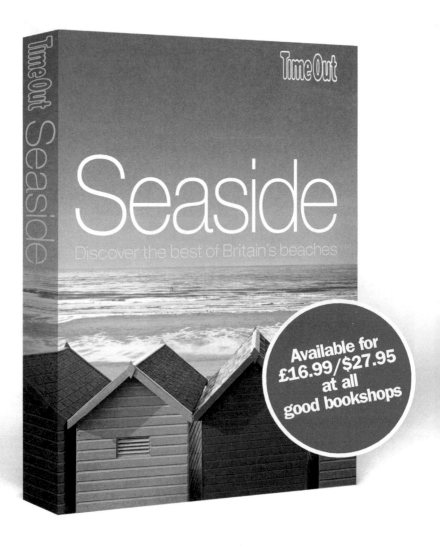

Festivals & Events

Norfolk

FEBRUARY

World Wetlands Day
www.rspb.org.uk, www.broads-authority.gov.uk,
www.norfolkwildlifetrust.org. Date 2 Feb.
Events are held throughout the Broads, Britain's most
important wetland, to celebrate World Wetlands Day,
which marks the signing of the Convention on Wetlands
in 1971. Contact the RSPB, the Broads Authority or the
Norfolk Wildlife Trust for more information.

Breckland International Film Festival
01362 656870, www.breckland.gov.uk/filmfestival.
Date early Feb-early Mar.
Launched in 2010, this small but sweet festival aims
to bring international releases to town and village halls
across rural Breckland. Author Louis de Bernières was
due to open the first festival.

King's Lynn Mart
Date Feb.
A huge funfair in the centre of King's Lynn. *See p29.*

Great Yarmouth Mardi Gras
01493 846550, www.seachangearts.org.uk.
Date Shrove Tue.
Held each year on King Street, this international street
party offers fun, fire, food and festivities.

UEA Spring Literary Festival
01603 508050, www.uea.ac.uk/litfest. Date Feb-May.
The University of East Anglia's annual literary festival
showcases the work of some of Britain's most
distinguished poets and novelists, in a series of
readings and talks throughout the spring. For £42,
a season passport gets you in to all eight events.
The 2010 line-up included Jim Crace, Esther Freud
and Simon Armitage.

MARCH

Aldeburgh Literary Festival
Date early Mar.
A small-scale event with big-name talents. *See p214.*

King's Lynn Fiction & Poetry Festivals
01553 691661, www.lynnlitfests.com. Date Mar
(Fiction), Sept (Poetry).
New and established writing talent. *See p29.*

APRIL

East Anglian Game & Country Fair
01263 735828, www.ukgamefair.co.uk.
Date 3rd weekend Apr.

Variety is the spice of life at this two-day, family-friendly
event, held at the Norfolk Showground in Norwich. Clay
shooting, archery instruction, dog jumping and ferret
racing are all on the agenda, along with trade stalls
and displays in the main arena.

1000 Guineas & 2000 Guineas
0844 579 3010, www.newmarketracecourses.co.uk.
Date late Apr-early May.
Two of the biggest fixtures in Newmarket's calendar
are the 1000 Guineas (for fillies only) and the 2000
Guineas. Hooves thunder down the Rowley Mile, while
excited punters throng the stands. For more on
Newmarket's busy racing calendar, check online.

MAY

Poetry-next-the-Sea Festival
www.poetry-next-the-sea.com. Date 2nd weekend May.
This mini literary festival sees national and international
poets performing alongside East Anglian talents in the
beautiful seaside setting of Wells-next-the-Sea on the
north Norfolk coast.

Norfolk & Norwich Festival
01603 766400, www.nnfestival.org.uk.
Date 1st-3rd week in May.
Norfolk's biggest arts festival, held every May, offers
a vibrant, impressively diverse programme of music,
theatre, dance, circus and visual arts.

Hunstanton Dance Festival
01485 535937, www.princesstheatrehunstanton.co.uk.
Date mid May.
Dance schools from all over the county submit pupils to
enter this one-day competition in Hunstanton, with locals
and visitors paying a small fee to watch.

Houghton International Horse Trials
www.houghtoninternational.co.uk. Date last week May.
See the world's leading riders compete at this four-day
event at Houghton Hall, in north-west Norfolk. Falconry
displays, bouncy castles and other entertainments are
laid on to amuse non-equestrian-minded visitors.

Fairy Fair
01328 710165, www.fairylandtrust.org. Date last
weekend May/Whitsun half-term.
Held at Holt Hall in north Norfolk, the fair is organised
by the Fairyland Trust, which helps families learn about
nature and conservation through workshops and crafts
(potion-mixing and wand-making might feature).

JUNE

Aldeburgh Festival
Date June.
Two culture-packed weeks at Snape Maltings. *See p214.*

Norfolk Food Festival

Three Rivers Race
Date 1st weekend June.
Boats race along the Rivers Ant, Bure and Thurne, in the northern Norfolk Broads. *See p109.*

Royal Norfolk Show
01603 748931, www.royalnorfolkshow.co.uk.
Date late June-early July.
The largest two-day agricultural show in the country, Royal Norfolk offers more than just livestock (although the farming industry is a large part of the equation). Sample some of Norfolk's finest produce in the food hall, have a go at archery in the countryside area or admire the work of around 150 local artists in the exhibition marquee.

Wymondham Music Festival
www.wymfestival.org.uk. Date late June-early July.
Founded in 1996, this annual music festival brings a fortnight of concerts, recitals and workshops to the market town of Wymondham. Highlights include a jazz picnic by the River Tiffy and the town busking day.

Festival Too
07932 114901, www.festivaltoo.co.uk.
Date late June-early July.
Free music festival in King's Lynn. *See p29.*

JULY

British Superbike Championship
0870 950 9000, www.britishsuperbike.com.
Date mid July.
Snetterton Circuit, in Thetford, plays host to a round of the UK's road-racing superbike championship. It's one of the fastest and most exciting stages of the competition, with riders reaching speeds of almost 200mph.

World Snail Racing Championship
01485 600650, www.snailracing.net. Date 3rd Sat July.
The undisputed highlight of Congham Fair, the World Snail Racing Championship is a hotly contested event. Around 200 snails are entered every year; the current record was set in 1995 by a gastropod named Archie, who completed the 13in course in a blistering two minutes.

Worstead Festival
01692 535620, www.worsteadfestival.org.
Date mid July.
The largest village festival in Norfolk, in Worstead, near North Walsham. *See p102.*

King's Lynn Festival
01553 764864, www.kingslynnfestival.org.uk.
Date mid July.
A fortnight-long celebration of music and the arts, with plenty of big-name performers. *See p29.*

Sandringham Flower Show
01485 541451, www.sandringhamflowershow.org.uk.
Date late July.
Attracting more than 22,000 visitors, Sandringham Flower Show is a highlight on the horticultural calendar. There are glorious show gardens, plant displays, stalls and talks; in the main arena, motorcycle stunts, dog and horse displays and a military band keep the crowds entertained. All profits go to charity.

Langham Street Fayre
01328 830696, www.langhamstreetfayre.com.
Date last weekend July alternate years.
A biennial street fair in the village of Langham, north Norfolk. The main street is lined with stalls, raffles, games and fluttering bunting, and festivities culminate with a hog roast and dancing at the Bluebell pub.

AUGUST

Theatre in the Forest
Date Aug.
Rendlesham Forest provides a bucolic, leafy backdrop to the Red Rose Chain's alfresco theatre performances. *See p214.*

British Touring Car Championship
www.btcc.net. Date 1st week Aug.
One of the ten rounds of this fast and furious touring car racing series takes place at Snetterton Circuit in Thetford.

Reepham Summer Festival
www.reephamfestival.co.uk. Date mid Aug.
A diverse array of music, from rock to pop, world music to punk, at this one-day event, plus arts and crafts, street entertainers and plenty of stuff for kids. Reepham is about 12 miles north of Norwich.

Hunstanton Kite Festival & Classic Car Rally
01485 533468, www.hunstanton-rotary.org.uk. Date 3rd week Aug.
Swooping kite displays and hands-on kite-based activities take place in the main ring, while stalls offer crafts and refreshments. Leave time to admire the resplendent line-up of gleaming classic cars and vintage Harley-Davidsons.

Cromer Carnival
www.cromercarnival.co.uk. Date 3rd week Aug.
The week-long shindig in the seaside resort of Cromer, with carnival day on the Wednesday, is one of the biggest carnivals in the county. Events run from fireworks and a fancy dress ball to the much-disputed knobbly knees contest.

Aylsham Show
01263 732432, www.aylshamshow.co.uk. Date bank holiday Mon.
More than 60 years old, the Aylsham Show is a vast, one-day agricultural event, held on the National Trust estate of Blickling Hall. The day's entertainments include showjumping, floral displays, dog agility shows and the children's sack race: in the morning, the more serious business of selecting prize-winning animals – cattle, sheep, goats, horses and ponies – takes place.

Barton Broad Regatta
01362 688727, www.bartonbroadopenregatta.co.uk. Date bank holiday Mon.
A flotilla of yachts take to the water at Barton Broad. This is one of several regattas that take place on the waterways in the Broads each year.

SEPTEMBER

North Norfolk Music Festival
01328 730357, www.northnorfolkmusicfestival.com. Date 1st 2 weeks Sept.
The North Norfolk Music Festival continues to entice top-level classical musicians to come and play in the region. Concerts are held in two churches, in South Creake and Burnham Norton.

King's Lynn Heritage Open Day
www.west-norfolk.gov.uk. Date 2nd weekend Sept.
A chance to see inside buildings that are usually closed to the public. *See p29.*

Norfolk Food Festival
www.norfolkfoodfestival.co.uk. Date 3rd week Sept-early Oct.
The first Norfolk Food Festival, in 2009, proved a great success. Alongside stalls, cookery demonstrations, tastings and competitions, expect more esoteric, village fête-style events – was the tallest jelly competition a flop? Find out by visiting the next festival. Many of the activities centre around Norwich.

Aldeburgh Food & Drink Festival
Date late Sept.
A ten-day feast of epicurean events. *See p214.*

OCTOBER

Norwich Beer Festival
www.norwichcamra.org.uk. Date last week Oct.
More than 200 real ales from Britain's independent breweries are on sale at this week-long festival, alongside 25 types of English cider and perry, and a selection of draught and bottled brews from further afield. It all takes place in the atmospheric medieval surrounds of St Andrew's & Blackfriars' Hall in Norwich.

Aldeburgh Poetry Festival. See p15.

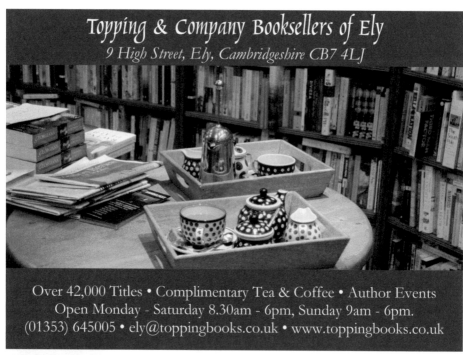

Aldeburgh Poetry Festival
Date early Nov.
Readings, discussions and workshops are on the agenda at this contemporary poetry festival. *See p214.*

Aldeburgh Documentary Festival
Date Nov.
Aldeburgh's documentary festival is a small but tremendously influential affair. *See p214.*

Suffolk

MAY

Wenhaston Vintage Tractor Run
01502 478266, www.wenhaston.net/tractorrun.
Date early May bank holiday Sun.
Hundreds of vintage tractors descend on this small village near Halesworth, and drive around the nearby country lanes. Some drivers attach a trailer, so that their family can come along for the ride. It's quite a sight.

International Suffolk Kite Festival
01359 270524, www.roughamairfield.org.
Date mid May.
Pack a kite and a picnic and prepare to gaze skyward at this two-day event, as numerous colourful contraptions take to the air at Rougham Airfield. Demonstrations feature international kite flyers and power kites, while build-your-own workshops mean no one need go without. There's a fairground and craft marquee too.

South & Heart of Suffolk Walking Festival
www.southandheartofsuffolk.org.uk.
Date mid May-early June.
Walks – some of which are free – are organised throughout the month. It's a great way to get to know some of this vast swathe of countryside, with refreshment stops and routes organised in advance by someone who knows the terrain.

Bury St Edmunds Festival
01284 757630, www.buryfestival.co.uk.
Date 2nd & 3rd weeks May.
Still going strong after a quarter of a century, Bury's big extravaga kicks off to the rousing strains of a Beating the Retreat ceremony, performed by a military band. Over the following fortnight, orchestral, jazz and choral concerts take place at various venues around town, along with comedy events, talks, workshops, theatre and more. The online programme is very user-friendly.

East Anglian Dragon Boat Festival
01780 470718, www.dragonboatfestivals.co.uk/eastanglia. Date 2nd weekend May.
Around 50 dragon boats take to the water at Oulton Broad for this colourful, noisy spectacle. Each boat has a drummer to beat out the strokes as it speeds towards the finishing line, and thousands of spectators line the banks at Nicholas Everett Park. A funfair, kids' activities and food stalls are laid on for a full family day out.

Suffolk Show
01473 707110, www.suffolkshow.co.uk.
Date 1st weekend June.
Held in Trinity Park, just south-east of Ipswich, this country show incorporates a large funfair, craft displays, a children's petting zoo and myriad refreshment stalls. The Grand Parade of livestock showcases the region's farming heritage, while motorcycle displays and an interactive sport zone keep thrill-seekers happy.

Woolpit Festival
01359 240655, www.woolpit-festival.com. Date mid June.
Founded in the 1970s, this arts festival in Woolpit, near Stowmarket, offers a pleasingly varied programme, running from chamber music and comedy to puppet shows and poetry.

Debenham Arts Festival
www.debenhamartsfestival.co.uk. Date late June.
An arts exhibition, street fair, talks from literary personages (Hilary Mantel made an appearance in 2009), drama and 'poets in the pub' sessions – all are on in Debenham in central Suffolk.

Haverhill Festival
01440 7141140, www.haverhillartscentre.co.uk.
Date late June.
Held during the last two weeks of June, this multifaceted festival – with comedy, music, street theatre, children's shows, dance and more – perks up the town of Haverhill no end. It's a community-led celebration, so most of the events are free.

Ip-art Festival
01473 432869, www.ip-art.com.
Date late June-early July.
This two-week arts fiesta brings a whole host of events to Ipswich and the surrounding area. In addition to film, theatre, dance, music and visual art shows, there are readings and workshops from local and national writers.

Spectacular Dancing Tent
01473 639230, www.danceeast.co.uk.
Date late June-early Aug.
Ipswich-based outfit Dance East sent its 'spiegeltent' travelling across East Anglia for the first time in 2009, with a range of classes, workshops and performances held inside it.

JULY

Bungay Summer Festival
www.bungay-suffolk.co.uk. Date 1st 2 weeks July.
Running for more than 20 years, Bungay's summer fiesta brings a variety of small-scale local events – ale and art trails, concerts, theatre shows, exhibitions and plenty of children's activities – to venues around town.

Newmarket Festival
01638 675500, www.newmarketfestival.wordpress. com. Date 1st 2 weeks July.
Like most of the excitement in this town, the festival largely takes place up at the racecourse, with some fringe

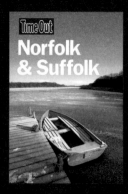

events at venues in town. Carnival floats proceed along the Rowley Mile, and there are special race meets at the July Course. Most events are aimed at local families.

Latitude Festival
www.latitudefestival.co.uk. Date mid July.
Southwold's Latitude is more than a music festival, with a bill that includes theatre, dance, cabaret, comedy and art. Attracting a spirited mix of hot new names and seasoned pros, it's a relatively small-scale, family-friendly affair (with 25,000 festival-goers in 2009). Day tickets are available, so you could incorporate some festival-going into a seaside break.

Dunwich Dynamo
www.southwarkcyclists.org.uk. Date last weekend July.
A convoy of intrepid cyclists sets off from London and pedals 120-odd miles through the night to Dunwich, arriving the next morning. It's a camaraderie- and adrenalin-fuelled ride, with a refreshment stop at Great Waldingfield; the following morning, sleeping cyclists litter Dunwich beach. Book ahead for the coach ride back.

AUGUST

Gig in the Park
www.giginthepark.co.uk. Date 1st weekend Aug.
This small, friendly, three-day music festival is staged in Halesworth's town park. The line-up tends towards big-name old-timers: in 2009, the headliners were Glenn Tilbrook, Chas and Dave and Nine Below Zero.

British Open Crabbing Championship
01502 478712, www.explorewalberswick.co.uk. Date early Aug.
Every year, the coastal village of Walberswick plays host to this crustacean-catching bonanza. Competitors have 90 minutes to catch the weightiest crab, armed with a single crabbing line and their bait of choice (equipment is available on site, for a small charge). An engraved silver salver and £50 goes to the winner, and the money raised funds the village's sea defences.

Lowestoft Air Festival
www.lowestoftairfestival.co.uk. Date 2nd week Aug.
Lowestoft's seafront is transformed, with stalls and rides along the shore, while Red Arrows and Spitfires take to the skies to perform precision manoeuvres – wing walkers and parachutists add to the wow factor.

Beccles Carnival
www.becclescarnival.co.uk. Date Aug bank holiday weekend.
There has been a carnival at Beccles for well over a century. The procession usually takes place on the Sunday; other attractions include a battle of the bands, a funfair, and fireworks on the Monday.

SEPTEMBER

Art on the Prom
01394 671033, www.artontheprom.org. Date 1st weekend Sept.
An outdoor exhibition along the promenade at Felixstowe. Professional and amateur artists sell their work, while the seafront gardens host arty workshops for people of all ages. Musicians and entertainers provide more fun.

Beccles Festival
www.becclesfestival.co.uk. Date mid Sept.
The main venue for this ten-day music festival is stately St Michael's Church, and the concerts are a harmonious blend of jazz, opera and classical offerings.

Fressingfield Music Festival
www.fressingfield.suffolk.gov.uk. Date late Sept.
Launched in 2005, Fressingfield's mini music festival brings some renowned classical musicians to this tiny Suffolk backwater. Concerts are held in the village hall, and St Peter & St Paul's church.

OCTOBER

Beccles Duck Race
www.becclesduckrace.org. Date early Oct.
For one weekend, Beccles is inundated with small plastic ducks. The race raises money for local charities, with the action taking place down at the Quay. Local bands and orchestras provide a lively musical accompaniment, and miscellaneous displays might range from gymnastics to skate stunts.

Halesworth Arts Festival
01986 874264, www.halesworthartsfestival.org.uk. Date 2nd & 3rd weeks Oct.
This fortnight-long cultural festival is organised by the town's arts centre, the Cut. It's usually a strong mix of classical and contemporary music, theatre, art exhibitions and workshops.

NOVEMBER

Ways with Words
01803 867373, www.wayswithwords.co.uk. Date mid Nov.
Novelists, historians, ex-politicians and journalists turn up for this literary festival in Southwold. In 2009, the bill included Shirley Williams, Libby Purves, Brian Keenan and Roy Hattersley. Tickets must be bought in advance.

Latitude Festival

Norfolk

Cromer Pier. See p73.

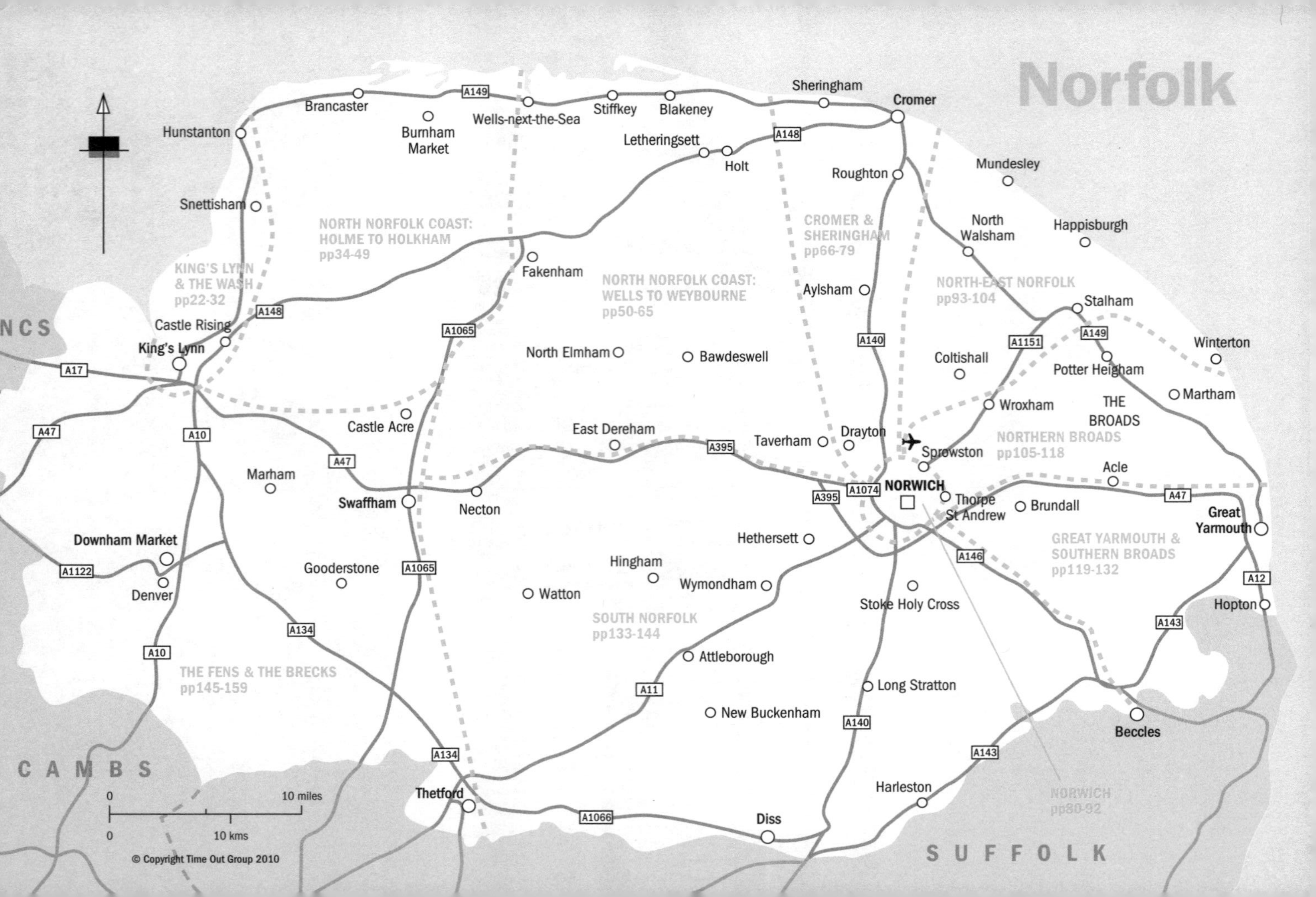

Norfolk

Winterton
Martham
Happisburgh
Stalham
Mundesley
North Walsham
Potter Heigham
THE BROADS
Acle
Great Yarmouth
Hopton
Beccles
Wroxham
Brundall
Colishall
Thorpe St Andrew
Spowston
Cromer
Roughton
Sheringham
Aylsham
Drayton
NORWICH
Stoke Holy Cross
Long Stratton
Harleston
Holt
Letheringsett
Blakeney
Stiffkey
Wells-next-the-Sea
Taverham
Hethersett
New Buckenham
Diss
Bawdeswell
Wymondham
Attleborough
Burnham Market
Fakenham
North Elmham
East Dereham
Hingham
Watton
Brancaster
Hunstanton
Snettisham
Castle Acre
Swaffham
Necton
Gooderstone
Thetford
Castle Rising
King's Lynn
Marham
Downham Market
Denver

NORTH-EAST NORFOLK
pp93-104

NORTHERN BROADS
pp105-118

GREAT YARMOUTH & SOUTHERN BROADS
pp119-132

NORWICH
pp80-92

CROMER & SHERINGHAM
pp66-79

NORTH NORFOLK COAST: WELLS TO WEYBOURNE
pp50-65

SOUTH NORFOLK
pp133-144

NORTH NORFOLK COAST: HOLME TO HOLKHAM
pp34-49

KING'S LYNN & THE WASH
pp22-32

THE FENS & THE BRECKS
pp145-159

SUFFOLK

CAMBS

LINCS

A12
A47
A143
A149
A151
A146
A140
A1074
A395
A11
A1066
A134
A1065
A10
A148
A17
A1122
A149

10 miles
10 kms
© Copyright Time Out Group 2010

Near Hickling Broad. See p105.

Norfolk

King's Lynn & the Wash

West Norfolk gets a raw deal. While near-neighbour north Norfolk lords it over the county with a reputation for glorious beaches, gastronomic delights and an outstanding coastline, the Wash is more likely to be thought of – if it's thought of at all – as a vast mudflat stretching between Norfolk and Lincolnshire. Yet this stretch of coast is magical, from the underrated and unsung charms of King's Lynn and the resort pleasures of Hunstanton ('sunny Hunny') on the coast to the delights of gorgeous villages such as Castle Rising on the 46-mile Peddars Way cross-county trail. There's a huge amount for the visitor willing to forgo metropolitan pleasures for a few days and instead explore a piece of Norfolk that's as timelessly beautiful as anything the north coast has to offer.

KING'S LYNN

This gem of a medieval town rewards the intrepid visitor who's willing to try the handle on a 15th-century panelled door just to see what's on the other side, or to nip down an unlikely looking alley in the hope of finding an unexpected watchtower. Doing the former on Queen Street will reveal Thoresby College, a beautiful 16th-century priests' college sited around a rectangular courtyard with a glorious old Judas tree at its centre; while nipping down King's Staithe Lane and taking a right through a private car park will bring you to the door of Clifton Tower, a five-storey Elizabethan building that is now the private residence of English Heritage head Simon Thurley. You can't get into the college, and the tower is open only sporadically (see www.clifton house.org.uk for details), but they are both part of the joy of wandering around King's Lynn.

It's fitting that such rewarding exploration lies at the heart of a town once home to George Vancouver – who in the 18th century mapped 5,000 miles of North America's west coast (and circumnavigated the island that would later be named in his honour) – and Samuel Gurney Cresswell, the Arctic explorer who was the first man to sail the Northwest Passage. The relaxed charms of this manageable town can easily keep you busy for hours.

Medieval magic

The major historic sites are all centred in the area around Purfleet Quay and South Quay, adjacent to the River Ouse. This is where you'll find the aforementioned buildings, as well as elegant private courtyards and quadrangles – such as Hampton Court (Nelson Street), built in the 14th century as a private merchant's house; Clifton House (Queen Street), with its spiralling barley-sugar mahogany columns; and the Hanse House (St Margaret's Place), once owned by the lucrative and influential Hanse League of German merchants. Just opposite the quay is Saturday Market Place, where, as you might expect, a market is held on Saturdays. It's also the site of one of the loveliest churches in Norfolk, and one of the largest town churches in the country: St Margaret's. A limestone beauty

founded in the 11th century, it sports a fetching three-storey leaning tower dating from the 12th, 13th and 14th centuries.

The medieval wonders continue 100 or so yards to the east of St Margaret's, with the Trinity Guildhall – now the Town Hall – marked by a fetching flint and stone chequerboard fascia. Venture further and you'll reach Greyfriars Tower, just off St James Street, founded by the Franciscans in 1230 and a rare survivor of the Reformation thanks to its importance as a marker guiding ships into port. Carry on to the end of St James Street and you reach the Walks park, the town's historic and extensive public green space that houses the imposing Red Mount Chapel (see p30) in its centre.

Other don't-misses await on the north-western side of town. The classical building just north of Purfleet Quay that would send Prince Charles into paroxysms of delight is the Custom House; designed by local architect Henry Bell as a merchant's exchange house in 1685, it was celebrated by Nikolaus Pevsner as 'one of the most perfect buildings ever built'. It's now home to the excellent tourist office (01553 763044, www.west-norfolk.gov.uk) and a sweet, free maritime museum, so you can explore the perfect doric and ionic pilasters, cupola and gallery to your heart's content. From here, head north on King Street and wander into the King's Lynn Arts Centre (no.29, 01553 764864, www.kingslynnarts.co.uk) to check out its programme of comedy, theatre, music, dance, film and visual arts. Part of it is located in the largest surviving medieval guildhall in Britain.

Head further north still and you'll reach vast Tuesday Market Place, an elegant Georgian square that's curious for the fact that it has no shops on it (barring one small chemist). It once thrummed to the noise of vendors who filled the entire space; now they rarely fill a third of the square, but good farmers' market produce can still be had here on Tuesday and Friday, along with picnic food, jams and Women's Institute goodies. For the rest of the week, it's used as a car park. Head across the square and east along St Nicholas Street to reach St Nicholas's Chapel (see p30), just off St Ann's Street – England's largest parochial chapel.

NORFOLK

The Wash

Once you've taken in all this medieval splendour at close quarters, catch the foot ferry (every 20 minutes from the quayside, 07974 260639) across the Ouse to admire the town's spires, towers and wharfs from the start of the Fen Rivers Way at West Lynn. A short walk from here brings you to St Peter's Church, famed for its rare medieval seven-sacraments font.

Adults might like a nose around the Old Granary (01553 775509, closed Sun) on King's Staithe Lane. This 'centre for antiques and collectables' is a warren of rooms stuffed with everything from gigantic architectural ironmongery to 1970s hippie-chic clothing and tableware – all at surprisingly good prices. Kids will definitely prefer a visit to Queenie's (122 High Street, 01553 766622, www.queeniessweetshop.co.uk, closed Sun), an old-fashioned sweet shop filled with 300 jars of sugary treats from yesterday's childhoods. The website lists all the sweets for sale in the shop.

A wealth of self-guided walks that help you to explore this lovely town with ease are available from the tourist office. Better still, enrol on a guided walk (see p26). The volunteer guides will bring medieval history alive for you – as well as opening all those doors and nipping down those alleyways you might otherwise have missed, unless your name's Vancouver.

Where to eat & drink

Many of King's Lynn's eating options are in attractive spots. The Bank House Hotel (see p26) holds pride of place, looking on to both the Ouse and Purfleet Quay; it's worth making a detour to sample its Modern British cuisine. Riverside (27 King Street, 01553 773134), located in a timbered building behind the Arts Centre with views over the Ouse, is a pleasant, upmarket restaurant that's particularly good for snacks and lunch, as is the dark and atmospheric Crofters Coffeehouse inside the arts centre itself.

The Green Quay café (01553 818500, www. thegreenquay.co.uk), housed in a converted Hanseatic warehouse on South Quay, does hearty salads made with local ham and cheese, while the Corn Exchange (01553 764864, www.kings lynncornexchange.co.uk) on Tuesday Market Place offers a decent lunch in a light-filled venue. And for real open space, stock up on picnic fodder at Norbury's Fine Foods (20-21 Tower Street, 01553 762804, closed Sun) and head to the nearby Walks park.

Bradleys
10 South Quay, PE30 5DT (01553 819888, www.bradleysbytheriver.co.uk). Lunch served noon-2.15pm daily. Dinner served 6.30-9pm Mon-Sat.
In a charming spot at the end of South Quay, facing the water to West Lynn, sits Bradleys: a quaint wine bar and restaurant in a former Georgian merchant's house. The ground-floor wine bar has a riverside terrace, and a lift clunks up to the first-floor restaurant, a lovely Georgian-style room complete with crystal chandeliers, quality cutlery and heavy drapes – a nice change from the ubiquitous tan, cream and black tones of too many 'boutique' restaurants.

Fillet of sea bass on braised fennel and celeriac with dry vermouth, and English sirloin steak with cherry tomatoes, flat mushrooms and hand-cut chips are typical dishes.

Luigi's

11 Saturday Market Place, PE30 5DQ (01553 771483, www.loveluigis.com). Lunch served 11am-2pm, dinner served 6.30-9pm Tue-Sat.
New Mediterranean with an eye to old Norfolk sums up this infamous space (infamous for being the former site of Rococo/Maggie's, which featured on *Ramsay's Kitchen Nightmares*, but still went under). Expect the likes of pork belly with black pudding, sea bass with pickled fennel, and linguine vongole with clams, tiger prawns and crab. The rooftop terrace is a pleasant spot for an aperitif.

Where to stay

Small independent hotels and B&Bs abound in King's Lynn, offering varying degrees of comfort, and prices that reflect the variety. The rambling Victorian Fairlight Lodge (79 Goodwins Road, 01553 762234, www.fairlightlodge.co.uk), a little way away from the old town's hustle and bustle,

has spacious, light-filled rooms at good prices. The Grange Hotel (Willow Park, South Wootton Lane, 01553 673777, www.thegrangehotelkingslynn. co.uk) is a more traditional establishment, as is the Maranatha Guest House (115-117 Gaywood Road, 01553 774596, www.maranathaguesthouse.co.uk); both offer good value.

Bank House Hotel ★

King's Staithe Square, PE30 1RD (01553 660492, www.thebankhouse.co.uk). Rates £100-£120 double incl breakfast.
This handsome 18th-century townhouse and former bank in the heart of historic King's Lynn faces across the Purfleet towards the Custom House on one side and the Ouse on the other. It has an appealing riverside terrace as well as a bar, brasserie and dining room that are intimate without being intimidating, and serve probably the best food in King's Lynn. Owner Jeanette Goodrich has designed 11 guest rooms with lovely fabrics and old finds that ensure each has its own character; all have very comfortable beds and Wi-Fi. The restaurant does 'gastropub' well: roasted cod with smashed new potatoes and cherry tomatoes was hearty and perfectly cooked. Lunchtimes see more adventurous dishes,

KING'S LYNN

Walking tours

King's Lynn's dedicated Red Badge guides enthusiastically volunteer their services, donating fees to conservation projects in the town. They offer a range of imaginative walking tours, among them the excellent Historic Lynn, charting the development of the town from 1100 to the present day, and Turbus' Town, which explores the 'new' (post-1180!) town and takes in North End, St Nicholas's Chapel and St George's Guildhall. It's not all old stuff, though: find out, for example, which recent Hollywood flop was shot in the town (when it stood in for turn-of-the-century New York). The guides can often get you inside buildings not usually open to the public. To book, call 01553 774297 or enquire at the tourist office.

Alternatively, the tourist office has maps for self-guided walks, such as Hanseatic King's Lynn, charting the town's prestigious and lucrative union with the Hanseatic League, and the Maritime Trail, which takes in wharfs, quays and merchant houses along a two-mile route.

HUNSTANTON & OLD HUNSTANTON

Searles Sea Tours ★

South Beach, Hunstanton, PE36 5BB (01485 534444, www.seatours.co.uk). Tours Mar-Oct 11am-6pm daily. Rates 30mins £7; free-£3.50 reductions. 2hrs £12; free-£6 reductions.
Taking a trip to Seal Island, the sandbanks or along the coast to the lighthouse and striped cliffs of Old Hunstanton is a great way to appreciate the unique coastline and marine life of the Wash. And doing it on the Wash Monster – a landing craft used by US troops in Vietnam – is enormous fun whether you're five or 50. It's just one of the Searles fleet; there's a wide range of regular tours on various vessels.

such as barley broth with haddock and dumplings, or black pudding and fried potatoes with mustard and bacon. And given the town's explorer and maritime heritage, it feels fitting to stay in the house in which Arctic adventurer Captain Samuel Gurney Cresswell died.

Old Rectory

33 Goodwins Road, PE30 5QX (01553 768544, www.theoldrectory-kingslynn.com). Rates £56 double incl breakfast.
A beautiful, rambling Georgian ex-rectory with three modern rooms, all with Wi-Fi, large comfortable beds and lots of tasteful neutral tones.

Stuart House Hotel

35 Goodwins Road, PE30 5QX (01553 772169, www.stuart-house-hotel.co.uk). Rates £89 double.
Just down the road from the Old Rectory, Stuart House has 18 lovely rooms – some dripping with rich brocades and deep vibrant colours, others in contemporary tones with deft and original touches. It's a great place to stay if you're happy to take a stroll across town to reach the sights – though with its own gardens, a restaurant and a CAMRA-listed bar with cosy fire, it would be easy not to venture out at all.

Heading north on the A149 from King's Lynn, the smart suburbs quickly give way to open countryside that positively undulates (who said Norfolk was flat?) – particularly as you near Castle Rising ★, a pretty little village topped by what appears from a distance to be a small hill. On closer inspection, it turns out to be earthworks surrounding the incredibly well-preserved remains of the 12th-century castle (*see p30*), which are a joy to explore. Clambering down the hill, it becomes apparent that there are further delights in the village itself. Simple, elegant St Lawrence's Church, for example, contains 17th-century furniture and some Norman elements (such as the west front and font), and a 15th-century 20-foot cross nearby. And if you manage to find the warden of the Grade I-listed single-storey red-bricked almshouses near the church, there's a good chance you'll be able to see the remarkable interiors of this Jacobean building and maybe even meet one of the inhabitants, the ladies of Trinity Hospital or Bede House, founded by the Earl of Northampton in 1614.

To this day the ladies still adhere to the conditions imposed on the recipients of the Earl's largesse – namely being single, able to read, at least 56 years old and not a 'harlot, scold, drunkard or frequenter of taverns, inns or alehouses'. They still attend church every Sunday wearing their scarlet cloaks and badges of the Earl of Northampton, adding a distinctive black steeple hat to the outfit once a year (on founder's day). Presumably, they stop for a post-church chat at the quaint local café Unique (*see p28*) rather than the Black Horse Inn, the equally quaint village pub.

From Castle Rising, the A149 wends its way past the tiny village of Wolferton – signposted near Sandringham and a must for royalists. Here you can snap the site of the Royal Families Railway Station, which operated from 1862 (when Queen Victoria bought Sandringham Estate as a Norfolk retreat for Edward VII) until the 1960s when it closed. It's fun to imagine all the royals and dignitaries who've stopped here – even Rasputin, apparently. It's now a private residence, but a friendly local might direct you to it. Sandringham Estate itself (*see p30*), where the Queen and Duke of Edinburgh spend Christmas, is open to the public in high season, while adjoining Sandringham Country Park (*see p30*) is open all year.

The next stop of any note is Snettisham ★, a pretty little village with a rambling second-hand bookshop, Torc Books (9 Hall Road, 01485 541188); a couple of excellent eating places – the Rose & Crown (*see p28*) and BYO café the Old Bank (*see p28*); and a gorgeous 14th-century church, St Mary the Virgin – look out for rare flying buttresses on the 175-foot spire. All these make Snettisham a good place for an overnight stay, particularly as it's close to the glorious beachside Snettisham RSPB Nature Reserve (*see p31*) – one of the most important twitchers' sites in the country, and a terrific place for a walk even if you wouldn't know a wading bird from a sparrow.

NORFOLK

Just before Heacham is popular Norfolk Lavender (01485 570384, www.norfolk-lavender.co.uk). 'England's premier lavender farm' is so good at marketing itself – pictures of purple lavender fields stretching to the horizon, for example – that coachloads of visitors stop off here. What they find is a small field of lavender bounded on two sides by main roads, a herb garden, a charmless tearoom and a lot of lavender tat in two shops. But there's more: cross the little wooden bridge (by going through the plant shop) and you'll enter a wondrous space, with a pretty pond, meadow garden, rose garden and woodland walk bordering a delightful rare breeds centre. Chickens predominate, but what chickens – you're unlikely to have seen such breeds before, some with glorious colours, others boasting plumage fabulous enough to make Gypsy Rose Lee green with envy. Wallabees, pigs, goats and more exotic animals also feature – and it's all free.

Heacham itself has few sights, though an interesting memorial to Pocahontas features in St Mary's Church. The Algonquin Indian princess, presented here in a Jacobean hat and neck ruff, had numerous ties to the area, saving the life of King's Lynn man Captain John Smith when she was just 12 years old and marrying John Rolfe of Heacham Hall in Virginia at 19. Sadly, she died after returning with him to England three years later in 1614. From here it's a few short miles to Hunstanton.

Where to eat & drink

The villages along the Wash contain some lovely spots in which to eat and drink, from quaint village pubs such as Castle Rising's Black Horse Inn (01553 631225) to top-class country hotel restaurants such as Congham Hall (see p29), where aperitifs are served with dainty canapés in a cosy lounge full of squishy sofas and chesterfields.

Old Bank

10 Lynn Road, Snettisham, PE31 7LP (01485 544080). Open 10am-2.30pm, 7-9pm Mon, Wed-Fri; 10am-2.30pm, 6.30-9.30pm Sat; noon-4pm Sun. No credit cards.
This small, friendly BYO establishment is a café, coffee shop and bistro rolled into one. Handmade pork sausage butties or breakfast snacks are substantial, sandwiches feature Comer crab and own-cooked ham, hot chocolate is served with fresh cream and chocolate flakes, and dinner features delicious unexpected treats such as appetiser pots of sweet roasted red peppers.

Rose & Crown ★

Old Church Road, Snettisham, PE31 7LX (01485 541382, www.roseandcrownsnettisham.co.uk). Meals served noon-2pm, 6.30-9pm Mon-Thur; noon-2pm, 6.30-9.30pm Fri; noon-2.30pm, 6.30-9.30pm Sat; noon-2.30pm, 6.30-9pm Sun.
This lovely 14th-century inn sprawls beguilingly, with seemingly unending rooms – some elegant dining spaces, others tiny snugs with huge fireplaces that look like they've been there for centuries, complete with locals to match. Three pretty and always busy dining rooms offer an appealing and selective gastropub menu that doesn't get

fancy, instead serving local dishes such as Brancaster crab and Norfolk marsh samphire simply and well. Hearty stalwarts such as steaks and bangers and mash, plus a good selection of fish dishes, should ensure something for everyone, and the desserts are delicious. Upstairs, 16 airy rooms (£90-£110 double incl breakfast) make you feel like you're at the beach, with bright blue and white paintwork and striped throws on the huge beds. Owners Jeanette and Anthony Goodrich also run the Bank House Hotel (see p26) in King's Lynn.

Unique Tea Room & Hat Shop ★

Castle Rising, PE31 6AF (01553 631211). Open 8am-5.30pm daily.
Sited in the former post office, this picturesque tearoom does a roaring trade to visitors who come to see the castle, then stay for a good range of daily specials, lunch and snack items as well as own-made cakes and scones, all served in a pretty interior and at even prettier garden tables. Head upstairs to see the fine hats made by owner Linda Crosby. All the furnishings and accessories displayed downstairs are available to buy at her nearby shop at Castle Farm Barn (01553 631500).

Where to stay

Snettisham's Rose & Crown (see left) is a great place to stay if you like rambling, raucous country inns – fortunately, the raucousness doesn't extend beyond 11pm. North Wootton's Red Cat Hotel (01553 631244, www.redcathotel.com) is equally lively and friendly. Slightly posher is the Victorian

Old Granary. See p24.

NORFOLK

Park House Hotel (01485 543000, www.park househotel.org.uk) on the Sandringham Estate; it has full disabled access and organises tours and group activities.

Appleton Water Tower
Near Sandringham House, PE31 6BB (01628 825925, www.landmarktrust.org.uk). Rates £97-£235 double.
This two-bedroom Landmark Trust property near Sandringham is a glorious structure: a red-brick, octagonal water tower designed by Robert Rawlinson in 1877. Each of the three floors contains just one room, and the building is topped by a water tank and a roof terrace, from which, on a clear day, you can see the Wash.

Congham Hall ★
Lynn Road, Grimston, PE32 1AH (01485 600250, www.conghamhallhotel.co.uk). Rates £125-£390 double incl breakfast.
This beautiful Georgian manor has amusing illusions of grandeur (you can charter a private jet at reception), but the 14 rooms are nicely appointed, the house comfortable and intimate and the grounds lovely. A walk after a very good breakfast reveals an orchard, a pretty herb garden and a wide number of activities: croquet, tennis or golf are all offered, with equipment available at reception. The setting, in 35 acres of tranquil, rolling (well, as rolling as Norfolk gets) countryside is delightful. As befits a country hotel, dinner here is a big deal: lots of modern French/English haute cuisine (jus and foam figure large), served in a bright, elegant space that's intimate rather than intimidating, by friendly staff who keep obsequiousness to a minimum.

Heacham Manor Hotel
Hunstanton Road, Heacham, PE31 7JX (01485 536030, www.heacham-manor.co.uk). Rates £85-£189 double incl breakfast.
Another country hotel, this time with an eye to modernity. Outside, the Grade II-listed 16th-century farmhouse is all traditional gables and manicured parkland; the interior has been restored and converted into a luxury, boutique-style hotel, with individuality to the fore. Some of the 14 rooms are four-postered, dark and cosy, others are bright and contemporary. There are a couple of self-catering barn cottages too.

Sandringham Camping & Caravan Club
Double Lodges, Sandringham Estate, Sandringham, PE35 6EA (01485 542555, www.campingand caravanningclub.co.uk/sandringham). Rates £7.14-£9.98; £2.64-£5.73 reductions.
Tell your friends you've slept at Sandringham by camping among the trees at this pretty woodland site within the royal estate, run by the estimable Camping & Caravanning Club. The pitches are large, facilities are plentiful and clean, the posh-looking shop sells a decent range of goods at reasonable prices, and there are lots of great walks.

Twitchers Retreat
9 Beach Road, Snettisham, PE31 7RA (01485 543581, www.twitchers-retreat.co.uk). Rates £75-£80 double incl breakfast. No credit cards.
Own-made cake on the tea tray, satin quilts on the beds, a wood burner in the cosy lounge and a lovely garden with a pond are just some of the extras at this little B&B. The

FIVE KING'S LYNN EVENTS

King's Lynn Mart
Tuesday Market Place. Date Feb.
For two weeks each year, starting on Valentine's Day, the town's main square turns into a massive funfair. It's the first in the showmen's calendar and a fitting homage to Victorian entrepreneur Frederick Savage, a King's Lynn engineer and inventor who brought steam power to fairground barrel organs then roundabouts, swings and other rides.

King's Lynn Fiction & Poetry Festivals
01553 691661, www.lynnlitfests.com. Date Mar (Fiction), Sept (Poetry).
Emerging and established contemporary poets and writers from around the world talk about their work in an informal and original setting (2009's festivals were held in Thoresby College), which usually offers plenty of opportunity for the public to meet participants.

Festival Too
07932 114901, www.festivaltoo.co.uk. Date end June/early July.
King's Lynn's annual free contemporary music festival continues to attract headline names like the Stranglers, Human League and 10cc. And with 2010 being its 25th anniversary, expect some top acts, as well as three weekends of street entertainment and family activities.

King's Lynn Festival
01553 764864, www.kingslynn festival.org.uk. Date mid July.
The fortnight-long festival of music and arts – established in 1950 – is an eclectic and enjoyable celebration of the arts, drawing big names in classical music and literature; 2009 saw concert appearances by the Berlin Symphoniker, Ukulele Orchestra of Great Britain, Martin Carthy and Dave Swarbrick, and talks by David Starkey and Stella Rimington. Many of the events take place in wonderfully atmospheric and unusual settings, including St Nicholas's Chapel, St Margaret's Church and St George's Guildhall.

Heritage Open Day
www.west-norfolk.gov.uk. Date Sept.
The second weekend in September sees many buildings usually closed to the public open their doors. Alongside the more famous historical buildings that can often be difficult to access – the Town Hall, Clifton House and Thoresby College, for example – Open Day regulars include the art deco Majestic Cinema and the Victorian Burkitt Homes almshouses. A vintage bus is on hand to ferry people to more far-flung sites of interest.

NORFOLK

Places to visit

Lynn Museum
Market Street, PE30 1NL (01553 775001, www.museums.norfolk.gov.uk). Open 10am-5pm Tue-Sat. Admission Mar-Sept £3.10; free-£2.60 reductions. Oct-Feb free.
The much-talked-of life-size replica of Seahenge, a Bronze Age timber circle discovered on the beach at Holme in 1999, isn't as impressive as it could have been, but this small museum is otherwise a pleasure to explore, not least for the insight into local engineer and inventor Frederick Savage and the development of his steam fairground rides.

Red Mount Chapel & The Walks
The Walks (01553 774297, www.west-norfolk.gov.uk). Open May-Aug 11am-3pm Wed, Sat. Admission £1; reductions free. No credit cards.
The impressive late 15th-century chapel for pilgrims on their way to the shrine of Our Lady in Walsingham is the second most important pilgrimage site in England after Canterbury. It stands like a beacon in the centre of the Walks, a lovely 18th-century park that is a gorgeous spot for a stroll and a picnic.

St Nicholas's Chapel ★
St Ann Street, PE30 1LR (01553 770479). Open June-Sept 10.30am-4.30pm Tue, Sat. Admission free.
The largest parochial chapel in England, founded in 1146, is a real stunner. Most of the building dates from the early 15th century; it houses some terrific 17th- and 18th-century merchant memorials, but it's the structure that really takes your breath away – from the stone star-vaulted porch to the beautiful wooden ceiling decorated with angels, all topped by George Gilbert Scott's 19th-century spire. If the church is closed, you can borrow the key from True's Yard Fisherfolk Museum or the Tudor Rose pub.

Town House Museum
46 Queen Street, PE30 5DQ (01553 773450, www.museums.norfolk.gov.uk). Open May-Sept 10am-5pm Mon-Sat. Feb-Apr 10am-4pm Mon-Sat. Admission £3.10; free-£2.60 reductions. No credit cards.
A social history museum charting the domestic life of the town from the Middle Ages to the 1950s through reconstructed rooms – including a medieval room, a Victorian nursery and an Edwardian school room.

True's Yard Fisherfolk Museum
North Street, PE30 1QW (01553 770479, www.truesyard.co.uk). Open 10am-4pm Tue-Sat. Admission £3; £1.50-£2.50 reductions.
Commemorating the fishing way of life in two beautifully restored Victorian fishermen's cottages – the only remainder of the once teeming North End fishing community – this little museum includes a smokehouse and a tearoom.

Castle Rising Castle ★
Castle Rising, PE31 6AH (01553 631330, www.castlerising.co.uk). Open May-Oct 10am-6pm daily. Nov-Apr 10am-4pm daily. Admission £4; £2.50-£3.30 reductions.

Castle Rising Castle

Hyperbole such as 'one of the most famous and important 12th-century castles in England' often sets visitors up for disappointment, but Castle Rising, or Castle D'Albini, really is spectacular. Heading towards the ticket-office-cum-shop, an impressively steep earthwork – in some places 120ft high – and deep (empty) moat surround and conceal a well-kept castle keep, which, when it comes into view, is breathtaking. The main section of the roof is gone, but all the walls and some of the rooms are fully intact, and the sense of medieval life is palpable.

Sandringham Country Park
Sandringham, PE35 6EH (01553 772675, www.sandringhamestate.co.uk). Open 24hrs daily. Admission free.
Once part of the Queen's private estate and covering nearly 600 acres, this wooded country park is a lovely spot, with two waymarked nature trails and plenty of paths for walkers and cyclists. From April to October, tractor-and-trailer tours take visitors to parts of the estate not usually open. The visitor centre contains a restaurant, a café, a plant centre and a gift shop, where you can pick up souvenir mugs and produce from the estate's farms.

Sandringham Estate
Sandringham, PE35 6EN (01553 612908, www.sandringhamestate.co.uk). Open Apr-Sept House 11am-4.45pm daily. Gardens 10.30am-5pm daily. Museum 11am-5pm daily. Oct House, museum 11am-4pm daily. Gardens 10.30am-4pm daily. Visitor Centre all year 10.30am-5.30pm daily. Admission House, museum & gardens £10; free-£5 reductions; £25 family. Museum & gardens £6.50; free-£3.50 reductions; £15.50 family.
The Queen's winter residence, a vast Victorian mansion, makes an intriguing day out. A number of ground-floor rooms are open to the public, their contents a strange mixture of styles that create the kind of home your gran would have if she'd been given tat by heads of state for the last 50 years and didn't have any taste. Does the queen really do the jigsaws of herself that are piled in the drawing room? You could ask one of the friendly and informative guides, who love

NORFOLK

to tell stories about what the royals like to do when they're in residence (watch 'family entertainment' such as *Atonement* was one snippet we gleaned). Visitors can also stroll the extensive gardens and visit the museum in the old stable block, which includes a collection of vintage royal motor vehicles. Admission includes access to Sandringham Country Park.

Snettisham Park
Park Farm, Snettisham, PE31 7NQ (01485 542425, www.snettishampark.co.uk). Open Feb-mid Dec 10am-5pm daily. Admission £5.50; free-£4.50 reductions.
Very much geared towards children, Snettisham Park encompasses 150 acres of farm and woodland. A highlight is the large herd of deer, which can be viewed on the 45-minute 'safari' by tractor and covered trailer. Other livestock include sheep (visit in March or April to bottle-feed the orphaned lambs), piglets and kid goats, as well as rabbits, guinea pigs and newly hatched chicks. There are also two adventure playgrounds, pony rides (book in advance on 01485 543815), a leather workshop and wildlife, archaeology and farming trails. You can bring your own picnic and eat it under the trees in the orchard, or buy lunch and cakes at the tearoom. The gift and farm shop sells everything from soft toys to fresh venison.

Snettisham RSPB Nature Reserve ★
Beach Road, off the A149, nr Snettisham (01485 542689, www.rspb.org.uk). Open 24hrs daily. Admission free.
The Wash is the most important estuary for birds in the UK, supporting more than 300,000 of them, thanks to a mix of marshland, shingle, mudflats and lagoon. The happy convergence of all these habitats at Snettisham beach makes this stretch of coast the best place to see waterfowl in huge numbers. Two of Britain's great wildlife spectacles take place here: at big tides, when tens of thousands of wading birds wheel over the mudflats and pack on to the islands in front of the reserve's hides; and at dawn and dusk, when the skies fill with pink-footed geese. Even if you're not interested in the birds, the reserve makes for a great walk and expansive views across the Wash.

HUNSTANTON & OLD HUNSTANTON
Hunstanton Sea Life Sanctuary
Southern Promenade, off Seagate Road, Hunstanton, PE36 5BH (01485 533576, www.sealsanctuary.co.uk). Open Summer 10am-5pm daily. Winter 10am-3pm daily. Admission £9.50; free-£9 reductions.
With a seal and fish hospital, otter and penguin sanctuaries and an underwater tunnel, this is seriously good educational fun for kids – and most adults will find themselves cooing over the convalescing marine animals brought here from around Britain's shores, or the small colony of Humboldt penguins bred here. Star attractions are the rescued seal pups, given names like 'Peter Crouch' and 'Houdini', and there's also an aquarium where you can get close to the likes of bamboo sharks, seahorses and skate.

location is fantastic for anyone wanting to explore the coast or wildlife – the RSPB reserve and beach are just five minutes' walk away.

HUNSTANTON & OLD HUNSTANTON

'Sunny Hunny' has a claim to fame, being England's only east coast resort that faces west. That may not sound like much, but it is quite peculiar, and rather thrilling, to watch the sun set from the east coast, particularly when it's setting over land (Lincolnshire, just across the Wash). Fortunately, the town's charms go further than just this geographical quirk.

An archetypal Victorian seaside resort, Hunstanton's rather austere buildings of dark brown local carrstone look down on a triangular green (with a bandstand for summer concerts), a wide expanse of sandy beach and the rump of a pier. Rebuilt after a 2002 fire, the latter no longer stretches out into the sea; it does, however, house an amusement arcade, a diner and bar and a ten-pin bowling centre. In summer, you can take pony rides on the sands or explore the coast and see the seal colonies in Searles' amphibious vehicles (*see p26*).

You won't find much in the way of fine dining or high fashion in Hunstanton, but prices are low and there's a fair range of shops, plus a market on Wednesday and Sunday at the Southend car park on the seafront. And although on first sight the town feels a bit tatty and tawdry, a couple of hours in and you begin to fall for the place; for the crazy golf course on Cliff Parade, for World of Fun on St Edmund's Terrace, 'England's largest joke shop', and even for the permanent funfair on the Southern Promenade, with its carousel, dodgems and other old-fashioned delights that hark back to a day when rides weren't named after drinks brands or made into films.

The Hunstanton Sea Life Sanctuary (*see left*) next door and the Boston Square Sensory Park just behind the bowling green offer more natural but equally enjoyable entertainment. Hunstanton also has a theatre, the Princess (The Green, 01485 532252, www.princesstheatrehunstanton. co.uk), where professional pantos play in winter and a varied menu of films, amateur dramatics and easy-listening music is offered the rest of the year.

Leaving Hunstanton on the A149, you soon come to the altogether less brash village of Old Hunstanton, where carrstone houses, an antiques, arts and crafts centre, an impressive medieval church and two clifftop pitch-and-putt courses offer enough entertainment for a pleasant afternoon. The sandy beach is peaceful and uncrowded, and the village shop, Old Hunstanton Stores (38 Old Hunstanton Road, 01485 533197, closed afternoon Thur, all Sun), has become a foodie attraction, with its deli selling a rich array of local grub.

Away from the main hub is the beautiful 14th-century church of St Mary the Virgin; of more interest to young children is the duck pond opposite. Le Strange Old Barns ★ (Golf Course

FIVE NORFOLK ICE-CREAMS

Holkham Hall
www.holkham.co.uk.
Forgo the dubious charms of Holkham Hall's tearoom in favour of one of its ice-creams from the nearby stall; the turkish delight is wonderfully delicate and creamy. The ice-creams also appear in desserts at the estate-owned Victoria (*see p43*) and Globe Inn (*see p55*).

Norfolk Country Fresh Cream
www.lakenhamcreamery.co.uk.
Traditional batch methods are used by Lakenham Creamery to produce a range of 24 ice-cream flavours; try award-winners such as rich butterscotch or Cointreau and mandarin or, our favourite, coconut and cream: velvety, coconutty and luscious enough to transport you straight to the Caribbean.

Norfolk Farmhouse
Pound Farm, North Tuddenham, NR20 3DA (01362 638116, www. norfolkfarmhouseicecream.co.uk). Open 9am-5pm daily.
The Dann family is understandably proud of its award-winning gooseberry and elderflower ice-cream, but don't discount other flavours made with local produce, such as blackberry and apple, and Norfolk fudge. There are flavours for diabetics too, and sorbets. The ices use eggs, fruit, milk and cream from the Danns' farm at North Tuddenham, near East Dereham, where you can buy the full range of flavours to take home.

Parravanis
www.parravanis.co.uk.
The Parravanis family has been making ice-cream in Norfolk for more than a century. Now based at Chedgrave in the southern Broads, the firm uses fresh local milk to create an adventurous range of 25 ice-creams (including coconut and chocolate, Italian marmalade and more traditional fruit-based versions) plus sorbets, which are sold from vans, a mobile ice-cream parlour and in farm shops throughout East Anglia.

Ronaldo's
www.ronaldo-ices.co.uk.
Available in most of the coastal resorts, including Cromer and Sheringham, Ronaldo's uses Norfolk produce – apples, strawberries, raspberries, blackberries and gooseberries – wherever possible. Try the blueberry, which contains fruit from King's Lynn's Fairgreen Farms, then have a go at re-creating the rich, colourful ice-cream by picking your own berries at the farm.

Road, 01485 533402, www.lestrangeoldbarns. co.uk) looks like a sprawl of unappealing crafts shops from the outside, but inside there are genuinely thrilling antiques finds to be had (two delicate Susie Cooper coffee cups were on sale for £11 each on our visit), and workshops house potters and jewellery makers who are happy to chat about their work and give demonstrations.

Down on the beach, you can explore the stunning candy-striped cliffs – layers of Norfolk carrstone and red and white chalk dating back to the Cretaceous period – and try to find a 135-million-year-old fossil at their base.

Hunstanton tourist office (Town Hall, The Green, 01485 532610) has a 50p map of three heritage trails: it's a thoroughly enjoyable way to explore the town centre, Old Hunstanton and the cliffs.

Where to eat & drink
This northernmost part of the coast is close to some of the fine dining to be found on Norfolk's north coast (*see p35*), which has also resulted in a trickle-down effect for this area. So there are plenty of great pubs in which to enjoy a pint and very good British food, often made with local ingredients – Sedgeford's King William IX Country Inn & Restaurant (01485 571765, www.the kingwilliamsedgeford.co.uk), for example, as well as a handful of more upmarket options, among them the Caley Hall Hotel (*see p33*) and the Best Western Le Strange Arms Hotel (01485 534411, www.abacushotels.co.uk), both in Old Hunstanton.

Cassie's Fish & Chip Restaurant
21 The Green, Hunstanton, PE36 5AH (01485 532448). Open Mar-Oct 10am-7pm daily.
In a pleasant site overlooking the green, this traditional chippie does a range of other meals too, including steak and kidney pie and roasts, fitting the bill for a family feed.

Neptune ★
85 Old Hunstanton Road, Old Hunstanton, PE36 6HZ (01485 532122, www.theneptune.co.uk). Lunch served noon-1.30pm Tue-Fri by arrangement; noon-2pm Sun. Dinner served 7-9pm Tue-Sun.
In 2009, chef Kevin Mangeolles gained a Michelin star for the lovely Neptune, an 18th-century coaching inn that replaces traditional olde worlde interiors with a refreshing New England style. Mangeolles sources as much as he can locally, using Thornham oysters and mussels, Brancaster lobsters, lamb from the Little Farming Company, pork from Courtyard Farm and even quinces grown on a neighbouring farm to deliver a menu that's as inventive and refreshing as the decor. There are six spick and span bedrooms, decorated in the same fresh style (£110-£185 double incl breakfast).

Salad Bowl Café & Ice Cream Parlour
Cliff Parade, Hunstanton, PE36 6DX (01485 534768). Open Apr-Sept 10am-6pm daily. Feb-Mar, Oct-Dec 10am-5pm Sat, Sun. No credit cards.
Catch a fabulous east coast sunset from the pretty Salad Bowl Café, situated on the cliff at the end of the promenade just past the sailing club. Good ice-cream, sandwiches and snacks should keep everyone in the family happy.

Rose & Crown. See p28.

Where to stay

Seaside B&Bs of dubious quality are plentiful in Hunstanton, but so too are owners who realise that nylon bedspreads and frilly curtains don't always cut the mustard; the Shellbrooke (01485 532289, www.theshellbrooke.co.uk) and Burleigh (01485 533080, www.theburleigh.com) are two good examples. If you'd prefer to be out of town, the Neptune (*see left*) is cosy and gorgeous, while Lakeside (01485 533763, www.oldwater works.co.uk) – a converted Victorian waterworks with its own lake, on the outskirts of Old Hunstanton – is a long way from the seaside buzz of Hunstanton proper.

Bays Guest House
31 Avenue Road, Hunstanton, PE36 5BW (01485 532079, www.thebays.co.uk). Rates £70-£90 double incl breakfast.
This Victorian seaside B&B has been modernised throughout, and boasts some decidedly untraditional touches – bathrobes, ceiling fans, Wi-Fi, DVDs, fluffy towels, sumptuous fabrics and a well-stocked mini fridge. There are just five rooms and it's deservedly popular, so book well ahead. No under-12s allowed.

Caley Hall Hotel
Old Hunstanton Road, Old Hunstanton, PE36 6HH (01485 533486, www.caleyhallhotel.co.uk). Rates £90 double incl breakfast.
This is a good option in Old Hunstanton, with 40 rooms in a sprawling and handsome manor house. Family rooms, dog-friendly rooms, disabled-accessible rooms and even a suite with a whirlpool bath are all available. There's also a restaurant, bar and attractive outdoor terrace.

Golden Lion Hotel
The Green, Hunstanton, PE36 6BQ (08445 560880, www.coastandcountryhotels.com). Rates £100-£120 double incl breakfast & dinner.
There are sea views from most of the 27 rooms at this impressive hotel perched next to the sea. Bold colours make a refreshing change from the neutral tones of so many hotels.

Lodge
Old Hunstanton Road, Old Hunstanton, PE36 6HX (01485 532896, www.thelodgehunstanton.co.uk). Rates £100 double.
The village location, proximity to Old Hunstanton beach, nice furnishings and decent restaurant make the 16-roomed Lodge a great base for exploring Norfolk's west coast.

North Norfolk Coast: Holme to Holkham

Nothing prepares you for the sheer scale and spectacular beauty of the 47-mile stretch of coast from Holme-next-the-sea right round to Cromer. Holkham beach is the star in this western half of the coastline, and a lure for location scouts: it's appeared in (among others) *The Eagle Has Landed*, *Shakespeare in Love* and, most recently, the ITV1 drama *Kingdom*. It's a knockout even on the dullest and dampest of days, when the palette of colours runs from dove grey to slate and the beach is perfect for long contemplative walks. But the rest of the coast is no less glorious: sand dunes, saltmarsh and nature reserves teeming with birdlife predominate, and there are plenty of coastal and rural footpaths to explore. Head inland to find equally rewarding landscapes, pretty sights and some excellent eating and drinking – particularly in gorgeous villages such as the Massinghams, or East Rudham and the Creakes, or the six villages that make up the Burnhams, complete with six medieval churches. A couple of grandiose stately homes also demand attention.

HOLME-NEXT-THE-SEA TO HOLKHAM

Holme-next-the-Sea

The attractive village of Holme-next-the-Sea marks the transition from the seaside resort style of Hunstanton and the Wash, with its coachloads of daytrippers taking in Sandringham and taking home Heacham lavender bags, to the more untamed isolation of the North Sea coast. It's a sweet village where chalk and flint cottages give way to golf links and a vast sandy beach that's a fine taster of what lies east. The gently undulating dunes are accessed via a boardwalk, and there's a shop selling Norfolk-made ice-cream, but little else, making for a lovely day at the seaside if your preference is for minimal amenities and a lot of sand between you and the next windbreak.

There's a choice of long-distance walks: the famed Peddars Way, following the course of a Roman road, begins – or ends – here; and the 47-mile Norfolk Coast Path runs west from Holme to West Runton. Less completist hikers might prefer the range of guided walks organised by the Norfolk County Council and the Ramblers' Association (see www.countrysideaccess.norfolk. gov.uk for details), or the numerous short walks along both long-distance paths. The coast path, in particular, is easily accessible thanks to the frequent CoastHopper bus service, which allows you to walk one way and return by bus (01553 776980, www.coasthopper.co.uk for timetables and coastal trails information). If you're driving, the A149 runs the length of the coast from Holme all the way to Cromer.

A couple of miles east of Holme lies the 35-acre Drove Orchards (Thornham Road, PE36 6LS, 01485 525652, www.droveorchards.com, closed mid Jan-Mar), worth visiting both for its farm shop – a great place to buy apples and freshly pressed juice from the orchards, as well as a huge range of other local produce – and the much-praised Yurt restaurant (*see p42*).

Thornham to Brancaster

Next door to Holme, Thornham is typical of the area; it's a tiny village with small cottages of clunch (a type of chalk), reddish-brown carstone and knapped flint on the High Street and more imposing homes down the lanes, plus a café, village shop, post office and two family-friendly pubs, the Lifeboat Inn (*see p40*) and the Orange Tree (*see p42*). Both offer accommodation, making the village a nice base for wild and windswept Brancaster Bay, just a mile away across the marshes and creeks. They may look bleak and desolate but this land teems with wildlife, and the area is a huge draw for birdwatchers.

A couple of miles east, the equally typical Titchwell is notable for the RSPB's Titchwell Marsh Nature Reserve (*see p47*), but most people head on to Brancaster. Here, homes ranging from the bijou to the pseudo-stately line the winding road leading to the excellent, unspoilt beach. Bar a snack shack opposite the car park, there's nothing here but sea, sky, marsh and one of the country's best golf links. Among golfing cognoscenti, the Royal West Norfolk club (*see p78*) is famous for having a waiting list that's longer than St Andrews', but for the rest of us, it's more famous for its

Great Bircham Windmill. See p47.

Brancaster. See p35.

Good things · HUMBLE PIE

Burnham Market. See p39.

mussels. During the season, bags of tender little bivalves are sold from fishermen's cottages in Brancaster Staithe, as well as from Letzers Seafood (Brancaster Staithe Harbour, 01485 525369, www.letzersseafood.com, closed Nov-Mar) on the harbour, where you can also buy more exotic seafood, including lobster and crabs in baguettes and impressive seafood platters.

The coastal path runs around the pretty harbour and close to the excellent White Horse pub (*see p44*), and there are some atmospheric walks across the marshes – to the National Trust-owned remains of the Roman fort at Branodunum (01485 210719, www.nationaltrust.org.uk), or a mile to Burnham Deepdale, where the backpackers' hostel and campsite at Deepdale Farm (*see p42*) is filled with walkers and families.

The Burnhams

A short detour inland leads to rather smart Burnham Market ★, the largest of a clutch of villages known as the Burnhams. In the 13th century, the River Burn was navigable by sea-going boats as far as Burnham Thorpe, now almost three miles inland. Silting of the river led to a decrease in the commercial importance of the Burnhams, but in the past 20 years there's been a curious and profound transformation in the fortunes of Burnham Market. It's a handsome old place with a long, tree-lined green at its centre and is at the very heart of north Norfolk's gentrification, with the impact being felt on towns and villages along the coast. Many of its properties are now second homes to folk from outside the county, and the newcomers' money has allowed some of Norfolk's most interesting shops to flourish.

Quality food is a highlight. Gather the ingredients for a picnic at the first-class deli Humble Pie (Market Place, 01328 738581, www.humble-pie.com, closed Sun), the traditional baker's W Groom (Market Place, 01328 738289, www.groomsbakery.co.uk, closed Sun) and Satchells Wines (North Street, 01328 738272, www.satchellswines.com, closed Sun). Gurneys Fish Shop (Market Place, 01328 738967, www.gurneysfishshop.co.uk closed Sun) is great for smoked fish, and Lucy's Tearooms (Market Place, 01328 730908) or Tilly's (Market Place, 01328 730300, closed Sun) are a must for cakes and pastries.

Food apart, there are two bookshops – Brazen Head (Market Place, 01328 730700, www.brazenhead.org.uk, closed Sun winter) for second-hand books and White House (Market Place, 01328 730270, www.whitehousebooks.co.uk, closed Sun, 1-2pm Mon-Sat) for new books and maps – not to mention the weekend Burnham Market Book festival each November. Other shops sell clothes, antiques and gifts; galleries include Saltwater (*see p43*), which shows Norfolk photography, the Fairfax (The Old Forge, North Street, 01328 730001, www.fairfaxgallery.com, closed Mon, Sun), which has contemporary painting, sculpture and ceramics, and Burnham Grapevine (Overy Road, 01328 730125,

www.burnhamgrapevine.co.uk, closed Sun), sister gallery to the excellent Grapevine in Norwich.

The other five villages that make up the Burnhams are smaller and, except for their churches, unremarkable. The round-towered churches of St Mary in Burnham Deepdale and St Margaret in Burnham Norton are both worth a look; the latter, in particular, is outstanding in both its structure and hilltop setting, and features a notable 15th-century painted wine-glass pulpit.

The little village of Burnham Thorpe, just east of Burnham Market, is the birthplace of Horatio Nelson. There's little here to mark the fame of this local boy made good, though Nelson held a farewell party at the village pub (now called the Lord Nelson, *see p49*) before returning to sea in 1793. If you detour here to pay homage, follow his example, then take the B1155 to rejoin the coast road, which you reach just west of Holkham.

Holkham

The land for miles around this area is owned by the Coke family (pronounced, with typical Norfolk linguistic idiosyncracy, 'Cook'), the Earls of Leicester. The grounds of the family's stately pile, Holkham Hall (*see p46*), stretch down to the famed Holkham beach ★. If you've ever seen a picture of a north Norfolk beach, it's likely to be this one. At high tide it's the perfect beach: immensely wide, sandy, backed by lovely pine woods and serviced by a lone snack truck in the car park (run by the Estate, it serves high-quality snacks such as venison sandwiches, own-made sausages and ice-cream).

The views are magnificent until the fog rolls in, and then the place acquires an eerie desolation magnified by the sound of unseen birds passing overhead. On a sunny day, sandcastles, swimming and beach games take priority; on windswept ones, walking, horseriding and kite-flying come to the fore. On such days Holkham beach may appear stark and bleak, but in fact it has an abundance of wildlife and is packed with interest for naturalists: sea lavender covers the salt marsh in the summer, and the dunes host a variety of flowers and grasses. The sand dunes are also popular with nesting birds – when necessary, sections of the beach are cordoned off to give colonies of little terns some space and a chance to rear their offspring.

The car park is just off the main coast road opposite the entrance to the Hall; pay, park and then walk along the boardwalk, through the woods, to the beach. Turn left at the end of the boardwalk and after about 20 minutes you get to the part of the beach used by naturists; turn right and the sand stretches away into the distance. If you keep walking, after about two miles you arrive at Wells-next-the-sea, identified by a jaunty row of beach huts. The colourful cluster comes as a surprise after the bare expanses of Holkham, and marks the beginning of a busier stretch of the coast, but one that's just as understated and enchanting.

Where to eat & drink

Local delicacies such as Holkham Estate venison, Morston and Brancaster mussels and Wells crabs and lobsters are made much of in the area, and were treasured even before gentrification set in.

Most of the hotels and inns with rooms have excellent food too, including the Hoste Arms, the Victoria, the White Horse, the Ship and Titchwell Manor; *see pp42-44* for all. For refreshments after a walk on Holkham beach, the Stables café on the estate (01328 713114, closed some of the winter – but phone to check in case it's open) is worth remembering.

Deepdale Café

Main Road, Burnham Deepdale, PE31 8DD (01485 211055, www.deepdalecafe.co.uk). Open 7.30am-4pm daily.

This modern café's location in a row of shops behind a garage forecourt gives little clue of what lies inside. Choose from all-day breakfasts made with local organic eggs, bread baked nearby and naturally smoked haddock to sandwiches, omelettes and cakes that are a cut above the norm. Lunches, from a blackboard list, are yet more ambitious: a smartly dressed salad of crayfish tails and bacon, or a fig, parmesan and red onion frittata for little more than a fiver.

Jockey

Creake Road, Burnham Market, PE31 8EN (01328 738321, www.thejockeyburnhammarket.co.uk). Lunch served noon-2pm Mon-Fri; noon-3pm Sat, Sun. Dinner served 6-9pm daily.

Quality pub food in a tiny and wonderfully cosy restaurant (book ahead if you can) that should appeal to traditionalists wanting the likes of good pork belly or liver and bacon. Two bars and outdoor tables are great for a post-beach walk pint, and there are four B&B rooms too (£60-£90 double incl breakfast).

Jolly Sailors

Main Road, Brancaster Staithe, PE31 8BJ (01485 210314, www.jollysailors.co.uk). Lunch served noon-2pm, dinner served 6-9pm Mon-Fri. Meals served noon-9pm Sat, Sun.

Highly likeable as a pub (serving its own-brewed beer in a congenial old bar), the Jolly Sailors also has a pretty garden and children's adventure playground area, all of which makes it a top choice for families. They're sure to find something they like from a menu that includes a wide range of pizzas and burgers as well as daily specials. The 312ft-long maltings that once stood here, built using blocks salvaged from the old Roman fort Branodunum, is long gone, but the brewery still produces three ales, all served here.

Lifeboat Inn

Ship Lane, Thornham, PE36 6LT (01485 512236, www.lifeboatinn.co.uk). Lunch served noon-2.30pm, food served 3-5pm daily. Dinner served 6.30-9.30pm Mon-Thur, Sun; 6-9.30pm Fri, Sat.

Fourteen spick-and-span, good-sized rooms, most of them with views out over Thornham harbour and the sea, make this a good option for a night or two. The 16th-century

Holkham Beach. See p39.

smugglers' inn is full of character and does a mean pile of mussels, served in one of the three bars, the pretty conservatory or the slightly more formal restaurant.

Orange Tree ★
High Street, Thornham, PE36 6LY (01485 512213, www.theorangetreethornham.co.uk). Breakfast served 8.30-9.30am Mon-Fri; 9-10am Sat, Sun. Lunch served noon-3pm Mon-Sat; noon-5pm Sun. Afternoon tea served 3-6pm Mon-Sat. Dinner served 6-9.30pm daily.
A pretty whitewashed pub set amid extensive gardens, serving a Modern English menu featuring tempting and inventive dishes such as Norfolk coast fish soup and marsh reared fillet of Norfolk beef. The slick, smart decor extends to the six bedrooms (£65-£120 double incl breakfast).

The Yurt ★
Drove Orchards, Thornham, PE36 6LS (01485 525108, www.theyurt.co.uk). Open Summer 9am-5pm, 6-9pm daily. Winter 9-5pm Mon, Tue, Sun; 9-5pm, 6-9pm Wed-Sat.
Just off the A1149, west of Thornham, this warm, light-filled yurt is a delightful lunch stop, from the wood burning stove at its centre and the wicker rockers and fake fur rugs circling it, to the friendly service and excellent food. Local shellfish and smoked fish feature

big on a menu that also lists a range of ploughmans and sandwiches, daily specials and mixed taster plates, and it's all served from an open kitchen area.

Where to stay

Deepdale Farm
Burnham Deepdale, PE31 8DD (01485 210256, www.deepdalefarm.co.uk/camping). Rates hostel £9.50-£13.50 per person; camping £4.50-£9 per person.
This environmentally friendly farm, right in the heart of an area of outstanding natural beauty, runs a backpackers' hostel in its stables and granary. It also has a famously quiet, family-friendly campsite that sits discreetly in two well-kept paddocks. A strict noise policy in the late evening means that party animals don't bother with Deepdale, and the caravan ban keeps it cosy (campervans are permitted). It's simple stuff, with no electrical hook-ups or generators.

Hoste Arms ★
The Green, Burnham Market, PE31 8HD (01328 738777, www.hostearms.co.uk). Rates £128-£208 double incl breakfast.
Paul and Jeanne Whittome's 17th-century inn on Burnham Market Green paved the way for the village's

Titchwell Manor

gentrification, and started a mini-empire that includes two equally delightful hotels/restaurants, the Vine House (*see p44*) and Railway Inn (*see below*), as well as a number of self-catering cottages, and a refurbished traditional railway carriage. What they all share is Jeanne's exuberant decor and love of art (there's even a small gallery), and each room is individually furnished with bold textures and fabrics to create an original space. On top of the 35 beautifully appointed rooms, the Hoste Arms is also known for its food. Local ingredients predominate in a happy mix of homely dishes (steak and kidney pudding, saddle of venison) and more international flavours (scallops with beetroot tempura, thai fish broth), served in a romantic, wood-panelled dining room.

Railway Inn & Cottages

Creake Road, Burnham Market, PE31 8EA (01328 738777, www.hostearms.co.uk). Rates £89 double incl breakfast.

A five-minute walk from sister property the Hoste Arms, the Railway Inn has smaller bedrooms, but shares the same attention to detail and love of good design. The old waiting room has been turned into a gorgeous and comfortable guest lounge, which leads on to a platform shared by a warm and luxurious wooden refurbished carriage. Breakfast is served at the Hoste.

Ship Inn

Main Road, Brancaster, PE31 8AP (01485 210333, www.flyingkiwiinns.co.uk). Rates £100-£150 double incl breakfast.

Scheduled to open in spring 2010, this is the latest in chef-hotelier Chris Coubrough's mini empire. Given his previous sympathetic restorations of pubs in the area (for example, the Crown Inn, East Rudham), we can expect a pub returned to its former glory, plus Coubrough's trademark excellent food. The Ship will major in fish and seafood, and there are nine en suite bedrooms planned.

Titchwell Manor

Brancaster Bay, Titchwell, PE31 8BB (01485 210221, www.titchwellmanor.com). Rates £110-£250 incl breakfast.

Overlooking the marshes of the RSPB reserve and just steps from the national coast path, Titchwell Manor is in a lovely location. After a long windswept walk, you'll be happy to collapse on one of the leather sofas for an afternoon pint or evening aperitif. The 31 rooms are spread over a number of buildings, chief of which is the big house, where rooms at the front have sea views. Two dining rooms serve good Modern European food often featuring local produce.

Victoria ★

Park Road, Holkham, NR23 1RG (01328 711008, www.victoriaatholkham.co.uk). Rates £120-£190 double incl breakfast.

In the endless sea of neutral colours most boutique hotels opt for, the Victoria stands out like a technicolour dream, creating a rare easy-going charm in this small hotel and restaurant. Decor is low-key but stylish, with furniture from Rajasthan mixing with modern TVs and gleaming bathrooms; there's a big fire in the lounge area, together with squashy, lived-in sofas and a bar. If you're looking for something a little private, three estate follies have been pressed into service as two-bedroom 'lodges'. Meals

Bringing the Outside In

Main Road, Holkham, NR23 1AD (01328 713093, www.bringingthe outsidein.co.uk). Open 10.30am-4pm Mon, Wed-Sun.

In an attractive studio space in Holkham village, Martin Billing exhibits and sells landscape photography that should please lovers of wild windswept seas and skies. Handmade coastal artefacts add to the browsability of this likeable venture.

Creake Abbey Studios

North Creake, NR21 9LF (07801 418907, www.creakeabbeystudios. co.uk). Open Summer 11am-5pm Tue-Sun. Winter 11am-4.30pm Tue-Sun.

A huddle of converted barns near the ruins of Creake Abbey (*see p47*) houses a small range of studios and shops selling an array of arts, crafts, old and new homeware, clothing and Provençal food (at Good Taste). The Abbey Café has outdoor tables and a good range of sandwiches and snacks, and on the first Saturday of each month a local food fair and farmers' market is held in the barn.

Norfolk Living

Market Place, Burnham Market, PE31 8HF (01328 730668, www.norfolk living.co.uk). Open 10am-5pm Mon-Sat.

Stylish home and garden accessories in a handsome (and very tempting) Georgian setting that seems to go on forever; once through the shop there's a courtyard with old stable, barn and cottage to explore too. Great for (extravagant) gifts.

Real Ale Shop ★

Branthill Farm, Branthill, NR23 1SB (01328 710810, www.therealaleshop. co.uk). Open Summer 10am-6pm Mon-Sat; noon-4pm Sun. Winter 10am-4pm Tue-Sat; noon-4pm Sun.

Just off the B1105 and set in a malting barley farm owned by the Holkham Estate and farmed by local tenant farmers, Teddy Maufe's Real Ale Shop is a thoroughly East Anglian affair (there's also a shop in Wrentham, Suffolk). The farm supplies 15 Norfolk brewers with much of the malt necessary to make an impressive 50 bottle-conditioned ales, and all of them are sold in this enticing shop. The farm also offers accommodation (£70-£75 double incl breakfast).

Saltwater Gallery

Ulph Place, Overy Road, Burnham Market, PE31 8HQ (01328 730382, www.saltwater.co.uk). Open 11am-5pm Mon, Tue, Thur-Sat; 11am-1pm Wed.

A nice space in which to peruse the photographs of Harry Cory Wright, whose affordable prints of the local area make great souvenirs.

NORFOLK

are served in the ground-floor dining room and in the bar, with both Modern British menus making use of local produce – often very local, such as Holkham steaks, organic chickens from a farm tenant or, in winter, wild game from family shoots.

Vine House

The Green, Burnham Market, PE31 8HD (01328 738777, www.hostearms.co.uk). Rates £137-£197 double incl breakfast.

On the other side of the green from the Hoste Arms (*see p42*), the Vine is smaller and quieter than its sister hotel, with no restaurant (breakfast is served at the Hoste) but a cosy study, drawing room and private garden, and seven large rooms.

White Horse

Brancaster Staithe, PE31 8BY (01485 210262, www.whitehorsebrancaster.co.uk). Rates £90-£194 double incl breakfast.

If the pretty beach-style blue and cream decor of the 15 rooms here (eight of them with their own terrace) weren't special enough, the location certainly would be, overlooking the marshland coastline of Brancaster Bay out to Scolt Head island. An engaging conservatory restaurant with a sun deck terrace offers a wealth of coastal dishes plus good gastropub standards.

INLAND TO GREAT MASSINGHAM

Given the lack of settlements along this stretch of the coast, gentrification has been forced inland, most obviously to the surrounding Burnhams, but also further afield. At Ringstead, Great Massingham, East Rudham and South Creake, gastropubs and inns with rooms – such as the Gin Trap Inn, the Dabbling Duck, the Crown (for all, *see p48*) and the Ostrich Inn (*see p49*) – offer great bases from which to explore the area. Villages such as Sedgeford, East Barsham, Great Bircham and the Weasenhams are home to medieval churches and pleasant pubs, and are surrounded by picturesque countryside criss-crossed by lots of trails and walks.

Such villages, often containing little more than just a glorious church and a cluster of knapped-flint thatched houses, are in some ways the most appealing; a fine example is Sedgeford, where the round-towered St Mary's Church adds a serene grandeur to the village. Harpley too is beautifully laid out and features some excellent houses alongside a church, St Lawrence, whose delicate angel roof and rustic medieval benches are just two of the features that help create a wonderfully atmospheric space.

But it's not all cute villages of little interest to historians; grand halls and mansions can be found near Tatterford, where the Palladian-style Houghton Hall (*see p47*) is located, and in East Raynham, home to the 17th-century Raynham Hall with its famous 'Brown Lady' ghost (Lady Dorothy, the supposedly mistreated wife of 'Turnip' Townshend, the estate's second viscount). She forms a nice link between the two houses, being sister to Britain's first prime minister, Robert Walpole and one of the

Walpoles of Houghton Hall. Raynham Hall is only very occasionally open to the public, usually by organised tour – check with the tourist office.

The villages lucky enough to have popular inns with rooms often thrive and draw other businesses too. At East Rudham, a pretty village centred around a large green, the popularity of Kiwi wonderboy Chris Coubrough's Crown Inn (*see p48*) has spawned the delightfully girly Brownies tea room and home accessories shop next door. All hot pink beach umbrellas on the outside and bright floral homeware inside, this is a lovely tea room serving cooked breakfasts and hot lunches as well as fairy cakes and brownies. The Creake Abbey Studios (*see p43*) in North Creake offers fun browsing of art, design, crafts, clothing and food, and just a couple of miles east the Real Ale Shop (*see p43*) stocks more than 50 Norfolk brewed beers.

Further south, the village of Great Massingham is one of the county's most attractive, with a huge green divided by little roads, a dizzying array of ponds (thought to be the fishing ponds for a long-gone 11th-century Augustinian abbey) and a famed son in Robert Walpole. He was educated here and built the majestic Houghton Hall. An atmospheric RAF wartime airfield near the village adds an unusual dimension, its dilapidated control tower calling to mind JG Ballard's tales of a dystopian future as well as echoing a sad past that saw the loss of 600 servicemen based here during World War II. Picturesque St Andrew's, in nearby Little Massingham, was the church of the RAF servicemen, and the graveyard has a number of simple but moving war graves.

A few miles east in Weasenham St Peter, fans of the *Today* programme might want to pay homage at presenter John Timpson's graveside; he settled in the village after 16 years on the show – though nearby Rougham offers more general interest in the church of St Mary, where there's a lovely screen and a plethora of brasses.

Dropping south from here brings visitors to one of Norfolk's greatest medieval sites, at Castle Acre (*see p151*), but heading back north towards the coast – possibly along the county-long trail Peddars Way, which bisects the area from Swaffham further south back to Holme on the coast – Great Bircham rewards exploration. There's a working windmill with a bakery (*see p47*) and, at St Mary's Church, a war graves plot for British, Commonwealth and German servicemen.

Beyond here the rolling folds of the Ringstead Downs valley, the largest area of chalk grassland in Norfolk, stretch to the village of Ringstead; best seen perhaps from the Norfolk Wildlife Trust site (NWT Ringstead Downs, 01603 625540, www. norfolkwildlifetrust.org.uk) just off the Ringstead/ Sedgeford road. It's a beautiful valley and part of the north Norfolk strip of Area of Outstanding Natural Beauty that stretches 40 miles from here to Mundesley; even if you don't walk any other stretch of the Peddars Way, the two miles between Ringstead and the ancient trail's end at Holme shouldn't be missed.

White Horse

Places to visit

Titchwell Marsh Nature Reserve

HOLME-NEXT-THE-SEA TO HOLKHAM

Holkham Hall ★
Holkham, NR23 1AB (01328 710227, www.holkham. co.uk). Open Holkham Hall Apr-Oct noon-4pm Mon, Thur, Sun. Bygones Museum Apr-Oct noon-5pm daily. Walled Gardens Apr-Oct 10am-4pm daily. Admission £11; £5.50 reductions; £27 family.
Home to the Earls of Leicester and the Coke family, this extensive, beautifully proportioned Palladian-style stately home was built during the 18th century on the site of a former family home. It's likely to be familiar to those who saw *The Duchess*, which was shot almost entirely on location here, and it is hugely impressive, from its jaw-dropping marble entrance hall and terrific collection of paintings to its opulent state rooms and servants' quarters. The 3,000-acre deer park in which the hall is set is worth a visit too, and there are extensive walks through it and around the mile-long lake. The estate also houses the Bygones Museum and History of Farming Exhibition, which will delight children who are into tractors, old steam engines and farmyard machinery. New for 2010 are the restored walled gardens that have been closed to the public since 2005. And note that there's some stylish shopping (pottery, a kitchen store, an Adnams wine shop and more) to be had at the North Gate entrance.

NWT Holme Dunes ★
Just west of Holme-next-the-sea, PE36 6LQ (01485 525240, www.norfolkwildlifetrust.org.uk). Open 10am-5pm daily. Admission £3. No credit cards.
Just at the point where the Wash meets the North Sea lies this exceptional Norfolk Wildlife Trust reserve, comprising a vast tract of mud flats, foreshore, sand dunes, scrub, pines, marsh and reedbeds. These all combine to make Holme Dunes one of the coast's most attractive landscapes, with a tangible air of fragility and emptiness. Of course, it's not empty at all; 320 species of birds have been seen from the three hides overlooking grazing marsh, pools and numerous paths, but even if you don't spot any of them, it's a wild and wonderful introduction to Norfolk's north coast.

Scolt Head Island
Brancaster Bay (0845 600 3078, www.natural england.org.uk). Open Summer 24hrs daily. Admission free; cruises may vary.
This offshore barrier island and nature reserve, run by Natural England, can be reached in summer via a ferry from Burnham Overy Staithe, or on a range of escorted cruises (try Branta on 01485 211132, www.brantacruises.co.uk). The mix of sand dunes, saltmarsh, shingle and intertidal sand and mud flats supports a wide range of birds. Much of the island is off-limits to human visitors in order to protect their nesting habitats, but a short nature trail with interpretation panels is a nice way of seeing this quiet and atmospheric site. You can get a terrific view of the island from Barrow Common and Burnham Deepdale Downs if you want to leave the birds in peace.

Sculthorpe Moor Community Nature Reserve
Turf Moor Road, Sculthorpe, NR21 9GN (01328 856788, www.sculthorpemoor.org). Open Apr-Sept 8am-6pm Tue, Wed; 8am-dusk Thur-Sun. Oct-Mar 8am-4pm Tue-Sun. Admission free (though this may change).
Created and managed by the Hawk & Owl Trust, this lovely reserve in the Wensum Valley is one that children in particular will enjoy. Birds of prey, woodpeckers, kingfishers and masses of insects and mammals are supported by a fertile habitat that includes wet and dry

woodland, reed beds, pools and riverbank. A boardwalk with bird feeders, nestboxes and three hides should help eager nature fans spot their targets.

Titchwell Marsh Nature Reserve ★
Signposted off the A149, just east of Titchwell village, PE31 8BB (01485 210779, www.rspb.org.uk). Open Mar-Oct 9.30am-5pm daily. Nov-Feb 9.30am-4pm daily. Admission free.
This RSPB wetland reserve is utterly absorbing, whatever your level of interest (or binocular power). Spanning an area rich in wildlife, thanks to a mix of deserted beach (where ancient peat beds, the remains of an age-old forest, are occasionally exposed), reed beds and shallow lagoons, the reserve houses a series of hides with pictures and information to enable close observation of a wide variety of wetland birds, including marsh harriers and avocets in summer and wigeons and brent geese in winter. You can hire binoculars at the visitor centre, where you'll also find a shop and café.

INLAND TO GREAT MASSINGHAM

Creake Abbey
Off the B1355, nr North Creake, NR21 9LF (www.english-heritage.org.uk/creakeabbey). Open 24hrs daily. Admission free.
Isolated in the middle of fields a mile or so from Burnham Thorpe with nothing for company but the tasteful and discreet Creake Abbey Studios (*see p43*) nearby, these extensive ruins of a 14th-century Augustinian abbey are great for moody, atmospheric pictures and a spot of gothic romance. The existing and impressive church of St Mary is worth a look for its wealth of artefacts and information about the original abbey.

Great Bircham Windmill
Great Bircham, PE31 6SJ (01485 578393, www.birchamwindmill.co.uk). Open Apr-Sept 10am-5pm daily. Admission £3.75; £2-£3 reductions.
Lovingly restored to its 19th-century grandeur, when it was one of more than 300 windmills in Norfolk, Great Bircham is an enjoyable place to spend an hour or two. It bustles with activity and various farm animals; there are pens housing happy-looking goats and sheep. The working mill is fun to climb (the fan deck offers great views), and there's also a bakery, tea room, art gallery and gift shop in which to fritter away time and money. Pitch up at the campsite (*see p49*) if you want to stay the night; and for those keen to explore further afield, the mill offers bike hire and a range of walking routes.

Houghton Hall ★
Just off the A148, nr Harpley, PE31 6UE (01485 528569, www.houghtonhall.com). Open Apr-Sept 1.30-4.30pm Wed, Thur, Sun. Admission £8.80; £3.50 reductions; £22 family.
Four miles west of the village of Tatterton, this palatial, Palladian-style hall was built in the 1720s by Britain's first prime minister, Sir Robert Walpole, with spectacular furniture and interiors designed by the coach painter turned stately home and furniture designer William Kent. From its pale golden exterior of Aislaby stone (quarried in North Yorkshire and transported by sea from Whitby to King's Lynn) to finely carved mahogany woodwork and sumptuous furniture, art and porcelain inside, Houghton is almost equal in splendour to Holkham Hall. It also boasts a walled garden that shouldn't be missed. New Houghton, the village built to replace the original Houghton (destroyed because it spoiled the views from the house), lies just a mile away.

Bircham Windmill Campsite

Where to eat & drink

Crown Inn ★

The Green, East Rudham, PE31 8RD (01485 528530, www.crowninnnorfolk.co.uk). Lunch served noon-2.30pm daily. Dinner served 6.30-9pm Mon-Thur, Sun; 6.30-9.30pm Fri, Sat.

The 2010 *Good Pub Guide* Norfolk Eating Pub of the Year award was a great accolade for owner Chris Coubrough, whose small but excellent Flying Kiwi Inns empire seems to be growing apace without the all-too-often attendant drop in standards. The Crown is as delightful and comfortable as its sister inns in Wells, Letheringsett and Brancaster. The menus major on inventive Modern British dishes bearing exotic twists: seared sea bream with chilli or Houghton Hall venison burger with curried cabbage and polenta, for example. The kids' menus are rather sweetly concocted by Coubrough's own offspring; cheese and beans on toast is always popular. Upstairs, six small but beautifully appointed rooms (£80 double incl breakfast) complete the compelling features.

Dabbling Duck

11 Abbey Road, Great Massingham, PE32 2HN (01485 520827, www.thedabblingduck.co.uk). Lunch served noon-2pm Mon-Sat; noon-3pm Sun. Dinner served 6.30-9pm Sun.

A sweet blue and white pub facing the huge green, the Duck's name comes from the village's many ponds. Inside, worn leather armchairs, scrubbed country tables and big fires make it the kind of place you could happily spend the day, eating pints of prawns, big bowls of moules marinière and above-par pub favourites such as burgers and

traditional puds. The three spick-and-span B&B rooms (£80 double incl breakfast) are named after notable World War II RAF servicemen stationed nearby.

Gin Trap Inn

6 High Street, Ringstead, PE36 5JU (01485 525264, www.gintrapinn.co.uk). Lunch served noon-2pm Mon-Fri; noon-2.30pm Sat, Sun. Dinner served Summer 6-9pm Mon-Thur; 6-9.30pm Fri, Sat; 6.30-9pm Sun. Winter 6.30-9pm Mon-Thur, Sun; 6-9.30pm Fri, Sat.

This pretty 17th-century coaching inn is a firm favourite with locals and visitors, and it's easy to see why. You'll find friendly staff, a traditional warm and cosy space (plus a lovely walled garden) and a no-nonsense menu that's heavy on local produce (Thornham oysters, Binham Blue cheese and Arthur Howell bangers). There are three country-style rooms too (£90-£120 double incl breakfast), all pretty florals and cream, with wrought-iron beds and excellent facilities.

Kings Head Hotel

Great Bircham, PE31 6RJ (01485 578265, www.thekingsheadhotel.co.uk). Lunch served noon-3pm daily. Dinner served 6-9pm (winter 7-9pm) daily.

Contemporary dining and bedrooms in a gorgeous whitewashed Grade II-listed 19th-century coach house make the Kings Head a good inland base: it's handy for the coast, but away from the hustle and bustle. Quality Modern British food is served in an elegant restaurant and courtyard, while the 12 individually styled rooms (£125-£175 double incl breakfast) are luxurious, with fresh flowers, a decanter of port and a plate of own-made biscuits to help you settle in.

Lord Nelson

Walsingham Road, Burnham Thorpe, PE31 8HL (01328 738241, www.nelsonslocal.co.uk). Lunch served noon-2.30pm Mon-Sun. Dinner served 6-9pm Tue-Sun.

There are more than 200 pubs in Norfolk bearing the name of the Trafalgar hero, but this one, in his birthplace, is positively shrine-like, with memorabilia adorning much of the whitewashed space, and lots of Lord Nelson souvenirs for sale behind the bar. Built in 1637, the classic boozer's high-backed wooden settles, stone-flagged floor, brick fireplace and comfortable snugs create the ideal setting to enjoy a pint of Nelson's Revenge and food that's of higher quality (and price) than your average pub grub: try Brancaster moules marinière or smoked duck salad, followed by rump steak or guinea fowl.

Ostrich Inn

1 Fakenham Road, South Creake, NR21 9PB (01328 823320, www.ostrichinn.net). Lunch served noon-2pm, dinner served 6.30-9pm daily.

A charming location in an equally charming village makes the Ostrich a good pint pit stop, even before factoring in the menu, which offers gastropub staples done well; monkfish tempura or chargrilled sardines for starters, liver and mash or duck breast for mains. Enjoy it all in a cosy olde worlde library room warmed by a log burner.

Rose & Crown

Nethergate Street, Harpley, PE31 6TW (01485 520577, www.harpleypub.net). Open 6.30-11pm Tue; noon-3pm, 6.30-11pm Wed, Thur; noon-3pm, 6.30pm-midnight Fri, Sat; noon-3pm, 7-10.30pm Sun. Lunch served noon-2pm Wed-Sun. Dinner served 6.30-9pm Tue-Sat; 7-9pm Sun.

Scrubbed wooden floors and a bright modern interior decorated with local artwork set the Rose & Crown apart from a run-of-the-mill village pub, and so does the food. The menu ranges from well-prepared and appealing pub dishes plus the odd dash of more international fare. There's a good range of wines by the glass, plenty of local ales, and an attractive garden for summer supping, all set in one of the area's prettiest villages.

Things to do

INLAND TO GREAT MASSINGHAM

Extreeme Adventure

High House, Weasenham, PE32 2SP (01328 838720, www.extreemeadventure.co.uk). Open Mar-Nov 9am-4pm daily. Admission £25; £23 reductions.

If you're over ten years old, more than 1.4m tall and have a good head for heights, you can experience the adrenaline-provoking pleasures of this extensive high-ropes course. The setting, south of Weasenham All Saints and just off the A1065 (though mostly away from the traffic noise), is impressive. The New Wood contains some of the highest trees in eastern England, which participants can clamber up using rope ladders to navigate their way along 20ft- or 40ft-high walkways before whizzing down a 1,000ft zipwire. Less intrepid adults can stay in the covered picnic pavilion, where refreshments are served and a log fire burns in cold weather.

Where to stay

As well as the B&Bs and campsites listed here, many of the inns listed above offer accommodation, including the Crown in East Rudham, the Kings Head in Great Bircham, the Gin Trap Inn in Ringstead and the Dabbling Duck in Great Massingham.

Bircham Windmill Campsite

Bircham Windmill, Great Bircham, PE31 6SJ (01485 578393, www.birchamwindmill.co.uk). Rates £10 per night for 2 people.

Freshly baked bread for breakfast, and waking to the noise of sheep and chickens are just a couple of reasons to stay at this small, friendly campsite; the gentle whirr of the sails sweeping round as you go to sleep is another. *See also p47.*

Church Farm House

Great Bircham, PE31 6RJ (01485 576087, www.church-farmhouse.com). Rates £70-£110 double incl breakfast.

A whitewashed period farmhouse on the outskirts of Great Bircham, Church Farm features four light-filled and cosy rooms. There are plenty of thoughtful and individual touches, including bright textiles and big breakfasts.

The Close

Station Road, East Rudham, PE31 8SU (01485 528925, www.closenorfolk.com). Rates £85 double incl breakfast. No credit cards.

An elegant ivy-clad Victorian family house that's now a B&B, set in a large garden with a stream running through it. It makes a great alternative to East Rudham's award-winning Crown Inn (*see p48*). The two large doubles are huge and well appointed, with pretty rugs and throws making them feel cosier than most.

Old School

South Creake, NR21 9JE (01328 823778). Rates £50-£70 double incl breakfast. No credit cards.

A cross between a B&B and self-catering accommodation, the Old School consists of a huge double bedroom (the ex-headmaster's study) and two interconnecting rooms, all with independent ground-floor access – and that's it. There's no breakfast room (continental breakfast is served in the bedroom) and no lounge, so this is one for people who like peace and quiet, and a quirky place to stay.

Oyster House

Lynn Road, West Rudham, PE31 8RW (01485 528327, www.oysterhouse.co.uk). Rates £75 double incl breakfast. No credit cards.

A lovely farmhouse garden setting makes the Oyster House B&B a great choice for families – particularly as the double and twin rooms set in the old dairy open directly on to a grassed courtyard. In the main house, a large double features a roll-top bath and lots of character, and breakfast is served in a traditional farmhouse parlour.

Valentine House

62 Back Street, South Creake, NR21 9PG (01328 823413). Rates £60-£80 double incl breakfast. No credit cards.

This B&B has two pretty adjoining rooms set in a garden studio. They're full of character and homely touches, such as patchwork quilts and exposed brick walls, with breakfast laid out on a huge farmhouse table.

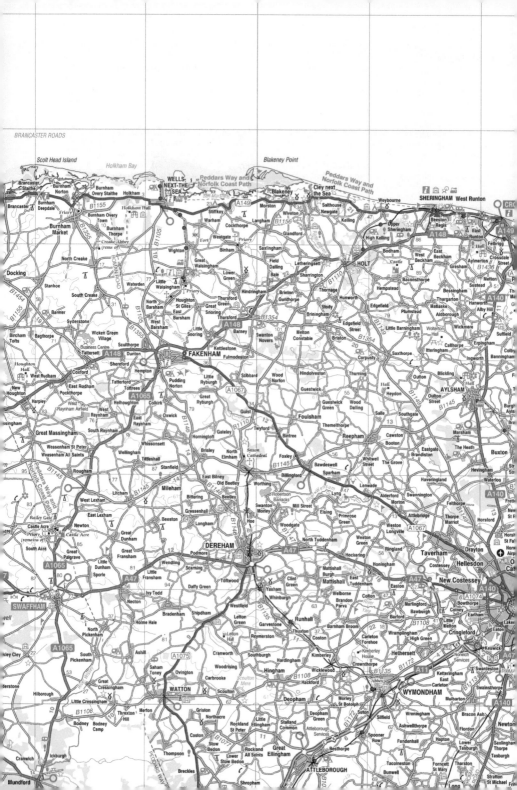

North Norfolk Coast: Wells to Weybourne

Where the western half of the north Norfolk coast is a huge empty expanse of sand, dunes and marsh, the eastern half is tamer, tidier and altogether more down to earth. In settlements such as Wells-next-the-Sea, Blakeney and Morston, fishing still plays its part, but as the A149 winds through Salthouse towards the Victorian town of Sheringham, the wide stretches of beach and marsh give way to pebbles and seaside resort pleasures. Inland, the towns of Little Walsingham and Holt are unmissable and offer some great shopping and eating opportunities. Dotted with numerous quaint villages, such as Salle, Reepham, Swannington and privately owned Heydon, as well as hundreds of Norman and Saxon churches, this inland area is great driving and walking terrain, with heath, wood, fen, pasture and even the odd small hill offering something for everyone.

WELLS TO WEYBOURNE

Wells-next-the-Sea

Less than two miles east of Holkham's vast, sparse, pine-backed beach, the little town of Wells-next-the-Sea manages to cram in a beach resort, a fishing port, a picturesque shopping street and a leafy green (the Buttlands, where the carnival is held in summer).

There's a wealth of things to do here, from sampling the fine dining at the Crown Hotel (see p54) or the Globe Inn (see p54) to browsing old-fashioned independent shops (butcher, baker, fishmonger, sweet shop, hardware store) along the Staithe, the narrow high street that runs uphill from the pretty quay lined with fishing and pleasure boats. There's a huge range of cafés and takeaways on the Staithe too, including the De-lish Deli, the Hamper, Nelson's Coffee House and the Picnic Hut (purveyor of Norfolk County Dairy ice-cream). Facing the quay, French's Fish Shop (10 Quayside, 01328 710396, closed Mon in winter) has been selling fish and chips for more than 75 years; a few doors away the Wells Deli (see p65) makes a mean crab sandwich.

Wells' sandy beach is a mile from the town centre; in summer, you can travel there via horse and carriage from the quay (around £1 per person) or on the narrow-gauge Harbour Railway that ferries passengers from the harbour to the beachside holiday camp, Pinewoods. At low tide it's a long walk out to the water. At high tide the sea rushes in (very fast – sirens sound to alert bathers to the danger of being cut off on the dunes), the beach shrinks dramatically, and crabbing boats flood into the harbour to unload their snapping cargo.

On the outskirts of town, the wonderful Norfolk design shop Big Blue Sky (see p64) is definitely worth the ten minutes' walk, and is a great stop if you're heading for the nearby Wells & Walsingham Light Railway (see p61). If you're visiting in May, look out for the annual Poetry-next-the-Sea Festival (01328 711813, www.poetry-next-the-sea.com).

Stiffkey to Blakeney

East of Wells, the coast road narrows as it passes through the small villages of Stiffkey (pronounced 'Stukey') and Morston, reflecting the change of mood to a more rural, homely feel. Look out for seasonal fruit and veg sold from roadside cottages, along with mussels, oysters, honeycomb and – that much sought after Norfolk speciality – samphire. Stiffkey boasts a good pub, the Red Lion (see p57); a great antiques and vintage lighting shop, Stiffkey Antiques (01328 830460, www.stiffkeyantiques.com, closed Wed, Thur Oct-Easter), housed in the former Methodist chapel; and the excellent Stiffkey Stores (01328 830489, www.stiffkeystores.com). Stock up on fabulous cupcakes and savoury snacks before heading a couple of miles south to the ruins of Elizabethan Stiffkey Hall (currently being restored, with gardens occasionally open to the public).

Morston's creeks are splendid for muddy paddling at low tide, but don't miss the tiny 11th- to 13th-century All Saints' Church. It doesn't have any electricity, so services and festivals are lit solely by candlelight from chandeliers made by parishioners Ned and Nick Hamond, creating a great atmosphere and beautifully illuminating the 15th-century painted rood screen.

Pub-lovers might want to make a small detour inland to the west of Stiffkey to pay homage to the Three Horseshoes at Warham (69 Bridge Street, 01328 710547), which has a classic old interior, plus well-kept ales, decent food (pies a speciality), and rooms. Or continue along the main coast road

Wells-next-the-Sea. See p51.

to Blakeney, where the two narrow streets leading down to the quay contain a handful of shops, pubs and restaurants, including the Blakeney Deli (30 High Street, 01263 740939, www. blakeneydeli.co.uk) and Westons fishmonger's (5A Westgate Street, 01263 741112, www. westonsofblakeney.co.uk). Here you'll find own-made enticements such as potted shrimps, resh crab and seafood quiches.

Blakeney is justly famous for its grey seal colony, best seen on a boat trip from Blakeney or Morston harbours (see p61), but it's also a lovely place to while away a few hours exploring the area's ancient relationship with the sea. In Back Lane, for

example, the vaulted cellars of the 14th-century Guildhall were used as a mortuary for drowned sailors in the 19th century, while the small turret on the north-east chancel of St Nicholas, a beautiful hilltop church, was for centuries a burning beacon guiding ships into harbour.

Cley-next-the-Sea to Weybourne

Continuing east along the A149, delightfully idiosyncratic Cley-next-the-Sea (pronounced 'Cly') makes a great base for hikes. There's no newsagent or grocer, but you will find a deli, smokehouse, lovely bookshop, pretty tearoom and three galleries, including Made in Cley (see *p64*). The energetic should take the lane east of the village down to the shingle beach and from there it's possible to trek to Blakeney Point (four miles there and back), keeping a seaward eye out for seals along the way. A more leisurely stroll starts from Church Lane (off the A149 by Picnic Fayre) and runs past Cley's enormous St Mary's Church, built in the 13th century, when the village was a prosperous port; the south porch, with its traceried battlements and lovely fan-vaulted roof, is stunning.

You can stock up on picnic goodies at Picnic Fayre (The Old Forge, 01263 740587, www.picnic-fayre.co.uk) and find presents for foodie friends at the Cley Smokehouse (High Street, 01263 740282, www.cleysmokehouse.com). Also on the High Street, the Pinkfoot Gallery (01263 740947, www.pinkfootgallery.com) has wildlife-inspired prints, paintings and sculptures, many by local artists.

Just east of Cley, the Cley Marshes Nature Reserve (*see p56*) is another good walking spot – head through the salt marshes and down to the beach. From here you can walk as far as Salthouse for lunch at Cookie's Crab Shop (*see p54*), a pint at the Dun Cow (Coast Road, 01263 740467, www.theduncow-salthouse.co.uk), a poke around another terrific church (St Nicholas), which holds a themed and curated contemporary art festival each year (usually in August), or a pleasurable stroll along the Salthouse Sculpture trail (01328 711426, www.salthousetrail.co.uk).

From here it's just a few miles to the more built-up charms of Weybourne, home to the Muckleburgh Collection (*see p56*) and the usual collection of tea shop, village store, pub and church backing a pretty and very steep pebbly beach known as Weybourne Hope (or Hoop). For paddling and castle-building, it's best to continue along the coast to the Victorian resort of Sheringham, where samphire and smoked fish give way to cotton candy floss and greasy spoons.

Where to eat & drink

Food along this stretch of the coast spans every budget, from shellfish and sandwich shacks on the quay (such as the Kabin Sandwich Bar at Blakeney) to pubs serving huge pots of mussels and local game (try Warham's Three Horseshoes; *see p51*), and more upmarket restaurants and bistros, such as the Moorings (01263 740054, www.blakeney-moorings.co.uk, closed dinner Mon, Sun, closed Mon-Thur Nov-Easter) in Blakeney and Morston Hall (*see p55*) in Morston. Thanks to a strong emphasis on local produce cooked on the premises, most of what's on offer is great.

Blakeney White Horse

4 High Street, Blakeney, NR25 7AL (01263 740574, www.blakeneywhitehorse.co.uk). Open 11am-11pm Mon-Sat; 11am-10.30pm Sun. Lunch served noon-2.15pm daily. Dinner served 6-9pm Mon-Thur, Sun; 6-9.30pm Fri, Sat.

Just up from the quay on Blakeney's quaint High Street, this ramshackle 16th-century pub is rightly renowned for its accomplished food, ranging from a crowd-pleasing bar menu to more inventive dishes, such as roast cod fillet with flageolet bean casserole. There's a B&B too: nine pretty, shabby-chic rooms decorated with tongue-and-groove panelling, seaside colours, roll-top baths and comfortable beds. A double room with breakfast costs £70-£140.

Cookie's Crab Shop ★
The Green, Salthouse, NR25 7AJ (01263 740352,
www.salthouse.org.uk). Food served Summer 9am-7pm
daily. Winter 9am-4pm daily, but times may vary.
No credit cards.
This jewel of a café keeps things simple. Seating is at cramped tables in a garden shed, or outside in a pagoda or beneath parasols. The menu is equally frills-free: a couple of soups (including the smoky kipper and tomato), takeaway sarnies and a wide array of seafood salads.

Corner House
Staithe Street, Wells-next-the-Sea, NR23 1AF
(01328 710701, www.cornerhouseatwells.com).

Wells & Walsingham Light Railway. See p61.

Lunch served 12.30-2.30pm Sat, Sun.
Dinner served 6-9.30pm Wed-Sat.
An alluring menu of seasonal and locally sourced Modern British food is served at this laid-back restaurant, bar and oyster bar, from Wells Quay crab soup (made using a whole crab, tomatoes, double cream and brandy) to pizza or local venison bourguignon.

Crown Hotel
The Buttlands, Wells-next-the-Sea, NR23 1EX
(01328 710209, www.crownhotelnorfolk.co.uk).
Open 10am-11pm daily. Lunch served noon-2.30pm,
dinner served 6.30-9.30pm daily.
Chris Coubrough's cream and blue, 16th-century coaching inn on Wells' elegant Georgian square is a smart affair. The restaurant serves great British food with Pacific Rim and Mediterranean influences, including plenty of fish. In the adjoining black-beamed bar, things are more low-key; heaped-high sandwiches, plus well-kept local ales and a good selection of wines by the glass. Upstairs, 12 rustic-minimal en suite rooms (£90-£155 double incl breakfast) come with attractive seaside themes and all mod cons.

George Hotel
High Street, Cley-next-the-Sea, NR25 7RN
(01263 740652, www.thegeorgehotelatcley.co.uk).
Open 10.30am-11pm Mon-Sat; noon-10.30pm
Sun. Lunch served noon-2.15pm Mon-Sat; 12.30-
2.30pm Sun. Dinner served 6.30-9pm Mon-Sat;
6.30-8.30pm Sun.
The enjoyable calm of this handsome country inn – under the same ownership as the Blakeney White Horse – makes it the perfect place to base yourself if you want to experience the tranquility of Cley. The modern restaurant proffers a wide range of dishes (including sandwiches), all reasonably priced. The dozen bedrooms (£50-£115 double incl breakfast) are unfussy, relying on natural light and neutral colours to provide understated simplicity. Rooms 3, 4 and 5 are the biggest and have the best views.

Globe Inn
The Buttlands, Wells-next-the-Sea, NR23 1EU
(01328 710206, www.holkham.co.uk/globe). Open
9am-11pm daily. Lunch served noon-2.30pm, dinner
served 7-9pm daily.
Owned by the Holkham Estate, the gorgeous Globe is located on the same grassy square as the Crown and is its equal in every respect. The excellent food is Modern British in style, employs as much local produce as possible, and is served as bar snacks and full meals. The seven contemporary styled B&B rooms (£80-£120 double incl breakfast) manage to be both pretty and stylish.

King's Arms
Westgate Street, Blakeney, NR25 7NQ (01263 740341,
www.blakeneykingsarms.co.uk). Open 11am-11pm
Mon-Sat; noon-10.30pm Sun. Food served noon-
9.30pm Mon-Sat; noon-8.30pm Sun.
A wonderfully old-school cosy pub near the Quay that's especially popular with walkers fresh from the salt marshes, who come to refuel on hearty dishes such as lamb shank on dauphinoise potatoes, and Thai green curry. Local fish and seafood is a speciality. There's accommodation upstairs (from £65 double incl breakfast), a real fire in the grate, and a family room out back.

NORFOLK

Blakeney. See p52.

Where to stay

As you'd expect from such a popular area, there's a huge choice of accommodation, from cute self-catering cottages (try the pretty blue and white Quayside cottages at Blakeney, 01462 768627, www.blakeneycottages.co.uk) to small and sweet B&Bs such as the Machrimore (Burnt Street, Wells-next-the-Sea, 01328 711653) and Arch House (50 Mill Road, Wells-next-the-Sea, 01328 710112, www.archhouse.co.uk), or the slightly more upscale Meadow View Guest House (53 High Street, Wighton, 01328 821527, www.meadow-view.net). Families might like a farmhouse B&B such as Branthill Farm (01328 710246), with access to an outdoor heated pool and tennis court. Upmarket options include the luxurious Blakeney House guest house (High Street, Blakeney, 01263 740561, www.blakeneyhouse.com) and country pile Bayfield Hall (Holt, 01263 713901, www.bayfield hall.com). In between, lots of great inns such as the Crown Hotel (*see p54*) in Wells, the George Hotel (*see p54*) in Cley and the White Horse (*see p53*) in Blakeney offer excellent accommodation.

Blakeney Hotel
Blakeney, NR25 7NE (01263 740797, www.blakeney-hotel.co.uk). Rates £142-£238 double incl breakfast.
This smart hotel's leisure features are a godsend in wet weather, with spa facilities, a heated pool, a gym and a games room. Sixty spacious rooms, some with balconies and private patios, others with wide-ranging views to the marshy estuary, will appeal to those who prefer hassle-free anonymity to B&B intimacy.

Cley Windmill ★
The Mill, Cley-next-the-Sea, NR25 7RP (01263 740209, www.cleymill.co.uk). Rates £78-£155 double incl breakfast.

This 18th-century windmill stands just outside the village (and away from the main road), and has supreme views of the reed-rustling salt marshes and the distant sea. Choose from five rooms in the circular mill itself or opt for seclusion in the former boat house, located across a small courtyard from the mill, and in two converted outhouses (which can also be let on a self-catering basis).

High Sand Creek Campsite
Greenway, Stiffkey, NR23 1QF (01328 830235). Open mid Mar-mid Oct. Rates £10-£15 2 people.
This lovely hillside campsite has fantastic views across the marshes, which are near enough to ensure plenty of birds and wildlife interest. The 80-pitch site is clean, has great facilities and friendly, helpful staff. It's a three-mile walk along the coast path to Wells (you can take the Coasthopper bus back).

Kelling Heath
Weybourne, NR25 7HW (01263 588181, www. kellingheath.co.uk). Rates Camping £16.75-£35.50 per pitch. Lodge £562-£1,362 per week. Holiday home £237-£819 per week.
Set in 250 acres of woodland and open heath, Kelling Heath has it all, from a campsite to attractive wooden lodges (sleeping up to six) and luxury holiday homes (sleeping six or eight). There's also a dizzying range of activities, including star-gazing nights, art workshops, cycling, swimming (in an indoor or outdoor pool) and tennis coaching, as well as plenty of entertainment for all ages.

Morston Hall
The Street, Morston, NR25 7AA (01263 741041, www.morstonhall.com). Rates £290-£340 double incl breakfast & dinner.
This award-winning country house hotel in Morston is a bastion of traditional comfort without being overbearingly old-fashioned; think English country house with all mod

WELLS TO WEYBOURNE

Cley Marshes Nature Reserve
Coast Road, Cley-next-the-Sea, NR25 7SA (01263 740008, www.norfolkwildlifetrust.org.uk). Open NWT members dawn-dusk daily. Non-members Mar-Oct 10am-5pm daily. Nov-Apr 10am-4pm daily. Admission Nature reserve £4; free reductions & NWT members. Visitor centre free.

One of Britain's top birdwatching sites has hides looking out over reed beds and pools, enabling you to spot avocets, bitterns, terns, marsh harriers, oystercatchers and more. The award-winning sustainable visitor centre incorporates a café, shop, observation area and displays on coastal history and stories. Coasthopper buses (01553 776980, www.coasthopper.co.uk) stop outside the reserve.

Muckleburgh Collection
Weybourne, NR25 7EH ((01263 588210, www.muckleburgh.co.uk). Open Apr-Oct 10am-5pm daily. Mar 10am-5pm Sat, Sun. Admission £6; £4-£5 reductions; £17 family.

Tanks, armoured vehicles, guns, aircraft (including a Harrier jump-jet), 54 model ships and more military gear than your average platoon has in Iraq are spread across eight exhibition halls. There's also a large gift shop and bookable tank rides. Outside, rusting vehicles and a radar station alongside crumbling concrete dormitories lends a bedraggled air of authenticity to the whole macho affair.

INLAND TO EAST DEREHAM

County School Station
North Elmham (01362 668181, http://web.ukonline. co.uk/Members/rj.cullen/Station.htm). Open Easter-Sept 11am-4pm Sun & bank hol Mon. Admission Free.

This wonderfully peculiar time-warp museum train station, designed to look like a station from 1941, is eerily realistic and evocative, with windows taped against bombs and posters bearing a grim-looking Winston Churchill calling for your support or demanding sternly whether your journey is really necessary. Thankfully, the tearoom forgoes powdered egg in favour of the real thing.

Gressenhall Farm & Workhouse ★
Gressenhall, NR20 4DR (01362 860563, www.museums.norfolk.gov.uk). Open Mar-Nov 10am-5pm daily. Admission £8.40; £6-£7.10 reductions.

Housed in an imposing workhouse, this social history museum evokes life in rural Norfolk with skill and flair, keeping things lively for children with a rare breeds farm, a Victorian photography studio and cart rides. Interpretive panels, interactive displays and audio-visual material mean there's something for all ages; a punishment cell for gore-fixated teenagers, workhouse trails and inmates' stories for the more thoughtful. There are lovely walks in the grounds and a decent tearoom.

Letheringsett Watermill
Riverside Road, Letheringsett, NR25 7YD (01263 713153, www.letheringsettwatermill.co.uk). Open Easter-Sept 10am-5pm Mon-Fri; 9am-1pm Sat.

Walsingham Abbey

Oct-Easter 9am-4pm Mon-Fri; 9am-1pm Sat. Admission £2.50; £1.50 reductions (£4; £2.50 reductions during working demonstrations). No credit cards.

Norfolk's only flour-producing watermill attracts thousands of visitors each year and is a regular on the tourist attractions awards circuit. It's justified; the 110-year-old mill is a lot of fun to explore and the riverside setting is magical. The regular working demonstrations and guided tours (on most weekday afternoons) offer fascinating insight into the production process. A well-stocked shop sells the spelt flour produced by the mill.

Natural Surroundings
The Wildlife, Wildflower & Conservation Centre, Bayfield Estate, Glandford, NR25 7JN (01263 711091, www.birdventures.co.uk). Open 10am-4pm Tue-Sun. Admission £3; £2 reductions; £8.50 family.

A lovely inland nature resource that has something for everyone, including ponds, wildlife gardens, wildflower meadows and a decent nursery. The tearoom is a must, not least for viewing birds and wildlife close up, thanks to window feeders and nest-box cameras.

Pensthorpe Nature Reserve
Fakenham Road, nr Fakenham, NR21 0LN (01328 851465, www.pensthorpe.com). Open Apr-Dec 10am-5pm daily. Jan-Mar 10am-4pm daily. Admission £8.50; £5-£7 reductions; £23 family.

The home of BBC's *Springwatch* is vast: a nature site in the Wensum Valley containing a wide range of areas, among them wildflower meadows, a bug walk and conservation centres. With 171 recorded wild bird species flitting about the sprawling wetlands, gardens and woodlands, it's of particular interest to birdwatchers.

Shell Museum
Church House, Glandford, NR25 7JR (01263 740081, www.shellmuseum.org.uk). Open Easter-Oct 10am-12.30pm, 2pm-4.30pm Tue-Sat. Admission £2; 50p-£1.50 reductions. No credit cards.
Built in 1915 to house a collection of shells assembled over a period of 60 years by Sir Alfred Jodrell, this tiny Dutch-style gem of a building contains thousands of exquisite seashells, fossils, birds' eggs, agate ware, local archaeological finds and the enjoyable tat only local museums ever seem to exhibit. Next to it stands St Martin's church, an equally arresting building that contains elaborate woodcarving and beautiful stained-glass windows; a carillon of 12 bells plays a hymn every three hours.

Slipper Chapel
Houghton St Giles, nr Walsingham (01328 820495). Open 8am-7pm daily; reduced opening hours in winter, phone for details. Admission free.
The pretty but unremarkable little 14th-century Roman Catholic Shrine of Our Lady, built as the last wayside chapel for pilgrims on their way to the Walsingham shrine, lies an attractive one-mile stroll from Walsingham. Be prepared to see people walking the route from the chapel to the village in slippers or bare feet, as Henry VIII supposedly did in 1511.

Thursford Collection ★
Thursford, NR21 0AS (01328 878477, www.thursford.com). Open Apr-Sept noon-5pm Mon-Fri, Sun. Admission £8; free-£7 reductions.
One of the strangest attractions in Norfolk was begun more than 50 years ago by George Cushing, who collected an eye-popping array of steam-powered and mechanical engines, fairground organs and carousels; look out for the steam-powered Venetian gondola ride, but whatever you do don't miss the 1931 Wurlitzer organ. Its 1,339 pipes create an astonishing array of sounds and effects, best experienced through daily recitals in the Wurlitzer cinema. Dickensian-style shops and cafés add to the olde worlde theme. Booking is obligatory for the Christmas Spectacular shows: see the website for details.

Walsingham Abbey Grounds
Entrance through Shirehall Museum, Common Place, Walsingham, NR22 6BP (01328 820259). Open Feb-Oct 10am-4.30pm daily. Nov, Dec 10am-4.30pm Sat, Sun. Admission £3.50; £2.50 reductions.
The 12th-century abbey ruins and lovely gardens are part of 20 acres of woodland and parkland, linked via beautiful little bridges and winding paths. Snowdrop walks in early spring are especially popular. The Shirehall Museum, which acts as the entrance to the grounds, houses the old courthouse as well as artefacts, photographs and an engaging history of the village's 1,000-year history.

cons – some rooms even have tile TVs in the bathrooms. But it's the hotel's gastronomic credentials that are the real draw; Michelin-starred chef Galton Blackiston (who runs the hotel with his wife Tracy) produces a daily set dinner and Sunday lunch that draws on local produce cooked simply but exquisitely. Non-residents are welcome to eat too.

Old Town Hall House
Coast Road, Cley-next-the-Sea, NR25 7RB (01263 740284, www.oldtownhallhouse.co.uk). Rates £85-£105 double incl breakfast.
A quietly charming B&B, with three rooms and one suite decorated in calming colours and kitted out with Roberts radios instead of TVs. Slap-up breakfasts include the likes of kedgeree with locally smoked haddock. A self-catering apartment sleeping two is also available.

Red Lion
44 Wells Road, Stiffkey, NR23 1AJ (01328 830552, www.stiffkey.com). Rates £80-£100 double incl breakfast.
A lovely village inn with big roaring fires, nooks and crannies and ten eco-friendly, chalet-style rooms a short way up the hill behind the pub, ensuring expansive views across to the River Stiffkey. The ground-floor rooms have little gardens, the upstairs ones large terraces; all are quiet and clean. The food is good-quality pub grub, featuring local ingredients.

Weybourne Forest Lodges
Sandy Hill Lane, Weybourne, NR25 7HW (01263 588440, www.weybourneforestlodges.co.uk). Rates £195-£795 per week.
This small cluster of timber lodges in a forest glade in the middle of nowhere (well, three miles from Holt and Sheringham) is perfect for a getaway, with no clubhouse or entertainment, just lots of beautiful countryside. Different styles of lodges include large, A-frame Scandinavian buildings and more humble two-person cabins, but all come with heating, games, books, a TV and parking for two cars.

INLAND TO EAST DEREHAM

Wiveton to Letheringsett
Inland north Norfolk has charms that are no less pleasurable than its coastal counterparts; they're just less obvious. The pretty little villages of Kelling and Wiveton are just a couple of miles from the sea; lovely views can be had from the pub garden at the Pheasant (01263 588101, www.pheasant hotelnorfolk.co.uk), set on rising ground in Kelling, and from the Wiveton Bell (01263 740101, www. wivetonbell.co.uk). The latter is next to a lovely church in the rolling landscape of Wiveton Downs and just a short walk from the magical Wiveton Farm Café (*see p62*).

Glandford too is a delight. It's a model village built at the start of the 20th century by Sir Alfred Jodrell, and contains flint and red-brick Dutch-style gabled houses; St Martin's Church, which has a beautiful roof and stained glass; Birdscapes Gallery (Manor Farm Barns, 01263 741742,

FIVE CRABBING TIPS

● Both Blakeney Quay and Wells Quay are ideal spots for crabbing (aka gillying). It's best to crab at high tide, when the sea is near the top of the harbour walls and you won't have far to reach down to grab your catch. Links to local tide tables can be found online at www.bbc.co.uk/weather. Times of high tides are also published in the *Eastern Daily Press* (Mon-Sat) and the *Lynn News* (Tue, Fri).

● You can get a weighted crab line for a few pence at local shops. Don't use a hook – which can get lost and injure seabirds – but simply tie your bait to the line or put it inside the little net provided.

● Instead of expensive bait, buy around £1's worth of bacon bits. These work just as well.

● Buy a landing net. A net is crucial, especially if you're crabbing near low tide: you don't want your snappers to drop off the line before you can haul them up to the quay.

● Use a decent-sized bucket (see-through, if possible), partially filled with seawater, to collect the crabs. When you're done, gently tip over the bucket and allow the little snappers to escape.

... AND WHERE TO BUY THE EDIBLE KIND

● Direct from fishermen's houses along the A149, particularly around Cley, Morston, Blakeney and Sheringham (look out for signs).

● Cookie's Crab Shop in Salthouse (*see p54*) – a wooden shack, a plastic pergola and a few rickety chairs and tables might not look like much, but the huge salads, sandwiches and takeway shellfish here are some of the best in the county.

● JWH Jonas (01263 514121, closed Mon, Sun, closed Wed & Sat after 2pm, all Dec-Mar) or J Lee Fisherman's crab stall for dressed crabs. Both are on New Street, Cromer.

● The Old Forge Seafood Restaurant (*see p61*) in Thursford always has Cromer crab on the menu – alongside plenty of other local fish and seafood.

● The Fair Maiden fishmonger in Happisburgh (*see p95*), where fresh and dressed crabs are joined by lobster and a terrific range of fresh and smoked fish – all the ingredients you need for a seafood salad or stonking fish pie.

www.birdscapesgallery.co.uk); and Norfolk's oldest purpose-built museum, the tiny and gorgeous Shell Museum (*see p57*). Sir Alfred lived at nearby Bayfield Hall (01263 713901, www.bayfieldhall. com). The 19th-century estate now houses a mini antiques mart in the Old Stables and has a picturesque series of ancient flint barns, one of which houses Bray's Cottage Pork Pies (phone ahead to buy the mouth-watering pies – 01263 860944, www.perfectpie.co.uk).

This is an area of rolling hills criss-crossed with public paths and bridleways, with something of interest at almost every turn. Just a couple of miles south-west of Wiveton, the village of Binham contains the evocative ruins of Binham Priory, plus a nice pub, the Chequers Inn (Front Street, 01328 830297). Nearby Langham is home to the biennial summertime Street Fayre (01328 830696, www.langhamstreetfayre.com).

Heading slightly further inland, Letheringsett's still-working flour watermill (*see p56*) is consistently voted one of the county's best attractions. Stop for lunch at the Kings Head (*see p62*), a rambling beauty of a pub in a lovely garden setting, before popping into the well-stocked farm shop and gallery Back to the Garden (*see p64*), just outside the village. From here it's just a mile to the Georgian town of Holt.

Holt ★

This handsome market town easily gives Burnham Market a run for its money. In some ways it's a better base and a more interesting town; less monied, more youthful and vibrant, with plenty to keep your interest for a weekend, as well as a pleasant escape route to Sheringham via the North Norfolk Railway, aka the Poppy Line (*see p77*). Most of the town was consumed by fire in May 1708; one of the few medieval buildings to survive is part of Gresham's public school. Christmas is a lovely time to visit Holt, as the town makes a huge decorative effort, and many consider the lights to be the best in the county.

The centre is pretty compact, with most shops and businesses on or near the High Street and Market Place, with an antiques enclave around Albert Street. Excellent independent shops range from department store Bakers & Larners (8-12 Market Place, 01263 712244, www.bakersand larners.com), which has a fine food hall, to clothing shops such as cult classic Old Town (*see p64*) and Annie & Boo. In addition, there are vintage shops such as Past Caring and Moo Moos, and great bric-a-brac, homeware and antiques to be found at the likes of Cottage Collectables, Great to be Green and Casa Andalus. Two galleries – Bircham (*see p64*) and Red Dot (2 Lyles Court, Lees Yard, 01263 710287, www.thereddotgallery.com) – are definitely worth a browse.

There's plenty of food too, with a dizzying range of restaurants and tearooms that span the gamut from good greasy spoon (Jambos' on Appleyard and the Owl Tea Room on Church Street) via pub grub (the Kings Head on the High Street, and the Pigs, *see p62*) to high-quality fare at Butlers (*see*

Cley Windmill. See p55.

p61), the tearoom and Number Ten restaurant in Bakers & Larners, and Byfords (*see p61*) – which also offers rooms at its Posh B&B.

Just three miles south-east of Holt, the extensive ruins of Baconsthorpe Castle, a moated and fortified 15th-century manor house run by English Heritage, are fun to explore, and you can chart the rise and fall of the once prominent Heydon family. A couple of miles out of Holt on the A148 towards Cromer, the rare bookseller Simon Finch's unusual Arts and Crafts house Voewood (*see p65*) is a must-see.

Little Walsingham to East Barsham

Further inland, to the east, lies Little Walsingham. This handsome medieval village, really more of a small town, has been an important place of Christian pilgrimage for almost 1,000 years. Even now, half a million devout members of the Catholic and Orthodox churches are drawn each year to the modern Anglican shrine of Our Lady of Walsingham, the 600-year-old Roman Catholic Slipper chapel (*see p57*), the ruins of the old Priory, and the Chapel of St Seraphim, a Russian Orthodox church housed in the old railway station. An enjoyable day can be spent in a variety of ways: wandering the narrow streets, admiring the half-timbered medieval buildings, popping into gift shops (religious souvenirs a speciality) and tea shops (the Walsingham tearoom does a mean pot of char and toasted teacake). For more substantial meals, the Bull on the High Street serves good grub, while

fish and chips and more adventurous dishes are on offer at the excellent Norfolk Riddle (*see p62*). Gather the makings of a great picnic at the Walsingham Farms Shop (Guild Street, 01328 821877, www.walsinghamfarmsshop.co.uk), and enjoy it amid the peaceful gardens of Walsingham Abbey (*see p57*). A Christmas fair is usually held in the village on the third weekend of November.

Poor old Great Walsingham, by contrast, is a misnomer if ever there was one, but it is worth a stop, not least for an enjoyable crafts and galleries mall next door to the Old Foundry, and some pretty-as-a-picture cottages. Heading south, park at the White Horse pub at East Barsham to check out the amazing battlemented red-brick Tudor manor house occupied by Henry VIII when he made the pilgrimage to Walsingham shrine – the house is closed to the public, but you can get fine views of the famed chimneys, towers, turrets and mullioned windows if you walk up to the rise facing it.

Fakenham & East Dereham

The market town of Fakenham is just a few miles further inland from here. The route is crossed by the pretty River Wensum, and further along the A1067 Norwich to Fakenham road is the magical Foxley Wood, Norfolk's largest area of ancient woodland, but the town itself offers few diversions or attractions. Its one-time Georgian grandeur is evident in the Market Square, but the place is blighted by ugly shops (many of them closed down) and a shabby demeanour. There's the odd

architectural delight, such as the cinema, the market cross and old gasworks (now the Fakenham Museum of Gas, www.fakenhamgasmuseum.com), plus a lively Thursday market.

On the outskirts of town, Fakenham racecourse (01328 862388, www.fakenhamracecourse.co.uk) makes a nice day out. The nearby Thursford Collection (*see p57*) and Pensthorpe Nature Reserve (*see p56*) offer good excursions for families – as does the Norfolk Wildlife Trust site at Thursford Wood, about three miles north-east of Fakenham (on the A148 road towards Cromer). The oaks here are some of the oldest in the county and provide refuge for an array of wildlife.

From Fakenham it's a short hop south to East Dereham, with a look at the ruins of North Elmham's 1,000-year-old Saxon cathedral on the way, but there's little reason to spend much time in the town nearest to Norfolk's geographical centre. It's key attractions are the marketplace, home to some elegant 18th-century houses (marred by insensitive shopfront conversions), a mad gothic revival Congregational chapel and, facing it, a corn hall turned into a cinema. Bishop Bonner's Cottage Museum of local history (01362 692009/695397, www.derehamhistory.com, closed Mon, Wed, Sun, closed Nov-Easter) is housed in a very pretty 1502 cottage at the bottom of Church Street. Best of all is the two-towered church of St Nicholas, a mainly 14th- and 15th-century structure with a 13th-century chancel and a wonderful font depicting the seven sacraments.

North-east to Reepham & the coast

Heading back towards the coast, a swathe of villages close to each other all reward exploration, whether you're into history, bucolic scenery, architecture or walking. Swanton Morley, lying in a hollow near the River Wensum, is famous for being home to the ancestors of Abraham Lincoln (the home of Richard Lincoln, who lived here in the 16th century, is now the Angel Inn, owned by the National Trust). Other favourites include Elsing, which contains one of the country's best church brasses (in 14th-century St Mary's) and 15th-century Elsing Hall, whose gardens are occasionally open to the public. Lyng is pretty as a picture and offers some great riverside walking; Lenwade has a highly rated Dinosaur Adventure Park (*see p61*; and the area around handsome Swannington further east offers some wonderful walks through terrain that takes in heathland, woods, fens, meadows and even a small hill.

The nicest area is around the conservation town of Reepham, a few miles north-west of Swannington. It's full of quaint thatched cottages and 18th-century brick houses tidily arranged around a neat marketplace, where a weekly Wednesday market and occasional antiques fairs (in the Old Reepham Brewery) are held. Even without them, the town contains a pleasing selection of independent shops: Very Nice Things has everything from art and crafts to homeware and books; Diane's Pantry is a health food shop and deli; and Melon Caulie Rose, as you might suspect, is a rather sweet greengrocer's.

Little Walsingham *See p59.*

There are two good pubs and a clutch of restaurants and tearooms (including one in a museum housed in what used to be Reepham train station; you can also pick up the long-distance Marriott's Way trail here). Of the two churches sharing the same churchyard, St Mary is worth exploring in some detail; highlights include a lovely ironwork door leading to the tower and a rather magnificent tombchest in the chancel.

But it's to Salle and Booton, just outside Reepham, that lovers of church architecture should head. St Peter & St Paul in Salle is built in splendid 15th-century Perpendicular style and is an awe-inspiring sight; it also has a beautiful interior. Booton's St Michael & All Angels is altogether more controversial, a gothic fantasy designed and built in the 19th century by Reverend Whitwell Elwin. He, magpie-like, took elements of all his favourite church architecture to construct a crazy-looking building that's also glorious, not least for its slender twin towers and central pinnacle.

The final village, Heydon ★, is possibly the most attractive, being a privately owned estate village that could be straight out of the pages of an Agatha Christie novel. Ranged around a delightful village green are the 13th-century St Peter & St Paul Church, the whitewashed Earle Arms (*see p62*), a tearoom (*see p62*) and a general shop, the smithy, and about 30 impossibly pretty houses. A mile away, Heydon Hall Park offers some great walks.

NORFOLK

Wending your way back to the coast, the charming villages of Melton Constable and the Snorings (Great and Little) are exactly as their names suggest; sleepy, ancient and picturesque villages that have changed little in the last century, and will probably change little in the next.

Where to eat & drink

Almost every village in this area has a pub; almost all of them are called the Crown, and almost all of them are worth at least a pint stop; some, like the Crown in Colkirk (Crown Road, 01328 862172) are even worth eating in. In Holt, try the Owl Tea Room (Church Street, 01263 713232) for a snack or the Lawns hotel (*see p65*) for a more refined setting.

Fish lovers should head to the Old Forge Seafood Restaurant (01328 878345, www.seafood.north norfolk.co.uk, bookings only Jan, Feb) in Thursford,

on the A148 between Fakenham and Holt, where most of the shellfish (crabs, oysters, lobsters, mussels) comes from Blakeney.

Butlers
9 Appleyard, Holt, NR25 6BN (01263 710790, www.butlersrestaurants.com). Lunch served noon-3pm, dinner served 6-9pm Mon-Sat.
Set in a large conservatory with a lovely terrace surrounding it, Butler's is a friendly and excellent bistro serving Modern European food that showcases Norfolk produce.

Byfords Café, Deli & Posh B&B ★
1-3 Shirehall Plain, Holt, NR25 6BG (01263 711400, www.byfords.org.uk). Café Food served 8am-11pm daily. Deli Open 8am-9pm Mon-Sat; 9am-8pm Sun.
Ideally located on the market square, Byfords is usually heaving, and it's easy to see why. The café is as cosy as they come and the food exemplary: a Mediterranean-influenced

Things to do

WELLS TO WEYBOURNE

Blakeney Seal Trips
Seals can be seen in a number of places along Britain's coastline, but the beauty of the beasts at Blakeney Point is their proximity. At high tide, boats from Morston Quay (try Beans Boats, 01263 740038, www.beansboattrips.co.uk, or Temples Seal Trips, 01263 740791, www.sealtrips.co.uk) take visitors out to a seven-mile shingle spit where a sizeable colony of seals can be viewed at surprisingly close quarters. Carry on to the idyllic coastal village of Blakeney and you can go out to the Point on foot, taking a desolate but wonderful two-and-a-half-mile hike along the coast path and back inland to Cley.

Wells & Walsingham Light Railway
Wells-next-the-Sea, NR23 1QB (01328 711630, www.wellswalsinghamrailway.co.uk). Open Apr-Oct times vary; check website for details. Tickets £6-£8; free-£6 reductions. No credit cards.
This is the world's longest 10.25in narrow-gauge steam railway, though at a little over five miles long, the half-hour journey is scarcely arduous. The diminutive train pulls its brightly painted carriages (some enclosed, others open-topped or part covered) through the Norfolk countryside, with stops at two

villages before its destination on the outskirts of Walsingham. Refreshments are sold at Wells station.

INLAND TO EAST DEREHAM

Dinosaur Adventure Park
Weston Park, Lenwade, NR9 5JW (01603 876310, www.dinosauradventure.co.uk). Open Summer 10am-6pm daily. Winter 10am-4pm daily. Admission £9.95; free reductions; prices change seasonally, check website for details.
This replica dinosaur theme park will obviously delight young visitors, but it's a hoot for grown-ups too. Trek along the dinosaur trail, have a round of Jurassic Putt and visit the secret animal garden for a close-up look at iguanas and all manner of creepy crawlies.

Whitwell Station & Reepham Railway
Whitwell Road, Reepham, NR10 4BA (01603 871694, www.whitwellstation.com). Open Summer 10am-6pm, winter 10am-4pm Sat, Sun. Weekday opening varies; call for details. Admission free.
This recently reopened steam railway hopes to be fully operational by summer 2010, with the station and tearoom restored to their 1940s heyday. There's a museum too. Special events are also planned; call or check the website for the latest information.

NORFOLK

selection with plenty of local ingredients. Takeaway food is available at the Deli (including a wide range of ready meals), and the 16 rooms in the Posh B&B (£150-£180 double incl breakfast) make stylish use of local materials.

Earle Arms ★
The Street, Heydon, NR11 6AD (01263 587376). Open noon-3pm, 6-11pm Tue-Sat; noon-11pm Sun. Lunch served noon-2pm, dinner served 6-8.30pm Tue-Sun.
This unspoilt, largely unmodernised village is popular with film and TV crews – *Jeeves and Wooster* was shot here, for example. Fittingly, the 16th-century village inn is all gnarled beams and wood panelling. Daily specials are cooked with flair and imagination, with local produce to the fore; book ahead if you want to sample them.

Heydon Village Teashop
The Street, Heydon, NR11 6AD (01263 587211, www.heydonvillageteashop.co.uk). Open Summer 10am-5pm Wed-Sat; noon-5pm Sun. Winter 10am-4pm Fri, Sat; noon-4pm Sun.
White lacy tablecloths, crockery decorating the walls and a warm terracotta flagstone floor tell you this is a totally traditional tearoom, and that's before you clap eyes on the gigantic sponges and slabs of chocolate cake. It's a surprisingly large space, with lovely views out to the village green, and staff couldn't be friendlier.

Hunny Bell
The Green, Hunworth, NR24 2AA (01263 712300, www.thehunnybell.co.uk). Open 11.30am-3.30pm, 5.30pm-midnight Mon-Sat; 12.30-4.30pm, 6.30-11.30pm Sun. Lunch served noon-2pm Mon-Sat; 12.30-3pm Sun. Dinner served 6-9pm Mon-Sat; 6.30-8.30pm Sun.
A beautiful village pub and restaurant that's part of the Animal Inns empire. Food is served in a dining room made cosy with warm tones of terracotta, brick, red textiles and golden wood, and also on a garden terrace. The Modern British, locally sourced menu won't disappoint, particularly if you're partial to game.

Kings Head ★
Holt Road, Letheringsett, NR25 7AR (01263 712691, www.kingsheadnorfolk.co.uk). Open 10.30am-10.30pm daily. Summer Food served noon-9.30pm daily. Winter Lunch served noon-2.30pm, dinner served 6.30-9.30pm daily.
Chris Coubrough continues to reap the benefits of a canny attitude to country inns: choose a good location; attract both locals and visitors with a wide-ranging menu that includes some bargain deals (£10 curry night, or pie and pint night); keep a good choice of local ales and wines by the glass; serve it all in a convivial, comfortable setting. Big flatscreen TVs are dotted discreetly among the bookshelves and squashy leather chesterfields. He makes it look easy.

Norfolk Riddle ★
2 Wells Road, Walsingham, NR22 2DJ (01328 821903, www.walsinghamfarmsshop.co.uk). Restaurant Lunch served noon-1.45pm Mon-Thur; noon-2.15pm Fri, Sat; noon-2.30pm Sun. Dinner served 6-8.45pm Tue-Thur; 6-9.30pm Fri, Sat; 6-8.30pm Sun. Fish & chip shop Lunch served 11.30am-2pm Mon-Thur; 11.30am-2.30pm Fri, Sat; 11.30am-2.30pm Sun. Dinner served 4.30-9.15pm Mon-Thur; 4.30-10pm Fri, Sat; 4.30-9pm Sun.

The likes of ox kidney and mushroom casserole or roast Walsingham partridge with sprouts are served in the restaurant, alongside stellar fish and chips (also served in the next door chippie). The spick and span Riddle is owned by Walsingham Farms Shop, which ensures a steady supply of Norfolk ales and ciders. Riddles, by the way, are agricultural implements for sorting and grading potatoes.

Pigs ★
Norwich Road, Edgefield, NR24 2RL (01263 587634, www.thepigs.org.uk). Open 11am-3pm, 6-11pm Tue-Sat; noon-4pm Sun. Lunch served 11am-2.30pm Tue-Sat; noon-3pm Sun. Dinner served 6-9pm Tue-Sat.
Wise diners take heed: the Modern British food served at this pretty village pub is worth travelling miles for. If the miles clocked up make you feel a tad guilty, you'll feel decidedly virtuous eating the carefully sourced mutton burgers, steaks and belly pork – the meat is locally reared, and comes via butchers and farmers who practise good animal husbandry. Snacks, Norfolk tapas (otherwise known as 'iffits') a piglets' menu and a decent drinks list complete the dining picture. There's a dartboard and a bar billiards table too.

Wheatsheaf
Church Road, West Beckham, NR25 6NX (01263 822110, www.wheatsheaf.ukpub.net). Open noon-2.30pm, 6-11pm Tue-Sat; noon-4pm Sun. Lunch served noon-2pm Tue-Sat; noon-3pm Sun. Dinner served 6.30-9pm Tue-Sat.
This sprawling, ivy-clad country pub just a few miles from Holt is a real gem. There's a pretty covered terrace and a large garden (with a great play area for kids). Inside is a cosy beamed bar area and two separate dining rooms warmed by a roaring fire. The food is hearty pub grub served in huge portions, and obviously popular – book ahead or risk disappointment.

Wiveton Farm Café ★
Wiveton Hall, 1 Marsh Lane, Wiveton, NR25 7TE (01263 740515, www.wivetonhall.co.uk). Food served Summer 9am-5pm Mon-Thur; 9am-8pm Fri-Sun. Winter 9.30am-8pm Fri, Sat; 9.30am-4pm Sun.
In and around a building reminiscent of a large beach shack, brightly painted rickety furniture, flowery tablecloths and pretty mismatched crockery create a distinctly rural Mediterranean feel, as though you're about to sit down for a long leisurely lunch with an Italian family. And the food is everything you could hope for: a great range of surprisingly delicate and sophisticated daily-changing meals and snacks that use as many ingredients from the farm as possible. The charming shop sells jams and produce made using the farm's own fruits, or you can pick your own.

Where to stay
The Kings Head in Letheringsett (*see above*), and Byfords Posh B&B (*see p61*) are two of the nicest places to stay in the area, but if they're full there are plenty of pleasant alternatives, particularly if you're fond of comfortable, intimate B&Bs. Plough House (59 Holt Road, Field Dalling, 01328 830017, www.oldploughhouse.co.uk); Field House (Moorgate Road, Hindringham, 01328 878726, www.fieldhousehindringham. co.uk); Number 45 Guest House (45 The Street,

NORFOLK

Wiveton Farm Café

Big Blue Sky

Back to the Garden ★
*Letheringsett, NR25 7JJ (01263 715996,
www.back-to-the-garden.co.uk). Open 9.30am-
5.30pm Mon-Fri; 9am-5pm Sat; 10am-4pm Sun.*
Just off the A149, Barney Farm produces a wide range
of organic meat, vegetables and fruit and sells it here
in a large barn. The huge ceilings and airy space are
a far cry from most farm shops, and the gallery/café is
a great place to stop for lunch or a snack – meals are
made using the shop's impressive range of cheeses,
deli goods, charcuterie, vegetables and breads.

Big Blue Sky ★
*Warham Road, Wells-next-the-Sea, NR23 1QA
(01328 712023, www.bigbluesky.uk.com). Open
Mid Mar-Oct 10am-5pm Mon-Sat; 11am-4pm Sun.
Nov, Dec 10am-5pm Wed-Sat; 11am-4pm Sun.*
This wonderful shop won the *Daily Telegraph* award
in 2009 for best independent shop in Britain, and it's
easy to see why. A large, light-filled space houses a
whimsical but wonderful range of goods made in Norfolk,
from delicate ceramic coasters and stylish stationery
to hefty jute beach bags, plus books and toys.

Bircham Gallery
*14 Market Place, Holt, NR25 6BW (01263 713312,
www.birchamgallery.co.uk). Open 9am-5pm Mon-Sat.*
A great contemporary art space showing and selling
the work of some 200 artists and craftspeople, with an
emphasis on modern work and a nice range of prices
– linos and prints start at around £45. The ceramics
and printmaking selections are particularly good.

Fakenham Antiques Centre
*Old Congregational Church, 14 Norwich Road,
Fakenham, NR21 8AZ (01328 862941,
www.fakenhamantiques.co.uk). Open 10am-
4.30pm Mon-Sat.*
More than 30 dealers sell everything from furniture,
lighting and homeware to prints, books and jewellery.
It's a fun space in which to browse and there's no
pressure to buy, just friendly dealers happy to talk
about their wares if you want them to.

Gallery Plus
*Warham Road, Wells-next-the-Sea, NR23 1QA
(01328 711609, www.gallery-plus.co.uk). Open
May-Oct 10am-5pm Mon-Sat; 11am-4pm Sun.
Nov-Apr 10am-5pm Wed-Sat; 11am-4pm Sun.*
This appealing art and design shop and gallery – next
door to Big Blue Sky – is owned and run by Trevor and
Joanna Woods, who display and sell a wide range of
2D art including prints, etchings, photos and paintings,
as well as 3D pieces such as jewellery and ceramics.

Ginger Rose
*3 Lyles Court, Lees Yard, Holt, NR25 6HS
(01263 711205, www.ginger-rose.co.uk).
Open 9.30am-5pm Mon-Wed, Fri, Sat.*
Accessories and homeware are stocked at this pretty
shop, where the emphasis is on carefully sourced
gifts you're unlikely to find anywhere else, including
vegetable candles, Lampe Berger household
fragrances, bathroom goodies and oddities such
as ropeball doorstops.

Made in Cley
*High Street, Cley-next-the-Sea, NR25 7RF
(01263 740134, www.madeincley.co.uk).
Open 10am-5pm Mon-Sat; 11am-4pm Sun.*
The bright yellow exterior draws you into a warm and
welcoming space where you can browse the hand-
thrown stoneware pottery for the home and garden
(made in the on-site workshop), as well as prints,
photography and jewellery.

Old Town ★
*49 Bull Street, Holt, NR25 6HP (01263 710001,
www.old-town.co.uk). Open 10am-5pm Tue-Sat.*
This wonderful clothing manufacturer and retailer
produces around 50 understated garments every
week from its workshop using beautiful British cottons,
woollens and linens. Along with a pleasing range of
accessories (the handsome ties make great gifts),
Old Town offers made-to-order items too. Choose
your fabric and garment from a range that includes
wraparound dresses, jackets, waistcoats and shirts.

Osozuku Gallery
*6 Albert Street, Holt, NR25 6HX (01263 711363).
Open 9am-5pm Mon-Sat.*
A colourful bazaar of goods from all around the globe, ranging from Rye pottery to Afghan glass and Persian ceramics, as well as ethnic and silver jewellery.

Salle Organics
Salle Moor Hall Farm, Salle, NR10 4SB (01603 879046, www.salleorganics.co.uk). Open 9am-5pm Mon-Fri; 10am-4pm Sat, Sun.
A lovely farm shop selling all the usual farm produce (you can even buy a whole organic sheep) as well as plenty of prepared organic food, including own-made soups, pasties, cakes and lemon and egg custard tarts. Lodge Cottage at the entrance to the farm is a self-catering cottage sleeping six.

Walsingham Farms Shop
Guild Street, Walsingham, NR22 6BU (01328 821877, www.walsinghamfarmsshop.co.uk). Open 9am-6pm Tue-Fri; 9am-5pm Sat; 9am-1pm Sun.
Local producers and farmers are showcased here, with a tantalising array of fresh and prepared food. The range includes salami from Suffolk, vegetables from nearby allotment holders, honey from Walsingham bees and a mouth-watering range of picnic goodies made in the shop's kitchen.

Wells Deli ★
15 The Quay, Wells-next-the-Sea, NR23 1AH (01328 711171, www.wellsdeli.co.uk). Open 9am-5pm Mon-Sat; 10am-4pm Sun.
The cornucopia of goodies includes a fantastic range of sandwiches and takeaway dishes using local meats and fish. There are also cured meats such as serrano ham, plus own-bottled olive oil, a decent wine selection and a wide and impressive range of local produce. The deli lets a charming holiday cottage in Wells too; contact matt@wellsdeli.co.uk for details.

Hindolveston, 01263 862527, www.number45. co.uk); and Park House (Brisley Road, North Elmham, 01362 668933, www.parkhousebedand breakfast.co.uk) are all peaceful B&Bs in lovely settings. For serious luxury in a unique building, gather together your friends and book Voewood (01263 713029, www.voewood.com), a splendid Arts and Crafts mansion with 14 bedrooms.

Holly Lodge
The Street, Thursford Green, NR21 0AS (01328 878465, www.hollylodgeguesthouse.co.uk). Rates £80-£110 double incl breakfast.
Decorated in a medieval style, this eccentric but wonderful B&B comes complete with Jacobean-style furniture, tapestries and a suit of armour in the main house. The three large and less fanciful bedrooms are in converted stables adjoining the house. The gardens are extensive, and there's also a sun deck and a conservatory.

Lawns
26 Station Road, Holt, NR25 6BS (01263 713390, www.lawnsatholt.co.uk). Rates £85-£110 double incl breakfast.
This elegant house is a great example of Holt's Georgian architecture, and is equally impressive inside. Owners Daniel Rees and Sue Catt have created a luxurious eight-bedroom hotel with a wine bar and dining room that are open to non-residents. Rooms are huge and filled with light, and decorated in period colours to create a real sense of warmth and comfort. In the pretty dining room, Modern British food comes nicely cooked and piled high.

Quakerhall Barns
Quaker's Hall, Haveringland, NR10 4QF (01328 821744, www.quakerhallbarns.co.uk). Rates from £705 per week.
Perfect for big groups, these two award-winning barns have been beautifully converted into contemporary living spaces available for a three-day weekend through to a week's stay. Pastel tongue-and-groove and wood-burning stoves brighten and warm large rooms that feature a fascinating array of materials, from flint-peppered walls and resin floors to granite worktops and exposed oak beams.

Sculthorpe Mill
Lynn Road, Sculthorpe, NR21 9QG (01328 856161, www.greenekinginns.co.uk). Rates £89.50 double incl breakfast.
Just six rooms, all with views of the tumbling River Wensum outside, make this charming 18th-century mill a great place to stay. Olde worlde beamed rooms, one with a four-poster, are comfortable and well appointed. Downstairs, good pub food and well-kept ales are served in a traditional restaurant and fire-warmed bar or, in good weather, in the garden.

Wensum Lodge Hotel
Bridge Street, Fakenham, NR21 9AY (01328 862100, www.wensumlodge.co.uk). Rates £85 double incl breakfast.
This 18th-century grainstore turned hotel and restaurant has a lovely riverside setting. Inside there are comfortable rooms, free Wi-Fi, a family-friendly restaurant and a games room. The Lodge is a good base for exploring nearby attractions such as the Thursford Collection (*see p57*) and Pensthorpe (*see p56*).

NORFOLK

Peddars Way and Norfolk Coast Path

Cley next the Sea
Salthouse
Newgate
Kelling
High Kelling
Upper Sheringham
Weybourne
SHERINGHAM   West Runton
Beeston Regis
East Runton
CROMER
Overstrand
Foulness

Letheringsett
Sharrington
Thornage
Hunworth
Stody
Briningham
Brinton
Melton Constable
Briston
Hindolveston
Guestwick
Guestwick Green
Wood Dalling
Foulsham
Themelthorpe
Reepham
Bawdeswell
Sparham

HOLT
Bodham
East Beckham
West Beckham
Baconsthorpe
Hempstead
Edgefield
Edgefield Street
Plumstead
Little Barningham
Matlaske
Aldborough
Saxthorpe
Corpusty
Thurning
Oulton
Heydon
Salle
Southgate
Cawston
Booton
Eastgate
Brandiston
Whitwell Street
The Grove

Castle
Gresham
Aylmerton
Crossdale Street
Metton
Sustead
Hanworth
Alby Hill
Wickmere
Wolterton Hall
Calthorpe
Itteringham
Ingworth
Blickling
Oulton Street
AYLSHAM
Marsham
The Heath

Felbrigg
Hall
B1436
Northrepps
Upper Street
Roughton
Thorpe Market
Gunton Station
Gunton Hall
Antingham
Suffield
Erpingham
Colby
Banningham
Felmingham
Tuttington
Burgh next Aylsham
Brampton
Lamas
Buxton
Little Hautbois
Great Hautbois

Sidestrand
Trimingham
Gimingham
Mundesley
Southrepps
Lower Street
Trunch
Bradfield
NORTH WALSHAM
Swafield
Honing
Spa Common
Crostwight
Worstead
Sloley
Scottow
Sco Ruston
Tunstead
Smallburgh
Ashmanhaugh
Neatishead

Paston
Knapton
Edingthorpe
Witton Bridge
East Ruston
Dilham
Pennygate

Hevingham
Stratton Strawless
Horstead
Hainford
Frettenham
Newton St Faith
Horsford
Waterloo
Haveringland
Swannington
Alderford
Morton
Lenwade
Lyng
Elsing
Primrose Green
Felthorpe
Attlebridge
Thorpe Marriot
Weston Longville
Costessey
Taverham
Hellesdon
Drayton
New Costessey
Easton

Coltishall
Belaugh
Wroxham
Wroxham Broad
Hoveton
Crostwick
Rackheath
New Rackheath
Woodbastwick
Salhouse
Little Plumstead
Panxworth
Blofield Heath
Broadlands Services
Great Plumstead

Horsham St Faith
Norwich Airport
Old Catton
Sprowston
Thorpe End
NORWICH
THORPE ST ANDREW
Spixworth

Honingham
Ringland
Hockering
Mattishall Burgh
Mattishall
East Tuddenham
North Tuddenham
Weston Green
Welborne
Brandon Parva
Colton
Marlingford
Bawburgh
Bowthorpe
Colney
Earlham
Little Melton
Great Melton
Cringleford
Eaton
Lakenham
Keswick
Trowse Newton
Postwick
Kirby Bedon
Surlingham
Bramerton
Rockland St Mary

Runhall
Barnham Broom
Coston
Carleton Forehoe
Wramplingham
High Green
Kimberley
Kimberley House
Crownthorpe
Wicklewood
Hethersett
Ketteringham
Norwich Services
Swardeston
Dunston
Swainsthorpe
ROMAN TOWN
Framingham Pigot
Caistor St Edmund
Arminghall
Framingham Earl
Hellington
Brundall
Blofield
Postwick
Arminghall

A148 A149 A140 A1150 A1151 A1042 A1074 A47 A146 A11 A1067 A1108 A1135 A1172 A1110 A1354 A1149 A1145

Cromer & Sheringham

As the north Norfolk coast curves around to the east, rolling dunes and nature-rich marshes give way to decidedly more traditional seaside views and landscapes, particularly in the once grand Victorian resorts of Sheringham and Cromer. In summer the towns' sandy beaches are packed, but winter is glorious too for windswept walks scored to the explosion of waves against the sea defences. At high tide, the sand is completely covered and only pebbles remain on view, backed by past-their-best hotels and fisherman's cottages. Inland, stately architectural wonders such as Blickling Hall and Felbrigg Hall, numerous round- and square-towered churches of singular design, two fabulous steam railways and the market town of Aylsham mean there's lots to do when you've had your fill of sand, crabs and watery sunsets.

And, finally, the area can lay claim to one very special attribute: the highest point in Norfolk. Take a trip on the Poppy Line or play a round on Sheringham golf course and it becomes clear that the land here is anything but flat, a fact attributable to the rolling nine-mile-long glacial Cromer Ridge that runs beside the coast. The apex of the ridge, Beacon's Hill, is just a 15-minute walk south from West Runton, and at 338 feet above sea level makes for a rare, knee-flexing Norfolk walk. Bring a picnic and enjoy the terrific views.

SHERINGHAM & THE RUNTONS

Sheringham

Arriving fresh from the abundant beauty and affluence of west Norfolk, the faded seaside resort of Sheringham may initially feel like a slap in the face with a cold wet fish, but wander round for half an hour and the quiet charms of this genteel town start to become apparent. It began as a fishing village, and the links with the sea remain – if you're lucky you might hear the Sheringham Shantymen (www.shantymen.com) singing in the pub one night. The town is easily accessible by train – the Bittern Line runs here from Norwich – but remote enough to have retained its independent shops.

And it has real character, from an esplanade with attractive public gardens, model-boating lake and gleaming pre-war tiled public toilets to fine sea views and a Blue Flag beach backed by sizeable cliffs. Walk along the top for glorious vistas, especially at sunset; head lower down and you'll pass colourful beach huts and small fishing boats. The Norfolk Coast Path runs through the town, but a short stroll along the front is pleasure enough, particularly at night when you can wander beneath the illuminations. The High Street climbing away from the sea is similarly appealing, chock-a-block with cafés, ice-cream parlours and seaside-tat shops that give way to better cafés, bistros, a butcher, greengrocer and, of course, charity shops.

Antiques and bric-a-brac fans can delve for knick-knacks in Crowes of Sheringham (Station Road), the Trading Post (Wyndham Street) and Sheringham Collectables (Melbourne Road), and everything else at the street market on Wednesday and Saturday. Food too is wide-ranging, from DIY options such as diminutive Richard's fish shop (Church Street) to the wondrous interiors of Crofters Austrian restaurant (High Street), with its blue gingham curtains and plush velvet cushions, dark rich wood, and beams taken from the old North Norfolk railway station.

A growing number of more modern bistros suggests the British hobby of keeping up with the neighbours seems to be having a positive influence, and pubs such as the Lobster (High Street) and the Wyndham Arms (Wyndham Street) offer excellent horizon-gazing, beer-supping spots. Opposite the Wyndham, a little nugget of history is commemorated by a blue plaque in the diminutive Whitehall Yard. Here, at 8.30pm on 19 January 1915, the first bomb was dropped on Britain in World War I (it didn't explode).

The Runtons

East of Sheringham, the tiny villages of West and East Runton offer excellent sandy beaches (reached via lanes off the A149) and little else, making them ideal for the quiet pleasures of sandcastle-building, rockpooling and clambering over sea-defence barriers at low tide, and immersing yourself in the waves at high tide. The rock beds that form the cliffs along this stretch of coast are almost two million years old in parts, and a haven for fossil hunters (evidence of rhinos, hyenas and, most famously, a 16-foot-high mammoth have been found here).

West Runton has a decent pint-and-grub stop in the form of the pretty Village Inn, while the Hillside Animal & Shire Horse Sanctuary (*see p70*) will entertain children for a couple of hours. Nearby, Beeston Regis village is the centre of 30 acres

of heath and woodland for walkers who prefer solitude to the seaside screams of seagulls and overexcited children. Next to St Mary's, a ruined Augustinian priory, is Priory Maze (*see p70*), combining enchanting gardens with a hedge maze, plant centre and tearoom.

East Runton is larger and has more facilities, including a village shop that stays open until 9pm (a rarity in these parts). A duck pond and large green with a play area add to the child-friendly appeal, and an attractive tearoom/newsagent, a chip shop and the Fishing Boat pub, on the High Street, should ensure a happy day for the grown-ups too.

Where to eat & drink

There's plenty of choice in Sheringham, though no outstanding pub. Of the numerous cafés, try Roy Boys (37 Station Road, 01263 822960, www.royboys.co.uk) for a decent bacon sarnie or cooked breakfast. On the High Street, Pungleberrys offers salads and other healthier options; Ronaldo's ice-cream parlour has a great range of flavours and often a queue; and 'Joyful' West's Shellfish Bar (01263 825444) serves the best crab sandwiches in Norfolk. The Wests, one of Sheringham's oldest fishing families, make the sandwiches to order from freshly boiled crustaceans. For fish and chips, Dave's (7-11 Co-operative Street, 01263 823830, www.davesofsheringham.com) is recommended.

The Runtons offer good beach-based options, from takeaway chips to tasty sandwiches and full-blown pub meals.

Constantia Cottage Restaurant
High Street, East Runton, NR27 9NX (01263 512017, www.constantiarestaurant.co.uk). Dinner served 7-10.30pm Mon-Sat.
Greek food – accompanied by live Greek music, of course – is the USP at this small restaurant housed in a charming flint cottage. The lengthy menu covers all the standards. Note that it's only open in the evening.

No.10 ★
10 Augusta Street, Sheringham, NR26 8LA (01263 824400, www.no10sheringham.com). Brunch served 11am-2pm Sat. Tea & coffee served 10am-noon, lunch served noon-2pm, dinner served 6.30-9pm Wed-Sat.
A husband-and-wife team run this attractive restaurant in the centre of town. The menu changes every few weeks, but has a Mediterranean slant: fish soup with gruyère, followed by tallegio and roast vegetable tart with avocado and tomato salad, for example. Tea and coffee is served in the morning.

Two Lifeboats
2 High Street, Sheringham, NR26 8JR (01263 822401, www.twolifeboats.co.uk). Open 11am-11pm Mon-Sat; noon-10.30pm Sun. Lunch served noon-2.30pm, dinner served 6-9pm daily.
Good pub grub and a daily carvery make this a decent inn for food, but it's the setting that's the main draw; the large bay windows offer great sea views. Accommodation (£70 double incl breakfast & dinner) is basic but affordable, and most rooms look out over the water.

Cromer. See p73.

Places to visit

SHERINGHAM & THE RUNTONS

Hillside Animal & Shire Horse Sanctuary
*West Runton, NR27 9QH (01263 837339,
www.hillside.org.uk). Open June-Aug 10am-5pm
Mon-Fri, Sun. Apr, May, Sept, Oct 10am-5pm Mon-
Thur, Sun. Admission £5.95; free-£3.95 reductions;
£18 family.*
More than 300 horses, ponies, donkeys and mules,
including the magnificent Ardennes breed of Shire
horse, are looked after here, as well as cows, sheep,
pigs and even a couple of ostriches – many of them
rescued from factory farms or the slaughterhouse.
There are harnessing demonstrations three times a
week in summer, but this is definitely not a petting
zoo; the emphasis is on the welfare of the animals
and campaigning against cruel farming methods.

Peter Coke Shell Gallery
*West Cliff, Sheringham, NR26 8JT (01263 824343,
www.sheringham-preservation.org.uk). Open Easter-
Sept noon-4pm Wed, Thur, Fri and by arrangement.
Admission free.*
Actor, playwright and sea shell sculptor Peter Coke
died at the age of 95 in 2008, leaving behind this
fascinating museum filled with more than 180 of his
weird and wonderful sea shell sculptures. Inspired
by the 'sailor's valentines' sculptures produced by
seafarers in the 18th century, the works include
incredibly intricate 'flower' arrangements, model
garden scenes and finely detailed pagodas – all made
from a variety of (often tiny) shells in natural colours.

Priory Maze & Gardens
*Cromer Road, Beeston Regis, NR26 8SF (01263
822986, www.priorymazegardens.co.uk). Open
10am-3.30pm Wed-Sun. Admission £5; £2.50-
£4.50 reductions.*
A quiz trail and enjoyably (but not frustratingly) difficult
hedge maze, based on the footprint of the nearby
ruined Beeston Priory, will keep youngsters happy.
Meanwhile, the grown-ups can delight in the formal
gardens, woodlands, meadows and tearoom.

Sheringham Park
*Wood Farm, Upper Sheringham, NR26 8TL
(01263 820550, www.nationaltrust.org.uk). Open
Park dawn-dusk daily. Visitor centre Feb-mid Mar,
Nov-Jan 11am-4pm Sat, Sun. Mid-Mar-Sept 10am-
5pm daily. Oct 10am-5pm Wed-Sun. Admission free.*
Humphry Repton's fabulous design for this vast park
takes in woodlands, parkland and stunning landscaped
gardens, where the displays of rhododendrons and
azaleas (from mid May to June) are legendary; see
them from the top of one of the viewing towers and
they are breathtaking. There are heaps of walks
and paths, but one of the nicest things to do is walk
through the length of the park to the coast and back
to Sheringham along the cliffs.

CROMER

Amazona Zoo
*Hall Road, NR27 9JG (01263 510741, www.amazona
zoo.co.uk). Open Apr-Nov 10am-5pm daily. Admission
£8.50; £6.50-£7.50 reductions.*

Big cats roam happily it seems in the feline forest
of this ten-acre zoo, where a wide range of critters,
including snakes, parrots, fish and monkeys, offer a
good couple of hours of amusement and education
for children. The one-time derelict woodland site
makes the most of pre-existing habitats; abandoned
brick kilns are now used as a winter hibernating
shelter for bats, for example.

Cromer Church & Tower
*30 Cromwell Road, NR27 0BE (01263 512000,
www.cromer-church.org.uk). Open June-Sept 10.30am-
4.30pm Mon-Fri, occasional Sat. Admission £1.50;
50p reductions.*
St Peter & St Paul boasts the county's highest church
tower, at 160ft; if your knees can take it, in the
summer you can climb the 172 steps to the top for
magnificent views over the town, pier and coast. The
lofty, light-filled interior has some some good modern
stained glass, including depictions of lifeboats, the
lighthouse and buckets and spades.

Cromer Museum
*Church Street, NR27 9HB (01263 513543,
www.museums.norfolk.gov.uk). Open Mar-Oct
10am-5pm Mon-Sat; 1-4pm Sun. Nov-Feb 10am-
4pm Mon-Sat. Admission £3; free-£2.50 reductions.*
If you're visiting Cromer Church, it's worth popping
next door into this small local history museum, housed
in a Victorian fisherman's cottage. There are plenty of
old photos, fossils and other items to gawp at, some
lovely old-fashioned wooden display cases and plenty
of themed events and dressing-up days for children in
the summer holidays.

RNLI Henry Blogg Museum
*The Rocket House, The Gangway, NR27 9ET
(01263 511294, www.rnli.org.uk). Open Apr-Sept
10am-5pm Tue-Sun. Oct-Mar 10am-4pm Tue-Sun.
Dec 10-4pm Sat, Sun. Admission free.*
Named after coxswain Henry Blogg, the RNLI's most
decorated lifeboater and a man who helped to save
873 lives around the Cromer coast, this little museum
about the town's lifeboat crews is a particular hit
with kids, who can practise Morse code, play with
model boats and follow a trail of quiz clues. The café
is worth a stop too.

INLAND TO AYLSHAM

Blickling Hall ★
*Blickling, nr Aylsham, NR11 6NF (01263 738030,
www.nationaltrust.org.uk/blickling). Open Hall
mid July-Aug 11am-5pm Mon, Wed-Sun; Mar-mid July,
Sept, Oct 11am-5pm Wed-Sun. Garden mid July-Aug
10.15am-5.15pm Mon, Wed-Sun; Mar-mid July,
Sept, Oct 10.15am-5.15pm Wed-Sun; Nov-Feb 11am-
4pm Thur-Sun. Park Dawn-dusk daily. Admission
Hall & Garden £9.30; £4.60 reductions; £26 family.
Garden only £6.30; £3.15 reductions; £18 family.
Park free.*
Beautifully laid out to present a stunning aspect and
approach from the moment it comes into view, this
magnificent Jacobean red-brick mansion has numerous
pleasures, from the Long Gallery to the glorious
plasterwork ceilings and excellent collections of

furniture, pictures, tapestries and books – the servants' library is a real eye-opener. Outside, there are superb formal gardens, including an orangery, and a huge park that features meadows, woods and an artificial lake surrounding the house. At one time the place belonged to the Boleyn family; look out for the ghost (headless, of course) of Anne Boleyn, Henry VIII's unfortunate second wife.

Felbrigg Hall ★
Felbrigg, nr Cromer, NR11 8PR (01263 837444, www.nationaltrust.org.uk/felbrigg). Open House Mar-Oct 11am-5pm Mon-Wed, Sat, Sun. Garden 11am-5pm daily. Admission House & Garden £7.80; £3.65 reductions; £19.40 family. Garden only £3.65; £1.60 reductions.
An impressive and fascinating mix of 17th-century architecture with 18th-century furniture and pictures and interior remodelling makes this elegant, good-sized country house a real pleasure to explore. The Chinese bedroom with its hand-painted 18th-century wallpaper is particularly fine. Movie-goers might recognise the place; it was used as a location for Michael Winterbottom's 2006 film *A Cock and Bull Story*. Outside, a walled garden, orangery and extensive park and woodland ensure plenty of photo-taking opportunities.

St Michael the Archangel
Church Road, Booton, NR10 4NZ (www.visit churches.org.uk). Open 10am-5pm daily. Admission free.
This eccentric, late 19th-century Gothic-style folly is the work of one Reverend Whitwell Elwin (a descendent of Pocahontas, no less), who cherry-picked all his favourite bits of churches around the country and, with no architectural input, constructed a structure that incorporates a minaret-like pinnacle and two skinny, soaring twin towers. Edwin Lutyens described it as 'very naughty but built in the right spirit'. The wooden angels were carved by James Minns, more famous for creating the bull's head that still features on Colman's Mustard packaging.

Wolterton & Mannington Estate
Mannington Hall, NR11 7BB (01263 584175, www.manningtongardens.co.uk). Mannington Gardens Open June-Aug 11am-5pm Wed-Fri; May-Sept noon-5pm Sun. Wolterton Park Open 9am-dusk daily. Wolterton Hall mid Apr-Oct 2-5pm Fri. Admission Mannington Gardens £5; free-£4 reductions. Wolterton Hall £5.
The estate of Lord and Lady Walpole provides 20 miles of waymarked footpaths and trails through two very different neighbouring estates of heath and landscaped gardens. Mannington, a medieval moated manor occasionally open to the public, has a stunning collection of roses, plus manicured lawns, a lakeside walk and a tea room that operates during garden opening hours. Wolterton Hall, a grander affair built by Thomas Ripley in the 1720s for Horatio Walpole (younger brother to Britain's first prime minister, Sir Robert Walpole), is open on Friday afternoons from spring to autumn. Its park includes an orienteering course and children's adventure playground, as well as spectacular views.

Where to stay
There are no boutique hotel options in this area, so the choice lies between cosy B&Bs or rather old-fashioned hotels. Sheringham's plethora of B&Bs means finding a decent, well-priced room shouldn't be hard; there are plenty of options on the Rise and Holway Road. Our favourites offer something a little special, whether it's as simple as a fridge with fresh milk or views that are as expansive as the never-ending horizons.

At the other end of the scale, the Links Country Park Hotel (01263 838383, www.links-hotel.co.uk, £130 double incl breakfast) in West Runton won't win any architecture or fashion awards, but it does have 35 acres of lightly wooded coastal parkland, a nine-hole golf course, an indoor swimming pool and a gym.

The Dales ★
Lodge Hill, Sheringham, NR26 8TJ (01263 824555, www.dalescountryhouse.co.uk). Rates £150 double incl breakfast.
Spacious rooms – 21 in total – stuffed with sumptuous fabrics and impressive oak furniture, alongside stained glass windows and big open fireplaces, make the interior of this Grade II-listed Victorian rectory cosy and luxurious. Outside, in the four acres of gardens, you can take a turn round the Norfolk-shaped pond or indulge in country pursuits such as tennis and croquet.

Incleborough House
Lower Common, East Runton, NR27 9PG (01263 515939, www.incleboroughhouse.co.uk). Rates £165-£185 double incl breakfast.
This handsome Grade II-listed house, built in 1687 and set in decidedly grand landscaped walled gardens, has just three splendid rooms. More unusual features include Sky TV and underfloor heating; opt for the Master Room and you even get a television embedded in the wall above the bath. The whole enterprise is overseen with lots of TLC by Nick and Barbara Davies.

Lodge Cottage
Upper Sheringham, NR26 8TJ (01263 821445, www.visitlodgecottage.com). Rates from £70 double incl breakfast. No credit cards.
This striking flint-and-brick house offers five rooms, all decorated differently and with obvious care. The public lounge is appealing too, with a small terrace for summer and an open fire for wintry days.

Manor Farm Camping & Caravan Site
Mill Lane, East Runton, NR27 9PR (01263 512858, www.manorfarmcaravansite.co.uk). Open Easter-Sept. Camping £12.50-£15 per pitch. No credit cards.
This campsite spreads across 18 acres of peaceful countryside on a working farm, but the rural setting doesn't mean roughing it; three fields share six amenity blocks with power showers, and two laundry rooms. Many of the pitches offer sea views.

Old Barn B&B
Cromer Road, West Runton, NR27 9QT (01263 838285, www.theoldbarnnorfolk.co.uk). Rates £64 double incl breakfast. No credit cards.

Sheringham. See p67.

A rambling house with an extensive garden, Karen Elliott's Old Barn is a charmer, from the comfortable beds in the three spacious bedrooms to the cosy beamed lounge and dining room, both of which lead directly to the garden.

CROMER

Four short miles connect Sheringham with Cromer, but the two have distinctly different characters. While Sheringham's growth from a fishing port to a tourist resort was slow, small-scale and late, Cromer – the self-styled 'gem of the north Norfolk coast' – became popular with visiting gentry in the late 1700s; nowadays, it's a splendidly old-fashioned seaside resort.

The beach, sandy then pebbly and backed by rows of brightly coloured beach huts, is the town's highlight. The pretty and popular pier, featuring the long-running Pavilion Theatre (*see p77*), a children's funfair, a modern café, a fishing area and a lifeboat station, adds hugely to its appeal, but away from the sea there are plenty of other attractions, among them a model-boating lake in North Lodge Park, a crazy golf course, an amusement arcade, the RNLI Henry Blogg Museum (*see p70*) and Cromer Church (*see p70*) with its impressively tall tower.

As with most seaside towns, Cromer is easily navigable and enjoyably explored in an afternoon, with plenty of shops offering poke-around pleasures. New Street, the tiny alley behind the front, is home to a wonderful second-hand bookshop, Bookworms. Around the corner on Church Street, more second-hand books and antiques are available at the charmingly named Much Binding Antiquarian Booksellers. In addition to books, it deals in all manner of fascinating bits and pieces, such as an embroidered silk handkerchief commemorating the Coronation for £15. The Crossways tobacconist on Chapel Street is another oddity, a lovely old-fashioned shop that still sells snuff and all sorts of pipe and tobacco paraphernalia (as well as the evil weed in hundreds of forms, of course).

But it's not all old junk and used books; Garden Street, adjoining New Street, is becoming rather swish these days, with old-timers such as Richard and Julie Davies' crab shack joined by the likes of Digby's Fine Chocolates (www.digbyschocolates.com) and the Garden House Gallery (01263 511234, www.garden-house-gallery.co.uk). Run by Hilary Hann, the latter stocks a winning mix of painting and photography by local artists, as well as home accessories.

More arts and crafts are available on Church Street: ceramics, wood sculptures, glass and limited edition prints at the Church Street Gallery (01263 510100, www.cromerart.co.uk); and Danish jewellery, Venetian carnival masks and Russian hand-painted brooches at Artyfax (01263 512233, www.artyfax.com). The increasing number of such lively independent shops suggests a growth in wealth and tone that's long overdue for this once grand and rather special resort – after all, where else in Britain can you see the sun both rise and set over the sea?

St Jude's Gallery

FIVE NORFOLK ART GALLERIES

Bircham Gallery
Holt's best art gallery stocks the work of more than 200 artists and craftspeople, including a wide range of very affordable prints. *See p64.*

Cat Pottery
Offering a mad mix of wild- and wide-eyed china cats sitting on every conceivable surface, and old railway memorabilia, this pottery-cum-shop in North Walsham is a photographer's dream. *See p98.*

Norwich Castle Museum & Art Gallery
From horses and bucolic countryside scenes by local old boy Alfred Munnings to contemporary works by photographer Richard Billingham and YBA Abigail Lane, the Castle's permanent collection and temporary exhibitions are always worth a look. *See p87.*

St Jude's Gallery
This north Norfolk gem specialising in modern British prints, located in the tiny village of Itteringham, would be worth trekking to even if it didn't have the excellent Walpole Arms pub nearby. *See p76.*

SCVA
Norwich's major art gallery, housed in an award-winning Foster building. Ancient figurative pieces that are teeny-tiny in size but huge in importance sit alongside paintings by Francis Bacon in an occasionally changing but always fascinating juxtaposition. *See p87.*

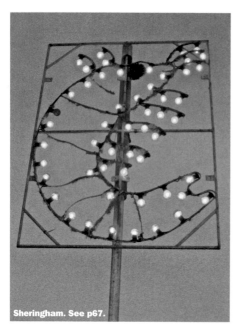
Sheringham. See p67.

Peggotty's Café
6 Hamilton Road, NR27 9HL (01263 511876).
Open 8am-3pm daily.
As authentic as they come, this gorgeous little café serves just what you'd expect, given the wooden tables, lace curtains, geometric 1960s carpet and Formica-clad walls. Crab sandwiches, liver and bacon, and spag bol figure large.

Mary Jane's ★
27-29 Garden Street, NR27 9HN (01263 511208).
Food served Apr-Oct 11.30am-8pm Mon-Sat; noon-7.30pm Sun. Nov-Mar 11.30am-3pm Mon-Fri; noon-5pm Sat, Sun. No credit cards.
With its pink walls and frilly net curtains, Mary Jane's dishes up a measure of feminine seemliness alongside its fish and chips. Family photos and landscape prints decorate the walls, and there's a small bar tucked in a corner (with fizzy keg beer). Queues often form at the adjoining takeaway, and tables in the restaurant are highly prized during the summer rush.

Tides
Cromer Pier, NR27 9HE (01263 511236, www.cromer-pier.com). Open 10am-4pm (8pm on show days) daily.
Situated at the land end of the pier, Tides offers essential beach snacks; come here for breakfast, soup and sandwiches at lunch or just a steaming cup of hot chocolate. The setting is atmospheric, particularly when the rolling seas are crashing outside and the slate grey sky seems endless.

Where to eat & drink
It's de rigeur to eat fish and chips on the seafront or buy dressed crabs to take home (from JWH Jonas or J Lee's, both on New Street), but more refined alternatives do exist, and their numbers are growing. For smarter crab dishes, try Bolton's Bistro at the Cliftonville Hotel (*see below*), or enjoy lunchtime sophistication at the curvy chrome and blue Rocket House Café in the RNLI Henry Blogg Museum (*see p70*). Sterling sea views are offered too, as they are at the Blue Sky Café, located in the clifftop car park at one of Cromer's highest points. You can also get excellent coffee and cakes.

Flint Cottage Restaurant
1A Church Street, NR27 9ER (01263 513178).
Lunch served 10am-2pm, dinner served 6-8pm daily.
A decidedly quaint café, with all-day breakfasts, a good range of snacks and sandwiches and daily specials.

Garden Street Grill
16 Garden Street, NR27 9HN (01263 515110). Food served noon-8pm Mon-Thur, Sun; noon-9pm Fri, Sat.
Truly trad and sporting wood as far as the eye can see, the Garden Street Grill is a haven for those who crave nothing more than a pile of peas and a dollop of mash next to a large portion of meat. Desperate Dans will love it.

La Griglia
2 Brook Street, NR27 9EY (01263 519619, www.la griglia.co.uk). Open 10am-11pm, lunch served noon-2.30pm, dinner served 6.30-9.30pm Mon-Sat.
Contemporary styling and a traditional menu are a winning formula at this popular modern Italian, which serves pizzas, pastas and risottos in a buzzy atmosphere.

Where to stay
As befits its retro feel, Cromer still boasts guesthouses of blessed cheesiness: flock wallpaper, candlewick bedspreads and tinned tomatoes with your egg and bacon. Look along Alfred Road and Cadogan Road (both off the A149) for some likely contenders.

Cliftonville Hotel
29 Runton Road, Cromer, NR27 9AS (01263 512543, www.cliftonvillehotel.co.uk). Rates £110-£144 double incl breakfast.
Edwardian splendour on the seafront, with stonkingly good views of both sea and town, make this independent hotel a great choice for fans of expansive vistas and old-fashioned design. Lots of original features give the place real character and originality (you can act out your *Gone with the Wind* fantasies in the main lobby). The elegant Bolton's Bistro serves a good range of seafood and big steaks.

Hotel de Paris
High Street, Cromer, NR27 9HG (01263 513141).
Rates £70-£78 double incl breakfast.
One for romantics and lovers of faded Victorian grandeur, the imposing Hotel de Paris could do with a brush-up, but has a terrific seafront location, rooms with tantalising views, some beautiful original features (particularly in the public spaces) and the kind of ambience that harks back to a more genteel age of tourism.

Link
The Lighthouse, Overstrand Road, Cromer, NR27 0JH (01386 701177, www.ruralretreats.co.uk). Rates from £241 for 2 nights.

NORFOLK

Book the children in at grandma's – babies and children aren't allowed at this former lighthouse keeper's cottage. Set in the base of the white octagonal tower of the working Cromer Lighthouse, it's a ten-minute walk from town via the coast path (a mile by road) and adjacent to the highly rated Royal Cromer golf course (*see p79*). There's room for just one couple.

Virginia Court Hotel ★

Cliff Avenue, Cromer, NR27 0AN (01263 512398, www.virginiacourt.co.uk). Rates £110-£160 double incl breakfast.

Just three minutes' walk from the seafront and pier, the rather grand Virginia Court was built at the end of the 19th century as a gentlemen's club for Edward VII and is set in its own gardens. It's currently being lovingly refurbished by owners Shawn Trumble and Martin Torrens, who are turning the 25 rooms into clean-lined, contemporary spaces. The restaurant is open to non-residents.

INLAND TO ALYSHAM

South of Cromer and Sheringham, simple seaside pleasures give way to grander attractions in the shape of imposing houses and gardens: privately owned Wolterton & Mannington Estate (*see p71*) and two wonderful properties now owned by the National Trust, Felbrigg Hall (*see p71*) and Blickling Hall (*see p70*).

Pretty villages lay claim to a clutch of churches with unusual features. St Peter's in the tiny village of Brampton, for example, is notable for its brick-crowned round tower; St Andrew's in Little Barningham is famed for its 17th-century wooden skeleton; St John the Baptist in Aylmerton boasts a round tower and some notable early 18th-century gravestones, including one decorated with a coffin, a skull and a snake devouring its own tail (symbolising eternity); and the Anglo-Saxon round tower of St Mary's in Bessingham is unique in

Buckinghamshire Arms. See p78.

being built of local carrstone rather than the more common flint or medieval brick.

Walkers and drinkers will appreciate the area's excellent trails and paths, and refreshment stops, in picture-perfect villages such as Erpingham, Heydon and Wolterton, and there's even good shopping to be had. For instance, the farm buildings at Alby Crafts (01263 761590, www.albycrafts. co.uk), located on the main A140 between Cromer and Aylsham, are home to ten craftsmakers, creating everything from wildlife habitats to ceramic wall plates, as well as a gallery, gift shop, furniture showroom and café.

The tiny village of Itteringham is home to the much-admired St Jude's Gallery (01263 587666, www.stjudes.co.uk). Fans of British design will be familiar with Angie Lewin's widely distributed but still fresh and winning dandelion clocks and wildflower designs, available as fabrics and prints (pictured on p73). The gallery also sells textiles, notebooks and prints by contemporary designers such as Mark Hearld, Alice Stevenson and Old Town, and hosts temporary exhibitions by the likes of printmaker Peter Greene.

And if you visit Blickling Hall, do make time for Samphire (01263 734464, www.samphireshop. co.uk), a terrific food shop in the grounds – but with its own car park, so you don't have to pay for National Trust parking. You can buy a fabulous range of ethically produced local foodstuffs from small-scale producers, including all the makings of a good picnic: daily baked bread, pâtés, sausage rolls, tip-top pies and a wide range of cheeses.

And then there's the market town of Aylsham. Located about ten miles south of Cromer, halfway to Norwich, this compact and attractive settlement is proud of its medieval heritage and long-held position as a thriving market town for the surrounding agricultural communities (and, more recently, its status as Norfolk's first plastic bag-free town). The general market on Monday and Friday, and farmers' market on the third Saturday morning

Things to do

Pavilion Theatre

Admission £3.40-£5.50; £2.40-£4.40 reductions; £13.40-£16 family .
A godsend on a wet day, this 25m pool features a beach area, a 150ft waterslide, a wave machine and a café, as well as a ball pit and soft play area.

CROMER

Pavilion Theatre
Cromer Pier, Cromer, NR27 9HE (01263 512495, www.cromer-pier.com). Box office Jan-Apr 10am-4pm Mon-Sat; 11am-3.30pm Sun. May-Oct 10am-6pm daily. Nov, Dec 10am-5pm daily. Tickets £10-£20.
Home of the famous 'Seaside Special' summer show, the theatre also hosts a season of celebrity concerts and performances, with tribute bands, themed songbook shows and local talent all firm favourites.

Sticky Earth Café
15 Church Street, Cromer, NR27 9ES (01263 519642, www.stickyearthcafe.co.uk). Open 10am-5pm Mon, Thur, Fri; 10am-5.30pm Sat; 11am-4.30pm Sun.
This well-equipped café and ceramics studio has friendly staff on hand to help children paint their own mugs, spoons, plates, animals and even T-shirts.

INLAND TO AYLSHAM

Aylsham Fun Barns
Spa Lane, Aylsham, NR11 6UE (01263 734108, www.aylshamfunbarns.co.uk). Open Mar-Oct 10am-5pm Thur-Sun. Nov-Feb 10am-4pm Sat, Sun. Admission £1; £6 child; £13 family.
It won't win any prizes for architecture or design, but on a rainy day the Aylsham Fun Barns may hit the spot. With a mix of farm animals, indoor and outdoor play areas, pony and donkey rides, and a child-centred menu at the café, little ones will find it a lot of fun.

Bure Valley Railway
Alysham station, Norwich Road, Aylsham, NR11 6BW (01263 733858, www.bvrw.co.uk). Open days vary; phone for details. Tickets £11 return; free-£6 reductions; £29 family.
The 18-mile round trip from Aylsham to Wroxham in the Broads on this narrow-gauge railway is a steamy adventure. Trains barrel alongside the River Bure through wood, pasture and heath, taking in mills, villages and pretty hump-backed bridges. There's a café and model train shop at Aylsham station.

Keys Auctioneers
Keys Aylsham Salerooms, off Palmers Lane, Aylsham NR11 6JA (01263 733195, www.keysauctions.co.uk). Open Mon varies, call for details; 9am-1pm, 2-4.30pm Tue-Fri; 9am-noon Sat.
General and specialist auctions are held regularly, and they're huge fun to attend, even if you have no intention of buying. Novices will find a useful beginner's guide on the website, but generally it's pretty straightforward: register for a bidding card, view the items, head for the auction room and see what happens. You might pick up an oak dining table for a bargain £18, a bag of vintage tennis racquets or a cricket bat for a fiver, or more specialist items such as books and paintings.

SHERINGHAM & THE RUNTONS

Poppy Line (North Norfolk Railway) ★
Sheringham station, Sheringham, NR26 8RA (01263 820800, talking timetable 01263 820808, www.nnrailway.co.uk). Open days vary; phone for details. Tickets £10.50 return; free-£9.50 reductions; £35 family.
The utterly enchanting, predominantly steam-driven Poppy Line takes passengers on a 20-minute trip between Sheringham and Holt, with a proper stop at Weybourne and a halt at Kelling Heath. It's a scenic route, hugging the coast and golf course before heading inland. The vintage carriages and genial staff in spick-and-span uniforms add to the charm, particularly during the various special days, including 'hands-on' kids' trips and Santa Specials in December. The buffet and gift shop at Sheringham station, which is close to the town centre (and near the national network station on the Norwich to Cromer line) is open daily. Holt station is about a mile outside the town, though the Holt Flyer, a vintage Routemaster bus, will (for an extra charge) take passengers into the centre.

Sheringham Little Theatre
2 Station Road, Sheringham, NR26 8RE (01263 822347, www.northnorfolk.org/littletheatre). Box office July-Sept 10am-9.30pm Mon-Sat; 10am-4pm Sun. Oct-June 10am-4pm Mon-Sat. Tickets £8-£15.
The delightfully tiny Little Theatre hosts a wide range of activities, including music, theatre, films, children's events and exhibitions, with highlights being a ten-week professional repertory season in summer and pantomime in winter.

Splash Leisure Centre
Weybourne Road, Sheringham, NR26 8HF (01263 825675, www.dcleisurecentres.co.uk). Open 7am-9pm Mon-Fri; 7am-6pm Sat; 9am-6pm Sun.

NORFOLK

TEN NORFOLK GOLF COURSES

Norfolk is blessed with more than 30 golf courses, many of them excellent, and a few among the best in the UK. Check each course's website for playing restrictions and prices.

FIVE FOR EXPERIENCED GOLFERS...

Hunstanton
Golf Course Road, Old Hunstanton, PE36 6JQ (01485 532811, www.hunstantongolfclub.com).
Hunstanton is very welcoming to visitors. It's a great course for winter golf as the greens are renowned for being fast and true all year round. Three- and four-balls have very limited availability, so check before travelling.

King's Lynn
Castle Rising, King's Lynn, PE31 6BD (01553 631654, www.club-noticeboard. co.uk/kingslynn).
A friendly club a few miles outside King's Lynn, with an attractive tree-lined course built on a seam of sand that makes for excellent, year-long playing conditions.

Royal West Norfolk
Brancaster, PE31 8AX (01485 210087, www.rwngc.org).
A lovely links course, with the sea on one side and the saltmarsh on the other, but attitudes here are 'old-school' and only the most persistent visiting golfers will manage to book a round. If you're able to reach the first tee, then a delightful experience awaits, especially if you're fortunate enough to catch the tide just right – it creates some interesting water hazards.

Sheringham
Sheringham, NR26 8HG (01263 823488, www.sheringhamgolfclub. co.uk).
Another links course with beautiful views from a clifftop position, where the welcome extended to non-members is similar to Hunstanton. The Sheringham to Holt steam railway runs the length of the course, adding to the magic.

Thetford
Brandon Road, Thetford, IP24 3NE (01842 752169, www.thetfordgolf club.co.uk).
A fabulous heathland course on the edge of the Breckland forest, on the county border with Suffolk. It's one of the best courses of its type, and something of a hidden gem. A warm welcome is guaranteed.

of the month, are very popular. We're also partial to Black Sheep (9 Penfold Street, 01263 733142, www.blacksheep.ltd.uk), which sells a small but desirable range of knitwear, accessories and gifts, notably a slinky black-wrapped wool-fat soap.

Good links – via roads, numerous paths, the lovely Bure Valley Railway (*see p77*) and a cycle path that links it to Wroxham in the heart of the Broads – have helped ensure it's a vibrant destination with plenty to offer visitors, including a couple of excellent places to stay.

Where to eat & drink

Pubs and tearooms are the norm in this area, which caters largely to walkers and families. The former will find much to enjoy at Aylsham's Black Boys Hotel & Restaurant and Wolterton's Saracen's Head (for both, *see below*), both of which also offer quality accommodation, while the Greens (01263 733085), on the A140 just south of Alysham, is a handy pie-and-pint option.

For families, the tearoom at Mannington Hall (*see p71*) offers a surprisingly wide range of locally sourced food; and youngsters can run around in the garden of Aylsham's Old Tea Rooms (18A Red Lion Street, 01263 732112, closed Sun). Best of all is the café at Aylsham Fun Barns (*see p77*), where children's faves such as beans on toast cost just £1.25.

Buckinghamshire Arms ★
Blickling Hall, Aylsham, NR11 6NF (01263 732133, www.bucks-arms.co.uk). Open Lunch served noon-2.30pm, dinner served 6.30-9pm Tue-Sat (June-Sept lunch also Mon). Meals served noon-8pm (Oct-May noon-3pm) Sun.
This Jacobean coaching inn just outside the gates of Blickling Hall will appeal to gourmets with its excellent and original British menu. There are three rooms too (£90 double incl breakfast) in vibrant colours and with four-poster beds, no less – if your visit to the mansion has left you with ideas above your station.

Food Lovers
3 Penfold Street, Aylsham, NR11 6ET (07929 180922). Open 9am-5pm Mon-Fri; 9am-4.30pm Sat. No credit cards.
Multi-tasking as a children's clothing shop, a small but thoughtfully stocked deli selling local produce and flour from Letheringsett Mill, and a likeable café, this is a pleasant place for a light lunch – though you might want to leave room for one of the tempting cupcakes.

Walpole Arms
The Common, Itteringham, NR11 7AR (01263 587258, www.thewalpolearms.co.uk). Open noon-3pm, 6-11pm Mon-Sat; noon-5pm Sun. Lunch served noon-2pm Mon-Sat; noon-2.30pm Sun. Dinner served 7-9pm Mon-Sat.
This Michelin Bib Gourmand winner impresses with a menu sporting pairings such as chickpea and chorizo stew with pork belly. The two-acre landscaped garden and vine-clad terrace make it a particularly lovely – and deservedly popular – lunch spot on a sunny day, so come early or be prepared for a long wait.

Where to stay

Of the many pubs in the area that offer accommodation, the handsome Buckinghamshire Arms (*see above*) is a fine choice – though it's only got three rooms.

It's worth looking into self-catering options too, via websites such as www.enjoyengland.com and www.norfolkcountrycottages.net; many places offer short and weekend stays at heavily discounted prices outside peak season.

Black Boys Hotel & Restaurant

Market Place, Aylsham, NR11 6EH (01263 732122, www.blackboyshotel.co.uk). Rates £57.50 double.
Four characterful and comfortable rooms in warm colours make the Black Boys one of the nicest places to stay in the area. Traditionalists will like the period pieces in the bedrooms as well as the resolutely English menu – generous portions of steak and kidney pie, lamb shank, and fish and chips – on offer in the bar/restaurant downstairs.

The Mill at Itteringham

The Common, Itteringham, NR11 7AR (01263 587688, www.itteringham-mill.co.uk). Rates £100 double incl breakfast. Self-catering £400-£600 per week for 4 people.
This handsome red-brick mill, in a beautiful setting on the banks of the River Bure, was sensitively refurbished in 2009 and now offers a range of accommodation options, from five B&B double rooms in the mill itself to two self-catering cottages (sleeping two and four) in the converted barn. The rear of the building now has floor-to-ceiling glazing, providing plenty of light inside and lovely views over the mill pond; eco-conscious visitors will also be pleased that the place is carbon-neutral. If you're visiting midweek, consider the 'eat-and-stay' deal, with meals provided at the nearby Walpole Arms.

Old Pump House B&B

Holman Road, Aylsham, NR11 6BY (01263 733789, www.theoldpumphouse.com). Rates £95-£115 double incl breakfast.
Book yourself into this lovely five-room B&B if you can. The cream-coloured Georgian building, complemented by a bucolic garden with statues and lily-filled ponds, is a stunner, and friendly owners Marc James and Charles Kirkman go out of their way to pamper their guests. The tastefully decorated bedrooms are ultra-comfortable, and particular praise goes to the lavish breakfasts (fresh fruit, porridge, kippers, hash browns and more).

Saracen's Head ★

Wall Road, Wolterton, NR11 7LZ (01263 768909, www.saracenshead-norfolk.co.uk). Rates £90 double incl breakfast.
Isolated, ivy-clad and instantly appealing from the outside, this former coaching inn (built to serve neighbouring Wolterton Hall) is just as charming inside. Rich bright colours mix with cosy rugs and attractive antiques to create a look that's the best of shabby chic through six bedrooms (all en suite) and a residents' lounge. The Modern British cuisine is equally original and tempting, with dishes such as baked Cromer crab with apple and sherry illustrating the enterprising cooking on offer. The business is currently up for sale, so visit while you still can.

Barnham Broom

Honingham Road, Barnham Broom, NR9 4DD (01603 757504, www.barnham-broom.co.uk).
On the outer edge of Norwich, these two 18-hole courses are attached to a four-star hotel and spa complex. It's an easy-going environment for visiting golfers; you can just turn up and play without being interrogated by a retired colonel.

Royal Cromer

145 Overstrand Road, Cromer, NR27 0JH (01263 512884, www.royalcromergolfclub.com).
Quality links more than 300ft above the beach, Royal Cromer is good at making visitors feel cherished. The course plays more parkland than links, but is almost always in excellent condition. If you have a good card in your hand, beware holes 14 and 15 by the lighthouse – they bite.

Royal Norwich

Drayton High Road, Hellesdon, Norwich NR6 5AH (01603 429928, www.royalnorwichgolf.co.uk).
Situated on the north edge of Norwich, this well-established club offers an interesting layout either side of the Drayton High Road. Non-members are welcome.

Sprowston Manor

Sprowston Park, Wroxham Road, Norwich, NR7 8RP (01603 254290, www.marriott.co.uk/hotels/hotel-information/golf-courses/nwigs-sprowston-manor-a-marriott-hotel-and-country-club/).
Part of a Marriott hotel complex – so again, not fusty – this course is created around a manor house and grounds. It's undergone major reconstruction fairly recently to USGA specifications, which makes it worth considering. Its proximity to Norwich may also be advantageous for non-golfers.

Weston Park

Weston Longville, NR9 5JW (01603 872363, www.weston-park.co.uk).
Based around an old country estate nine miles from Norwich, Weston is set in beautiful parkland. The place is also a wedding and conference centre, so the vibe is friendly. It's less established than some Norfolk courses, but don't let this deter you – its reputation is growing.

NORFOLK

Norwich Cathedral. See p87.

Norwich

Despite good links via road and rail, Norwich feels slightly removed from the rest of Britain, and can often give the impression of being somewhere far away, rather than a city less than two hours from London by rail. This sense of isolation gives it a more individual character than many of England's homogenised civic centres, and means that the inhabitants make much of what they have here, rather than looking to London for entertainment.

The lovely city centre is compact enough for you to really get to know it in a couple of days, though there's so much packed in that you could easily stay for a week and not run out of things to do. There's an impressive clutch of historical and cultural attractions, a dizzying array of good pubs and decent eating options, and some very nice places to stay. Shopping is fun here too – there are many interesting independents – and best of all, there's no need for a car in the centre of town.

Rural escape is also hassle-free; there are a number of enjoyable villages and market towns within reach, and fast access to the natural wonders of the Norfolk Broads (*see p105*) to the east and the Norfolk coast to the north (*see p34*).

The centre

It's easy to orientate yourself: the cathedral, castle, market square, railway station and even the football ground on Carrow Road are an easy stroll away. In the very heart of Norwich is Michael Hopkins's Forum (2 Millennium Plain, 01603 727950, www.theforumnorwich.co.uk), a millennium project built after the Central Library was destroyed by fire in 1994. It's home to a variety of organisations including the Millennium Library, an excellent tourist information centre, the BBC, Fusion (a digital screen gallery) and Pizza Express. The broad façade of this airy and transparent building acts as a useful meeting and orientation point. Opposite is the largest medieval church in the city, St Peter Mancroft (The Chantry, 01603 610443, www.stpetermancroft.org.uk).

Centuries overlap everywhere in Norwich, which is hardly surprising given its age. By 1004 the city's meandering River Wensum had helped turn it into a thriving centre for trade and commerce in the east of England. Nowadays, remains of this past can be seen wherever you look: along the riverside path, home to the Cow Tower medieval brick lookout and the stone arch of Pull's Ferry (once a 15th-century water gate); and on Chapelfield, where the 14th-century city walls stand. Beneath a Georgian façade you're quite likely to find a Norman building; medieval beauties include the Guildhall, Dragon Hall (*see p86*) and the Norwich Castle Museum & Art Gallery (*see p87*). Tudor relics are evident at Armada House on St Andrew's Plain, supposedly built with timber from Spanish Armada ships wrecked on the East Anglia shore, and throughout the delightful, cobbled area of Elm Hill (www.elmhill.co.uk).

More modern architectural attractions include local hero George Clipper's breathtaking art nouveau Royal Arcade shopping centre (*see p85*);

the impressive art deco City Hall & Clock Tower (*see p86*) that Hitler vowed – but failed – to destroy; and the city's two stunning cathedrals: the Cathedral Church of St John the Baptist (*see p86*) designed by George Gilbert Scott, and Norwich Cathedral (*see p87*), one of 32 pre-Reformation churches in the city.

Shopping

Norwich has a large number of deconsecrated churches, and on Saturdays many of them open their doors to stallholders of all hues, transforming the city into a vast flea market. You can certainly expect a tea and cake stall, and you'll often find a minstrel strumming a guitar in the nave.

At the other extreme, in the sparkling, chic Chapelfield mall (www.chapelfield.co.uk), there's a whole range of smart shops, including an Apple store. Close by is the superbly stocked independent Jarrold's department store (01603 660661, www.jarrold.co.uk); the chi-chi Norwich Lanes (*see p85*); quaint Elm Hill (check out the Jade Tree – 15 Elm Hill, 01603 664615, www.thejadetree.co.uk – for classy crafts); a broad range of big-name high-street shops along the length of Gentleman's Walk and London Street; heaps of charity shops; and a great market (*see p85*) six days a week.

Culture

Nowadays, a visiting Steve Coogan will find a city that's a far cry from the cultural backwater so mercilessly lampooned by Alan Partridge. The independent Cinema City (St Andrew's Street, 0871 704 2053, www.picturehouses.co.uk) screens a wide variety of films, including children's movies on Saturday mornings. The Theatre Royal (Theatre Street, 01603 630000, www.theatreroyalnorwich.co.uk) shows opera and ballet as well as plays;

Norwich Cathedral. See p87.

there's also the smaller Maddermarket Theatre (St John's Alley, 01603 620917, www.madder market.co.uk), and the Playhouse (42-58 St George's Street, 01603 598598, www.norwich playhouse.co.uk), which hosts regular comedy nights. Children will love Norwich Puppet Theatre (*see p90*). And then there are the many and varied options provided by the University of East Anglia, not only art exhibitions at the Sainsbury Centre (*see p87*), but also concerts, readings and other cultural activities – have a look at their very useful website, www.ueaticketbookings.co.uk.

Golden Triangle
A good area to base yourself in if you want to be outside the centre of town, the Golden Triangle (www.thegoldentriangle.co.uk) is the area between the interestingly named Unthank Street, and the Ipswich and Newmarket Roads. It's home to galleries, cafés, bars, pubs, restaurants and a mixed bag of independent hotels and guesthouses. The excellent Grapevine Gallery (*see p85*) can be found here, conveniently next to the much lauded 103 bistro (*see p91*), and on seemingly every corner there's a pub with a resolutely trendified sign. The leafy streets are home to middle-class young families, professionals and students.

Where to eat & drink
Norwich folk are proud of the fact that they reputedly have a pub for every day of the year and a church for every week of the year, but they're also gladdened by the city's increasingly impressive restaurant scene. Well-regarded chains such as Wagamama (408 Chapelfield Plain, 01603 305985, www.wagamama.com) and Loch Fyne Fish Restaurant & Oyster Bar (30-32 St Giles Street, 01603 723450, www.lochfyne.com) have outlets in Norwich, but they are just part of a scene that includes an array of lively independents.

International cuisine is well covered. You can eat Mexican at Mambo Jambo (14-16 Lower Goat Lane, 01603 666802, www.mambojambo restaurant.com), Belgian at the Waffle House (39 St Giles High Street, 01603 612790, www. wafflehouse.co.uk), Japanese barbecue at Sakura Yakiniku (5 White Lion Street, 01603 663838, www.sakura-norwich.com) and Italian at Pinocchio's (11 St Benedicts Street, 01603 613318). All are buzzy and rammed at weekends.

The trendy Golden Triangle area groans with good gastropubs and bars too; notables include the Langtry (79 Unthank Road, 01603 469347, www.thelangtry.co.uk), the Rose Valley Tavern (111 Unthank Road, 01603 630930, www.norwich-rosevalleytavern.co.uk) and the Fat Cat (*see p92*).

But the big daddy when it comes to eating out is undoubtedly the Tombland/Queen Street area, aka Restaurant Row, where many of the city's best restaurants are located. In addition to the ones listed below, honourable mentions should go to Beluga (2 Upper King Street, 01603 624042, www.mybeluga.co.uk), Orgasmic Café (6 Queen

Elm Hill. See p81.

Street, 01603 760650, www.orgasmic-cafe.com)
and Reeds Restaurant & Bar (27-28 Tombland,
01603 665660, www.reedsnorwich.co.uk).

Britons Arms Coffee House & Restaurant

*9 Elm Hill, NR3 1HN (01603 623367). Open 9.30am-
5pm Mon-Sat. No credit cards.*
Tudor beams feature large in this 15th-century thatched
coffee house and restaurant on Norwich's prettiest cobbled
street. Should the old-fashioned kitsch be a bit too much,
there's a pretty terraced garden in which to enjoy your tea
or traditional British dishes.

By Appointment

*25-29 St Georges Street, NR3 1AB (01603 630730,
www.byappointmentnorwich.co.uk). Open 7.30-9pm
Tue-Sat.*
Walk past any of the four dining rooms spread across three
15th-century beamed merchants' houses and you'll feel like
a Dickens street urchin gazing in at the opulent interiors,
stuffed with antiques, chandeliers and shiny silverware. A
meal here is a real feast for the senses, and the food – Modern
British with an emphasis on meat – looks a treat too.

Café 91

*Upper St Giles Street, NR2 1AB (01603 627422,
www.beecheshotelnorwich.co.uk/dining). Open 8.30am-
6pm Mon-Sat; 8.30am-4pm Sun.*
Owned by Beeches hotel, this lovely turn-of-the-20th-century
coffee shop serves everything from yummy breakfast
pastries and brunch dishes to pasta mains and cartoonishly
giant own-made cherry bakewells – a snip at £1.50.

NORFOLK

Mackintosh's Canteen. See p89.

Caley's Cocoa Cafe

Guildhall, Gaol Hill, NR2 1NF (01603 629364, www. caleys.com). Open 9am-4.30pm Mon-Sat; 11am-4pm Sun.
Located in the 15th-century Guildhall, this gorgeous tearoom and café is as traditional as they come, which is the least you'd expect from a company that's been making chocolate drinks and bars for more than 120 years. Back then, Norfolk landscape and horse painter Alfred Munnings decorated the wrappers; they're less picturesque nowadays, but the Help for Heroes Fairtrade bars are definitely worth a takeaway.

Cinema City Dining Rooms ★

Cinema City, St Andrews Street, NR2 4AD (07504 356378, www.picturehouses.co.uk). Meals served Bar noon-9pm Mon-Thur; noon-6pm Sat, Sun. Dining Rooms 6-9pm Fri, Sat.

Three gorgeous medieval spaces paved with huge flagstones make this a great place to eat, and that's before tasting the excellent Modern British and European food served in the bar and restaurant. The £7.95 soup and sandwich combo is a winner at lunch, but make the most of it by visiting for a weekend dinner and treat yourself to dishes such as bouillabaisse or roast cod with shellfish and veg minestrone.

Crypt Café Bistro

St Andrews & Blackfriars Hall, St Andrews Plain, NR3 1AU (01603 627950). Open 10am-3.30pm Mon-Sat. No credit cards.
Enjoy good café fare and simple, well-prepared specials in a stunning hall that dates back to 1307; it's worth coming just to explore the building, which is otherwise closed to the public.

Drunken Prawn stall, Norwich Market

Grapevine Gallery

109 Unthank Road, NR2 2PE (01603 760660, www.grapevinegallery.co.uk). Open 10am-5.30pm Tue-Sat.
A great place to browse, or buy lovely crafts and art, from little felt kits to gorgeous ceramics and jewellery. There's another branch in Burnham Market.

The Lanes

www.norwichlanes.co.uk
A vibrant independent retail scene spread over several streets, with the best shops not actually on the picturesque lanes, but the larger cross-streets they link: St Benedicts Street, St Giles Street and Pottergate. You'll find music, vintage and contemporary fashion and homewares. Upper St Giles Street is a highlight, with Verandah (01603 666137, www.verandah-norwich.co.uk) for homewares, Pavilion (01603 761862) for jewellery, shoes and accessories, and Louis Deli (01603 763377) for amazing foodstuffs.

Norwich Market ★

01603 213537, www.norwich-market.co.uk.
The 190-stall market is a lovely traditional one, the like of which it's hard to find these days. Wristwatch straps? Check. Wincyette pyjamas at £3.99? Check. Big jars of boiled sweeties and chocolate mice? Check. Plus bacon butties, dress fabrics, second-hand books, CDs and fruit and veg, alongside organic produce from Salle Organics, a Brazilian groceries stall, a great cheese stall, local Aldous ice-cream and sparkling shellfish from the Drunken Prawn stall. It's open Monday to Saturday, from 9am to 4pm.

Royal Arcade ★

This 1988 art nouveau shopping arcade opposite the market, designed by local star George Skipper, is a real beauty, with Doulton tiles, Italian terrazzo stone flooring, decorative pillars and stained glass. And that's before you check out the cute Colman's Mustard Shop (*see p86*), Langleys toy shop (nos.12-14, 01603 621959) Penita's deli/café (no.3, 01603 625757) or Digby's of Holt chocolate shop (01603 765924). Or blow the budget at fine-leather shop Marrs (no.6, 01603 766299, www.marrsleather.co.uk).

Tombland Antiques Centre with Collectables

14 Tombland, NR3 1HF (01603 619129). Open 10am-5pm Tue-Sat.
In an appropriately olde worlde building – Augustine Steward House, built in 1549 – is a wonderful warren of rooms selling antiques from a number of dealers: everything from art deco homewares and art nouveau jewellery to books, ceramics, clocks, toys and, of course, furniture.

NORFOLK

Cathedral Church of St John the Baptist

Cathedral House, Unthank Road, NR2 2PA (01603 624615, www.stjohncathedral.co.uk). Open 7.30am-8pm daily. Admission free.

George Gilbert Scott's 20th-century Gothic Revival building – the city's Roman Catholic cathedral – stands imposingly at the top of Grapes Hill. A stunningly decorated, elegant cruciform in shape, it's breathtaking both outside and in, particularly if you stand at the junction of the north and south transepts and gaze at the soaring space above. On summer Saturdays tower tours twice a day offer marvellous views of the city.

City Hall & Clock Tower

St Peter's Street, NR2 1NH (01603 727927, www.norwich.gov.uk). Open City Hall 8.45am-5pm Mon-Fri. Clock Tower by arrangement. Admission free.

While it's easy to admire the imposing exterior of Norwich's 1938 City Hall, it's worth taking a Blue Badge guided tour of the building (contact the tourist office for dates), when you can explore the art deco interior and timber-panelled rooms. If you can't manage that, sneak a peak into the ground-floor entrance hall and first-floor landing, both lined with Italian marble.

Colman's Mustard Shop

15 Royal Arcade, NR2 1NQ (01603 627889, www.colmansmustardshop.com). Open 9.30am-5pm Mon-Sat.

Located in the spectacular Royal Arcade, the Colman's shop is a must for cheap, original gifts, but the things you're most likely to want to buy aren't for sale: locked away in the three cabinets that make up the museum are gorgeous cruet sets and mustard holders, plenty of Colman's packaging from yesteryear and a (mercifully) brief history of the company.

Dragon Hall

115-123 King Street, NR1 1QE (01603 663922, www.dragonhall.org). Open 10am-5pm Mon-Fri, Sun. Admission £5; £3-£4.20 reductions; £12 family.

Discovered in the 1970s, this medieval merchant's trading hall raises some interesting questions about history and its preservation, having been stripped of centuries of partitioning and conversions to create two halls topped with a timber crown post roof and intricately carved and painted dragon. It's spectacular and well worth a visit.

Eaton Park

South Park Avenue, NR4 7EH. Open 24hrs daily.

Opened in 1928 by the then Prince of Wales, this pretty park would probably mightily please the current Prince of Wales, with its classical features, ornamental gardens, lily and model boating ponds, and domed mosaic fountain. He might be less enamoured of the miniature train, skate park and sports facilities, which include tennis, bowls and pitch and putt.

Inspire Discovery Centre

St Michael's Church, Oak Street, NR3 3AE (01603 612612, www.inspirediscoverycentre.com). Open 10am-4pm Mon-Fri; 11am-5pm Sat, Sun. Admission £4.50; £4 reductions.

Housed in a medieval church, Inspire is a small interactive science museum that should keep children entertained for at least a couple of hours. As well as plenty of hands-on exhibits and an under-fives area, there are regular science demonstrations and themed weekends.

John Jarrold Printing Museum

Whitefriars, NR3 1SH (01603 677183, www.johnjarroldprintingmuseum.org.uk). Open 9.30am-12.30pm Wed; other days by appointment. Admission free.

Look at the entrance tiles in Jarrold's department store and you'll see they say Jarrold Press – the Norfolk mini-magnate made a fortune by publishing (among other books) Anna Sewell's *Black Beauty*. The story is engagingly told at this little museum – open only on Wednesdays – which ambitiously also covers the history of printing in general. Specialists will love the wealth of old presses and the explanations provided by on-site enthusiasts, but it's worth a half-hour of anyone's time.

Norwich Cathedral

Sainsbury Centre for Visual Arts

Norwich Castle Museum & Art Gallery
Castle Meadow, NR1 3JU (01603 493625,
www.museums.norfolk.gov.uk). Open 10am-4.30pm
Mon-Fri; 10am-5pm Sat; 1-5pm Sun. Admission £6;
£4.40-£5.10 reductions.
From pretty much anywhere in central Norwich you'll
catch beguiling glimpses of the 900-year-old castle keep
that's now the centrepiece of this excellent museum
and art gallery. The squat but elegant Norman structure,
built of dazzling Caen limestone (and refaced with Bath
stone in the 1830s), is equally arresting inside. You'll
find the likes of Snap the dragon, the centuries-old star
of Norwich's mayoral processions, plenty of gibbets,
torture instruments and other ghoulish exhibits that will
appeal to kids, and various interactive displays – plus
a chilling well that descends more than 120ft. Next
door are a dizzying array of galleries covering everything
from Egyptian and Viking history to decorative arts and
fashion. You really need more than one visit to take it
all in; if time is limited, aim for the ceramics collections,
the paintings by equestrian artist Alfred Munnings,
the wonderful display of teapots in the Twining Teapot
gallery, and the Treasure, Trade and the Exotic gallery,
which includes two terrific Eric Ravilious mugs.

Norwich Cathedral ★
12 The Close, NR1 4DH (01603 218300,
www.cathedral.org.uk). Open 7.30am-6pm daily.
Admission free. Tours £4.
Founded in 1096 and constructed of Caen stone,
this stunning Romanesque cathedral has a number
of standout features, including the fan-vaulted roof,
the transepts, Thomas Gooding's skeleton tomb, the
monastic cloister, the presbytery and the surprisingly
contemporary decoration on the spire, England's
second highest. The Cathedral Close and grounds are
worth exploring too. Look out for the statue of Nelson
gazing at the school he attended; the memorial to local
hero Edith Cavell, who was executed by the Germans
in World War I and is buried in the cathedral; and the
saint-studded Erpingham Gate. On the north side of
the cathedral, on Bishopsgate, is the Bishop's Garden,
a walled gem open to the public on certain days from
May to July, when there are also teas and a plant stall
(see www.norwich.anglican.org/gardens for details).

Plantation Garden ★
4 Earlham Road, NR2 3DB (01603 219630,
www.plantationgarden.co.uk). Open 9am-6pm
daily. Admission £2.
These three acres of glorious gardens, in a medieval
chalk quarry next to the Roman Catholic cathedral,
are a fantastic place to spend an hour or two. Gothic
fountains, an Italianate terrace, a summer house, a
sculptured terrace wall and numerous walkways link
imaginatively planted flower beds, ensuring a visual
natural feast that's unrivalled in the city.

Sainsbury Centre for Visual Arts (SCVA) ★
University of East Anglia, Earlham Road, NR4 7TJ
(01603 593199, www.scva.org.uk). Open 10am-5pm
Tue, Thur-Sun; 10am-8pm Wed. Admission free.
Sir Norman Foster's elegiac building may look like
an aircraft hangar dropped into the middle of a rural
university campus, but there's no doubting that it works
brilliantly in presenting a collection that resembles a
mini version of the British Museum with a bit of Tate
thrown in. The focus is very much on the educational,
but it's done in an understated and visually compelling
manner – even the school groups seem engaged with
the work. Imaginative, beautifully designed temporary
exhibitions are held in a basement space that draws
the eye to the parkland vistas in unexpected ways.

Strangers Hall
Charing Cross, Norwich NR2 4AL (01603 667229,
www.museums.norfolk.gov.uk). Open Feb-Christmas
10.30am-4.30pm Wed-Sat. Admission £3.30; free-
£3.80 reductions; £9.10 family.
One of Norwich's oldest buildings (dating from
1320) houses a range of historical displays in a
series of interlinked rooms decorated with textiles
and period pieces. Costumed invigilators provide
plenty of fascinating detail about daily life in Tudor
and Stuart England.

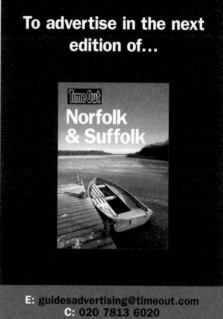

Old Rectory. See p92.

Delia's Restaurant & Bar/Yellows

Norwich City Football Ground, Carrow Road, NR1 1JE (01603 218704, www.deliascanarycatering.com). Open Delia's 7-9pm Fri, Sat. Yellows noon-11pm Mon-Wed, Sun; noon-10pm Thur-Sat.

With limited opening hours and serious competition in the city centre, it's hard to imagine why you'd make the trek to Carrow Road until you taste Delia's no-nonsense but delicately prepared classics (boeuf bourguignon, calf's liver with onions, grilled plaice) served in an elegant white space decked out with crisp linen and the kind of comfortable touches you'd expect from the everywoman chef. New York-style diner Yellows offers warming plates of chilli, clam chowder and buffalo wings, alongside, as you'd hope, a wide range of burgers, steaks and salads. The excellent three-course children's menu costs £8.95.

Elm Hill Brasserie ★

2 Elm Hill, NR3 1HN (01603 624847, www.elmhill brasserie.co.uk). Lunch served 12.30-2.30pm, dinner served 5.45-10.30pm Tue-Sat.

At this award-winning brasserie, chef/proprietor Simon Turner likes to mix things up, serving contemporary and classic European and British dishes, with an emphasis on East Anglian produce. So you might get bouillabaisse with local cod and smoked haddock, say, or Suffolk skate wing with pepper, bean and Toulouse sausage stew.

Ivory's Restaurant & Café

Assembly House, Theatre Street, NR2 1RQ (01603 627526, www.assemblyhousenorwich.co.uk). Open 10am-7pm Mon-Sat; noon-3pm Sun.

The gorgeous interiors of this Georgian mansion are best enjoyed over an hour or two in the stunning restaurant (named after its architect, Sir Thomas Ivory), which serves morning coffee, high tea and brasserie staples for lunch and early suppers. Not surprisingly, the traditional Sunday roasts are very popular in winter.

Last Wine Bar

76-78 St George's St, NR3 1AB (01603 626626, www.lastwinebar.co.uk). Lunch served noon-2.30pm, dinner served 5-10.30pm Mon-Sat.

Sited in a former Victorian shoe factory, this swish but affordable restaurant serves tempting Modern British and French dishes – such as cod fillet with saffron mash and buttered kale – in an airy and elegant space that still manages to feel intimate and personal.

Library Bar & Grill

4A Guildhall Hill, NR2 1JH, (01603 616606, www.rafflesrestaurants.co.uk). Lunch served noon-2pm, dinner served 6-10pm Mon-Sat. Meals served noon-4pm Sun.

Norwich isn't short on grand locations for restaurants, and this has to be one of the best, housed in what was Britain's first public library. Smart black leather chairs provide a modern counterpoint to the lovely original wood panelling and bookcases. Food is Modern British, with much of it cooked on a wood-fired grill.

Mackintosh's Canteen

Unit 410, Chapelfield Plain, NR2 1SZ (01603 305280, www.mackintoshscanteen.co.uk). Open 10am-10pm Mon-Fri; 9am-10pm Sat, Sun.

Located in a former sweet factory, this bright, two-storey restaurant is part of the Animal Inn stable. Staff are friendly, the ambience lively and the deft Modern British menu, which emphasises local produce, offers crowd-pleasers such as haddock and chips or salmon and samphire as well as an appealing range of risottos, burgers and salads.

Mad Moose & 1up ★

2 Warwick Street, NR2 3LD (01603 627687, www.themadmoose.co.uk). Open noon-11.30pm Mon-Sat; noon-10.30pm Sun.

Things to do

Bittern Line

www.bitternline.com (National Rail enquiries 08457 484950, Anglia Railways tickets 08700 409090). This 30-mile scenic railway connects Norwich with the north Norfolk coastal towns of Cromer and Sheringham via the Norfolk Broads at Salhouse, Hoveton and Wroxham. If you're bringing a bicycle, arrive early: trains can take only four bikes.

Blue Badge walking tours ★

Tourist Information Centre, The Forum, Millennium Plain, NR2 1TF (01603 213999, www.visitnorwich. co.uk/blue-badge.aspx). Blue Badge guides conduct a number of regular themed walks around the city, covering general history (City of Centuries, for example) to the more specific, such as Tales of the Riverside, and the downright weird – anyone for the Dead Parrot Tour?

City Boats

Griffin Lane, Thorpe St Andrew, NR7 0SL (01603 701701, www.cityboats.co.uk). Open Easter-Sept 10am-4pm daily. Admission varies; check website for details. The River Wensum forms a convenient loop around the city, so a boat trip is a great way to see the sights. A range of daily cruises, lasting from 20 minutes to three hours, leave from three quays in and around Norwich.

Norwich City FC

Carrow Road, NR1 1JE (01603 760760, tickets 0844 826 1902, www.canaries.co.uk). Tickets £17-£34. The home ground of Norwich's popular Canaries (named after the singing canaries introduced by 16th-century Dutch weavers to keep them entertained as they worked at their looms) shouldn't be missed. Buy a ticket to a match here and join some of the country's most loyal – and long-suffering – fans.

Norwich Puppet Theatre

St James, Whitefriars, NR3 1TN (01603 629921, www.puppettheatre.co.uk). Open varies; check website for details. Admission £7; £5-£5.50 reductions; £20 family. This lovely theatre is housed in a medieval church. Touring puppet companies offer a wide range of shows, from Perseus to the Snow Queen, for kids of all ages, as well as an imaginative programme of craft-based workshops for both children and grown-ups.

UEA Sportspark

University of East Anglia, Earlham Road, NR4 7TJ (01603 592398, www.sportspark.co.uk). Open 7.30am-10.30pm daily. Admission varies; check website for details. Follow a visit to the Sainsbury Centre with a workout: facilities include an Olympic-sized swimming pool, astro pitches, squash and tennis courts and a climbing wall.

Norwich City FC

NORFOLK

Henry Watt's Animal Inn mini empire of Norfolk eateries has amassed two Michelin Bib Gourmand awards, including one for 1up, the splendiferous first-floor restaurant above the Mad Moose pub. It's a delightful place for a special meal, and the food, Modern Anglo-French, is possibly the best you'll eat in the city. Downstairs, the velvet and gilt gives way to stripped floors, with a gastropub menu to match, though the dishes still punch well above their weight.

103
103 Unthank Road, (01603 610047, www.103unthank. com). Breakfast served 8.30-11am, lunch served noon-2.45pm daily. Dinner served 6-9.30pm Mon-Sat.
Billed as a bistro and deli, this recent addition to the vibrant Golden Triangle food scene is winning plaudits galore with its appealing mix of old-style British dishes such as ham, egg and chips and more imaginative fare (smoked eel with beetroot relish; artichoke, celery and sage soup; oysters with hot chorizo – for breakfast!). Even better, few of them bust the £10 mark. The space is bright but small, and you can't book, so prepare to queue – it's worth every minute.

Pulse Café Bar
The Old Fire Station Stables, Labour in Vain Yard, Guildhall Hill, NR2 1JD (01603 765562, www.raffles restaurants.co.uk). Open 10am-4pm Mon; 10am-10pm Tue, Wed; 10am-11pm Thur-Sat; 11.30am-4pm Sun.
Come here for inventive vegetarian cooking in a lovely open-plan setting above the Rainbow Wholefoods shop. The menu draws on flavours from eastern Europe, Africa and Asia to deliver appealing dishes that span breakfast through to main evening meals.

Red Lion
52 Eaton Street, Eaton, NR4 7LD (01603 454787, www.redlion-eaton.co.uk). Breakfast served 8-10am daily. Lunch served noon-2.15pm, dinner served 6.30-9pm Mon-Sat. Meals served noon-8.30pm Sun.
The bygone decor – Dutch gables, beams, panelled walls and inglenook fireplaces – and Modern British cuisine make this 17th-century pub and hotel worth leaving the city for – it's on the outskirts of Norwich. Expect local ingredients such as Cromer crab, a good range of steaks and a daily specials board featuring big meat favourites such as steak and kidney suet pudding and Norfolk lamb's liver. Six comfortable rooms upstairs and in a stable annex make this a popular B&B option too (£54 double incl breakfast).

Tatlers
21 Tombland, NR1 3RF (01603 766670, www.butlers restaurants.co.uk). Lunch served noon-2pm Mon-Sat. Dinner served 6-9.30pm Mon-Fri; 6-10pm Sat.
With vibrant red walls, simple wooden tables and chairs and ingredients sourced from Norwich Market, this laid-back bistro is a great Tombland feature. The inventive Modern European cooking – risotto of wild garlic and crumbled goat's cheese, say, or roasted fillet of beef with oyster fritter – is very popular, so booking is a must.

Where to stay
The compact nature of Norwich's city centre means that hotels are usually within easy range

of almost everything you'd want to visit, and plenty of competition ensures keen pricing. Further afield, on the south-west edge of the city, the Red Lion gastropub (*see p91*) also has rooms.

If you'd prefer to self-cater, try Norwich City Breaks Apartments (0800 011 4006, http://norwichcity breaks.co.uk). Centrally located two-bedroomed apartments cost from £158 for two nights midweek.

Beeches Hotel
2-6 Earlham Rd, NR2 3DB (01603 621167, www.beecheshotelnorwich.co.uk). Rates £80 double.
Arranged over three Grade II-listed houses next to the Roman Catholic cathedral, the Beeches offers smart, spacious rooms that have the air of a cheered-up gentlemen's club; dark wood furniture, floral curtains, chequerboard bathrooms and crisp white linen.

Dunston Hall
Ipswich Road, NR14 8PQ (01508 470444, www.devere.co.uk). Rates from £171 double incl breakfast & dinner.
Pretend you're one of the country set at this Elizabethan-style red-brick mansion, built in 1859 and now run by the upmarket De Vere chain. Facilities include an indoor swimming pool, sauna, steam room and fitness suite, an 18-hole golf course and acres of parkland. The rooms (150 in total) are as plush and comfortable as you'd expect.

Gothic House
King's Head Yard, Magdalen Street, NR3 1JE (01603 631879, www.gothic-house-norwich.com). Rates £95 double incl breakfast. No credit cards.
This beautiful Grade II-listed Regency house in the heart of the city is a real treat, but it has only two rooms (one double, one twin), so you'll need to book well in advance. Each room has its own private bathroom, with Molton Brown toiletries, bathrobes and fluffy white towels.

The Grove
59 Bracondale, NR1 2AT (01603 622053, www.the grovenorwich.co.uk). Rates £80-£90 double incl breakfast. No credit cards.
There are only three rooms at this attractive B&B, but all are spacious, comfortable and pleasantly decorated, with open fireplaces, roll-top baths and views over gardens and city rooftops.

Maids Head Hotel
Tombland, NR3 1LB (0870 609 6110, www.folio hotels.com). Rates £79-£105 double.
The 13th-century Maids Head Hotel is Britain's oldest hotel, apparently; Elizabeth I was once a guest. It's obviously being doing something right over the centuries and is now a regular award-winner – including Norfolk Hotel of the Year in 2008, when it was completely refurbished. With 84 vastly differing rooms and suites (including the one Bess is reputed to have stayed in), it should have something to suit most tastes.

Marriott Sprowston Manor
Wroxham Road, NR7 8RP (01603 410871, www.marriott.co.uk). Rates from £118 double.
This Marriott Hotel & Country Club on the outskirts of town (thus great for exploring both the city and the Broads)

FIVE NORWICH PUBS

Adam & Eve
Bishopgate, NR3 1RZ (01603 667423, www.adamandevenorwich.co.uk).
Open 11am-11pm Mon-Sat; noon-10.30pm Sun.
Norwich's oldest pub is proud of its 800-year history, and equally proud of its fine range of beers and annual listing in the *Good Pub Guide*.

Cidershed
98-100 Lawson Road, NR3 4LF (01603 413153, www.theshednorwich.co.uk).
Open noon-11.30pm Mon-Fri, Sun; 11am-11.30pm Sat. No credit cards.
Cider fans should hotfoot it to this light, airy space, where they'll find a rosewood bar, vintage road signs, great bands and a terrific range of ciders made by landlord Ryan Burnard, including Monty's Dog Dry, named after the pub dog.

Delaney's Irish Bar
41 St Andrew's Street, NR2 4TP (01603 305995). Open 11.30am-2am daily.
Big, brash and raucous, Delaney's is not the place for a quiet pint. Party hard and enjoy genuine Dublin Guinness.

Eagle
33 Newmarket Road, NR2 2HN (01603 624173, www.theeaglepub.co.uk). Open 11am-11pm Mon-Sat; noon-6pm Sun.
An oldie in the Golden Triangle area, this friendly Georgian pub also offers excellent, reasonably priced food (local game pie, Brancaster mussels). Summer barbecues are served on the terrace, and it's very child-friendly for a city boozer.

Fat Cat Freehouse
49 West End Street, NR2 4NA (01603 624364, www.fatcatpub.co.uk). Open noon-11pm Mon-Wed, Sun; noon-midnight Thur, Fri; 11am-midnight Sat. No credit cards.
The winner of the the *Good Pub Guide's* Beer Pub of the Year 2010 may not look like much from the outside, but it's heartily recommended for its excellent drinks list (including its own brews, numerous guest ales on tap and 50 bottled beers from around the world) and friendly punters.

And 700 more...
Norwich once had more than 700 pubs, a figure dwindling to less than 140 at the last count. On the Blue Badge guided walk 'A pub for every day of the year', you can learn the history of some of them. No beer stops, unfortunately, but there's nothing to stop you coming back and sharing your new-found knowledge with the locals. Book tickets and get more information from the tourist information centre (01603 213999, www.visitnorwich.co.uk).

comes with 170 acres of mature parkland to wander around, a health and beauty spa, indoor pools for children and grown-ups, and one of Norfolk's best golf courses.

Number 17 ★
17 Colegate, NR3 1BN (01603 764486, www.number 17norwich.co.uk). Rates £72 double incl breakfast.
This recent addition to Norwich's B&B scene is a real gem, both in terms of its city centre location and its sumptuously appointed rooms. Converted from a derelict printing mill by former builder Jim Clark, with decor by his wife, Glynis, it has eight rooms, some of which face on to a courtyard for alfresco breakfasts or chilling out with a bottle of wine. There's even a hot-tub should chilling out get a bit chilly. Breakfast is a highlight, featuring plenty of fresh fruit and pastries alongside excellent cooked dishes.

Old Rectory
103 Yarmouth Road, Thorpe St Andrew, NR7 0HF, (01603 700772, www.oldrectorynorwich.com). Rates £120-£150 double incl breakfast.
Situated on the eastern edge of the city, this atmospheric, creeper-clad Georgian house has eight lovely rooms – five in the main building and three in the adjacent former coach house. Past guests have nothing but praise for the place, from the large, luxurious sleeping quarters and the excellent cooking (breakfast, afternoon tea, dinner – with own-grown and local produce to the fore) to the beautiful gardens and the outdoor swimming pool, complete with its own sun terrace.

St Giles House Hotel ★
41-45 St Giles Street, NR2 1JR (01603 275180, www.stgileshousehotel.com). Rates from £130 double incl breakfast.
Gorgeous hotel, cool bar, Elysium spa and top-class restaurant... you could stay here and never get out to explore the classy boutiques on this happening street. Designed by renowned local architect George Skipper in 1906, the building is now a striking mash-up of old and new, with 24 individually designed rooms.

38 St Giles
38 St Giles Street, NR2 1LL (01603 662944, www.38stgiles.co.uk). Rates £120-£150 double incl breakfast.
Owned by Jan and William Cheeseman, this stylish Georgian house has just five rooms, so reserve early if you want to sample the own-made cakes, friendly service and excellent facilities, including Bang & Olufsen TVs with Virgin Media, and Wi-Fi. The location is ideal, in the centre of town near the Market and the Lanes.

Wedgewood House
42 St Stephens Road, NR1 3RE (01603 625730, www.wedgewoodhouse.co.uk). Rates £65 double incl breakfast.
This small, friendly B&B is a five-minute walk from the centre and two minutes from Chapelfield, which means a peaceful night's sleep and easy access to buses for the Sainsbury Centre. The eight rooms are comfortable and cosy, and all have Wi-Fi. Owners Elspeth and Nigel Evans will happily point you in the direction of good food and attractions nearby.

North-east Norfolk

Normally sleepy Norfolk is positively in a coma in this isolated part of the county, which isn't to say there's nothing here – though if coastal erosion continues unchecked, there will be considerably less than there is today. Here, erosion not only means the washing away of cliffs but also whole communities, particularly in fast-disappearing Happisburgh and some of the villages around it.

Star attractions in the area include huge sandy beaches at Waxham, Horsey and Winterton-on-Sea, stretching for mile after empty mile and more than a match for the famed beaches of the north Norfolk coast. Handsome (currently) inland villages, such as Trunch and Knapton, and borderline Broads villages such as East Ruston, offer the timeless pleasures of flint cottages, pretty pubs and singular medieval churches. They act as delightful counterpoints to the kiss-me-quick charms of the seaside towns and the isolated beauty of the vast beaches nearby.

OVERSTRAND TO HEMSBY

Overstrand
If you judged Norfolk's coastline by the reams of tourist pamphlets, accommodation guides and tourist board-sanctioned attractions available, you'd be forgiven for thinking the coast ended at Cromer. Consequently, most people make it as far east as Cromer and then turn inland to head towards Norwich and civilisation. But just two miles further east is the wonderful village of Overstrand, home to three Edwin Lutyens buildings (Overstrand Hall, the Methodist Church and the Pleasaunce), lovely St Martin's Church, the terrific Clifftop Café (*see p99*) overlooking a glorious beach, some great places to stay, a decent pub and an excellent range of walks – whether coastal, rural or a combination of the two.

The village was a fashionable, upmarket holiday destination by the late 19th century – Winston Churchill holidayed here just days before the outbreak of World War I – and was dubbed Poppyland owing to the profusion of poppies in the area. The nearby villages of Sidestrand and Trimingham are equally underrated pleasure spots offering expansive and empty beaches – plus, of course, chips or sand-speckled sandwiches to go with them.

Mundesley & Bacton
A few miles further east, Mundesley steps things up a gear. This sizeable village is something of an oddity, exhibiting as it does the vestiges of a once illustrious past in a handful of fading Victorian hotels and an attractive promenade and gardens, and a crazy golf course (Adventure Island, *see p104*). The North Norfolk Railway used to serve the village, bringing holidaymakers in their thousands to explore the town and its pretty millpond, but mostly to enjoy the sea air and the excellent beach (a regular Blue Flag winner). The branch line was axed in 1964, though part of the old railway track is still visible inland near North Walsham, at Pigneys Wood local nature reserve (www.pigneys-wood.co.uk).

The lack of easy public transport has resulted in a quiet and appealing village with more amenities than most. There's the Maritime Museum (Beach Road, 01263 720879, closed Sept-Easter), surely the world's smallest, housed in a coastal look-out station; C21 art gallery (High Street, 01263 720473); and some interesting buildings – notably the whimsical Bar Victoriana (Beach Road, 01263 720309) and the unusual Coronation Hall, home to the Mundesley Players who stage regular shows and musicals. A handful of cafés includes the Tea Caddy Tea Rooms (High Street, 01263 721751, closed Thur, Fri), Café B, Café Lilia (for both, *see p98*) and a pleasant beach café on the promenade. Clifftop pub the Ship (Beach Road, 01263 722671, www.mundesleyship.co.uk) claims to have 'probably the best beer garden in Norfolk'.

Gather picnic ingredients at Country Pickings delicatessen (19 High Street, 01263 720054, closed Sun) and the Lobster Pot seafood stall in the village car park and make the most of the coast; with its eye-catching if dilapidated groynes, gaily painted beach huts and wide sandy beach, it's a real winner. Just beyond the village, on the coast road, are the four white sails of Stow Mill (*see p98*), an 1820s corn mill that continued operating until 1930.

Thanks to the plethora of caravan parks along this stretch of coast, there's no shortage of pubs, cafés and fish and chip shops heading out of Mundesley, but because of the sheer length of that coastline – just over 35 miles from Sheringham to Great Yarmouth – it's easy to escape the crowds once you get past frankly horrible Bacton (surely the reason the coastline beyond has remained such a secret).

Lacking Mundesley's Victorian charm, Bacton is resolutely 20th century, a shambolic string of tawdry-looking B&Bs and guesthouses. It's best avoided by heading inland to North Walsham and returning to the coast at Happisburgh (pronounced, in typical Norfolk fashion, 'Haisbro').

Happisburgh to Hemsby

Visible for miles, red and white striped Happisburgh Lighthouse (*see p98* – which turned a fetching pink in 2008 when a sudden summer storm ruined the latest touch-up) is just one reason to stop at this lovely village; a great pub, fine church, sweet tearooms, well-stocked wet fish and shellfish shop, and exhilarating walks along the crumbling clifftop or beach below are the others. Erosion is a major problem here, as is evident from the wooden sea defence barriers stretching the length of the beach.

Expansive beaches are the norm for the next 20 miles, some the focus for miniscule Blackpool-esque resorts (Sea Palling and Hemsby), others glorious expanses of nothing but clean sand, big blue skies and seemingly endless sea (Waxham, Horsey and Winterton-on-Sea). All have something to recommend them; Sea Palling, in particular, is great for families who want an understated mini-resort with child-friendly facilities such as ice-cream stands and doughnut parlours, a good café and a tiny amusement arcade, while the stretch between Waxham and Winterton-on-Sea is a birdwatching hotspot. Twitchers shelter in the beach cuttings and hunker down in the dunes to catch sight of chiff-chaff, stonechat, cranes and red-throated and black-throated divers.

Around the old smugglers' village of Horsey – worth a look for the thatched, round-towered All Saints' Church and a pint and a pie at the Nelson Head (*see p99*) – the beach is particularly quiet, visited only by birdwatchers, dog walkers and the colony of grey seals who come every year to bask on the beach. Sitting on the sea defence wall with no other soul around, just watching the 100 or so new pups born each winter is a real joy (and beats a packed boat at Blakeney into a cocked hat).

The pleasures (and seals) continue south at Winterton-on-Sea ★. Served by an excellent beach café and backed by the pastel-painted Hermanus roundhouses (*see p100*), Winterton-on-Sea has one of the area's best beaches. The water is deep enough to attract windsurfers from around the country and the extensive dunes provide a great habitat for all manner of wildlife, including terns, natterjack toads and the odd adder. The attractive streets, filled with neatly-thatched cottages and white picket-fenced gardens, a cute village store, a good fish and chip shop and a picturesque 300-year-old pub, make it one of the prettiest villages, too.

Make the most of it; south of here, 'lively' Hemsby, all fast food joints, amusement arcades, discos and seaside tat shops, is something of a culture shock after the quiet emptiness of the rest of east Norfolk's breathtaking coastline... but a very good introduction to the charms of Great Yarmouth (*see p119*).

Winterton-on-Sea. See p95.

Places to visit

Happisburgh Lighthouse
Happisburgh, NR12 (www.happisburgh.org/lighthouse).
Open Easter-Aug 11am-4pm Sun, bank hols. Admission
£2; £1 reductions. No under-8s. No credit cards.
East Anglia's oldest working lighthouse, dating from
1790, is also Britain's only independently run one.
There are regular open days in summer, a gift shop
and a starring role in the occasional TV drama, most
recently Stephen Fry's Kingdom. The 112-step climb to
the lantern room is definitely not for vertigo sufferers;
indeed, the spiral stone staircase is hair-raising for
anyone. Views from the top are as far-reaching and
glorious as you'd expect – on a clear day you can see
for about 13 miles.

Horsey Windpump & Mere
Horsey, NR29 4EF (01263 740241, www.national
trust.org.uk). Open Apr-Sept 10am-5pm daily; Nov-
Mar see website for details. Admission £2.50;
£1 reductions.
Just south of Horsey, the elegant five-storey Horsey
drainage windpump hoves into view on the land side
of the beach road, and offers a great couple of hours'
entertainment that could stretch into a whole day if
the weather is good. The mill itself is fun to explore,
and there's a lovely three-mile circular walk that skirts
part of Horsey Mere on the easternmost fringes of
the Broads, before cutting through flat Norfolk fields
to emerge at the Nelson Head pub (see right).

Stow Mill
Stow Hill, Paston, NR28 9TG (01263 720298,
www.stowmill.co.uk). Open 10am-dusk daily.
Admission £1.50; 50p-£1.25 reductions.
No credit cards.
Built as a flour mill by James Gaze in the 1820s, this
traditional Norfolk windmill is a great example of its
kind, and one that kids will love, from the steep ladders
that lead up through its four floors to the small shop
selling all things windmilly.

Waxham Great Barn
Waxham Road, Sea Palling, NR12 0DY (01692
598824). Open May-Oct 10.30am-4.30pm daily.
Admission £3; £2.50 reductions.
This impressive, Grade 1-listed 180ft long barn
(Norfolk's biggest, built around 1570) is constructed
from the remains of several dissolved monasteries.

It contains a small museum and a popular café,
housed in the converted cow shed. Child-friendly
activities are held in the summer months.

Cat Pottery
1 Grammar School Road, North Walsham, NR28 9JH
(01692 402962, www.winstanleycats.uk.com). Open
9am-5pm Mon-Fri; 11am-1pm Sat (11am-3pm Sat
July-Sept).
Down a wee cobbled lane, what were tinsmiths'
workshops are now filled with old railway and transport
paraphernalia and hundreds of wide-eyed ceramic cats
(and the odd dog) made by Jenny Winstanley and her
family. The felines look down from battered display
cases, peek from old fire hydrants, and sit like ranks
of soldiers on rickety shelves, creating one of the
maddest little museums (and shops – most of the
pottery is for sale) you're ever likely to visit.

East Ruston Old Vicarage Gardens ★
East Ruston Old Vicarage, East Ruston, NR12 9HN
(01692 650432, www.e-ruston-oldvicaragegardens.
co.uk). Open Apr-Oct 2-5.30pm Wed, Fri-Sun, bank
hols. Admission £6.
The 30 acres of coastal garden here are utterly
magical, largely due to the sheer horticultural
exuberance created by owners and designers Alan
Gray and Graham Robeson. The duo bought the
house in the mid 1990s, inheriting what they call a
'blank canvas', and have turned it into an imaginative
extravaganza taking in everything from a wildflower
meadow to formal Dutch gardens and towering ferns
to a Californian border of explosive colour. It's all the
more impressive considering the exposed nature of
the site. Clever peepholes and topiary bring views of
the surrounding area, and a pretty tearoom completes
what is surely Norfolk's best garden.

Norfolk Motorcycle Museum
Railway Yard, North Walsham, NR28 0DS (01692
403342, www.mc-museum.freeserve.co.uk). Open
Easter-Sept 10am-4.30pm daily. Oct-Easter 10am-
4.30pm Mon-Sat. Admission £3.50; free-£3
reductions. No credit cards.
Strictly one for two-wheel enthusiasts, this unlikely-
looking museum has a collection of more than 80
motorcycles from the 1920s to the '60s, as well as
old bicycles and die-cast toys.

Where to eat & drink

This section of coast may be quieter than elsewhere
in Norfolk, but it's still the seaside, so there are
traditional caffs, greasy-spoons and chippies galore.
Poppylands Café at Delph Farm (01493 393393,
closed Mon-Fri), a converted barn on the coast
road between Sea Palling and Waxham, is worth
a weekend stop if you don't fancy pub grub or caff
staples, while Jonet Restaurant (17 Beach Road,
Mundesley, 01263 720903) serves breakfasts,
lunches and afternoon teas and hefty Sunday roasts.
   On the B1159 near Walcott, the Lighthouse Inn
(01692 650371, www.lighthouseinn.co.uk) is a
sprawling, popular pub that welcomes children.

Café B
2 Cromer Road, Mundesley, NR11 8BE (07786
572334). Open 10am-4pm Tue-Sun. No credit cards.
This bright little café serves good coffee, Dutch hot chocolate
and various teas, accompanied by cakes, pastries and panini.
Second-hand books and knitting yarns are stocked too.

Café Lilia
Station Road, Mundesley, NR11 8JH (01263 722282).
Open 9.30am-3pm Tue-Fri; 12.30-2.30pm Sun.
No credit cards.
A good selection of snacks, including baguettes and jacket
potatoes, plus breakfasts and daily specials, are produced
in this friendly, family-run café.

NORFOLK

This deservedly popular pub specialises, as you might guess from the name, in fish dishes – the fish pie, and seafood omelette with prawns and smoked salmon are both terrific. Bar snacks and real ales (Adnams, Woodforde's and guests) are available, and there are also three B&B rooms (£80 double incl breakfast).

Hill House ★
North Walsham Road, Happisburgh, NR12 0PW (01692 650004). Open noon-3pm, 7-11.30pm Mon-Wed; noon-11.30pm Thur-Sun. Lunch served noon-3pm, dinner served 7-9.30pm daily.
Located on a small hill, the Hill House is a Grade II-listed, 16th-century inn rightly lauded for its well-kept ales (around six, with occasional visitors) and good pub food, and famous for its one-time guest, Arthur Conan Doyle. The menu includes ploughman's, local crab and fish dishes, and pile-'em-high meat and three veg options, and there's an annual Solstice Beer Festival in June. Four rooms (£60 double incl breakfast) are available, one of them housed in a converted 1901 signal box.

Nelson Head
The Street, Horsey, NR29 4AD (01493 393378, www.nelsonheadhorsey.co.uk). Open 11am-9pm daily. Lunch served noon-2.30pm, dinner served 6-8.30pm daily.
A very welcome sight after a fine circular walk from Horsey Windpump (*see p98*) to the beach, the Nelson Head offers Woodforde's beers and excellent roasts and pies in front of a roaring log fire – perfect on a winter's day. Dogs are welcome, though not at meal times.

Old Hall Inn
Coast Road, Sea Palling, NR12 0TZ (01692 598323). Open 11.30am-11pm daily. Lunch served noon-2.30pm, dinner served 6.30-8.30pm daily.
A pretty 17th-century farmhouse with two cosy bars, a restaurant and a beer garden; meals often feature crab and lobster caught by the village fishermen. There's accommodation too (six rooms; £50-£60 double incl breakfast). Keep an eye out for the resident ghost; the figure of a woman dressed in grey, sitting on a window ledge in the television lounge.

Smallsticks Barn Café
Cart Gap Road, Happisburgh, NR12 0QL (01692 583368). Open Summer 10am-5pm Tue-Sun. Winter 10am-5pm Sat, Sun.
This new café is a godsend for walkers enjoying the isolated stretch of beach between Happisburgh and Lessingham. Located in a converted barn some 100 yards from the Cart Gap lifeboat station, it's open for breakfast, lunchtime snacks, cakes and cream teas, and offers expansive views from its enclosed terrace.

Where to stay
The coast road (B1159) from Cromer to Great Yarmouth has a range of accommodation options with great locations and views; in Mundesley, try Whincliff B&B (01263 721554) for the former and the once grand Manor Hotel (01263 720309, www.manorhotelmundesley.co.uk) for the latter. Most of the village pubs dotted along the coast

East Ruston Old Vicarage Gardens

Clifftop Café ★
22 Cliff Road, Overstrand, NR27 0PP (01263 579319). Open Easter-Oct 8am-5pm Tue-Sun. Nov-Easter 8am-4pm Tue-Sun. No credit cards.
There's been a café on this spot since 1925, though probably not always painted bright yellow and furnished with pretty pine tables. The current incarnation does great full English breakfasts, homely cooked lunches and cakes.

Fishermans Return
The Lane, Winterton-on-Sea, NR29 4BN (01493 393305, www.fishermans-return.com). Open Summer 11am-10.30pm daily. Winter 11am-3pm, 5-10.30pm daily. Food served noon-2pm, 6-9pm daily.

have B&B rooms too, including Hill House in Happisburgh, Old Hall Inn in Sea Palling and Fishermans Return in Winterton-on-Sea (for all, see p99) .

If you're looking to self-cater, Shoal Cottage (01263 576996, www.clifftopholidays.co.uk), which sits next to the Clifftop Café in Overstrand, has expansive sea views and sleeps eight.

TEN NORFOLK DELICACIES

Booja-Booja chocolates
www.boojabooja.com.
Let's face it, if you think of posh chocolates, you don't immediately think of down-to-earth Norfolk. And yet the Booja-Booja Company has won more than 25 awards for its small range of organic chocolate truffles and ice-cream, possibly because of its inventive bold flavour combos; anyone for cognac flambéed banana truffles?

Bray's Cottage pork pies ★
www.perfectpie.co.uk.
Home-reared Saddleback rare-breed pigs, a dash of onion marmalade and seasoning are all you need to create the perfect pork pie, according to Bray's Cottage proprietors Nell Montgomery and Sarah Pettegree. Test their theory with the ready-cooked version on a picnic, or take home the frozen variety.

Breckland Orchard soft drinks
www.brecklandorchard.co.uk.
Claire Martinsen's old-fashioned sodas have been garnering praise from all quarters: the ginger beer with chilli was highly rated by Observer Food Monthly in 2009. If ginger beer's not your thing, the cloudy lemonade or blackcurrant and raspberry will tumble you into Enid Blyton territory faster than you can say 'those pesky kids'.

Chillis Galore sauces
www.chillisgalore.co.uk.
Wilf and Kathy Thompson have been growing chillis in Norfolk for 20 years, bottling them as own-made jellies, sauces and relishes with some tantalising and original flavours – among them jalapeño, lime and coriander chilli jelly, and Caribbean mustard chilli sauce.

Cley Smokehouse
www.cleysmokehouse.com.
Smoked prawns, eels, kippers, haddock, potted shrimp, pickled herrings, cured meats, smoked cheese... they smoke a lot of stuff at Cley Smokehouse (see p53), and have been doing so for more than 30 years, trying as much as possible to use locally sourced ingredients. There's a great range of own-made pâtés too.

Danum House
22 Pauls Lane, Overstrand, NR27 0PE (01263 579327). Rates £50 double incl breakfast. No credit cards.
This handsome house with five en-suite rooms is just minutes from the sea and will delight fans of olde worlde interiors, not least for its original oak panelled walls.

Green Lawn House
35 High Street, Overstrand, NR27 0AB (01263 576925, www.greenlawnhouse.co.uk). Rates £130-£195 double incl breakfast.
An intriguing, Lutyens-style Edwardian residence with three nicely decorated and kitted-out suites (sleeping two or four) with full cooking facilities. They're bookable on a self-catering basis from two nights to a week. Pets are welcome, with advance notice, as are children (cots and high chairs can be provided on request).

Hermanus Holiday Camp ★
The Holway, Winterton-on-Sea, NR29 4BP (01493 393216, www.hermansholidays.com). Rates £287 single roundhouse per week.
The story goes that the owner of this terrifically located holiday camp (overlooking the dunes and a golden beach) constructed the fairytale-like thatched roundhouses after seeing similar ones on a visit to Hermanus Bay in South Africa. Although quite basic (think cute caravans), the pastel-painted cottages are well equipped and recently refurbished, and enchanting. In addition, there's an outdoor heated pool from late May to mid September, lovely gardens, family entertainment, games and an on-site restaurant and bar.

Sea Marge Hotel ★
High Street, Overstrand, NR27 0AB (01263 579579, www.seamargehotel.co.uk). Rates £142 double incl breakfast.
A clifftop location and four acres of gardens and terraced lawns leading down to the foreshore make this elegant Edwardian building a beauty. The 25 bedrooms (all en suite) include original features in contemporary settings. Food is served in the bar and two restaurants; non-residents are welcome. There's also a lounge with games.

NORTH WALSHAM & AROUND
No village in east Norfolk rivals the likes of Burnham Market on the north Norfolk coast – but given the sheer abundance of them (there's a village or hamlet every mile or so), it's easy to find a sizeable number that have a notable attraction, whether it's a stunning church, a great pub, a particularly harmonious aspect or a picture-perfect village pond. And there are signs that the Farrow & Ball effect is gathering pace: Northrepps, for example, a typical flint cottage-heavy village just

inland from Overstrand, has acquired Northrepps Cottage (see p104), a boutique country hotel and restaurant owned and run by Deborah Gurney, a member of the august Norfolk family that included prison reformer Elizabeth Fry and noted scholar Anna Gurney.

The busy market town of North Walsham is the heart of this area (known as 'Griffon Country' after the arms of the Paston family, who once owned most of it) and has a number of decent accommodation options, as well as a handsome market square, a 14th-century wool church, a tiny row of shops that began life as medieval stalls (in Pope's Passage, on the north side of the churchyard), and Paston College, now a sixth-form college but in the 1760s the school attended by Horatio Nelson. The shopping is forgettable, but it's a pleasant place with some attractive streets and houses, a Cat Pottery (see p98) that's a real one-off, and a local artists' gallery, the Griffon (32 Vicarage Street, 01692 407509).

The noted Paston Way starts out here too; beginning in the Market Place, the 20-mile waymarked trail takes in 15 churches and villages en route to Cromer, through quiet lanes, along high cliffs and across arable fields and grazing pastures. There's more good walking (and cycling) on the Weavers' Way, a 60-mile trail between Cromer and Great Yarmouth, which also passes through the town.

North Walsham is also not a bad base for exploring the surrounding villages of Trunch, Knapton and Worstead, each of which makes for a good half-day excursion. Trunch stands out for its thatched 17th-century manor house and late

Nelson Head. See p99.

Houghton Hall venison

Largesse from the Marquess of Cholomondley, whose Norfolk estate supplies selected local butchers with the meat of the rare white fallow deer that roam the 450 acres of parkland surrounding the hall (see p47).

Mrs Temple's Cheese ★

Catherine Temple produces a number of Norfolk cheeses, the most famous of which is probably binham blue, a subtle, soft-veined blue cheese, but there's also crumbly walsingham, gouda-style warhans and even a melton mozarella. All the cheeses are handmade from the family's own dairy cow herd and widely available at farmers' markets, delis and farm shops.

Norfolk Lavender shortbread

www.norfolk-lavender.co.uk.
You'll find lavender shortbread in many of Norfolk's tearooms, where it's worth trying for its wonderfully delicate flavour. Buy some of the ingredients at Norfolk Lavender (see p28) if you're smitten, or bags of the ready-made variety at various farm shops.

Samphire sausages

www.samphireshop.co.uk.
Made from outdoor-reared rare-breed pigs and subtly flavoured with nutmeg, sage, coriander and ginger, Samphire's sizzling range of sausages were once described by Gary Rhodes as the best he'd ever tasted. Buy them at either of the two Samphire shops in Blickling (see p76) and Wymondham (see p140) or online.

Stoneground flour & bread

Letheringsett Watermill (see p56) near Holt produces a range of stoneground wheat, including whole wheat and spelt, that's available across Norfolk, both as flour and in pastries, loaves and cakes. Denver Mill (see p152) also makes its own bread and cakes, on sale at the mill tearoom and shop.

NORFOLK

Beechwood Hotel. See p104.

14th-century St Botolph's Church. The latter is notable for a highly carved wooden font canopy (one of only four in England) and an impressive angel hammerbeam roof, only outdone in the area by the church of St Peter & St Paul in Knapton, which has an even more beautiful double-hammerbeam roof with 138 angels. And if you like a good round tower, don't miss St Mary's Church in Roughton, which boasts a particularly lovely one, built partly of ironstone.

Nearby, in the extensive grounds of Gunton Park, the hard-to-find church of St Andrew is definitely worth visiting. This Palladian, chapel-like building is the only church designed by the great Robert Adam, and the hunt for it, through a large wooded estate with a deer park, fishing lake, an observatory tower, the shell of the original Gunton Hall (gutted by fire in 1882) and an occupied hall of private apartments, makes for a great walk, particularly when you eventually spy the light, beautifully proportioned church in its perfect setting. It's now cared for by the Churches Conservation Trust (www.visitchurches.org.uk).

Heading south, the village of Worstead – heart of the area's 14th-century weaving trade and the origin of the word 'worsted' – is another good halting point, not least for the impressive scale of its 14th-century wool church, St Mary's. The convivial village pub, the New Inn (see p103), is at the heart of the three-day Worstead Festival (www.worsteadfestival.org) in July, which bills

itself as the largest village festival in Norfolk and offers an intriguing mix of terrier racing, sheep shearing, folk music and ceilidhs.

A few miles east, the Broads/Griffon borders hold a few more pleasant sights: in the village of East Ruston, St Mary's Church lies in a great open fields setting and the Old Vicarage Gardens (see p98) offer one of Norfolk's best attractions, while the tiny traditional hamlets of Ingham and Lessingham are home to a lovely church apiece and two good pubs with rooms: the Swan Inn (see p104) and the Star (see p103). Both of them make good bases for exploring the coast and the Broads.

Where to eat & drink

North Walsham is the best bet for lunch, with coffee shops and cafés such as Madisons (6 Kings Arms Street) and Butterfingers (Mitre Tavern Yard) doing a brisk trade – though perhaps not as brisk as Kelly's Plaice fish and chip shop on the market square.

There's still a pub in most villages, many offering a good selection of real ales and pub grub. For Modern British food in a grander setting, country hotels Beechwood and Northrepps Cottage (for both, see p104) won't disappoint.

Chubby Panda
22 Market Street, North Walsham, NR28 9BZ (01692 500920). Lunch served 11.30am-2.30pm daily. Dinner served 5-10.30pm Mon-Thur, Sun; 5-11pm Fri, Sat.

Above-average international food is rare in small towns, so all hail the Chubby Panda, which serves decent Thai and Chinese food in an understated, elegant space with leather armchairs and damask tablecloths.

Crown Inn
Smallburgh, NR12 9AD (01692 536314, www. smallburghcrown.co.uk). Open 5.30-11pm Mon; noon-3pm, 5.30-11pm Tue-Fri; noon-3pm, 7-11pm Sat; noon-4pm Sun. Lunch served noon-2pm daily. Dinner served 6.30-9pm Mon-Fri; 6.30-9.30pm Sat.
The Crown is a sprawling, 15th-century thatched coaching inn with a pretty dining room and classic beer garden. There are real ales and homely food, plus two guest bedrooms (£60 double incl breakfast).

Liaison
5 Market Street, North Walsham, NR28 9BZ (07787 786707). Open 8.30am-3.30pm Mon-Fri; 10am-2pm Sun. No credit cards.
A bright café with a cosy sofa area (with a TV that keeps children transfixed), a decked terrace and friendly staff serving a wide range of sandwiches and snacks.

New Inn
Front Street, Worstead, NR28 9RW (01692 536296). Open noon-3pm, 6.30-11pm Mon-Fri; noon-11pm Sat; noon-10.30pm Sun. Lunch served noon-3pm, dinner served 6-11pm Mon-Fri; food served noon-11pm Sat, Sun.
This handsome pub looks after its real ales (from Deuchars and Adnams, as well as regularly changing guest beers) and visitors in equally good measure. Daily blackboard specials are offered in a pleasant space that includes a small bar with a big fire, two lounges, a summer garden and a cosy dining area. Occasional hog roasts are another draw.

Olive Tree Restaurant ★
1 Bacton Road, North Walsham, NR28 0RA (01692 404900, www.theolivetreenorfolk.com). Open noon-11pm Tue-Sat; noon-6pm Sun. Lunch served noon-3pm Wed-Sun. Dinner served 6-9pm Tue-Sat.
This relative newcomer to the area is a rarity, with its airy, clean-lined, modern decor and matching 'bistro-gastro' food served from an open kitchen. The interior is pleasant enough, but it's the exterior, with its large deck and water feature leading to a summer bar area and open-air swimming pool, that provides the wow factor. A typical dish might be Norfolk pork belly, stuffed with figs and thyme, on chorizo, creamed potatoes and Madeira sauce.

Star
School Road, Lessingham, NR12 0DN (01692 580510, www.thestarlessingham.co.uk). Open 6-11pm Mon; noon-3pm, 6-11pm Tue-Fri; noon-11pm Sat, Sun. Lunch served noon-2.30pm Tue-Sat; noon-3pm Sun. Dinner served 6-9.30pm Tue-Fri; 6-9pm Sat.
Taken over by a friendly local couple in 2009, this cosy village inn serves a small range of well kept Norfolk ales and changing guest ones, and a daily specials menu that often includes locally caught fish and shellfish, as well as gigantic T-bones, local pork and, on Sundays, excellent roasts with all the trimmings. Eat in the small restaurant or better still, nab the table next to the giant inglenook fireplace in the lounge.

TEN NORFOLK GARDENS

East Ruston Old Vicarage Gardens ★
A 30-acre gem packed with colour and interest, plus a pretty tearoom. If you only have time to visit one garden, make it this one. *See p98.*

Gooderstone Water Gardens ★
Waterlogged grazing ground transformed into a six-acre water garden. A charming tearoom completes the idyll. *See p153.*

Hoveton Hall Gardens
Imaginative planting makes the woodland and lakeside walks a treat; kingfishers are often seen by the lake. *See p112.*

Narborough Hall ★
Wild and formal gardens are entwined to great effect, and all surrounded by ancient parkland, lakes and woods. *See p154.*

Plantation Garden ★
Near the centre of Norwich, but hidden away in a medieval chalk quarry, this 'secret' garden features Gothic fountains, an Italianate terrace, a summer house and numerous walkways. *See p87.*

Priory Maze & Gardens
Formal gardens, woodlands and meadows, plus a hedge maze based on the footprint of nearby ruined Beeston Priory. There's a tearoom too. *See p70.*

Raveningham Gardens
A set of gardens that includes huge herbaceous borders, an Edwardian rose garden, a lake and an 18th-century walled kitchen garden. *See p131.*

Sheringham Park
A vast, Humphry Repton-designed park, where the displays of rhododendrons and azaleas (from mid May to June) are stunning. *See p70.*

Walsingham Abbey Grounds
Snowdrop walks in early spring are just one of the highlights of these 20 acres of woodland, parkland and gardens. *See p57.*

West Acre Gardens
A garden centre unlike any other, set in the walled garden of a manor house. The display gardens are hugely inspirational. *See p154.*

NORFOLK

Swan Inn
Sea Palling Road, Ingham, NR12 9AB (01692 581099).
Open noon-3.30pm, 6-11pm daily. Lunch served 11am-
2pm, dinner served 6-9pm Tue-Sun.
Dating back to the 14th century when it was part of the
Ingham Priory, this well-sited pub next to a fine church
serves Woodforde's ales and no-nonsense traditional
English dishes such as liver and bacon, and steak and
kidney pudding. Five en suite rooms are also available, set
in a converted barn just across the road (£70-£100 double
incl breakfast).

Vernon Arms ★
2 Church Street, Southrepps, NR11 8NP (01263
833355, www.vernonarms.com). Open 11am-11pm
daily. Lunch served noon-2pm, dinner served 6.30-
9pm daily.
A charming, ultra-friendly pub, which serves good food
cooked entirely on the premises. Straightforward lunchtime
grub includes hot baguettes, jacket potatoes, ploughman's
and salads; come the evening, dishes range from pork with
red onion marmalade, melted stilton and mash to the pub's
signature dish, the Vernon Arms Black and Tan – a beef,
Guinness and ale pie with gravy, proper chips and mushy
peas. There's a good collection of beers too.

Where to stay
There are plenty of B&Bs, inns and hotels in this
area. Self-catering places are often available for
as little as one or two nights out of season – it's
always worth asking.
  Elderton Lodge (01263 833547, www.elderton-
lodge.co.uk), a small hotel occupying the former
shooting lodge of Gunton Hall, was being
refurbished by new owners as this guide went
to press; check the website for updates.

Things to do

OVERSTRAND TO HEMSBY

Adventure Island
Beach Road, Mundesley, NR11 8BG (no phone).
Open Summer 10am-10pm daily. Admission £3;
£2.50 reductions.
A great, old-fashioned 12-hole themed crazy golf
course, with lakes and waterfalls, pirates, monsters
of the deep and all manner of inventive papier mâché.
Floodlit too, should you fancy an after-dark round.

NORTH WALSHAM & AROUND

Bittern Line
www.bitternline.com (National Rail enquiries 08457
484950, Anglia Railways tickets 08700 409090).
The Bittern Line may not have cute steam engines,
but this 30-mile railway linking Cromer with Norwich
is well worth taking if you want to get a real sense of
rural Norfolk and a land's view of the Broads villages.
Stops at North Walsham, Gunton and Worstead
make the line great for exploring this area, bikes
are welcome (though it's essential to book ahead
in summer) and a 20p through ticket enables you
to use the area's buses too.

Beechwood Hotel ★
Cromer Road, North Walsham, NR28 0HD (01692
403231, www.beechwood-hotel.co.uk). Rates £80-£160
double incl breakfast.
The 17 rooms in this smart country hotel are vibrantly
decorated and feature numerous welcome touches, among
them Molton Brown products, bathrobes and free-standing
bathtubs. The restaurant is equally appealing, as is the
Modern British food: cauliflower and binham blue soup or
Norfolk lamb, for example, with ingredients sourced as
much as possible within a ten-mile radius. The hotel was a
great favourite of Agatha Christie. No under-tens.

Deers Glade Caravan & Camping Park
White Post Road, Hanworth, NR11 7HN (01263
768633, www.deersglade.co.uk). Open All year. Pitch
£10.50-£14.50 2 people.
A great family-friendly campsite and caravan park in a
woodland setting. There's a natural play area for children,
a fishing lake, two large, clean shower/toilet blocks, a shop
and even Wi-Fi access from your tent. In August, tent-only
Muntjac Meadow opens for campers wanting a more low-
tech, back-to-nature vibe; at night there's a communal
campfire to gather round.

Mill Common House
Mill Common Road, Ridlington, NR28 9TY (01692
650792, www.millcommonhouse.co.uk). Rates £64-£84
double incl breakfast. No credit cards.
There are two large B&B rooms in this stately Georgian
farmhouse. Think spacious and comfortable beds, open log
fires, a conservatory, a walled garden and flowers
everywhere. A flint and brick-built self-catering cottage
(sleeping four) is also available.

Northrepps Cottage ★
Nut Lane, Northrepps, NR27 0JN (01263 579202,
www.northreppscottagehotel.co.uk). Rates £110 double
incl breakfast.
A small, luxurious country house hotel and restaurant,
where seven smart en-suite rooms feature underfloor
heating, power showers, flatscreen TVs and ultra-fluffy
towels. The setting and extensive gardens are gorgeous, and
the restaurant serves imaginative Modern British food:
wild boar, Norfolk pork and pistachio terrine with rhubarb
chutney is a typical dish.

Old Rectory
Ridlington, NR28 9NZ (01692 650247, www.old
rectory.northnorfolk.co.uk). Rates £55-£70 double.
No credit cards.
This charming Georgian rectory is set in four acres of
gardens and woods, with just two guest rooms: a huge, light-
filled room in the main house and a separate garden room
with its own kitchen, sitting room and terrace.

Scarborough Hill Hotel
Old Yarmouth Road, North Walsham, NR28 9NA
(01692 402151, www.arlingtonhotelgroup.co.uk/scarhill).
Rates £70 double incl breakfast.
Eight individually decorated bedrooms make up this
country house hotel; some border on the OTT, but all are
well appointed and very comfortable. The restaurant, set in
a twinkling glass conservatory, serves an extensive menu,
often using local fish and game.

NORFOLK

Northern Broads

If there's one Norfolk attraction most people have heard of, it's the Norfolk Broads, the sprawling network of seven rivers (the Ant, Bure and Thurne in the north and the Yare, Wensum, Waveney and Chet in the south) and 63 shallow inland lakes fringed by reeds, marshland and woodland on which water-bound holidaymakers spend happy weeks. These ancient flooded pits, ranging in width from a few feet to several miles, were created by the large-scale excavation of peat, an important and valuable fuel – first by the Romans, then by local monasteries in the Middle Ages. Over the centuries, rising sea levels and newly formed channels created 117 square miles of wetland that, since their discovery by Victorian sailing enthusiasts looking for the latest thrill, have become one of England's most popular 'natural' wonders.

This is a landscape that feels a long way from civilisation and its manifold distractions. Walking gingerly through the wetlands or sitting on a boat travelling at four miles an hour slows the world right down, enabling water, trees, marsh, sky and wildlife to create a very special landscape. Add in the sound of rustling reeds, soft breezes in the trees and water sucking against the banks of 125 miles of tranquil rivers, tributaries and lakes, and you're bound to feel at peace. On land you'll find medieval stone bridges, picturesque drainage windpumps, beautifully proportioned flint churches and a wealth of other man-made but naturally harmonious structures. You don't have to sleep aboard a boat to appreciate the beauty, tranquillity and leisurely pace of life of the Broads, but if you only explore the area by car, bike or foot, you'll definitely miss out – so at the very least hire a day-boat and take to the water.

HICKLING & BARTON BROADS

Hickling Broad

If you only have time to get out on one Broad, make it the biggest, Hickling, which covers more than 320 acres. This serene stretch of water is magical, and the surroundings quieter than the area around Hoveton and Ranworth Broads further west.

The starting point, the Broads Haven marina at Potter Heigham (pronounced 'Potter Ham') has a well-stocked information centre, a couple of decent places to eat and its very own department store, Lathams. Although a key Broads hub, it's surprisingly quiet, thanks to the Potter Heigham Old Bridge, a medieval hump-backed bridge whose six-foot eight-inch headroom makes it impassable by big boats, thus keeping the stretch of the River Thurne between here and Hickling (and further to Horsey Mere) as peaceful as possible. Swirling currents beneath the bridge make navigating it a little tricky, but the fearless day-boater is rewarded with the sight of pretty fretworked wooden cottages topped with the reed thatch and sedge that are cut back regularly from the waterways, to keep them open for both man and beast. Downstream of the bridge, keep an eye out for the Dutch Tutch, a 12-sided black and white house and adjacent shed made up of two sections of a 19th-century helter-skelter from Great Yarmouth.

Once the houses have vanished, a deep tranquility descends, broken only by the sound of ducks, geese and swans on the river and, further back from the reed and sedge banks, numerous other species; kingfishers, kestrels, tits, warblers and bittern all live in this rich landscape of marsh, wood and water. The names of the areas they inhabit are just as lyrical and lovely as the birds themselves: Sound Plantation, Whispering Reeds, Deep-Go Dyke, Candle Dyke and Hundred Acre Marsh. Many have little moorings, where you can stop to listen and look; a motor boat travelling at just four miles an hour creates enough noise to frighten off wildlife. At Candle Dyke junction, turn left for Hickling Broad. (If you turn right, there's an enjoyable diversion to Horsey Mere for some great walking and a look around the National Trust windpump – see p98.)

The wide expanse of water can be unnerving after the restraining riverbanks, but follow the marked channels and you'll be fine, soon arriving at the far end of the broad, at the Pleasure Boat Inn, where you can stop for some landside exploration. A 20-minute walk past the thatched boathouses at Hickling Staithe will bring you to the Hickling Broad National Nature Reserve (see p112). Hickling village, split between waterside Hickling Heath and Hickling Green inland, has little of note beyond the Greyhound Pub (see p107) and Whispering Reeds boatyard (if you're hiring

a boat here, it's useful to know that they're all able to pass under Potter Heigham Bridge).

An alternative option is to continue straight on at the Candle Dyke junction, rather than turning left. This leads to Martham Broad National Nature Reserve, a hotspot for swallowtail butterflies. Adjacent is West Somerton, a lovely village with some fine riverside walks and a beautiful 900-year-old church, St Mary. Perched on a hill, it provides great views over the countryside and towards Winterton-on-Sea. Martham village has various shops and a decent pub set around a green, and a wonderfully eccentric scarecrow festival every May.

Barton Broad

Back on dry land, the roads radiating from Potter Heigham offer a number of different Broads experiences. Head west on the A1062 or north-west on the A149 to the area around Barton Broad. The villages of Irstead and Barton Turf offer something special in their churches, both called St Michael (including a glorious, brightly coloured rood screen at Barton Turf), but have few other enticements. Nearby Neatishead is bigger; it's a lovely Georgian village with a shop, a decent restaurant, a homely pub and a comfortable guesthouse. The spectacular waterside homes north of the village are known locally as Millionaires' Row. Thanks to their waterside but slightly off-the-beaten-track settings, all three villages are pretty and unspoilt. At Gays Staithe (between Neatishead and Irstead), you can follow the Barton Broad Boardwalk for sweeping views across the broad, or take a boat trip on the solar-powered *Ra* (*see p114*).

Travelling north from Barton Broad on the River Ant brings you to Stalham Staithe, home to the award-winning Museum of the Broads (*see p112*), and pretty Sutton Staithe. Tiny Sutton village has a church, a pottery (*see p112*) and a (non-working) cornmill built in 1789. A whopping nine storeys high, it's the tallest windmill in England. The market town of Stalham is rather rundown, but useful if you need a supermarket, or want to stock up on wet weather gear and all manner of other items at the Original Factory Shop (129 High Street, 01692 580882). The Swan Inn (*see p108*) is a good lunch stop, and the town hall hosts a farmers' market and an enjoyable bric-a-brac market on alternate Saturdays.

If you're travelling by road, the A149 runs past Sutton and Stalham, and on to upmarket hotel/restaurant Wayford Bridge Inn (*see p108*), before heading south (as the A1151) to decidedly more upbeat and bustling Wroxham.

Where to eat & drink

This region is a long way from the foodie mecca of the north Norfolk coast, but there are plenty of picturesque pubs, often by the water, serving hearty and reliable food. Try the popular Falgate Inn (Ludham Road, 01692 670003) in Potter Heigham; the Greyhound (The Green, 01692 598306, www.greyhoundinn.com) in Hickling Green, which has a beautiful garden; the White Horse (The

Thurne Dyke Mill. See p116.

Street, 01692 630828) in Neatishead, where huge portions are served in a handful of tiny slate-floored bars or a nice dining room; or the pretty Victoria (12 Repps Road, 01493 740774) in Martham.

For more special occasions, there are upmarket restaurants in the Wayford Bridge Inn (*see p108*) and the Sutton Staithe Hotel (*see p108*). If you just want good fish and chips, try Harry's (Bridge Road, 01692 670415) in Potter Heigham, or Broadland Fish & Chips ★ (27 High Street, 01692 580247, closed Sun) in Stalham.

Crown Inn ★
41 The Street, Catfield, NR29 5AA (01692 580128). Open noon-2.30pm, 7-11pm Tue-Fri; noon-3pm, 7-midnight Sat; noon-3pm, 7-10.30pm Sun. Lunch served noon-2.30pm Tue-Fri; noon-3pm Sat, Sun. Dinner served 7-9pm Tue-Sun.
Just one mile from Catfield Staithe, off Hickling Broad, this is a proper village pub in a very attractive village, with well-kept ales and hearty food. Inside is a cosy bar, outside a lovely garden. There are also two rooms (£50 double incl breakfast).

Mermaids Slipper
The Staithe, Stalham, NR12 9BY (01692 580808). Lunch served 11.30am-3pm Tue-Sat; noon-3pm Sun. Dinner served 6.30-9pm Tue-Sat.
Visit this delightfully located waterside restaurant for very good French food that makes the most of local produce. It opened in summer 2009 and meal times may change, so it's a good idea to call first.

NORFOLK

Swan Inn
*90 High Street, Stalham, NR12 9AU (01692 582829,
http://stalhamswan.co.uk). Open 11am-9pm Mon-Sat;
noon-9pm Sun.*
Luckily, the only pub in Stalham serving food does a good
job of it, offering the likes of toasted sandwiches, liver and
bacon, and beef and Guinness pie. You can eat in the
spacious, modern lounge bar, a small, summery restaurant
or on the back patio. There's free Wi-Fi too for email fiends.

Ye Olde Saddlery
*The Street, Neatishead, NR12 8AD (01692 630866,
www.thesaddleryrestaurant.com). Dinner served
6-8.30pm Thur-Sun.*
This cosy restaurant and bar offers Modern British food
that's a cut above average pub fare, with lots of tempting
fish dishes and a good range of bar snacks. In the summer
months (May-September), there's usually a Sunday
lunchtime carvery, plus dinner served on more than just
Thursday to Sunday – phone to check exactly when they
plan to open. Prices are at pub rather than restaurant levels.

Where to stay
You'll find a decent number of B&Bs – generally
of the chintz and pine variety. Two standouts are
Black Horse Cottage (The Green, 01692 598691,
www.blackhorsecottage.com), next door to the
Greyhound pub in Hickling; and the 18th-century
Regency Guest House (The Street, 01692 630233,
www.regencyguesthouse.com) in Neatishead. For
campers, the tiny Causeway Cottage Caravan Park
(Bridge Road, 01692 670238, closed Nov-Mar) in
Potter Heigham is close to the water and shops,
and has good amenities and friendly staff.

Sutton Staithe Hotel
*Sutton, NR12 9QS (01692 580244, www.sutton
staithehotel.co.uk). Rates £59.95 double incl breakfast.*
This largeish hotel next to the River Ant (with 13 rooms,
ranging from single to family in size) won't win any design
prizes for its decor, but it's comfortable and well located.
Food is dependable and recommended by Broads regulars.

Wayford Bridge Inn ★
*Off A149, nr Stalham, NR12 9LL (01692 582414,
www.maypolehotels.com). Rates £60-£105 double
incl breakfast.*
Fifteen comfortable, contemporary-styled, river-facing
rooms, a restaurant serving a traditional menu of burgers,
seafood and steaks, and a peaceful but handy location make
this a good alternative to a B&B. In summer, the large
waterside terrace is a great spot for dinner or a drink.

RANWORTH BROAD & AROUND

Wroxham & around
Wroxham, the so-called capital of the Broads,
thanks to its location near the head of the navigable
River Bure (the westernmost of the region's four
rivers and thus the 'beginning' of the Broads), is
the antithesis of the region in general. Where the
waterways can be placid and relaxing, the town –
actually two towns, Wroxham and Hoveton, linked

by a hump-backed bridge – is heaving, especially
in the summer holidays. It's also on both the
Bure Valley (*see p77*) and Bittern Line (*see p104*)
railways, which brings in more visitors. Fortunately,
there's little to reason to linger here once you've
poked your head into Roy's department store,
had a pleasant stroll around the bridge area and
along the river, and sampled a lovely ice-cream
from Wroxham Ices in the precinct on the riverside,
or fish and chips from Ken's takeaway/restaurant
next to the bridge. Better to head out of town,
west towards Coltishall or east towards Ranworth
(via the delightful villages of Salhouse and
Woodbastwick on the B1140 or Horning on the
A1062 – or all of them if you're on the river).
   Coltishall, set on the Bure at the far western
tip of the Broads, and the starting point for most
cruises, is large, pretty and distinctly upmarket,
with lots of elegant Dutch-gabled houses and a
thatched church. There's plenty to explore here,
including two thriving riverside pubs, a chippie,
tearooms, an antiques outlet and various
independent shops. It's also a halt on the
Bure Valley Railway.
   Salhouse has its fair share of 18th-century
thatched cottages. You pass some of them on
the ten-minute walk from the village car park
to Salhouse Broad, where the (unusual) sandy
shoreline is backed by bluebell woods. You can
hire canoes here or catch the summer water
taxi to reach the nature trail around Great
Hoveton Broad.
   A couple of miles further on is the village of
Woodbastwick ★, where stern notices warn of
private roads barred to 'anglers and scouts', the
village blacksmith watches strangers with a beady
eye, and you suspect the gunsmith does a roaring
trade. Woodforde's brewery, maker of the highly
praised Wherry and Sundew bitters, certainly does;
it's located behind the popular Fur & Feather pub
(*see p114*) and scents the air with a delicious
heady hit of malt. The visitor centre and shop are
open daily and evening brewery tours (£10) are
available on selected days; call 01603 722218
or check www.woodfordes.co.uk for details. The
village is picture-postcard pretty: a glorious array
of thatched cottages, almshouses and a large flint
church are grouped around a triangular green that
contains a canopied well; away from the green, the
houses get even grander. Covered with a generous
dollop of snow, the whole scene would resemble
something out of a Richard Curtis film.
   From Woodbastwick, it's just a couple of miles
by road to the beautiful village of Ranworth, which
sits next to Malthouse Broad (a popular sailing
spot) and is a short distance from Ranworth Broad
– now a NWT nature reserve (*see p112*) and closed
to boats. The other main attraction here is obvious:
imposing St Helen's Church (*see p113*) dominates
the skyline, and provides an unmissable bird's-eye
view of the Broads region from its tower. A mile
further on, Fairhaven Woodland & Water Garden
(*see p112*) in South Walsham offers boat trips to
the St Benet Abbey ruins that are otherwise only
really visible from the River Bure.

Horning & around

On the other (north) side of the River Bure, Horning ★ is one of the Broads' most attractive villages, with a positive panoply of reed-thatched cottages (with cutely matching boat houses) and half-timbered Edwardian buildings lining the banks of the Bure. With assorted restaurants and riverside pubs, an art gallery, a delicatessen and a clutch of little shops and tearooms, the village is a terrific base, perfect for rural or river forays, or visits to nearby attractions such as the RAF Air Defence Radar Museum (see p113) and Bewilderwood (see p112). There's even a colourful paddle-steamer, Southern Comfort, which runs regular cruises along the Bure.

For a lovely walk beside the Bure, follow Lower Street out of the village for about a mile towards Horning Ferry (a seasonal foot ferry across to Woodbastwick Staithe), and on to the impressive village church of St Benedict, dating from around 1220. From here you'll have a clear view of splendid St Helen's Church on Ranworth Broad.

If you're planning to visit Horning in June, you'll need to book well ahead; the village is the starting point for the famous Three Rivers Race, a gruelling 45-mile test along the Ant, Bure and Thurne.

Four miles east of Horning is Ludham, the last village of note in the Wroxham/Ranworth ring. After the perfection of Woodbastwick and Horning, it might disappoint at first, but its church, St Catherine, houses two excellent restored 15th- and 16th-century painted screens, and what the village lacks for in charm it makes up for in amenities. There are a couple of good pubs, as well as the pretty Alfresco Tea Rooms (Norwich Road, 01692 678384, www.alfrescotearooms. co.uk, closed Mon-Fri Jan-Mar, Nov, all Dec). At the excellent Throwers grocery store, you can pick up local produce, including flour and muesli from Letheringsett Mill, How Hill honey and Brays Cottage pies, plus 60 types of cheese and other deli fare.

Nearby, How Hill House (01692 678555, www. how-hill.org.uk) is a grand Edwardian house that operates as a privately owned study centre. On certain days, the public can visit the estate, which is home to Toad Hole cottage, a traditional 19th-century marshman's home, as well as a nature trail and riverside walks. You can also explore the tiny dykes of adjacent How Hill Nature Reserve on the Electric Eel, a six-seater, Edwardian-style boat (01692 678763, www.broads-authority.gov.uk, closed Nov-Mar). While there, pop into Grove Farm Studio & Gallery (Sharp Street, 01692 670679, www.grovefarmgallery.co.uk, open Mon, Tue, Sun by appointment only), which displays and sells work by local artists. A two-mile walk across the grazing marshes on the outskirts of Ludham will bring you to the isolated and atmospheric ruins of St Benet's Abbey, on the north bank of the Bure. From Ludham, it's just over a mile to Potter Heigham.

Where to eat & drink

The year-round appeal of gorgeous villages such as Horning and Woodbastwick ensures a wide variety of food along this stretch of the Bure. You'll find

FIVE PICK-YOUR-OWN FARMS

Fairgreen Farms
Hill Road, Middleton, nr King's Lynn, PE32 1RN (07928 533846, www.blueberrypicking.co.uk). Open Mid July-Sept 9am-5.30pm Mon-Sat.
They scorn such humdrum soft fruits as strawberries and raspberries at Fairgreen, opting instead for big, delicious blueberries, available as PYO in summer or frozen all year round.

Grange
Fleggburgh Road, Rollesby, NR29 5AJ (01493 740236). Open Mid June-Sept 10am-5.30pm daily.
Next to the A149 in the northern Broads, the Grange has an unusually wide range of PYO vegetables, including asparagus, beetroot, sweetcorn, courgettes, cucumbers, onions, tomatoes and potatoes, as well as the more common raspberries, strawberries and gooseberries.

Groveland Fruit Farm
Thorpe Market Road, Roughton, NR11 8TB (01263 833777, www.farm-shop-norfolk.co.uk). Open June-Sept 9am-4.30pm daily.
Set on the B1436 near Roughton, south of Cromer, Groveland Farm has a farm shop and deli if you're too lazy to opt for the PYO apples, strawberries and other soft fruits available in its extensive fields. Groveland also has a PYO farm at Felbrigg, near Holt.

Leith House Plum Orchard
Leith House Farm, nr Burnham Overy, PE31 8JL (01328 738311, www.pmfarming.co.uk). Open Mid July-mid Sept 10am-4.30pm daily.
A lovely plum orchard in north Norfolk containing 3,000 plum trees and more than 35 varieties, both ready-picked and PYO. Apple juice and jams are also for sale.

Wiveton Hall Fruit Farm
Wiveton Hall, 1 Marsh Lane, Wiveton, NR25 7TE (01263 740525, www.wivetonhall.co.uk). Open May-Sept 9.30am-5.30pm daily.
PYO strawberries, raspberries, blackcurrants and asparagus from the Wiveton Estate on the north Norfolk coast near Cley. The lovely farm shop sells jams, chutneys, cordials and pork products, and the charming café (see p62) is fast becoming a must.

Hickling Broad. See p105.

Places to visit

HICKLING & BARTON BROADS

Museum of the Broads ★
The Staithe, Stalham, NR12 9DA (01692 581681, www.northnorfolk.org/museumofthebroads). Open 10.30am-5pm daily Apr-Oct. Admission £4; £3.50 reductions.
This award-winning museum telling the human history of the Broads, from medieval peat diggers to 21st-century holidaymakers via reedcutters, boat builders, thatchers and sailors, manages to engage the imaginations of both children and adults. There's an excellent programme of activities (among them painting, quizzes and playboat events) and a permanent display that evokes the history of the Broads meticulously and entertainingly.

NWT Hickling Broad National Nature Reserve
Hickling, NR12 0BW (01692 598276, www.norfolk wildlifetrust.org.uk). Open Reserve dawn-dusk daily. Visitor centre Apr-Sept 10am-5pm daily. Admission £3.50; free reductions. Boat trip £8-£10; £4-£6 reductions.
Being on the water is great, but an equally terrific way to explore the marshland of the Broads is via this wonderful nature reserve, run by the Norfolk Wildlife Trust. A range of short trails and boardwalks gives you close-up access to all sorts of wildlife, including wading birds, otters and lizards. For a final sense of how amazing this area is, take the two-hour Water Trail boat trip through the backwaters of the Broad (not navigable any other way) and climb the galvanised steel staircase up to the tree tower.

Sutton Pottery
Church Road, Sutton, NR12 9SG (01692 580595, www.suttonpottery.com). Open 9am-1pm, 2-6pm Mon-Fri.
Potter and ceramicist Malcolm Flatman has been crafting tableware and vases for more than 20 years. His fascinating workshop is piled high with the tools of his trade and a wide range and style of wares for sale. He's equally happy to let you, er, potter around to your heart's content or talk in depth about the process. He also runs classes ranging from three-hour lessons to two-day residential courses.

RANWORTH BROAD & AROUND

Bewilderwood ★
Horning Road, nr Horning, NR12 8JW (01603 783900, www.bewilderwood.co.uk). Open Feb half-term, end Mar-Oct 10am-5.30pm daily; closed some Tue, Wed, so phone to check opening times. Admission free-£11.
Every child we know who's been here has loved every minute spent clambering around Bewilderwood's beautiful, magical treehouses, following its imaginative and inventive trails and marsh walk, crossing its jungle bridges and whizzing down its zipwires. Parents are encouraged to get down and dirty with their offspring, and there are lots of special events throughout the year, making this one of the best days out for families in Norfolk. Even the food is great. Don't miss it.

Fairhaven Woodland & Water Garden
School Road, South Walsham, NR13 6DZ (01603 270449/270683, www.fairhavengarden.co.uk). Open May-Aug 10am-5pm Mon, Tue, Fri-Sun; 10am-9pm Wed, Thur. Mar, Apr, Sept-Nov 10am-5pm daily. Dec-Feb 10am-4pm daily. Adults £5; £2.50-£4.50 reductions.
A great place for nature lovers, with 131 acres of ancient woodland, water gardens and a private broad. Gnarled ancient oaks – including a 950-year-old king oak – feature on a lovely three-and-a-half-mile woodland walk, and from everywhere you get superb views across South Walsham Inner Broad. The 50-minute boat trip on the private broad to the ruins of St Benet's Abbey (open Apr-Oct, £6.50) is a delight, especially for birdwatchers.

Hoveton Hall Gardens
Hoveton, NR12 8RJ (01603 782558, www.hoveton hallgardens.co.uk). Open July, Aug 10am-5pm Wed-Fri, Sun. May, June 10am-5pm Wed-Sun. Mar 10am-5pm Sun. Apr Days vary, check website for details. Admission £5; £2.50 reductions.
An ornamental wrought-iron Spider's Web gate leads to 15 acres of woodland and lakeside walks, plus a 1920s water garden and lake (a great place to spot kingfishers). The imaginative formal and informal planting dates from the early 20th century.

NWT Ranworth Broad Nature Reserve
Ranworth, NR13 6HY (01603 270479. www.norfolk wildlifetrust.org.uk). Open Reserve 24hrs daily. Visitor centre Apr-Oct 10am-5pm daily. Admission free.

NWT Upton Broad & Marshes Nature Reserve

A pretty boardwalk trail that meanders through oak and carr woodland and reedbeds, studded with information and interpretation boards, makes this reserve a particularly good option for children. At the end of the boardwalk, the floating visitor centre – topped with reeds and very picturesque – offers plenty of hand-on learning opportunities for the kids and expansive views across the tranquil water (no boats are allowed) for the grown-ups.

RAF Air Defence Radar Museum
Royal Air Force Neatishead, nr Horning, Norwich, NR12 8YB (01692 631485, www.radarmuseum. co.uk). Open Apr-Oct 10am-5pm Tue, Thur. Nov-Mar 10am-5pm 2nd Sat of mth. Admission £4.50; free-£4 reductions.
An engaging and lucid collection that uses a range of imaginative displays – among them an original Cold War operations room (used until 1993), a nuclear bunker and a Night Blitz room – to show the history and development of radar from the 1930s to the present.

St Helen's Church ★
Ranworth, NR13 6HT (01603 270769, www.ranworth.churchnorfolk.com). Open 9.30am-dusk daily. Admission free.
The entrance to the tower of 14th-century St Helen's Church, aka the Cathedral of the Broads, warns that it contains '89 uneven steps, 2 ladders, 1 trapdoor'. And as you'd hope in a church, they don't lie. The stairs are dark, narrow and irregular, the ladders are unnerving and the final trapdoor is likely to hit you on the top of your head as you emerge blinking into the light – but boy, is it worth it. The views are terrific and as far-reaching as you'd expect; five broads are visible from the top, and on a clear day you can see the spire of Norwich Cathedral. Don't miss the church itself, which houses what many experts say is England's finest painted chancel screen, dating from 1419, and a 15th-century illuminated service book.

Wroxham Barns Craft Centre
Tunstead Road, Hoveton, NR12 8QU (01603 783911, www.wroxhambarns.co.uk). Open 10am-5pm daily. Admission Barns free. Junior Farm £3.75; free reductions.
This curious crafts-themed amusement park has a large number of family-focused activities, enabling adults and children to learn about, watch and even occasionally have a go at activities such as apple-pressing, wood-turning, pottery, quilting and jewellery-making. If the little ones tire of crafts, there's a funfair, animal farm, picnic area, mini golf and lots of country fayre on sale in the various food shops and cafés.

TRINITY BROADS

Caister Castle & Car Collection
Castle Lane, Caister-on-Sea, NR30 5SN (01572 787649, www.caistercastle.co.uk). Open Mid May-Sept 10am-4.30pm Mon-Fri, Sun. Admission £9; £4.50-£8 reductions; £24 family.
The atmospheric ruins of this 15th-century castle, built by Sir John Fastolf (supposedly the inspiration for Shakespeare's Falstaff) provide a pleasing backdrop to the biggest private car collection in Britain. Both are bound to prove a hit with dads and small boys, who can climb the 90ft castle tower for great views before gawping at the rare and vintage vehicles from the likes of Lotus, Bugatti, Ford and Harley-Davidson. The French-made Panhard et Levassor from 1893 is claimed to be the world's first 'real' car. A woodland walk, café and picnic area provide respite from all the machinery.

NWT Upton Broad & Marshes Nature Reserve
Low Road, Upton, NR13 6EQ (01603 625540, www.norfolkwildlifetrust.org.uk). Open 24hrs daily. Admission free.
Windpump remains, a medieval broad and primeval-looking alders make this reserve of open water, fen, reedbed, woodland and marsh a pleasure to wander round, via a series of waymarked trails and boardwalks. The reserve is one of the UK's top ten sites for dragonflies.

Thrigby Hall Wildlife Gardens
Thrigby Road, nr Filby, NR29 3DR (01493 369477, www.thrigbyhall.co.uk). Open Mar-Oct 10am-5pm daily. Nov-Feb 10am-4pm daily. Admission £9.50; £7.50-£8.50 reductions.
A curious selection of animals – from big cats to cockatoos and red pandas to monkeys – can be found in the pleasant gardens here, making it an enjoyable half-day attraction for both grown-ups and kids. The latter will love the swamp house crocs and snakes.

NORFOLK

New Inn, Horning

TEN WAYS TO EXPLORE THE BROADS

BOAT HIRE

Canoe
Explore the tiny tranquil channels off the main waterways (and see more wildlife than you ever would on a larger craft) with the help of the Canoe Man (01603 499177, www.thecanoe man.com). You can just hire a canoe for a day, take a weekend camping and canoeing trip or embark on longer guided and unguided B&B canoe holidays. Gear is supplied and food can be arranged en route.

Motor boat
Norfolk Broads Direct (01692 670711, www.broads.co.uk), operating out of Wroxham and Potter Heigham, has everything from small motor boats that can be hired by the hour through to luxury holiday cruisers. The day-boats are easy to manage and enable you to get very close to the water, with easy mooring at pubs and along the rivers and broads, but you'll have to trade up a bit if you want to make a cup of tea.

Yacht
If you want to get out on the water, but would rather sail than motor along, do it in style on a beautiful 1930s wooden yacht, bookable from a half day to a week at historic Hunter's Yard (01692 678263, http://huntersyard.co.uk, closed Nov-Easter) in Ludham. With no engine or electricity on board, this is a low-tech, eco-friendly way to explore the broads.

BOAT TOURS

Barton Broad
Climb aboard the unusual-looking, solar-powered catamaran *Ra* (named after the Egyptian sun god) for a 75-minute trip around Barton Broad. Trips leave from Gay's Staithe at Neatishead, and run from April to October. Book ahead on 01603 782281.

Horsey Mere
Take a one-hour guided cruise on the tranquil waters of Horsey Mere with Ross' River Trips (01692 598135, www.rossrivertrips.co.uk) on the *Lady Ann*, a pretty wooden boat that seats a dozen passengers. You can then stretch your legs on the three-mile nature trail around the mere. Trips run several times a day from May to September; well-behaved dogs are allowed.

everything from posh nosh at proper hotels – including the Broad House Hotel (*see p116*), Norfolk Mead Hotel (*see p116*) and Wroxham Hotel (*see p115*) – to adventurous dishes in lovely little restaurants, as well a broad range of pubs serving reasonably priced, own-cooked food.

In Coltishall, the Rising Sun (28 Wroxham Road, 01603 737440) has a lovely riverside garden. Next door but not next to the river, the Kings Head ★ (26 Wroxham Road, 01603 737426, www.kingsheadcoltishall.co.uk) makes up in decor for what it lacks in watery delights. The raised wooden deck is a great spot from which to enjoy some of the best pub food in the area, and the four smart bedrooms are a good place to recover from a gastronomic blowout.

In Horning, the friendly New Inn (Lower Street, 01692 631223, www.newinn-horning.co.uk/horning-pub.htm) offers free moorings and a riverside garden with play area; and the distinctive Swan Inn ★ (01692 630316, www.vintageinn.co.uk/theswaninnhorning) dishes out standard pub grub in a terrific setting on a sharp bend in the river. It also has B&B rooms.

The Kings Head (Station Road, 01603 782429) in Hoveton is highly rated by Broads aficionados and it too has rooms; the Fur & Feather (Slad Lane, 01603 720003, www.thefurandfeatherinn.co.uk) in Woodbastwick is next door to Woodforde's brewery, so ideal for real ale fans; the Ship Inn (18 The Street, 01603 270049, www.theshipsouth walsham.co.uk) in South Walsham has a decked terrace and a varied menu; the King's Arms (High Street, 01692 678386, www.kingsarmsludham.co.uk) in Ludham is great for children, with a playground and beer garden, as well as a model train running around the beamed ceiling inside; and the Malsters (01603 270900, www.themaltsters.com) in Ranworth has a good beer garden.

Bure River Cottage Restaurant
27 Lower Street, Horning, NR12 8AA (01692 631421). Dinner served 6.30-9.30pm Tue-Sat.
A fine Modern European restaurant, specialising in fish and seafood dishes, with many ingredients locally sourced. Service is excellent, and the the quality of the cooking sings out. The glass frontage provides good views of the hustle and bustle on the river and of this lovely village.

Old Mill Restaurant
8 The Old Mill, Wroxham, NR12 8DA (01603 783744). Food served Summer 9am-7pm daily. Winter 9am-4pm daily.
The riverside terrace makes the Old Mill a pukka lunchtime choice for well-made traditional English food, but hungry boat folk also come here for breakfast (served all day), tea and takeway dishes.

Recruiting Sergeant
Norwich Road, Horstead, NR12 7EE (01603 737077, www.recruitingsergeant.co.uk). Open 11am-11pm Mon-Sat; noon-11pm Sun. Lunch served noon-2pm Mon-Sat. Dinner served 6-9pm Mon-Wed; 6-9.30pm Thur-Sat. Food served noon-9pm Sun.
This large and lovely whitewashed pub near Coltishall is one of the best in the area for gastropub fare that makes the most of local produce. The variety of daily specials (around 20 a day) makes choosing fiendishly hard. And the shaded back terrace, leafy garden and indoor dining room are all so well designed you'll have a hard time deciding where to sit.

Staithe 'N' Willow ★
16 Lower Street, Horning, NR12 8AA (01692 630915, www.broads-norfolk.com). Open/food served 10am-8pm daily.
With its riverside location and lovely garden, this thatched cottage would make a great lunch spot even if the food wasn't good. Fortunately, it is, thanks to an enterprising use of local produce to create a menu that ranges from breakfast dishes to sandwiches, cakes and full-blown meals.

Where to stay
If you plan to spend a lot of time on the water, Wroxham isn't a bad base. Reliable B&B options include the Coach House (96 Norwich Road, 01603 784376, www.coachhousewroxham.co.uk) and Wroxham Park Lodge (142 Norwich Road, 01603 782991, www.wroxhamparklodge.com) – though the decor in both might be too flouncy for some tastes – while the smart, modern Wroxham Hotel (The Bridge, 01603 782061, www.arlingtonhotel group.co.uk/wroxham) has 18 rooms, some with riverside balconies, plus a bar and restaurant.

Otherwise, Coltishall is a good bet, thanks to the Kings Head pub (*see p114*) and two fine B&Bs: the Old Railway Station B&B (31 Station Road, 01603 737069, www.theoldrailwaystation.co.uk) has three double rooms in a converted Victorian train station, with breakfast served on the platform; and Bridge

Malthouse Broad
Travel on an eight-person reed lighter – traditionally used to transport bundles of reeds and now powered by electricity – on a one-hour tour of Malthouse Broad with the *Helen of Ranworth* (01603 270453). There are two morning trips from Easter to October. In the afternoon, the boat operates as a ferry, running from Ranworth Staithe to the wildlife centre at NWT Ranworth Broad Nature Reserve (*see p112*).

ON FOOT & BICYCLE

Bike hire
You can hire bikes for adults (£14 a day) and children (£8), as well as tagalongs, baby seats and trailers, from Broadland Cycle Hire (07887 480331, ww.norfolkbroadscycling.co.uk), based at Bewilderwood (*see p112*). The comprehensive 'Broads by Bike' leaflet – available from tourist information centres or downloadable from www.the broadsbybike.org.uk – details nine circular routes, with information on cafés, pubs, attractions and sites of interest.

Boardwalk trails
For a close-up look at the vegetation, insects, birds and other wildlife on the edge of the water, follow the boardwalk nature trails set up at many of the key broads, including Barton, Ranworth, Hickling and Upton – all managed by the Norfolk Wildlife Trust (01603 270479, www.norfolkwildlife.org.uk).

Weavers' Way
This long-distance path runs between Cromer and Great Yarmouth, taking in part of the northern broads. From Stalham it loops around Hickling Broad to Potter Heigham, then follows the River Thurne to the waterside hamlet of Thurne and further south to Acle. You can download maps and details from www.countryside access.norfolk.gov.uk.

Wherryman's Way
The Wherryman's Way follows the River Yare for 35 miles from Great Yarmouth to Norwich, running through various southern broads villages, nature reserves and landmarks such as eerie Breydon Water, the pretty village of Reedham and isolated Berney Arms Mill. Download a brochure showing the whole trail plus 12 smaller circular routes from www. wherrymansway.net/circularwalks.html.

House (1 High Street, 01603 737323, www. bridgehouse-coltishall.co.uk) offers rooms in a 300-year-old ex-coaching inn and converted barns. There's also pretty Broadland B&B (West End Lodge, Norwich Road, 01692 678420, www. bedbreakfast-norfolkbroads.co.uk) in Ludham.

Broad House Hotel
The Avenue, Wroxham, NR12 8TS (01603 783567, www.broadhousehotel.co.uk). Rates £171-£231 double incl breakfast.
This handsome Queen Anne red-brick house, set in 24 acres of secluded gardens and woodland, is a delight if money's no object. Choose from six rooms and three suites, all individually designed, with rich colours, sumptuous fabrics and country house furniture. The bathrooms are equally luxurious. The restaurant serves top-notch British food, with most of the vegetables coming from the hotel garden.

Norfolk Mead Hotel ★
Coltishall, NR12 7DN (01603 737531, www.norfolk mead.co.uk). Rates £100-£190 double incl breakfast.
An elegant, creeper-covered Georgian country mansion set in extensive, relaxing grounds on a quiet stretch of the Bure (with moorings available for boaters). Decor in each of the dozen rooms is different, but all have a pretty, homely vibe. There's an outdoor swimming pool, and the restaurant is recommended for its classy Modern European cooking and imaginative use of local seasonal ingredients.

Seven Acres House
Seven Acres Lane, Great Hautbois, NR12 7JZ (01603 736737, www.norfolkbroadsbandb.com). Rates £75-£82 double incl breakfast. Cottage £206-£502 per week.
It's the seven acres of grounds surrounding this handsome late Edwardian house near Coltishall that are so enticing: from the two south-facing B&B rooms, the rolling green lawns seem to stretch for ever. There's also a cute single-storey cottage with a kitchen and a patio, which sleeps three.

TRINITY BROADS

Acle
Heading east from South Walsham brings you inexorably towards Acle, where the road forks: east towards Great Yarmouth, and north towards Thurne and three more broads – Ormesby, Rollesby and Filby, collectively known as the Trinity Broads. At first sight, the large village of Acle isn't much to look at – but it grows on you. Its position close to the River Bure and its railway station (on the Norwich to Great Yarmouth line) combine to make it a key centre for boaters, cyclists, and walkers, but it's always been important – 1,000 years ago it was a wealthy fishing and trading port on a sandbank surrounded by sea and estuary, and in the 19th century was the heart of a thriving boatbuilding trade.

The village centre – a huddle of shops, tearooms and pubs around a green – is worth exploring. The Thursday market dates back to the 13th century, and the splendid Norman church, St Edmund's, is one of the best in the area, with a turreted round Saxon tower and a 15th-century belfry topped with eight figures looking down on the nave's thatched

roof. Acle Coffee Shop (01493 741000, closed Mon) houses a newsagent, general store and second-hand bookstall. Horners (0800 9754416, www.horners.co.uk) holds a household and general goods auction every Thursday and an antiques auction every sixth Saturday, and there's a farmers market in the church every second Saturday. The little blue- and white-painted Acle Bridge Stores, adjacent to the bridge over the Bure just north of the village, is one of the Broads' sweetest sights.

There are pleasant walks in the various woods around Acle (detailed on boards around the village or you can download a Burlingham Woodland Walks guide from www.countrysideaccess.norfolk.gov.uk). Alternatively, stroll to nearby Upton for a pint in the White Horse pub (*see p118*) or to spot dragonflies at Upton Broad & Marshes nature reserve (*see p113*).

Thurne to Caister-on-Sea
Five miles north of Acle, the peaceful waterside hamlet of Thurne and its staithe are home to a striking whitewashed drainage mill (Thurne Dyke Mill), pretty cottages, a little gift shop with work by local artists, and a pub that doubles as the village shop. There's also a small campsite, Woodside Farm (*see p118*). The long-distance Weavers Way footpath runs through the village; while its 56 miles may be a step too far for most, the three-mile riverside stretch to Potter Heigham is lovely.

From Thurne the obvious route is east towards the final group of northern broads, the Trinity Broads (officially five broads: Ormesby, Rollesby, Filby and the much smaller Ormesby Little and Lily). The Muck Fleet Dyke links them with the River Bure, but is not navigable by boat – resulting in a tranquility that's hard to find on the other waterways. Most of the surrounding villages are unremarkable, though Stokesby is sweet and has two waterside eating and drinking options. Five miles further east, elegant Ormesby St Margaret, centred around a green, offers some relief from quaint thatched cottages with some distinctly modernist-looking 1960s buildings.

Eastwards, as the Broads give way to the coast, big holiday parks begin to blight the landscape, stretching the length of the coast from Hemsby to Caister-on-Sea. Caister is a modern residential town that's largely indistinguishable from Great Yarmouth to the south – the racecourse is all that separates the two towns. A few attractions are worth seeking out: to the north, just off the A149, the foundations of a Roman fort (now run by English Heritage) might interest history buffs. The Caister Castle & Car Collection (*see p113*) is a must for petrolheads, and the ruined medieval castle to which it's attached is impressive. A few miles inland, Thrigby Hall Wildlife Gardens (*see p113*) near Filby has an impressive array of primates, big cats and reptiles, as well as fine views over the most remote northern broads.

Where to eat & drink
Pubs offer the best food in this rural area. They mostly come frills-free, but are usually cheap, cheerful and very careful with their cask- and bottle-conditioned ales.

Hickling Broad. See p105.

Next to Acle Bridge, the Bridge Inn (Old Road, 01493 750288, www.maypolehotels.com) is a popular lunch venue thanks to its extensive riverside seating. The Lion Inn (The Street, 01692 670796, www.lion-inn-thurne.co.uk) in Thurne is known for hearty steaks cooked on a proper chargrill, while the recently revamped Ferry Inn (The Green, 01493 751096, www.ferryinn.net) in Stokesby occupies an idyllic riverside setting, and serves a pleasing array of dishes from red mullet in spicy Thai curry to ham, egg and chips.

Places worth a pint stop include the Eel's Foot Inn (Eels Foot Road, 01493 730342) on the banks of Ormesby Broad, and the White Horse (17 Chapel Road, 01493 750696, www.whitehorseupton.co.uk) in Upton. Smokers get sofas and wicker armchairs in a covered barn outside the pub. Non-smokers will enjoy the snug interior and well-kept beers.

Hermitage Restaurant
64 Old Road, Acle, NR13 3QP (01493 750310, www.thehermitageseafoodrestaurant.co.uk). Lunch served noon-2.15pm, dinner served 6-9.15pm Tue-Sun.
It may not look a hot prospect from outside, but this popular fish restaurant is a winner, with a wide-ranging, unfussy menu that uses local produce as much as possible: crabs and lobsters from Wells, whitebait from Lowestoft, mussels from Morston and the Wash, and locally grown fruit and veg.

Kings Head Inn
The Street, Acle, NR13 3DY (01493 750204, www.kingsheadinnacle.co.uk). Open 11am-11.30pm daily. Lunch served noon-2.30pm Mon-Sat. Dinner served 6.30-9pm Mon-Sat. Food served noon-9pm Sun.
This recently refurbished 16th-century coaching inn in the middle of Acle is a good choice for walkers and cyclists. Food is pub standards done well. There's a leafy garden and six bedrooms (£69 double incl breakfast).

Riverside Tea Rooms & Stores
The Green, Stokesby, NR29 3EX (01493 750470). Open Tea Rooms 7.30am-6.30pm Mon-Sat; 7.30am-5.30pm. Shop 7am-7pm Mon-Sat; 7am-6pm Sun.
Make a day of it on the nearby riverbank with takeaway own-made pies and cakes, a bottle of wine and some fishing tackle and fresh bait from this cute white and yellow tearoom and shop. Breakfasts (including a veggie version) and light lunches are also served, should the fish fail to bite.

Where to stay
The remote setting of the Trinity Broads means accommodation options are less varied than elsewhere, but comfortable and affordable B&Bs are plentiful. Set in a former drainage mill north of Acle, St Margaret's Mill (01493 752288, www.st margaretsmill.co.uk) is a holistic centre and B&B that offers a range of alternative therapies. The Kings Head Inn (*see left*) in Acle also has rooms.

Amber Lodge Hotel
South Walsham Road, nr Acle, NR13 3ES (01493 750377, www.amberlodgeacle.com). Rates £70-£85 double incl breakfast.
This pleasant, rambling former rectory set in four acres of grounds has ten recently refurbished bedrooms. All are en suite, and have Wi-Fi and great countryside views.

Clippesby Hall ★
Clippesby, NR29 3BL (01493 367800, www.clippesby. com). Rates Camping Easter-Oct £10.50-£26.50 per pitch. Chalet £267-£422 per week. Lodge £446-£936 per week. Cottage £494-£1,277 per week.
A range of accommodation, including camping, cottages and wooden lodges, in an excellent location three miles north of Acle. The tent and caravan pitches are spread over eight areas, including secluded woodland sites and family-oriented lawns, and the facilities are comprehensive, with swimming and tennis during the summer and a very well-stocked information centre. The self-catering buildings (sleeping up to eight) are appealingly varied in style, set in individual glades and furnished to a high standard.

Woodside Farm
Common Lane, Thurne, NR29 3BX (01692 670367, www.woodside-farm.co.uk). Rates Easter-Oct £17 per pitch.
With just a dozen pitches (mainly for tents) on the outskirts of the charming village of Thurne, Woodside Farm is ideal for a spot of back-to-basics camping. There are two showers, a washing-up room – and that's about it, though electric hook-ups can be provided for a small fee.

NORFOLK

Great Yarmouth & Southern Broads

For many people, the Norfolk Broads end at the A47, the horizontal slash of dual-carriageway that bisects the county from Great Yarmouth in the east to King's Lynn in the west. Virtually the whole of Norfolk's coastline and all its most popular broads lie north of this road. The handful of broads south of it – Surlingham and Rockland on the western stretch of the River Yare, the villages that line the banks of its eastern stretch and the Chet tributary, and those that border the Waveney into Suffolk's Oulton Broad – tend to be forgotten, like embarrassing hicksville relatives of the city boy made good. For this reason, the waterways of the southern broads tend to be more tranquil and less touristy than their northern counterparts. Alternatively, for old-fashioned bucket-and-spade fun, and some surprising pockets of historical character, there's the brash seaside resort of Great Yarmouth.

GREAT YARMOUTH

Like Blackpool without the roving gangs of drunken lads and hen parties, Great Yarmouth offers seaside tat all the way from the pier along the length of Regent Road and up to the shopping precinct. And yet, you can't help but like this town. It's partly to do with the down-at-heel but not down-on-its-luck feel of the place – the sense that people flock here not because they can't afford anything else, but because they like paddling in the sea, building sandcastles, eating familiar food and taking in the seaside air, just as holidaymakers have done since the town's late-Victorian rise as a popular seaside resort.

Great Yarmouth's prosperity and importance stretches back much further, however. The settlement developed in the tenth century around herring (known as 'silver darlings') fishing, expanding through the Middle Ages to become England's fifth richest town; as recently as 1913, it still supported more than 1,000 herring fishing boats. And it retains an impressive architectural history that's still evident – if you can find it. Mid 20th-century urban planning has not been kind to the town's heritage quarter, with uninviting alleyways (some of them remainders of the 145 medieval 'rows' that formed the east/west links with the north/south main streets) that are more Thatcher's Britain than thatched Britain, leading to grim council estates. But it's worth making the effort to seek out attractions such as one of the most complete medieval town walls in England (seen at its best in the north-west tower at North Quay); the 12th-century St Nicholas's Church (England's largest parish church); a 300-year-old smokehouse; and a heritage quarter containing merchant houses that are more than 400 years old. Fortunately, navigation is easy thanks to the town's compact size and a rectangular street grid that has drawn comparisons with Manhattan.

Heritage quarter

It's tempting to see the seafront as the focus of Great Yarmouth, but most of the old town was built not facing the sea, but looking inland towards the River Yare – specifically the channel parallel to the coastline that has for centuries provided a safe harbour and lucrative port. It's in this sliver of land between the river's banks on the west and the sea to the east that the handful of period properties and museums that make up the heritage quarter lie; most are on or near South Quay. The best are the Nelson Museum (see p130), Time & Tide (see p131) and the Elizabethan House Museum (see p130).

Other places are worth visiting too, including the Great Yarmouth Potteries (18-19 Trinity Place, 01493 850585, www.greatyarmouthpottery.co.uk, closed Sat, Sun), and the Great Yarmouth Row Houses and nearby remains of a 13th-century Franciscan friary (South Quay, 01493 857900, www.english-heritage.org.uk/greatyarmouthrow houses, closed Oct-Mar). The Tolhouse (Tollhouse Street, 01493 745226, www.museums.norfolk. gov.uk, closed Dec-Mar), located in one of the oldest (12th-century) buildings in East Anglia, has some imaginative interpretive ways of looking at the history of crime and punishment in Great Yarmouth over the centuries.

To find out about the various buildings and their accessibility – some are open only by appointment or on a guided tour – visit the tourist information centre on the seafront (25 Marine Parade, 01493 846346, closed Sat, Sun). You can also join in a historical tour with Heritage Guided Walks (details on 01493 846346 or 07901 915390). The tourist

Great Yarmouth beach

office will also be able to direct you to such sights as the timber-cottage birthplace of *Black Beauty* author Anna Sewell; the 18th-century St George's Church, now a theatre and arts centre; and the 1930 *Lydia Eva* steam drifter, the last vessel built at the King's Lynn shipyard. For refreshments, Quayside Plaza (9 South Quay, 07500 740827) is a pleasant little bistro with an intriguing (and cheap) arts and crafts shop.

The seafront

Heading from South Quay towards the sea, the streets broaden out to create the more familiar look of a genteel English seaside resort, with grand Victorian and Edwardian houses (now gaily painted B&Bs) leading to masses of interchangeable restaurants and greasy spoons, pound-shops, fast-food outlets and the occasional oddity. Take Regent Road, the street leading directly to the pier. Traditional grill restaurants and souvenir shops are interspersed with shops selling mock Crocs, air rifles, goth gear and personalised everything. You can also buy cowboy gear at Klobbers Western Wear and gawp at the notoriously bad waxworks at the endearingly naff House of Wax. There's even a few modern-looking cafés.

Pockets of more innovative and inventive commerce are close at hand, however. The recently refurbished Victoria Arcade houses a number of indie boutiques, while Market Row and neighbouring rows are reminiscent of Brighton's

Lanes, filled with eminently browsable shops such as Waldens Antiques & Collectibles (41 Market Row, 01493 857898, closed Thur, Sun) and the Wonderful World of Books (8-10 Broad Row, 01493 858646, closed Sun). East Anglian department store Palmers (37-39 Market Place, 01493 844291, www.palmerstores.com, closed Sun) is worth a poke around, as are the stalls at the Wednesday and Saturday market.

But no one comes to Great Yarmouth for its shopping, and all the resort clichés and tat are quickly forgotten once you reach the front and its glorious expanse of sand and sea. Donkey rides under the Britannia Pier and strongman photo-ops on top of it will send older folk down memory lane, while younger visitors will enjoy the funfair rides and amusement arcades. The beach is terrific: miles of golden sand broken by three piers. At the northern end, fun-filled Britannia Pier (www.britannia-pier. co.uk) has been rebuilt a number of times in its 160-year history (twice after being cut in two by ships); the quiet Jetty, a popular fishing spot, is said to have been where Horatio Nelson landed on his return from Copenhagen in 1801; and the 1854 Wellington Pier (www.wellington-pier.co.uk) at the southern end of the strip, is the oldest of the three.

Marine Parade, the wide seafront promenade, is home to a dizzying range of attractions, including the Pleasure Beach amusement park (South Beach Parade, 01493 844585, www.pleasure-beach. co.uk, closed Nov-Feb – featuring 70 rides, the

NORFOLK

Great Yarmouth seafront. See p121.

Row Houses. See p119.

Arnold Palmer mini-putting course and the Pirate's Cove crazy golf course), the Sea Life Centre (*see p130*), the Amazonia World of Reptiles (*see p130*) and the wonderful Merrivale Model Village (*see p130*). There are also horse-drawn carriage rides, boat trips to the grey seal colony and wind farm at Scroby Sands and, of course, plenty of perfect spots to paddle, scoff fish and chips, or soak up the sun in a deckchair while gazing beyond the wind farms to the horizon.

Look inland too; a scan of the front reveals some fine architectural constructs, such as the grand 1911 Empire Cinema (sadly closed), and towering Nelson's Monument. The latter's grim setting belies its splendour: more than 144 feet tall, it was erected in 1819, predating Nelson's Column in Trafalgar Square by 24 years, as perhaps befits his status as a Norfolk hero. Oddly, it's not topped by the local boy himself, but by the figure of Britannia.

Near Great Yarmouth

When you tire of sand in your sandwiches, the incessant noise of amusement arcade automata and the smell of fried food, there are a clutch of attractions just outside town. North of town, on the way to Caister, is Great Yarmouth Racecourse ★ (Jellicoe Road, 01493 842527, www.great yarmouth-racecourse.co.uk). Time your visit to coincide with one of the popular flat race meetings (April to October) – hugely exciting and a great way to spend a day. Greyhound and motor racing fans should head to nearby Yarmouth Stadium (01493 720343, www.yarmouthstadium.co.uk, closed Sun), which looks like something you'd find in the Midwest. Keep an eye out en route to it for the lovely bus station, its art deco façade decorated with large tile-mosaics of modes of transport through the ages, including a penny farthing.

Alternatively, head south across the River Yare towards the sweetly old-fashioned town of Gorleston, where you'll find part of a medieval priory, a serene yacht pond, an Edwardian music hall, a traditional seaside theatre, gently clambering cliffs and even a small-scale version of Liverpool Cathedral. It's a laid-back, genteel resort and a perfect transition from the brashness of Great Yarmouth to the gentle waterways of the southern broads and Suffolk.

Where to eat & drink

You'll be hard-pressed to find outstanding cooking in Great Yarmouth, with a couple of notable exceptions: Andover House (*see below*) and 3 Norfolk Square (*see p125*). Otherwise, carefully peruse greasy-spoon menus and choose one you like, or opt for predictable pub food: the White Swan (North Quay, 01493 842027) does a good range of own-cooked standards, and the Rumbold Arms (Southtown Road, 01493 653887, www.therumboldarms.co.uk) smokes its own fish and has a Sunday carvery.

Olive Garden ★
42 Regent Road, NR30 2AJ (01493 844641, www.olivegardenrestaurant.co.uk). Open 6-9pm Mon; noon-2pm, 6-9pm Tue-Thur; noon-2pm, 6-10pm Fri, Sat; 1-8pm Sun.
Looking sparse, modern and distinctly different from its old-fashioned neighbours, the Olive Garden draws in eager punters with a varied menu that uses locally sourced produce whenever possible. You'll find dishes here unseen elsewhere on the street: baked crab, tiger prawns with chilli, mussels and prawn linguine, say, as well as a nice range of clay-baked Mediterranean dishes such as beef stifado.

Where to stay

The streets leading off the front are packed with B&Bs; Trafalgar Road has some particularly spick-and-span ones painted in gay mixes of white and pink, white and yellow, and white and blue, their gardens tumbling with hanging baskets and pansies.

Classic Lodge (13 Euston Road, 01493 852851, www.classiclodge.com) has rich fabrics and original Victorian features in good-sized rooms. Barnard House B&B (2 Barnard Crescent, 01493 855139, www.barnardhouse.com) is more stylish and modern, with three well-appointed rooms (two double, one family) that come with bottled mineral water and Wi-Fi. There's also a self-catering cottage in the garden that sleeps two.

Andover House
28-30 Camperdown, NR30 3JB (01493 843490, www.andoverhouse.co.uk). Rates £81-£99 double incl breakfast.

Funky design and attitude (steel and leather bar stools, black wallpaper, stripped wooden floors and young friendly staff) make this place a rare treat in Great Yarmouth. The restaurant serves very good Modern British food, much of it using local produce, such as rack of Norfolk lamb, Thetford Forest venison and slow-stewed oxtail.

Kensington
29 North Drive, NR30 4EW (01493 844145, www.kensington-hotel.co.uk). Rates £59-£90 double incl breakfast.
Looking out over the sea-facing landscaped gardens of North Drive to the water beyond, the detached Kensington has 26 rooms, with reasonably contemporary furnishings, that are comfortable and bright; many have DVD players. The hotel has free Wi-Fi.

Southern Hotel
46 Queens Road, NR30 3JR (01493 843313, www.southernhotel.co.uk). Rates £68-£75 double incl breakfast.
From the outside, the Southern, set in a terrace, looks indistinguishable from its neighbours. But the large, sunny rooms are comfortably furnished in imaginative colour schemes and sympathetically retain original features – room 14, for example, still has an original balcony from its days as a ballroom.

3 Norfolk Square ★
3 Norfolk Square, Albemarle Road, NR30 1EE (01493 843042, www.3norfolksquare.co.uk). Rates £60-£90 double incl breakfast.
A no-kids policy and just eight rooms make this beautiful hotel a haven of peace and quiet, aided by a good location

that's a short walk from the seafront and town centre. All the rooms are large and smartly decorated, with DVD players, dressing gowns, slippers and Wi-Fi.

AROUND BREYDON WATER
Just to the west of Great Yarmouth lies the natural wonder that's responsible for keeping the southern broads as quiet as the grave: the vast Breydon Water – the tidal confluence of the Rivers Yare, Waveney and Bure. Tricky channels, shallow water and tides make this four-mile-long, one-mile-wide body of water difficult to navigate, which effectively turns it into a barrier between the northern and southern broads, but it is passable at the right times.

Berney Arms & Burgh Castle
If you're on the water, the tiny settlement of Berney Arms, in the middle of the windswept Halvergate Marshes, at Breydon Water's western end, is an ideal place to moor. Its 19th-century windmill is the tallest in Norfolk, standing nearly 70 feet high. It houses a small museum, and the little tearoom/ gift shop and store are worth a look, but an even better destination is the Berney Arms Inn (*see p127*), one of Norfolk's most isolated pubs. The hamlet is more than two miles from a road and can only be reached by boat, on foot, or – incredibly – by rail. The station is Norfolk's remotest, part of the wonderfully atmospheric Wherry Lines railway ★ (www.wherrylines.org.uk) that runs from Norwich and Acle, with trains stopping at Berney Arms on request.

Arnold Palmer mini-putting course

Paths around the area, including the RSPB's Breydon Water & Berney Marshes reserve (01493 700645, www.rspb.org.uk), are numerous. Railway, river and footpath also take you quite close to the stumpish yet evocative remains of the third-century Roman fort of Gariannonum, at the village of Burgh Castle on the southern side of the River Waveney. Civilisation encroaches here, not only with roads but with two good pubs, as well as a pretty campsite and marina. All have great views over Breydon Water and across the marshes to Halvergate. This magical area offers a sense of peace and wonder; you'll feel a long, long way from the hurly-burly of Great Yarmouth, just a few miles to the east.

Haddiscoe & Reedham

From Burgh Castle, the Waveney and Yare take off in different directions across the county. The Waveney heads southward, flowing through some nice villages and attractions as it heads to Beccles, Bungay and beyond. For much of its length, it forms the boundary between Norfolk and Suffolk.

In Haddiscoe, a few miles south of Burgh Castle, the church of St Mary ★ has an intriguing round tower. Dating from around 1100, the church has both Saxon and Norman elements. The telescope-like banded tower is four storeys high; its crenallated 15th-century top features a distinctive knapped flint and stone chequerboard pattern. The spare simplicity of the interior reflects the elegance of the exterior, and the checked, tiled floor echoes the banding on the tower. Nearby riverside pub the Crown Inn (see right) is a good stop before embarking on a short walk to Herringfleet Marshmill – the last full-size working windmill in the country – on the far bank of the Waveney, or wending your way the three miles to Reedham beside the River Yare.

Reedham★ is a great place to spend a few hours. It's a substantial village, and a sprawling one: the four-mile circular walk around it takes in a train station; the Humpty Dumpty microbrewery (Church Road, 01493 701818, www.humptydumptybrewery. co.uk, closed Nov-Easter); the Cupcakes tearoom (48 Riverside, 01493 700713); an award-winning post office and craft shop, the Garage Café & Gallery (36 Station Road, 01493 700790, www.thegaragecafe.com, closed Oct-Mar); a craft outlet in the Old Brewery; and Pettitts Adventure Park (see p131). There's also the chain ferry: the Broads' last remaining ferry and, at £3.90 for a crossing of some 20 feet, surely the most expensive way to travel in Britain. The village's three pubs – the Ferry Inn (see right), the Ship (see right) and the Nelson Head – all have lovely riverside settings. If you're heading inside the Nelson, beware the chirpy pub song excerpts; despite a pretty fire, great (if slightly bonkers) decor, a book exchange, bar billiards and a good range of beers, the music will drive you out in less time than it takes to knock back a half.

Where to eat & drink

You'll find good food here. The Queens Head (High Road, 01493 780363, www.queensheadbc.co.uk)

is a decent lunch stop if you're in the Burgh Castle area, while the Red Lion at Halvergate (Marsh Road, 01493 700317) is a great choice if you're doing the circular walk to Berney Arms. At St Olaves, the 16th-century Bell (Beccles Road, 01493 488249, www.bellinn-stolaves.co.uk) offers hearty pub grub and a grand riverside garden in which to enjoy it.

Berney Arms Inn ★
Berney Arms, NR30 1SB (01493 700303). Open Mar-Nov noon-11pm Mon-Sat; noon-10.30pm Sun. Lunch served Mar-Nov noon-2.30pm daily. Dinner served Mar-Nov 6-8.30pm daily.
The most remote pub in Norfolk can only be reached by boat, train (request stop) or on foot, but it's definitely worth making the effort to get here. You'll find a wonderfully friendly and idiosyncratic pub with good beer (including ales from Reedham's Humpty Dumpty brewery), lots of outdoor seating in a picturesque spot, and a warm, cosy space inside. Food is of the superior pub kind (lamb shank, pies, steaks) and portions are huge.

Crown
The Street, Haddiscoe, NR14 6AA (01502 677368, http://thecrownathaddiscoe.co.uk). Open Summer 11am-midnight Mon-Thur, Sun; 11am-1am Fri, Sat. Winter noon-11am Mon-Thur, Sun; noon-1am Fri, Sat. Lunch served noon-3pm, dinner served 6-9pm daily.
The requisite wooden beams and original features make this 17th-century coach house an attractive, pleasant place for a very good lunch or supper, with robust dishes such as cajun roasted salmon, beef bourguignon and own-made steak, ale and mushroom pie. There are also three comfortable rooms, brightly painted and individually decorated; all have Wi-Fi.

Ferry Inn
Ferry Road, Reedham, NR13 3HA (01493 700429). Open 10.30am-3pm, 6-11pm Mon-Fri; 10.30am-11pm Sat; 11am-11pm Sun. Lunch served noon-2.30pm, dinner served 6-9pm Mon-Fri. Meals served noon-9pm Sat, Sun.
High-quality pub standards – bangers and mash, fish and chips – join the likes of fish stew and Brancaster mussels on the menu at this characterful pub. It would be fun even without the mad decor. But the thousands of business cards, stuffed animals and assorted oddities such as divers' helmets give you something entertaining to look at while supping the well-kept ales.

Priory Farm Restaurant
Beccles Road, St Olaves, NR3 9HE (01493 488432). Lunch served noon-2pm, dinner served 6-10pm daily.
The charming location makes Priory Farm a nice lunch stop, especially if you have kids, who'll love tearing around the priory ruins and cooing over the llamas and deer in the garden. The daily-changing specials of traditional English dishes should keep them happy, and the vast selection on the standard menu will ensure something for everyone.

Ship
Riverside, Reedham, NR13 3TQ (01493 700287). Open 11am-11.30pm daily. Lunch served noon-2.30pm, dinner served 6.30-9.30pm daily.
A terrific riverside setting, next to the swing railway bridge, and a huge beer garden make this a top pick for summer evenings, and there's a nice play area too. Food, served in

NORFOLK

NINE NORFOLK CHURCHES (AND ONE ABBEY)

Churches of the Fens ★

A triumphant triumvirate of goodies in adjoining villages. St Mary the Virgin, in Wiggenhall St Mary, has the best 15th- and 16th-century carved benches in Norfolk, if not England. In Walpole, St Peter (the biggest of the three churches) has the most impressive features, including fine medieval bosses, a spectacular nave and medieval paintings of saints, while St Andrew has unusual octagonal turrets. *See p145.*

St Nicholas's Chapel, King's Lynn

This chapel was founded in 1146, although most of the existing building dates from the early 15th century. The structure is breathtaking: look out for the carvings and star-vaulted ceiling in the porch, and the wooden ceiling decorated with angels playing musical instruments. There's an interesting collection of 17th- and 18th-century monuments and memorials, as well as George Gilbert Scott's 19th-century spire. *See p30.*

Norwich Cathedral ★

One of Britain's most stunning cathedrals. The interior of this Romanesque structure (founded 1096) is dominated by a gorgeously ornate and beautifully proportioned fan-vaulted roof. The monastic cloister is beautiful and there's some surprisingly contemporary spiral stone decoration on the spire, England's second highest. Don't miss the quirky, spooky-looking skeleton tomb of Thomas Gooding. *See p87.*

St Helen, Ranworth

Spacious St Helen's, aka the Cathedral of the Broads, has a 14th-century tower that provides amazing views of five broads and, on a clear day, the spire of Norwich Cathedral. The downside, especially for those with no head for heights, is the 89 uneven steps, two ladders and one trapdoor you'll have to negotiate to get to the top. *See p113.*

St Margaret, Hales

Located in the middle of open countryside, with a thatched roof and an impossibly

Andover House. See p124.

the bar and a separate restaurant space, consists of good own-cooked seasonal dishes alongside pub standards such as steak pies, roasts and seafood bakes.

Where to stay

Accommodation can be sparse once you get outside Great Yarmouth, so it's a good idea to book ahead. The Crown (*see p127*) in Haddiscoe and the Queens Head (*see p127*) in Burgh Castle both offer rooms, but if you get stuck, try the Burgh Castle Marina & Caravan Park (Butt Lane, 01493 780331, www.burghcastlemarina.co.uk), a quiet holiday park with a summer swimming pool that has a number of caravans to rent for short breaks.

Manor House

Tunstall Road, Halvergate, NR13 3PS (01493 700279, www.manorhousenorfolk.co.uk). Rates £80 double incl breakfast. No credit cards.

The accommodation in this 300-year-old working farmhouse is in a private wing. There are just two guest rooms, so expect plenty of peace and quiet, interrupted only by the sound of the honking geese on the pond in the extensive gardens. Rooms are comfortable, with traditional decor. Breakfast is served in a dining room where the decoration echoes the elegant style of the rooms.

The Pyghtle
26A The Hills, Reedham, NR13 3AR (01493 701262, www.reedham-thepyghtle.co.uk). Rates £60 double incl breakfast. No credit cards.
Book well ahead if you want to stay at the Pyghtle, as the entirely self-contained cottage B&B – converted from two small holiday cottages – is very popular. It comes with its own front door, two floors (there's a sitting room downstairs, and a double en suite bedroom upstairs); breakfast is included, nevertheless.

Reedham Ferry Touring Park & Campsite
Reedham Ferry, NR13 3HA (01493 700999, www.archerstouringpark.co.uk). Rates £12-£18 per night.
Set over four acres bordering the Yare, this is a campsite for those who like their home comforts. Top-notch facilities, including electric hook-ups, laundry room, bar, restaurant, barbecue area and a private fishing lake, mean it's very popular. There are just 20 pitches, so it's a good idea to book ahead. Proximity to the Ferry Inn (*see p127*) is another draw.

WEST OF REEDHAM

Loddon & around
From Reedham, it's a few short miles north-west to the Norwich broads of Surlingham and Rockland, but it's well worth making a short detour south-west to the lively Chet riverside villages of Loddon ★ and Chedgrave. Loddon, a popular boating centre for the southern broads, is an attractive small market town, with a good chippie, a community shop, a lovely weatherboard watermill spanning the river, a waterside picnic area and – standing high over the town – the impressive 15th-century Holy Trinity Church, a great example of the Gothic Perpendicular style. Good examples of Georgian and Victorian buildings abound, but Loddon offers a rare modern treat for architecture fans in a sweet collection of 1960s housing by Lowestoft architects Tayler and Green, whose delicate, well-proportioned bungalows between the Low and High Bungay Roads are standout examples of post-war public housing.

It's well worth hiring a day-boat here to follow the enchanting three-and-a-half-mile stretch of the River Chet to Hardley Cross, the 1556 boundary marker between the city of Norwich and the borough of Great Yarmouth. The route takes in pretty wooded riverbanks before turning into a canal bordered by expansive views of grazing marshes. If you prefer to stay on dry land, a number of Wherryman's Way circular walks at Loddon and Chedgrave follow the Chet footpath past the Hardley Flood, fantastic for spotting water birds and wildlife – including otters.

cute round tower, this Grade I-listed Norman church will knock your socks off. Little has changed since it was built in the 12th century. Highlights include the magnificent carved and columned Norman doorway, an octagonal 15th-century font and the wall paintings. See p130.

St Mary, Barton Bendish ★
Tiny St Mary's, with its thatched roof and delicate simplicity, is a real delight. Inside is an ethereal, spare space, decorated only with a 14th-century wall painting and some carved pieces, all bathed in pure white light. The key is available from the big house opposite the church's entrance. See p152.

St Mary, Haddiscoe
Dating from around 1100, and containing both Saxon and Norman elements in its structure, this round-towered church stands out for its notably tall tower. The tower's distinctive crenallated top, with a chequerboard pattern in flint, is from the 15th century. Inside, the space is simple and elegant. See p127.

St Michael & All Angels, Booton
A Gothic fantasy designed and built in the 19th century by Reverend Whitwell Elwin, who took elements of all his favourite churches and put them together to construct a building that's mad but also glorious and gorgeous. Traditionalists might prefer the distinctly more restrained churches at nearby Cawston and Salle. See p60.

St Peter, Forncett St Peter
A typical round-towered flint Norfolk church, set in a tiny village. The exterior is particularly lovely, especially the Saxon tower – possibly the finest example in England. To get inside, you'll need to get the key from the churchwarden. See p136.

Wymondham Abbey ★
The torrid history of this huge and splendid Norman abbey, founded in 1107, includes a centuries-long dispute between parishioners and monks and the grisly death of William Kett on the walls of the western tower. See p141.

NORFOLK

Places to visit

GREAT YARMOUTH

Amazonia
Central Sea Front, NR30 3AH (01493 842202,
www.amazonia-worldofreptiles.net). Open Feb-Nov
10am-5pm daily. Admission £4.95; £3.95 reductions;
£15 family.
One for fans of creepie-crawlies, this jungle rainforest
zoo houses more than 70 species of reptiles in
evocative displays, including snapping turtles,
hissing cockroaches, royal and burmese pythons,
bird-eating tarantulas and myriad geckos.

Elizabethan House Museum
4 South Quay, NR30 2QH (01493 745526,
www.museums.norfolk.gov.uk, www.national
trust.org.uk). Open Apr-Oct 10am-5pm Mon-Fri;
noon-4pm Sat, Sun. Admission £3.30; free-£2.80
reductions.
This well-crafted National Trust museum convincingly
evokes different aspects of domesticity in the 16th
century with a series of period rooms that illustrate
life both above and below stairs. It also houses the
Haddiscoe Hoard, a collection of more than 300
silver coins that form part of a display on life in
Great Yarmouth during the Civil War.

Merrivale Model Village ★
Wellington Pier Gardens, Marine Parade, NR30
3JG (01493 842097, www.greatyarmouthmodel
village.co.uk). Open Apr-Oct daily; times vary,
check website for details. Admission £6; £4.50-
£5.50 reductions; £18.50 family.
With more than 200 miniature shops, houses and
buildings set in sweet landscaped gardens, Merrivale
is an utter delight, particularly when it's lit up by the
tiny street lights at dusk. Play areas, rides, a shop
and a café ensure fun for all ages.

Nelson Museum
6 South Quay, NR30 2RG (01493 850698,
www.nelson-museum.co.uk). Open Apr-Sept 10am-
5pm Mon-Fri; 1-4pm Sat, Sun. Jan-Mar, Oct, Nov
10am-4pm Mon-Fri; 1-4pm Sun. Admission £3.40;
£2 reductions; £9 family. No credit cards.

RSPB Strumpshaw Fen

This museum, dedicated to Britain's great naval hero,
is set in a Grade II-listed Georgian merchant's house.
The potential for stuffiness in the likes of the Naval
Room (detailing Nelson's career chronologically) and
the Georgian Life Room is offset by a number of
engaging and child-friendly exhibits, including the
Below Decks recreation of a man-of-war. The Maritime
Courtyard, an outdoor exhibit filled with large versions
of sailors' games and a rolling, swaying 'deck imitator',
is excellent for both picnicking and tearing around in.

Sea Life Centre
Marine Parade, NR30 3AH (01493 330631,
www.sealife.co.uk). Open 10am-3pm Mon-Fri;
10am-4pm Sat, Sun. Admission varies, phone
for details.
A terrific aquarium that includes an underwater
tunnel for viewing sharks and sea turtles, a pirate
cove, fisherman's wharf, rock pool, jellyfish tank and
– of course – a shop and café. It's also a seahorse
breeding centre and does conservation and rescue
work, so there's plenty of information and activities
around those subjects. The newest arrival is a colony
of Humboldt penguins.

The village of Hales, just to the south, is
unremarkable but for one feature: the tiny
Norman church of St Margaret ★. The building,
along with St Gregory in neighbouring Heckingham,
are glorious examples of East Anglian Norman
church architecture, with classic round towers,
thatched roofs, magnificent Norman doorways and
idyllic open field settings. Garden fans will want to
continue along the B1136 to Raveningham, famous
for the lovely Raveningham Gardens (*see p131*)
and home to the sweet Cinnamon Gallery (Beccles
Road, 01508 548441, closed Mon-Wed), which
sells and exhibits local artefacts and crafts and
also has a coffee shop and antiques centre.

Surlingham, Lingwood & around
Heading north-west towards Norwich, the villages
of Surlingham and Lingwood – both around six
miles from Loddon, on different sides of the Yare –

are worth a stop. Each has thatched cottages
and a riverside pub; the former has a shop,
and there are grander 17th- and 18th-century
houses in the latter. Either is a good base for
botany and wildlife fans, given their proximity
to Surlingham Church Marsh (01603 715191,
www.rspb.org.uk), with its lovely short trail
through a former grazing marsh, with pools
and dykes to explore. For others, Surlingham's
picture-perfect location on a horseshoe bend
of the Yare and range of good pubs gives it
the edge; it's also closer to Wheatfen Nature
Reserve (The Covey, 01508 538036, www.
wheatfen.org), which has a great two-mile walk
over the fenland tidal marshes and carrs on
the Yare.
   More excellent nature trails lie near Buckenham,
just a mile or so south of Lingwood and notable
for its church, St Nicholas, which is one of only

period costume, a ride on a Victorian carousel, a street of traditional shops (including an ironmonger and an apothecary) and life-sized models of famous Victorian characters and historical figures.

AROUND BREYDON WATER

Pettitts Adventure Park
Church Road, Reedham, NR13 3UA (01493 700094, www.pettittsadventurepark.co.uk). Open Apr-Oct 10am-5.30pm daily. Admission £9.95; £7.95 reductions; £39 family.
Children and adults will fall in love with the tiny African pygmy goats and miniature horses here, but the rabbits, owls, raccoons, pigs and lemurs will elicit lots of 'aahs' too. And when you're done with feeding and petting, there's a half-mile-long miniature railway, heaps of rides and numerous activities and playgrounds.

WEST OF REEDHAM

Time & Tide Museum ★
Blackfriars Road, NR30 3BX (01493 743930, www.museums.norfolk.gov.uk). Open Apr-Nov 10am-5pm daily. Dec-Mar 10am-4pm Mon-Fri; noon-4pm Sat, Sun. Admission £4.50; £3.30-£3.80 reductions.
This award-winning museum, housed in a restored Victorian herring curing works, features some excellent re-creations of bygone days. There's a Victorian terrace and fisherman's home, a 1950s quayside and a seaside holidays gallery that will have older visitors tripping happily down memory lane. The interactive displays will keep children amused, and the Silver Darlings café (open to all, not just museum-goers) serves a nicely fishy selection of snacks, such as kipper paté and marinated herrings, alongside the more usual sandwiches, soups and cakes.

Yesterday's World
34 Marine Parade, NE30 2EN (01493 331148, www.yesterdaysworld.co.uk). Open Feb-Oct 10am-5pm daily. Admission £7; £6 reductions; £20 family.
Eschewing the strictly educational in favour of the experiential, this re-creation of a century of British history includes a Victorian tearoom with staff in

Raveningham Gardens
Raveningham, NR14 6NS (01508 548152, www.raveningham.com). Open Easter-Aug 11am-4pm Mon-Fri. Admission £4; £3.50 reductions. No credit cards.
Priscilla Bacon lived at Raveningham for 50 years and in that time developed a garden that's a joy to visit, from its impressive borders to its rose beds and Edwardian summerhouse. Sympathetic contemporary touches include a new herb garden, lake and sculptures.

RSPB Strumpshaw Fen
Low Road, Strumpshaw, NR13 4HS (01603 715191, www.rspb.org.uk). Open Reserve dawn-dusk daily. Visitor Centre Summer 9am-5pm daily. Winter 9am-4pm daily. Admission £2.50; 50p-£1.50 reductions; £5 family. No credit cards.
A wonderful habitat of reedbeds, woodland and meadows, plus a good range of walks and activities, as well as three hides from which to spy the likes of marsh harriers, bitterns and kingfishers. There's plenty here for kids and non-twitchers too, with activity rucksacks available for the former and a range of guided walks for birdwatching beginners.

five churches in Suffolk with a hexagonal church tower. Attractions here include two RSPB reserves at Buckenham Marshes and Strumpshaw Fen (*see above*), Strumpshaw Steam Museum (01603 714535, www.strumpshawsteammuseum.co.uk, open daily July-Sept, check for other times) and the little village of Strumpshaw.

The nearby riverside village of Brundall is well worth a stop, not least for one of the best restaurants in the area, Lavender House (*see p132*). There are also several places to hire boats – Swancraft (01603 712362, www.swancraft.co.uk) offers discounts for Wherry Lines ticket holders – and a high street with a pub, small shops and a post office that's a real step back in time. After looking round the village, a gently meandering boat trip up the Yare to the outskirts of Norwich seems the perfect way to end any exploration of this region's quiet charms.

Where to eat & drink
Pubs serving good traditional British dishes are the best options for food in this part of the world. Standouts include the Swan Hotel in Loddon (Church Plain, 01508 520239), where everything from beef stew to tottering yorkshire puds to tottering knickerbocker glories is made in the kitchen; the newly refurbished Coldham Hall Tavern in Surlingham (Coldham Hall Carnser, 01508 538366, www.coldhamhalltavern.co.uk), which occupies a terrific riverside spot on the Yare; Ferry House, also in Surlingham (Ferry Road, 01508 538659, www.surlinghamferryhouse.co.uk), which provides fresh, resolutely traditional dishes such as steak and ale pie, beer-battered cod and Sunday roasts; and the New Inn in Rockland St Mary (12 New Inn Hill, 01508 538403, closed Mon, dinner Sun winter), which does much the same fare.

NORFOLK

Garden House

Yarmouth Road, Hales, NR14 6SX (01508 548468, www.halesgardenhouse.co.uk). Open 7-11pm Mon; noon-2pm, 7pm-midnight Tue-Sat; noon-midnight Sun. Lunch served noon-2pm Tue-Sun. Dinner served 7-9pm daily.
With a large garden and an open, pleasant bar and restaurant divided by a big wood-burning stove, the Garden House is a solid choice for a locally brewed pint or a hearty meal. The menu consists mainly of crowd-pleasing dishes – from own-made chilli, pies and burgers to steaks and fish and chips. There are also daily-changing specials such as pork fillet with plum and marsala sauce.

Lavender House ★

39 The Street, Brundall, NR13 5AA (01603 712215, www.thelavenderhouse.co.uk). Open/food served 6.30-11.30pm Tue-Sat; noon-5pm Sun.
Set in a gorgeous 16th-century thatched and whitewashed house, Lavender House is one of the best places to eat in south Norfolk. Chef Richard Hughes's 'Modern Norfolk' cuisine uses produce sourced almost exclusively from the county, and features the likes of tortellini of smoked eel, Edgefield venison and terrine of local game birds. For a real blow-out, find a bunch of friends and book the Opitz room, where a nine-course tasting menu, plus canapés, cookbook, glass of champagne and memorabilia, costs £385 for six.

Where to stay

If you don't fancy a B&B, the two self-catering cottages at the 15th-century thatched barn and fortified manor Hales Hall (Loddon, 01508 548507, www.haleshall.co.uk) might appeal; renting them gives you access to the Hall's glorious gardens. If you can't do without a great British breakfast, Braydeston House in Brundall (91 The Street,

01603 713123, www.braydestonhouse.co.uk) offers two rooms in a Georgian house set in woodland gardens with views of the River Yare; breakfast, with own-made bread and preserves, is served in the conservatory. The two rooms at Pottles Barn (Ferry Road, Surlingham, 01508 538117, www.britainsfinest.co.uk) occupy a comfortable barn conversion in a half-acre garden.

For a boutique-style B&B experience, Little Willows (Nursery Road, Chedgrave, 01508 528525, www.littlewillows.co.uk) is pretty, has Wi-Fi in both bedrooms and also offers self-catering. Raveningham's Orchards (Beccles Road, 01508 548322, www.orchardsretreat.com) is a former rectory set in three lovely acres, while Lingwood's Station House (Station Road, 01603 715872, www.stationhouseonline.com) is one for railway fans: its three rooms are in a restored Victorian station house on the Wherry Lines railway.

Chedgrave House

Norwich Road, Chedgrave, NR14 6HB (01508 521095, www.chedgrave-house.co.uk). Rates £60-£65 double incl breakfast. No credit cards.
A great base for Loddon and the southern broads, this Victorian B&B is tastefully decorated and serves excellent cooked breakfasts, with its own free-range eggs.

Hall Green Farm ★

Norton Road, Loddon, NR14 6DT (01508 522039, www.hallgreenfarm.co.uk). Rates £75 double incl breakfast. No credit cards.
This elegant listed Georgian farmhouse, set in secluded grounds, has three large, nicely decorated rooms – the English country room, the African themed room and the Moroccan room – in a converted former dairy. All are en suite and open on to a private garden.

Reedham. See p127.

South Norfolk

Norfolk's undisputed architectural wealth lies in its 800-plus churches, some 700 of them medieval and 124 with round towers; the best examples are found in the southern half of the county, a 50-mile-long swathe of land running the length of the A47 and stretching 20 miles south to the Suffolk border. But there are other pleasures here too. Market towns and villages such as Diss, Harleston, Attleborough, Wymondham and Hingham are some of the oldest and most charming in Norfolk. The terrain of South Norfolk is varied too, from marshy fens and scrubland in the far west to the broads in the east, in between encompassing river valleys, woodland, forest and grazing meadows, sometimes dotted with Roman remains. It makes for a rich mix of attractions for all manner of visitors, including walkers, fishing fans, church buffs and amateur historians – just don't expect most children to go crazy for it.

HARLESTON & AROUND

Villages & churches

Day-trippers from Norwich rarely head south, opting instead for the Broads to the east or the coast to the north, but for those who do venture here, immediate reward lies in the privately owned village of Framingham Pigot, just off the A146. It retains the kind of traditional village appeal that makes it a total charmer, from the Dickensian shopfronts to St Andrew's, a church that's a fine example of rural Victorian architecture.

Signs directing you to nearby Caistor St Edmund's Roman town (Venta Icenorum) promise a bit more than the remains actually deliver: a large field with some information panels showing the layout of the town that once stood here. You download a guided walk to your mobile phone – details are on the noticeboard at the entrance – which allows a decent reconstruction of the town, if you're imaginatively inclined. If not, just head instead for Poringland, a mile and a half away, to see the village sign that depicts Norfolk artist John Crome working on *The Poringland Oak* (the painting is on display at Tate Britain). Three miles west is Stoke Holy Cross, an impressive village with some fine examples of grand English village architecture, including Gothic revival and mock Tudor mansions near the church. The huge million-pound weatherboard mill is where Colman's Mustard was first produced. It's now a restaurant, but food lovers should head for the local pub, the Wildebeest Arms (*see p135*), or travel a few miles south to Brooke, a sweet village set around two lakes and woodland, containing the terrific, 800-year-old, round-towered church of St Peter and popular gastropub the King's Head (*see p135*).

This area is stuffed with similarly attractive villages with impressive churches. At Shotesham, a clutch of lovely thatched cottages and houses are overlooked by the 16th-century All Saints' Church. Peek inside to view the wall paintings (including a red naked woman burning in the flames of hell, two eerie-looking heads and a delicate tree of life

fragment), as well as some geometric-patterned stained glass. Saxlingham Nethergate is equally picturesque, with more thatched dwellings, another church, St Mary – famous for its 13th-century stained glass, some of the oldest and best in East Anglia – and a parsonage built in 1784 by Sir John Soane. The church buff should continue south to Shelton, where St Mary's is regarded as one of the best examples of perpendicular architecture in Norfolk. The banded red-brick porch is arresting, and the stained glass in the soaring east window is particularly fine.

Four miles south, Pulham Market is worth a visit if you like quintessentially English conservation villages: pretty thatched cottages, church, shop and post office are set around a village green, where you'll also find the whitewashed Crown Inn (*see p135*). Gables Yard next to the green is home to a few craft workshops; visit Kate Fisher (07733 230191, www.katefisher.co.uk, closed Mon, Tue, Sun) for a delicate array of blue and white thrown pots and dishes inspired by coastal landscapes. St Mary's Church in the next-door village of Pulham St Mary is definitely worth a stop for its stonework; check out the trumpet-blowing angels on the 15th-century porch and the story of local king and saint St Edmund carved in the parapets.

Harleston

From Pulham Market it's a ten-minute drive to the area's hub and the heart of the Waveney Valley, the market town of Harleston, admired by Pevsner for its excellent timbered and Georgian architecture. The focus of the town is the elegant market square (still home to a weekly Wednesday market), but the streets radiating from it deliver treats too – Old Market Place, in particular, has some fine houses. The shops aren't quite as impressive, though a wander will reveal a few gems, such as the Millhouse Pottery (1 Station Road, 01379 852556, closed Mon, Tue), where you'll find majolica garden- and homeware; deli Cooke & Co (25 The Thoroughfare, 01379 853173); traditional

butcher's Frank Spurgeon (29 The Thoroughfare, 01379 852230); and, tucked behind the Cardinal's Hat pub, the Adnams Cellar & Kitchen Store (23 The Thoroughfare, 01379 854788, http://cellar andkitchen.adnams.co.uk). The last three are all closed on Sundays. Diminutive Harleston Museum (3 Old Market Place, 01379 854423, closed Oct-Apr) is worth a look if it's open (Wed, Sat); if not, you could go for fish and chips at one of the town's three chippies – Norman's (12 London Road, 01379 852242, closed Mon) is the best, and offers a pretty space if you want to eat in.

Pick up a leaflet featuring three local walks (available in most pubs and hotels) and take a stroll through the Waveney Valley, much loved by Edwardian painter Alfred Munnings, born just across the border in Suffolk. The walks take in scenes that would have been very familiar to the artist, including the 17th-century Needham Mill, Cuckoo Hill (offering terrific views up and down the valley) and Munnings's birthplace, the quaint village of Mendham.

West from Harleston, the Upper Waveney Sculpture Meadow (01379 668552, www.upper waveneysculpturemeadow.co.uk) in Brockdish hosts occasional art events and organised trails; while Scole is notable for the 17th-century Scole Inn (see below), an imposing red-brick monolith with high gables and squat chimney stacks. The nearby Crossways Inn (see below) is cosier.

Where to eat & drink

If you're staying in Harleston, JD Young (see right) offers gastropub standards at very good prices in a genial, comfortable space. In Framingham Pigot, Brasted's (Manor Farm Barns, 01508 491112, www.brasteds.co.uk, open Fri, Sat only) has an inventive menu, and uses plenty of local produce. In Pulham Market, the Crown Inn (Harleston Road, 01379 676652, www.thepulhamcrown.co.uk) is perfect if you crave trad pub food in a proper thatched village pub on a green. In Brooke, the King's Head (6 Norwich Road, 01508 550355, www.kingsheadbrooke.co.uk) – under the same ownership as the popular Unthank Arms in Norwich – is an inviting, modern spot with a large garden. Food runs from morning coffee to weekend breakfasts, Sunday roasts and the likes of chicken liver and chorizo salad or risotto cakes.

Crossways Inn
Bridge Road, Scole, IP21 4DP (01379 740638, www. crosswaysscole.co.uk). Open noon-11pm daily. Lunch served 12.30-2.30pm, dinner served 6.30-8.30pm daily.
This beamed building is a delight inside and out, with dark nooks and crannies, red leather armchairs and big hearths and fireplaces combining to create the kind of village pub that townies dream of. Decent pub food and regular music and events evenings put it firmly at the heart of village life.

Wildebeest Arms ★
82-86 Norwich Road, Stoke Holy Cross, NR14 8QJ (01508 492497, www.thewildebeest.co.uk). Open 11am-4pm, 6-11.30pm Mon-Sat; 11.30am-4.30pm,

6-11.30pm Sun. Lunch served noon-2pm Mon-Sat; 12.30-2.30pm Sun. Dinner served 7-9pm daily.
The Wildebeest Arms is one of a handful of pubs in Norfolk to have received a Michelin Bib Gourmand (one of the others, Norwich's Mad Moose & 1up – see p89 – is also owned by the Animal Inns group). À la carte prices aren't cheap, but the set lunch and dinner menus are great value and include an imaginative range of Modern European dishes, such as grilled lemon and thyme smoked mackerel.

Where to stay

Rural accommodation close to Norwich is plentiful, ranging from B&Bs such as Salamanca Farm Guest House in Stoke Holy Cross (Norwich Road, 01508 492322, www.a1tourism.com/uk/salamanc.html) to corporate country houses such as Caistor Hall in Caistor St Edmund (01508 494998, www.caistor hall.com), which has 21 large luxurious bedrooms. You'll need to book well ahead for Hillside Farm in Bergh Apton (Welbeck Road, 01508 550260, www.hillside-farm.com), a gorgeous 16th-century thatched farmhouse with just two rooms, and the Old Rectory in Framingham Pigot (01508 493082, www.norfolkoldrectory.co.uk), an elegant Georgian house with a lovely spacious garden once owned by the Bishop of Norwich.

JD Young Hotel
2-4 Market Place, Harleston, IP20 9AD (01379 852822, www.jdyoung.co.uk). Rates £90 double incl breakfast.
A 15th-century coaching inn with 11 comfortable rooms. The restaurant is equally charming, with a menu of English standards that are well cooked and keenly priced, not to mention a better-than-average wine selection.

Old Bakery ★
Church Walk, Pulham Market, IP21 4SL (01379 676492, www.theoldbakery.net). Rates £75-£85 double incl breakfast.
You can't miss the Old Bakery, thanks to its pale pink exterior. Inside, the 1580 listed building is pleasingly sedate, with wattle and daub walls, exposed internal beams and three attractive, chintz-free rooms, all en suite.

Scole Inn
Ipswich Road, Scole, IP21 4DR (01379 740481, www.oxfordhotelsandinns.com). Rates £85 double incl breakfast.
A Jacobean hand-carved staircase and original hand-painted sundial are just some of the period features in this grand 17th-century coaching inn. The 12 rooms in the main building come with their own working fireplace; 12 more modern rooms are located in adjoining converted Georgian stables. There's also a restaurant and a bar.

DISS & ATTLEBOROUGH

Diss
West of the A140 – which bisects the county from Cromer in the north to Scole in the south – a wealth of traditional Norfolk villages are packed together like peas in a pod, each with their own individual quirks and appeal. Tucked in the south-east corner

Wymondham Abbey. See p141.

of the area is Diss, a particular favourite of Sir John Betjeman. It's easy to see why. Norfolk's most southerly town is a delight, ranged around a large mere (lake) with a park on its southern side where numerous waterfowl come to feed. The town's commercial area is north of the lake, from where you get tantalising glimpses of the water from little alleyways and pubs such as the aptly named Waterfront Inn. Buildings span a range of styles and periods (Tudor, Georgian, Victorian) and there are plenty of independent shops. If you're here on a Friday, don't miss the auction at TW Gaze (Roydon Road, 01379 650306, www.twgaze.com), which could include anything from modern 20th-century furniture to medieval pieces – and don't be surprised if auctioneer Elizabeth Talbot looks familiar: she's a regular on BBC2's *Flog It!*.

The heart of the shopping area is Market Place (once the poultry market and still home to a Friday market), where the tiny Westgate department store is dwarfed by the giant Georgian post office next door. Diss Museum (*see p141*) is housed in the Victorian Shambles, a pretty building with Tuscan columns set on a cast-iron verandah; the impressive half-timbered Tudor coaching inn behind it is now a Nepalese/ Indian restaurant. A wander up Market Hill and St Nicholas Street, home to grand St Mary's Church, reveals more architectural delights, such as the 1854 Corn Exchange and numerous half-timbered houses and buildings, including the impressive Saracen's Head (*see p139*). The Diss Publishing Bookshop (40 Mere Street, 01379 644612, www.diss publishing.co.uk, closed Sun) resembles a boathouse and is stuffed with books, gifts and a coffee shop.

The only thing lacking is a good food and drink scene. If the pubs don't appeal, try the various restaurants in Norfolk House Yard, including Les Amandines (vegetarian) and Singtong (Thai).

Diss to Attleborough

Heading west from Diss on the A1066, it's only a few miles to the excellent Bressingham Steam & Gardens (*see p141*). Nearby are two churches of note, both called St Andrew. The tower at South Lopham is a massive, squat Norman affair, while Fersfield's version is tall and slim, surrounded by graceful yew trees and open fields.

A few miles north at Kenninghall, the friendly Red Lion (*see p139*), located opposite another appealing church, is a good pit stop. The sprawling layout of the village is ideal for a post-lunch stroll; do look round the 18th-century panelled Baptist church that's now home to the oddly named Suffolk Potteries (Lopham Road, 01379 687424, www.suffolkpotteries.co.uk, closed Sat, Sun).

Further west, Brettenham is noteworthy for its unusual red-brick estate houses and a High Gothic Victorian pile designed by Samuel Sanders Teulon that sports all the architect's best features, including a cluster of wonderfully over-the-top Gothic towers and spires. It's privately owned, but the gates are often open, so you might get a peek at the rooftop and the lake. Consolation for fans of the architect lies in the local church of St Mary, rebuilt by Teulon in 1852, though it's an understated example of his style, and in his bridge over the Little Ouse at nearby Rushford.

This part of Norfolk is just jammed with notable churches. Yet another impressive example is at East Harling: 15th-century St Peter & St Paul is one of the county's best Perpendicular chuches, with a number of interesting features; pick up a leaflet at the door to make sure you don't miss any. The late medieval stained glass in the east window is stunning.

More points of interest lie north of Diss. Social history enthusiasts can drop into the Burston Strike School (*see p141*) to pay their respects, while World War II enthusiasts can visit the 100th Bomb Group Memorial Museum (*see p141*)

NORFOLK

in Dickleburgh. If you have kids in tow, Banham Zoo (see p141), seven miles north-west of Diss, is probably a better bet.

Banham is a hop, skip and jump from New Buckenham, a 12th-century example of town planning whose wealthy-looking but unpretentious air, as well as some fascinating buildings, reward exploration. Ranged around a green on which sits the curious Market Cross – a tiny 16th-century building that was raised up on Tuscan columns a century after it was built – are two pubs, including the George (see p138), and a cluster of medieval cottages. For a pleasant walk, head down King Street to twee gift shop La Maison (01953 860713, www.lamaisongiftsandinteriors.com); its first-floor café resembles something out of Alice in Wonderland, all gingham curtains and delicate wrought-iron furniture covered in polka-dot oilcloths, and the setting for delicious own-made cakes and sandwiches. Continue past a lovely group of almshouses to the remains of the 12th-century 'new' castle built by Norman baron William D'Albini

as a replacement for his previous fortress at Old Buckenham. 'Remains' could be slightly overstating the grassy site; what was once an impressive round keep – the first known example in England – surrounded by a large castle, is now mainly a series of depressions, small mounds and ditches. The common to the east of the village has been untouched grazing land for 800 years.

A couple of miles away, Old Buckenham has a huge village green – the largest in England, it's claimed – a 19th-century cornmill (01603 222705, this used to be open to the public on occasional weekends, but it's currently closed until further notice) and a great pub, the Gamekeeper (see p138).

Further east lies Forncett St Peter, home to a round-towered church that's beautiful in both setting and design. Wander around the overgrown graveyard to admire the exterior, notably the superb Saxon tower and imposing north porch. Inside – you'll need to get the key from the churchwarden, Bev Poole (01953 788036) – are some very convincing faux-medieval Victorian bench ends and two 15th-century

Wymondham. See p140.

Wildebeest Arms. See p135.

engraved tomb chests. Nearby twin Forncett St Mary contains the quirky Forncett Industrial Steam Museum (*see p141*), which is open on occasional Sundays. Otherwise, the villages are unremarkable, so it's best to push on to Tasburgh, five miles north-east, for some bucolic rolling scenery and a walk along the banks of the River Tas, taking in the Elizabethan manor house of Rainthorpe Hall and the quaint hamlet of Newton Flotman with its fine 16th-century bridge.

Attleborough

Wymondham and Attleborough sit on the A11, seven miles from each other. Both are fairly typical Norfolk market towns, but for shopaholics and foodies, Attleborough has the edge, thanks to the Mulberry Tree (*see p138*), and a main road crammed with heaps of independent retailers, charity shops and tearooms. Many of the buildings are relatively new for Norfolk, the town having expanded around the railway line built here in 1840, but a few quaint oldies still exist: the whitewashed Griffin Hotel on the High Street is an elegant example of the town's medieval past. The businesses on the High Street are housed in cute bow-fronted buildings or more handsome two- and three-storey Georgian blocks, all combining to create a great example of an unspoilt Georgian market town.

Things to do

HARLESTON & AROUND

Playbarn

Westgreen Farm, Shotesham Road, Poringland, NR14 7LP (01508 495526, www.theplaybarn.co.uk). Open 9.30am-3.30pm Tue-Fri; 10am-5pm Sun. Admission £1-£1.50; £4-£6 reductions.
A rainy-day saviour in the form of an indoor and outdoor playcentre for under-7s, with pedal tractors, climbing apparatus, sandpit, ball pool and soft play inside, and a small farm, pony rides, tractor rides, and picnic and play areas outside.

The church, St Mary, is a knockout. Built in Norman and Early English styles, the exterior is imposing rather than charming. But inside is a delicately carved, 15th-century oak screen that spans the church's entire 52-foot width. The panels still contain wonderful colours, as do the fragments of wall painting above the crossing arch. The windows and a stone font with humorous faces are worth examining too, and if the organ's blasting triumphantly as you explore, it makes the experience all the better.

Outside, a six-foot pyramid marks the grave of local Egyptologist Melancthon William Henry Brooke. It's not the county's only one: in the woods at Blickling Hall (*see p70*) in north Norfolk, a pyramid modelled on the Roman tomb of Caius Cestius contains the remains of John Hobart, the 2nd Earl of Buckinghamshire, and his two wives. It predates the 1929 tomb of Brooke by almost 140 years.

On the eastern edge of Attleborough is Besthorpe Hall (01953 450300, http://besthorpe.com). In spring thousands of bluebells carpet the grounds, but there's year-round interest for horticulture buffs in this 16th-century home of the Drury family, who gave their name to London's Drury Lane. Visiting is by appointment only.

Where to eat & drink

There's no shortage of traditional village pubs serving tasty, inventive own-cooked food in this part of the county. Standouts include the Burston Crown in Burston (Mill Road, 01379 741257, www.burstoncrown.com); the George (01953 860043, www.thegeorgenewbuckenham.co.uk) in New Buckenham; and the Gamekeeper (01953 860397, www.thegamekeeperfreehouse.com) in Old Buckenham.

Mulberry Tree ★

Station Road, Attleborough, NR17 2AS (01953 452124, www.the-mulberry-tree.co.uk). Open 11am-11pm Mon-Sat. Lunch served noon-2pm, dinner served 6.30-9pm Mon-Sat.

Boutique hotel-restaurants are rare round these parts, making the Mulberry an unexpected and luxurious oasis. Food is Modern British done simply and well – venison steak with bubble and squeak, pickled pear and stilton salad or smoked haddock with cauliflower cheese – all served in a space that's warm and cosy. There's a good wine list too. Upstairs are five comfortable bedrooms (£90 double incl breakfast), decorated in a low-key, stylish manner.

Red Lion
East Church Street, Kenninghall, NR16 2EP (01953 887849, www.redlionkenninghall.co.uk). Open noon-3pm, 5.30-11pm Mon-Thur; noon-11pm Fri, Sat; noon-10pm Sun. Lunch served noon-2pm Mon-Sat; noon-2.30pm Sun. Dinner served 7-9pm Mon-Thur, Sun; 7-9.30pm Fri, Sat.
A pink-painted village pub with a small bar and snug and equally tiny dining alcoves where own-cooked food is served daily. Bar snacks such as olives, houmous and pitta bread are available, as well as standards such as local gammon and steak and kidney pudding. B&B accommodation consists of four simple rooms (£65 double incl breakfast).

Saracen's Head
75 Mount Street, Diss, IP22 4QQ (01379 652853, www.saracensheaddiss.co.uk). Open 10am-3pm, 6.30-11pm daily. Lunch served noon-2.30pm, dinner served 6.30-9.30pm daily.
This striking timber-framed building, parts of which are more than 500 years old, is a beauty. The food's good too: traditional pub grub is given a nice twist in dishes such as peppered calves' liver, but purists will appreciate the likes of Lowestoft fish and chips and Norfolk gammon steak. The single, double and family rooms (£60 double incl breakfast) are pub standard too, comfortable and cosy.

Where to stay
Three of the area's best places to eat – the Mulberry Tree (*see p138*) in Attleborough, the Red Lion (*see above*) in Kenninghall and the Saracen's Head (*see above*) in Diss – also offer rooms.

In North Lopham, Church Farm House (Church Road, 01379 687270, www.churchfarmhouse.org) offers three rooms in the Grade II-listed farmhouse, all featuring antique furniture, rich textiles and views of the church. The sitting and dining rooms are cosy and warm, particularly when the log fire is blazing away. A candlelit evening meal is also available.

In Great Moulton, Oakbrook House (Frith Way, 01379 677359, www.oakbrookhouse.co.uk), formerly the village school, is now a friendly, comfortable, nine-bedroom guesthouse, with decor that's easy on the eye and evening meals served on request; bring your own wine for just £1 corkage.

Dickleburgh Hall
Semere Green Lane, Dickleburgh, IP21 4NT (01379 741259, www.dickhall.co.uk). Rates £85 double incl breakfast. No credit cards.
Set in extensive open countryside that includes an 18-hole private golf course, old-fashioned Dickleburgh Hall has comfortable, cottagey-style en suite rooms, as well as a sweet self-contained cottage in the grounds. There's also a croquet lawn, billiards table and indoor badminton court.

CULTURAL CONNECTIONS

● Holkham Beach appears in the final scene of *Shakespeare in Love*, with Gwyneth Paltrow strolling across the expansive sands.
● American travel writer and self-confessed Anglophile Bill Bryson has lived in the market town of Wymondham since 2003.
● Great Yarmouth features heavily in *David Copperfield*. Dickens visited the town in 1849, staying at the Royal Hotel on Marine Parade.
● Steve Coogan's 1990s spoof presenter Alan Partridge is a Norfolk local, broadcasting his *Up with the Partridge* show on Radio Norwich.
● Sir John Betjeman was a frequent visitor to Diss from the early 1960s. The town inspired his poem 'A Mind's Journey to Diss', addressed to Harold Wilson's wife Mary, who was born in the town. 'Dear Mary, yes, it will be bliss, to go with you by train to Diss', it begins.
● Although born across the border in Mendham, Suffolk, Edwardian artist Alfred Munnings spent much of his formative years in Norfolk, receiving formal training at the Norwich School of Art. His early paintings are filled with scenes of rural East Anglia.
● Stephen Fry's *Kingdom*, an ITV drama about a small-town solicitor in the fictional Norfolk town of Market Shipborough, was shot mainly in Swaffham, though Wells-next-the-Sea, Holkham and Hunstanton also appear.
● Distinguished author and academic WG Sebald set up home in the town of Wymondham and later the village of Poringland, after emigrating from Germany to work at the University of East Anglia in the 1970s. He died in a car crash near Norwich in 2001.
● Sir Arthur Conan Doyle wrote his Sherlock Holmes mystery story *The Dancing Men* while staying in the 16th-century Hill House in Happisburgh.
● Parts of Stanley Kubrick's 1987 film *Full Metal Jacket* were filmed around the Norfolk Broads, which stood in for the paddy fields of Vietnam.

NORFOLK

Gissing Hall
Upper Street, Gissing, IP22 5UN (01379 677291, www.
gissinghall.co.uk). Rates £55-£75 double incl breakfast.
This handsome red-brick 15th-century mansion, five miles
north of Diss, makes a great rural retreat. It has 22 rooms
of varying sizes and prices, from small doubles to four-
posters. All are decorated in tasteful tones (you'll look in
vain for chintz) and the grounds are great for a post-
breakfast amble.

Park Hotel
29 Denmark Street, Diss, IP22 4LE (01379 642244,
www.parkhotel-diss.co.uk). Rates £65 double incl
breakfast.
Within walking distance of Diss town centre, the Park offers
20 individually designed rooms, furnished with nice
wrought-iron or wooden sleigh beds, and spread across
two buildings. The restaurant is popular for its carvery and
set menus.

WYMONDHAM & HINGHAM
The triangular parcel of land that lies between the
A11 and the A47 splits into two types of terrain:
the heaths and forests of the Brecks that stretch
from Attleborough to Swaffham in the west, and the
more affluent villages near Norwich. The former area
is great for walking and wooded adventures, while
the latter has more to offer those whose outward-
bound activities tend towards a post-prandial
village amble rather than a long-distance hike.
There are the market towns of Wymondham, Watton
and Hingham, plus a slew of eminently enjoyable
villages such as Shipdham, Kimberley, Bawburgh,
Hethersett, Great Hockham and Great Ellingham.

Wymondham & around
Wymondham – pronounced 'Windum' – is the
largest and most historically interesting town in
the area, with a huge and splendid twin-towered
abbey (*see p141*) that's visible for miles around.
There are good places to eat, including the 15th-
century Green Dragon pub (*see p144*) and the
award-winning Brief Encounter Refreshment
Room (*see p143*) at Wymondham Station. This is
also where the volunteer-run Mid-Norfolk Railway
(01362 690633, www.mnr.org.uk) operates.
Trains (sometimes with steam engines) travel
the 11 miles to Dereham on weekends and bank
holidays; check the website for exact days of
operation. In the town centre is the pretty Market
Cross, on Market Place, built in 1617-18 and
home to the local tourist office (01953 604721,
www.south-norfolk.gov.uk, closed Sun Apr-Oct,
closed Tue-Thur, Sun Nov-Mar). The nearby streets
are lined with charity shops, independent gift and
food stores – including an outpost of the award-
winning Samphire farm shop (*see p76*) – assorted
tearooms, a supermarket and the Wymondham
Heritage Museum (*see p141*). Market day is Friday,
and there's also a monthly farmers' market.
   The museum contains information on Robert
and William Kett, leaders of the peasants' uprising
in 1549 that would become known as Kett's
Rebellion; the rebellion's reputed rallying point is a
few miles outside town, at Kett's Oak, just before
Hethersett. This large village has some interesting
Tudor, Stuart and Georgian buildings, an impressive
church in the form of St Remigius (14th century in
origin but mainly Victorian inside) and the upmarket
Park Farm Country Hotel (*see p144*).

Mulberry Tree. See p138.

Places to visit

DISS & ATTLEBOROUGH

Banham Zoo
Kenninghall Road, Banham, NR16 2HE (01953 887771, www.banhamzoo.co.uk). Open 10am-4pm daily. Admission £9.50; £6.95 reductions.
From big cats to meerkats and Shire horses to giraffes, this is traditional zoo territory, all 35 acres of it. So you get feeding sessions and talks, close-up presentations, birds of prey displays and plenty of other interactive experiences, as well as a café and gift shop.

Bressingham Steam & Gardens ★
Thetford Road, Bressingham, IP22 2AB (01379 686900, www.bressingham.co.uk). Open Mar-Oct 10.30am-5pm daily. Admission £8-£12; £4.50-£10.50 reductions.
This mix of spectacular gardens and impressive collection of steam engines and locomotives (including a Victorian steam carousel and the famous 6100 Royal Scott locomotive) shouldn't work but it does. Possibly because tootling around the former in one of the latter (via not one but four narrow-gauge railway rides) is a delightful way to admire the work and dedication that horticulture and steam enthusiast Alan Bloom put into the project from its inception in the 1940s. Kids will adore the fire museum too – almost another attraction in its own right – while older folks might like the memorabilia relating to TV show *Dad's Army*.

Burston Strike School
Church Green, Burston (01379 741337). Open phone for details.
This tiny school in a tiny village is the site of the longest strike in history, a 25-year boycott of a state school that began in April 1914 when pupils of the Burston village school walked out to protest the dismissal of their teachers, Tom and Kitty Higdon. In 1939 the school became a museum and archive, and it hosts an annual festival at which Tony Benn is a regular speaker.

Diss Museum
The Shambles, 4 Market Place, Diss, IP22 4AB (01379 650618). Open May-Aug 2-4pm Wed, Thur; 10am-4pm Fri, Sat; 2.30-4.30pm Sun. Mar, Apr, Sept-Nov 2-4pm Wed, Thur; 10am-4pm Fri, Sat. Admission free.
This tiny museum tells the story of the town through memorabilia including the Old Rectory Doll's House, sepia photos and information panels.

English Whisky Company
Harling Road, Roundham, NR16 2QW (01953 717939, www.englishwhisky.co.uk). Open 10am-5.30pm daily. Admission £4.75; £2 reductions.
Take a tour and find out how whisky is made (using locally grown malting barley), then sample the only whisky distilled in England. The shop stocks the finished results, plus more than 200 other whiskies.

Forncett Industrial Steam Museum
Low Road, Forncett St Mary, NR16 1JJ (01508 488277, http://oldenginehouse.users.btopenworld.com). Open May-Nov 11am-5pm 1st Sun of mth; other times by appointment. Admission £6; £5 reductions. No credit cards.

English Whisky Company

A collection of large industrial steam engines (including one that used to open London's Tower Bridge), plus a pretty rooftop tearoom.

100th Bomb Group Memorial Museum
Common Road, Dickleburgh, IP21 4PH (01379 740708, www.100bgmus.org.uk). Open Mar-Oct 10am-5pm Sat, Sun. Admission free.
Sited at the wartime base of the 100th Bomb Group and B17 Fortress Bomber, this fascinating museum – spread across a site that includes a Nissan hut, control tower and engine shed – contains an impressive collection of models and memorabilia evocatively telling the moving story of the American airmen and ground crew based here from 1943-45.

WYMONDHAM & HINGHAM

Wymondham Abbey ★
Church Street, Wymondham, NR18 0PH (01953 607061, www.wymondhamabbey.com). Open phone or check website for details. Admission free.
The story of the two towers (one ruined, one unfinished) of this magnificent Norman abbey, founded in 1107, is one of the most fascinating in its history, involving centuries-long bitter disputes between parishioners and Benedictine monks. But there are plenty of other tales to discover, about the gorgeous angel roofs, the two 18th-century organs, the beautiful nave made of Caen stone, the grisly death of rebel William Kett on the walls of the western tower and the glistening gilded screen built by Sir Ninian Comper as a memorial to the local men killed in World War I. The best way to see it all is on one of the regular guided tours, but you'll get a huge amount just from looking around the abbey, where various leaflets and church guides are available.

Wymondham Heritage Museum
10 The Bridewell, Norwich Road, Wymondham, NR18 0NS (01953 607494, www.wymondham heritagemuseum.co.uk). Open Mar-Oct 10am-4pm Mon-Sat; 2-4pm bank hol Mon, 1st Sun of mth. Admission £3; 50p-£2 reductions. No credit cards.
Located in the former Bridewell, which has seen service as various prisons, a police station and a court in its 200-year history, the Museum offers an engaging history of the town.

For more information, visit www.country-markets.co.uk.

Aylsham
Market Place, NR11 6EL (01263 733354, www.aylsham-tc.gov.uk). Open General market 9am-5pm Mon, Fri. Farmers' market 8am-1pm 1st & 3rd Sat of mth.
The weekly Town Hall market sells a fine range of cooked foods and preserves. The deservedly popular farmers' market adds organic meat, eggs and plants to the mix. *See also p76.*

Fakenham
Corn Hall, Market Place, NR21 9AQ (01328 850104, http://fakenham towncouncil.org.uk). Open Charter market 8am-noon Thur. Farmers' market 8am-noon 4th Sat of mth.
Running for more than 35 years, this outdoor market is one of Norfolk's oldest Women's Institute markets, and still one of the best; the chutneys and preserves are ace. The monthly farmers' market offers cheeses from local producer Catherine Temple (*see p101*), locally sourced partridge, pheasant and wild venison, soups, wines, pastries and a whole host of other tempting goodies. *See also p59.*

Harleston
General market: Market Place, IP20 (01379 854519, www.harleston-norfolk.org.uk). Open 6am-3pm Wed. Farmers' market: Swan Hotel, The Thoroughfare, IP20 9AS (01379 852221, www.harlestonswanhotel. co.uk). Open 9am-1pm 3rd Sat of mth.
The weekly general market is a traditional outdoor one, the monthly farmers' market is held indoors, so a nice option for rainy days. Arrive early to get the best choice of the scrumptious home-made cakes. *See also p133.*

King's Lynn
Tuesday Market Place, IP30 1JL (01553 616202). Open 8am-3pm Tue, Fri.
Produce sells out fast at this popular outdoor market, so rock up early to pick up delicious own-made sausage rolls and pies, as well as plenty of produce direct from farms. *See also p23.*

North Walsham
St Benets' Hall, Vicarage Street, NR28 9DQ (01603 667940). Open 9am-12.30pm 2nd & 5th Sat of mth.
This friendly, twice-monthly market stocks a great range of local seasonal produce, including baked goods, fish, game, salad, honey and beeswax products, pies, ready-meals and preserves. *See also p101.*

A few miles north on the River Yare is Bawburgh, definitely worth a visit to see the cone-topped round tower, late medieval stained glass and fascinating mish-mash of building styles at the church of St Mary & St Walstan, and for the excellent King's Head pub (*see p144*). Ketteringham (south of Hethersett and the A11) is worth a stop too; this estate village has some lovely neo-Tudor cottages and another church, St Peter, notable for its monuments and stained glass. From the tower you get a great bird's-eye view of stately Ketteringham Hall, a Tudor/mock Gothic pile owned by Colin Chapman, chairman of the Lotus car group, and now used as a business centre.

Head west for the riverside mill buildings of Barnham Broom and the thatched cottages and Regency lodge houses of Kimberley; both are likeable, picturesque sites good for walking. If you're after some pampering, check out Barnham Broom hotel, golf and country club (*see p144*) or, more unusually, the upmarket tipi garden at Kimberley Hall (*see p144*).

Hingham & around
The small market towns of Watton and Hingham vie for attention in a competitive fashion. The former contains a couple of oddities: a curious 1679 clocktower on the High Street and, inside St Mary's Church, an engaging 1639 poorbox in the form of a carved wooden grinning priest with the inscription 'Remember the poore', whose hand drops your contribution through to a bag. The round church tower is Norman, topped by a later octagonal band with some lovely stonework.

But in the battle of the picturesque, Hingham ★ wins hands down, thanks to a breathtaking display of Georgian town houses that made it one of the most fashionable places in the area in the 18th century. A century earlier, people couldn't get out fast enough: the charming town sign commemorates the exodus of the many parishioners who followed in the footsteps of Robert Peck, the village's one-time vicar and Puritan, who left for America in the early part of the 17th century, founding a new Hingham in Massachusetts. Samuel Lincoln, ancestor of Abraham, was one of the emigrants.

Today, Hingham has the appeal of a substantial village, with an interesting array of shops, pubs and restaurants. Standouts include Lincoln's Tea Shoppe & Bistro (*see p143*) on the smaller of the two greens; architectural salvage shop Mongers ★ (15 Market Place, 01953 851868, www.mongers ofhingham.co.uk, closed Sun), which has a wealth of wonderful stuff sprawling across gardens, sheds and a yard outside and a warren of rooms inside; and Harrods of Hingham general store (7 Church Street, 01953 851455, closed Sun), which specialises in local produce. The White Hart Inn (*see p144*) is huge; you can't miss the 14th-century church of St Andrew either, thanks to its colossal 120-foot-high tower; it also has an impressive 15th-century tomb and some notable stained glass.

Another equally arresting church, All Saints, can be found six miles north at the village of Shipdham – which is notable for being the very centre of Norfolk. The church tower is topped by a very unusual and delicate cupola made of lead and wood, which looks distinctly at odds with the solid Norman features beneath it. A few miles south of Hingham, another clutch of villages – Great Hockham and the Elllinghams – offer something of interest for the weary village wanderer. There are yet more lovely churches at Great and Little Ellingham, while Great Hockham is a textbook south Norfolk village if ever there was one. Thatched cottages nestle around a triangular village green; there's a primary school and popular local pub; lively village customs exist in the form of the Horn Fair in May and the dancing Clodhoppers; and on the village outskirts is a grand Queen Anne mansion, Hockham Hall, and a large church with some striking medieval wall paintings.

Where to eat & drink

Wymondham has two fine cafés: the Coffee Shop (25 Market Street, 01953 423482, closed Sun), which serves towering slices of victoria sponge, and the tearoom at the Heritage Museum (*see p141*) in what was the prisoners' exercise yard.

In Hingham, Lincoln's Tea Shoppe & Bistro (The Fairlands, 01953 851357, www.lincolns-of-hingham.co.uk, closed Sun), is great for lunch or dinner, and features lots of fish.

Pub enthusiasts will enjoy the food, drink and decor at the 16th-century Ye Old Buck Inn (29 The Street, 01603 880393, www.honinghambuck.co.uk) in Honingham, while the White Hart (47 The Street, 01953 483361, www.thewhitehartrocklands.co.uk, closed Mon) in Rockland All Saints makes up for its lack of outward charm with a great menu whose ingredients are sourced as much as possible from a five-mile radius. Country hotels Barnham Broom (*see p144*) and Park Farm (*see p144*) both have restaurants that offer something a bit special.

Angel Inn
Sallow Lane, Larling, NR16 2QU (01953 717963, http://larlingangel.moonfruit.com). Open 10am-11pm daily. Food served noon-9.30pm Thur-Sat.
This whitewashed freehouse just off the A11, halfway between Thetford and Attleborough, is a regular in the *Good Pub Guide* for its changing range of well-kept real ales from Norfolk and elsewhere and its August beer festival. It's also a good place to eat, with own-cooked traditional dishes and an oak-panelled dining room that's full of warmth and original features. There are also B&B rooms (£80 double incl breakfast) and camping from March to October.

Brief Encounter Refreshment Room & Restaurant ★
Station Approach, Wymondham, NR18 0JZ (01953 606433, www.wymondham-station.com). Open 8am-3pm daily.
Unremarkable from the outside, the interior of Wymondham railway station is given over to the jaw-dropping Brief Encounter restaurant, a faithful homage to the classic stiff-upper-lip wartime weepie. The traditional British food, from snacks to a full à la carte menu, is surprisingly good. There's also a tiny museum and bookshop.

Norwich
Gentlemans Walk, NR2 1ND (01603 213537, www.norwich-market.co.uk). Open 9am-4pm Mon-Sat.
A fabulous, old-school daily market with more than 190 stalls, including organic produce from Salle Organics, a Brazilian groceries stall, herbs and spices, a very good cheese stall, local Aldous ice-cream, shellfish at the Drunken Prawn and even a little deli. *See also p85.*

Produced In Norfolk Farmers' Market
Wroxham Barns, Tunstead Road, nr Hoveton, NR12 8QU (08458 951096, www.producedinnorfolk.com). Open 10am-1pm 2nd Sat of mth.
This award-winning enterprise, set up to promote and revitalise Norfolk's rural economies, is a must if you want to sample and buy food direct from local producers. At its monthly market at Wroxham Barns (*see p113*), you'll find rare-breed pork and pork products, pickles and preserves, dairy goods and a dizzying array of fruit and vegetables.

Sheringham
St John's Hall, Wyndham Street, Sheringham, NR26 8BA (01263 822213). Open General market Wed (Apr-Nov), Sat. Country market 10am-11.30am 1st & 3rd Thur of mth.
Two popular markets that between them offer a wonderful selection of products. Visit the general market for fruit and veg, plants, clothing, electrical goods, music, art and even gemstones, and the country market for yummy foodstuffs such as spicy Jamaican marmalade, lavender honey and piles of cakes and pies. *See also p67.*

Swaffham
Market Place, PE37 7AB (01760 722922, www.swaffhamtown council.gov.uk). Open 9am-1pm Sat.
Some 90 stalls fill what must be one of Norfolk's loveliest Georgian market squares; come for the traditional produce and prepared foods, as well as crafts and second-hand bric-a-brac. *See also p150.*

Wayland Farmers' Market
High Street, Watton, IP25 6AR (01953 883915, www.wayland.org.uk/ farmersmarket.html). Open Feb-Dec 8.30am-12.30pm 1st Sat of mth.
This terrific not-for-profit farmers' market in Watton, nine miles south-east of Swaffham, stocks produce exclusively sourced within a 30-mile radius. Stallholders offer heaps of tasting opportunities and special seasonal events, as well as organising occasional art shows and craft fairs.

Green Dragon
6 Church Street, Wymondham, NR18 0PH (01953 607907). Open noon-3pm, 5-11pm Mon-Fri; noon-11.30pm Sat; noon-10.30pm Sun. Lunch served noon-3pm, dinner served 5.30-8.30pm Mon-Fri. Meals served noon-8pm Sat; noon-7pm Sun.
The oldest pub in Wymondham features beams and timber everywhere, as well as leaded Tudor windows, roaring fires in rickety bars and a pretty walled garden. Wi-Fi and en suite rooms (£55 double incl breakfast) put it firmly in the 21st century. Traditional food and a selection of real ales complete the picture.

Kings Head
Harts Lane, Bawburgh, NR9 3LS (01603 744977, www.kingshead-bawburgh.co.uk). Open 11am-11pm Mon-Sat; 11am-10.30pm Sun. Lunch served noon-2pm daily. Dinner served 5.30-9pm Mon-Sat.
The King's Head was nominated for two categories (Best Norfolk Menu and Chef of the Future) in the 2009 Eastern Daily Press Food Awards. Deservedly so: chef Lewis Burrell creates excellent, beautifully presented gastropub fare, at very reasonable prices. Local produce is to the fore; in fact, the suppliers are listed on the menu. The interior is charming too, with wooden settles, leather sofas, low-beamed ceilings and inglenook fireplaces.

Where to stay

A number of pubs offer accommodation, including the Green Dragon (*see above*) in Wymondham, the Angel Inn (*see p143*) in Larling and the White Hart (3 Market Place, 01953 850214) in Hingham, where a recent change of hands and refurbished rooms have resulted in good reviews. Elm Lodge (Downham Grove, 01953 607501, www.smooth hound.co.uk/hotels/elmlodge) offers comfortable B&B accommodation in a large red-brick country house with two acres of garden and woodland on the edge of Wymondham.

For something completely different, consider Kimberly Hall Tipi Garden (01603 759447, www.kimberleyhall.co.uk). Set in an 18th-century walled garden are six well-equipped tipis (each one sleeping six), two pavilion tents and a field kitchen, with toilets, showers and seasonal swimming pool close by. You'll need a large group and bank balance, though, as the site is only hired as a whole.

Barnham Broom Hotel
Honingham Road, Barnham Broom, NR9 4DD (01603 759393, www.barnham-broom.co.uk). Rates £85-£140 double incl breakfast.
Ideal for traditionalists looking for a very relaxing break in a top-notch country hotel, with spa and golf packages available. The 46 bedrooms and suites are decorated in a smart corporate style, and the restaurant offers an inventive menu of British dishes, such as roast Norfolk pork loin and bread and buttter pudding.

Park Farm Country Hotel
Norwich Road, Hethersett, NR9 3DL (01603 810264, www.parkfarm-hotel.com). Rates £130-£185 double incl breakfast.
One for lovers of space, this Georgian building is set in 200 acres and offers 53 well-appointed rooms, ranging from standard to boutique-style, as well as a spa and gym facilities. There's also a bar and a restaurant serving Modern British food with the emphasis on local fish and meat.

Sallowfield Cottage ★
Wattlefield, NR18 9NX (01953 605086, www.sallowfieldcottage.co.uk). Rates from £60 double incl breakfast.
Three nicely decorated rooms (two en suite, one with a private bathroom) are available in this lovely former dairy three miles outside Wymondham. What makes the place special are the expansive, award-winning gardens, set around a large pond and with plenty of outdoor seating.

Barnham Broom Hotel

The Fens & the Brecks

There's a bench in the WWT Welney Wetland Centre in the heart of the Fens that paraphrases a popular local saying: 'Any fool can appreciate mountains, it takes a discerning eye to appreciate the beauty of the Fens'. And it's true. As you look out across the flat, featureless terrain broken only by old windmills and new wind turbines, it's hard to imagine there's anything here worthy of more than an afternoon's exploration. But, gradually, you discover there's more to the landscape than meets, literally, the eye. Along a quiet road, acres of bright orange pumpkins, looking as if they've just landed from space, delight with their vibrant incongruity; a working windmill serves terrific sandwiches made from its own flour in a pretty tearoom; medieval churches and charming villages offer rich pickings for history and architecture fans; and even if you can't understand their fiendishly complex workings, it's easy to appreciate the Victorian engineering feats used to tame the tides at Denver. Further west, the marshy peat of the Fens gives way to the sandy heaths, pine forests, farms and Neolithic mines of the Brecks, a vast playground spanning two counties, with 370 square miles that have something for everyone.

DOWNHAM MARKET & THE FENS

Looking out across the vast open Fens that stretch west from Downham Market, the flatness pierced only by the occasional church spire, it's not hard to imagine that just over 200 years ago – before the area was successfully drained – much of it was a massive bog. Long before that, millennia ago, it was covered in oak forest, which became flooded after the last Ice Age and eventually rotted down to form the rich peat soils cultivated so aggressively today. Take a walk along any of the numerous paths traversing the Fens and you might trip over proof; the gradual erosion of the soil is revealing the preserved remains of ancient bog oaks, coloured in rich hues of red and blue from the minerals they have absorbed. They're just one of nature's surprises to be discovered in this rich, fertile landscape.

The Fens are also home to an impressive array of Churches Conservation Trust sites (www.visitchurches.org.uk), with three ★ that are definitely worth visiting. Two are in the village of Walpole on the Lincolnshire border: Walpole St Peter and Walpole St Andrew. The former is undoubtedly the big daddy of the three at 160 foot tall, and its highlights could – and do – fill a small book (available in the back of the church). Check out the medieval bosses, among the finest in Norfolk, and the spectacular nave, complete with centuries-old paintings decorating its screens. Smaller St Andrew is celebrated for its unusual octagonal turrets. St Mary the Virgin at Wiggenhall has the best collection of 15th- and 16th-century carved benches in the county, if not England.

Downham Market

The area's main settlement is Downham Market, capital of the Norfolk Fens and one of the county's oldest market towns. These days, the market (held on Fridays and Saturdays) is a lacklustre affair, with just a few uninspiring Poundbuster-style tat stalls bolstered by the occasional continental farmers' market and a fortnightly craft market on summer Saturdays, but there's still enough here to make it a good base for a weekend of pleasurable walking and sightseeing. There are some decent eating and drinking options too.

Nicknamed the 'Gingerbread Town' because of the distinctive yellow brick and rust-brown carrstone used in many of its older buildings, Downham Market sits on rising ground on the edge of the Fens and is surprisingly hilly. The main landmark is the 1878 cast-iron clock tower in the town square. A miniature Big Ben, it's a piece of pure nursery rhyme whimsy, with distinctive black and white panels (originally green and white) and a gothic roof with gold-leaf tracery. Free cardboard miniatures are available from the town's Heritage Centre (see p152). The Tourist Information Centre (Priory Centre, 01366 383287, closed Sat afternoon, Sun) is just south of the square, off Priory Road.

The parish church of St Edmunds is the next building of any note. Dating from Norman times, it has some fine medieval stained glass in the tower and a 15th-century font, but is nowhere near as eye-popping as the Castle Hotel (see p148), a handsome building whose black and white exterior is festooned with overflowing hanging baskets.

Across the border

Peckover House in Wisbech, Lincolnshire (www.nationaltrust.org.uk/peckover) is that rare thing: a historic house that doesn't feel stuffy and museum-like. Imagine you're in a Jane Austen novel and take a turn in the garden too, but don't forget your fan. It's closed Thursday, Friday and November to mid March.

Shopping options are old-fashioned. There's the musty but fascinating Antiques & Collectables (47 Bridge Street, 01366 387700, closed Sun), 1960s-styled My Fair Lady boutique (10 London Road, 01366 383452, closed Sat afternoon) and teeny-tiny, one-time department store AT Johnson. Best is Smallbottom (26 High Street, 01366 380762, closed Sun), a higgledy-piggledy shed selling all manner of 20th-century bric-a-brac. Expect lots of 'my gran had one of those' teapots and dinner services, but also stunning lamps, furniture, clocks and furnishings, all reasonably priced. A number of farm shops are not far away, with notably large ones in the villages of Hilgay and Stowbridge and on the A1122 south of town.

Walkers can access the Fen Rivers Way (www.countrysideaccess.norfolk.gov.uk), a 50-mile path that connects Cambridge with King's Lynn, tracing the course of rivers that drain slowly across the Fens into the Wash. It runs through the town on the west side of the Great Ouse river – get there by strolling down Bridge Street/Railway Road and past the train station.

Denver

If you follow the path south along the river for less than two miles, you'll reach Denver, home to a working windmill (see p152) and a decent pub, the Jenyns Arms (see right), where you can sit in the riverside garden and admire the strutting peacocks while trying to figure out how the fiendishly complex-looking Denver Sluice works. This impressive waterways control system controls river flow, diverts floodwaters and acts as a lock gate between the tidal Ouse to the north and the freshwater rivers to the south. Part of it hails from 1834, though there's been a sluice here for much longer – since 1651, when Dutch engineer Cornelius Vermuyden pioneered a scheme to drain the fenland owned by the Duke of Bedford. For another look at the Fens' unique watery landscape, visit the WWT Welney Wetland Centre (see p152), a few miles further south.

The sluice is not Denver's only claim to fame – pop into the Downham Market Heritage Centre to learn about the grisly Denver murderer, executed in 1837 for killing a local fortune-teller (you'd think she'd have seen it coming).

Villages nearby

As you move east from Downham Market, away from Lincolnshire and into Norfolk proper, there are perceptible shifts in the landscape – and the villages are undoubtedly prettier than their western Fens counterparts. Take Hilgay, a few miles south of the town. Recorded as just one of two settlements in the Norfolk Fens in the Domesday Book, when it was an 'island' (a hilly knoll), time feels as if it has stood still here. There's a pleasing church, of course, All Saints, worth a look for the curious memorial to Denver-born inventor George William Manby, which contains the sad words, 'The public should have paid this tribute.' The walk to the church, which is set some way from the village, is pleasant, via an elegant avenue of

mature lime trees, but you might be just as tempted to chill out on the banks of the peaceful River Wissey or stroll around Hilgay Heronry, a copse designated a Site of Special Scientific Interest for the 40 or so herons that nest there.

Stow Bardolph, a couple of miles north of Downham Market on the A10 (the main road between Cambridge and King's Lynn), is equally enjoyable. Children will love the Church Farm Rare Breeds Centre (see p152), while adults will prefer the excellent Hare Arms (see p148), and both will be creeped out by the alarmingly life-like wax effigy of parishioner Sarah Hare adjacent to Holy Trinity Church – it's been in a mahogany cupboard in the north-west corner of the 1624 Hare Chapel since her death in 1744.

A few miles east lies another lovely village, Barton Bendish. It's worth a visit to examine the unusual decoration on the austere but fascinating village hall, flanked by matching houses in an elegant piece of architectural symmetry, and to pop into the gorgeous little church of St Mary (see p152). Refreshment (and accommodation) is available at the sterling Spread Eagle Inn (see p148).

Where to eat & drink

The Andel Lodge in Tottenhill, and Timbers Hotel in Fincham (for both, see p148) offer typical hotel dining at reasonable prices, but, given the calibre of village pubs in the area and their commitment to using good-quality Norfolk produce, you might want to follow the examples of the locals and head for their locals. The Chequers (7 Church Road, 01366 387704) in the sweet village of Wimbotsham, the Jenyns Arms (01366 383366, www.jenyns.co.uk) in Denver, and the Heron (The Causeway, 01336 384147) in Stow Bridge impress with their extensive range of ales and piles of hearty own-cooked food.

The area's restaurants and tearooms tend to cluster around Downham Market, which has assorted hotel restaurants, as well as Dangs Thai restaurant (51-53 Bridge Street, 01366 388147), where the highly decorative interior will make you feel you're much further east than East Anglia. Denver Mill (see p152) also has a tearoom.

Crown Hotel

12 Bridge Street, Downham Market, PE38 9DH (01366 382322). Open 9.30am-11pm daily. Lunch served noon-2.45pm Mon-Sat; noon-4pm Sun. Dinner served 6-8.45pm daily.

This 16th-century coaching inn has a pleasant outdoor seating area in the old carriage entrance. But if you want to avoid the smokers, best head indoors to the restaurant, which serves old-school classics such as gammon, steaks and fish cakes, and a good selection of beers and wines. You can also eat in the separate Stable bar.

Fenland Express

Downham Market Railway Station, Railway Road, Downham Market, PE38 9EN (01366 386636). Open Café 5am-5pm Mon-Fri. Bar 10am-5pm Mon-Wed; 10am-11pm Thur-Sat. No credit cards.

This sweet café, located in the former station master's office at Downham station, is a terrific spot to enjoy a hearty sausage bap washed down with a half-pint, thanks to a bar that's open during the day and three evenings a week. There's a wide array of snacks, sandwiches and cakes – and second-hand books to browse – but no cooked dishes.

Hare Arms
Stow Bardolph, PE34 3HT (01366 382229, www.the harearms.co.uk). Bar Open 11am-2.30pm, 6-11pm Mon-Sat; 11am-2.30pm, 6-10.30pm Sun. Lunch served noon-2pm, dinner served 7-10pm Mon-Sat. Food served noon-10pm Sun. Restaurant Dinner served 7-11pm Mon-Sat.

Peacocks and chickens wandering round the lovely garden, a roaring fire and great food inside, wonderfully friendly staff, and a bill that doesn't break the bank – it all adds up to what is possibly the perfect pub. The extensive bar menu has plenty of vegetarian dishes and daily specials such as crab salad, but the dinner-only restaurant is the place if you want to push the boat out – it's exceedingly popular, so do book. The £9.50 Sunday roasts are highly recommended, and served all day, hurrah.

Hop & Hog
1 High Street, Downham Market, PE38 9DA (01366 386658). Open 9am-5pm daily. No credit cards.

Local produce is to the fore in the delicious sandwiches and teas served in this friendly, old-fashioned café. It produces its own pickles and chutneys and brews real ale too; so you could try beetroot, organic ginger or apple chutney with a chunky cheese sandwich, accompanied by a glass of stout.

Palmers Restaurant Brasserie
45 High Street, Downham Market, PE38 9HF (01366 388124, www.palmersrestaurant.co.uk). Open noon-3pm, 7-9.30pm Tue-Sat.

The cod art deco branding doesn't bode well, but this is a bright spot – all polished blond wood and blue paintwork – for lunch or dinner if the town pubs don't appeal. An imaginative range of vegetarian dishes includes the likes of roasted butternut squash and wild mushroom risotto.

Spread Eagle Inn ★
Church Road, Barton Bendish, PE33 9GF (01366 347995, www.spreadeaglenorfolk.co.uk). Open 6.30-11pm Mon-Wed; noon-2.30pm, 6.30-11pm Thur-Sat; noon-8pm Sun. Lunch served noon-2.30pm Thur-Sat; noon-6pm Sun. Dinner served 6.30-9pm Mon-Sat.

This village pub manages to be modern yet cosy, and offers plenty of daily specials as well as an appealing bar menu – free-range chicken caesar salad, perhaps, or own-made steak burger with caramelised onion marmalade. All produce is sourced as much as possible in Norfolk. There's also a commendable drinks list and a huge grassy garden in which to relax. If you're in need of accommodation, the five rooms cost from £75 double incl breakfast.

Where to stay

Windy Miller fans might want to check out the self-catering accommodation at Denver Mill (*see p152*): two red-brick Victorian millers' cottages, called 'Wheat' and 'Barley', both sleeping four. The Spread Eagle Inn (*see above*) in Barton Bendish

has five well-appointed rooms converted from the old stable block, with small seating areas outside – excellent for sitting in the sun with a pint while taking advantage of the free Wi-Fi.

Andel Lodge Hotel & Restaurant
48 Lynn Road, Tottenhill, PE33 0RH (01553 810256, www.andellodge.co.uk). Rates £77.50-£97 double incl breakfast.

Well placed for both the Fens and the Wash, Andel Lodge is a small, family-run hotel, with individually decorated rooms, a comfortable, well-stocked bar and a red-velvet restaurant modelled on local Indian meets *Fawlty Towers* – and that's a definite compliment.

Castle Hotel
High Street, Downham Market, PE38 9HF (01366 384311, www.castle-hotel.com). Rates £95 double incl breakfast.

This exuberent, black and white coaching inn has 11 en suite rooms. All have character, and two have four-poster beds and jacuzzis. The decor ranges from plain to elaborate, and the photo-filled lounge bar is a great place for an aperitif before heading out for dinner.

Chestnut Villa
44 Railway Road, Downham Market, PE38 9EB (01366 384099, www.chestnutvilla-downham.co.uk). Rates £25-£60 double incl breakfast.

June and Ted Plumb aren't afraid of colour; the rooms in their homely abode boast lovely bright satin comforters, colourfully painted walls and all the mod-cons you'd expect at a top-quality guest house.

Dial House ★
12 Railway Road, Downham Market, PE38 9EB (01366 385775, www.dialhousebnb.com). Rates £60 double incl breakfast. No credit cards.

Robert and Jacquie Shrimpton bought the late 18th-century Dial House in 2007 and have turned the former maltsters and academy for young gentlemen into a smart B&B, while keeping many of the original features. The three bedrooms are named after the Mumford sisters who ran the academy, just one clue to the obvious delight the owners take in their new venture.

Timbers Hotel & Restaurant
Lynn Road, Fincham, PE33 9HE (01366 347747, www.timbershotel.co.uk). Rates £58.50 double incl breakfast.

The 17 chalet-style rooms in this converted barn complex work well if you want a bit of space and somewhere to sit apart from the bed. All the doubles have separate lounge areas, some with sofa beds (good for kids). The three restaurants have menus to suit all budgets too; for example, from the Simply Timbers menu, you can choose a main course for £6.50 and add a starter or dessert for £1.

Westhall Cottages
20-22 Sluice Road, Denver, PE38 0DY (01366 382987, www.westhallcottages.com). Rates £50 double incl breakfast.

Four rooms set in sweet, old-fashioned Grade II-listed cottages offer a lovely rural base from which to explore the Fens. The local pub and village store are minutes away.

NORFOLK

NORFOLK

West Hall Farm Caravan Park & Fishing Lakes

Sluice Road, Denver, PE38 0DZ (01366 387074, 07790 272 978, www.westhallfarmholidays.co.uk). Rates £10 tent pitch; £7-£14 caravan pitch.

These three camping areas in waterside locations are particularly popular with fishing fans, though only the main Lakeside site takes tents. Facilities (including Wi-Fi) are excellent. Denver Mill is close at hand for daily fresh bread, and the campsite shop and farm shop sell a wide range of local produce. Self-catering options, in cottages and caravans, are available too.

SWAFFHAM & THE BRECKS

Swaffham

If you've seen the Stephen Fry TV series *Kingdom*, you'll be familiar with Swaffham: the Georgian market town doubles as the show's fictional Market Shipborough. However, you might be somewhat disappointed with the real deal; judicious editing and close-cropped shooting work wonders with Swaffham's dowdier aspects.

The best day to visit is Saturday, when the elegant triangular marketplace is abuzz with action. Unlike many country markets, which have been reduced to a few sad stalls, Swaffham's is thriving, with bric-a-brac, books and accessories nestling happily next to local fruit and veg and dairy products, all watched over by the statue of Ceres, Roman goddess of the harvest, who adorns the domed Market Cross.

London Street, the main drag, is home to the diminutive Swaffham Museum (*see p154*), which is also the tourist information centre, and a great café/bookshop, Ceres (no.20, 01760 722504, closed Sun), where you can browse an impressive range of new and used books while scoffing own-made cakes and downing big mugs of tea.

A handful of distinguished buildings, including the Georgian Assembly Rooms, some smart town houses and the grand 15th-century church of St Peter & St Paul (*see p154*) should keep architecture fans happy for an afternoon. There are more churches of interest in nearby villages: All Saints in Necton bears ancient and Victorian motifs and styles in a fascinating architectural mash-up; thatched St Mary's in Beachamwell features some of the best-preserved medieval graffiti in Britain and an 11th-century round tower, one of the earliest in Norfolk; and St Mary's in Houghton-on-the-Hill (*see p154*) contains some remarkable 11th-century wall paintings.

For walkers and cyclists, the long-distance Peddars Way (www.nationaltrail.co.uk/peddarsway), which runs for 45 miles from Knettishall Heath in Suffolk along a Roman road to Holme-next-the-Sea on the north Norfolk coast, is just a mile from the town. There are also plenty of enjoyable villages with striking distance.

Denver Sluice. See p147.

A few miles to the north is Castle Acre ★. One of the prettiest villages in Norfolk, with some key sights and a number of excellent places to eat and stay, it makes a great weekend base. Its attractions are manifold: the picturesque cottages and diminutive versions of Georgian town houses; the massive flint Bailey Gate and the long, manicured Stocks Green; the dramatic ruins of the Norman castle and Cluniac priory (for both, see p153).

Next door is West Acre village, where another ruined priory, the tall chimney of a lime-burning kiln, All Saints' church with adjacent 14th-century priory gate, and West Acre Gardens nursery (see p154) provide a happy couple of hours' exploration. More horticultural pleasures await at Narborough Hall (see p154).

South to Thetford
Heading south from Swaffham, it's not far to the attractive hamlet of Cockley Cley and its reconstruction of an Iceni Village (see p154). Further on are delightful Gooderstone Water Gardens (see p153) and Oxburgh Hall (see p154), a wonderful moated manor house that has belonged to the Bedingfeld family since 1482 and is now run by the National Trust.

Further south towards the Suffolk town of Brandon, Feltwell is worth a stop for the church of St Nicholas, a strikingly elegant and imposing building with its massive Norman tower and huge,

clear glass windows. In the southern Brecks, the amazing prehistoric Grimes Graves (see p153) seems to have landed from another planet altogether, while Thetford Forest (see p154) is a welcome vertical diversion for eyes that have become too used to the horizontal plane. In the underwhelming town of Thetford itself, the Dad's Army Museum & Trail (see p153) offers the chance to learn more about a part of British culture that is as popular as fish and chips. And if you haven't had enough of religious ruins by this point, Thetford Priory (www.english-heritage.org.uk/thetfordpriory), once one of the most important monasteries in East Anglia, also awaits. Though if you've visited Castle Acre Priory, it will disappoint: there's very little to see apart from some wall fragments and an almost-complete 14th-century gatehouse.

Finally, on the county border, Weeting Heath is a wonderful area of Breck heath famous for its rare stone curlews, resident between April and September. It's run by the Norfolk Wildlife Trust (01842 827615, www.norfolkwildlifetrust.org.uk).

Where to eat & drink
Award for best pub name has to go to Cockley Cley's Twenty Church Wardens (01760 721439), which gets packed to the gills on Sunday – perhaps by churchwardens enjoying a well-earned half. The rambling Olde Windmill Inn (01760 756232, www.oldewindmillinn.co.uk) in Great Cressingham is popular for its great choice of real ales and proper pub grub; it also has rooms. In Swaffham, Strattons Hotel (see p159) is the place for a special occasion. Mother Hubbard's (91 Market Place, 01760 721933, www.mother-hubbards.com) offers giant portions of fish and chips, and Rasputin (23 Plowright Place, 01760 724725, closed Mon, dinner Sun) specialises, as you might expect, in Russian cuisine.

Café at Brovey Lair
Carbrooke Road, Ovington, IP25 6SD (01953 882706, www.broveylair.com). Open 7.45pm daily.
Chef Tina Pemberton and husband Mike moved to Norfolk from London in 2000 to open a fish restaurant that marries the cooking of the Pacific Rim with flavours closer to home – and it's worked a treat, as the plaudits attest. The restaurant's success is largely down to Tina cooking things she likes – there's just one four-course set menu each evening, for £47.50. Booking is essential. You can also stay over: two junior suites (£135 double incl breakfast) with private sunny terraces sit in the attractive garden, which also has a heated outdoor pool.

Chocolate Mirror
1 Guildhall Street, Thetford, IP24 2DT (07503 752852). Open 9am-10pm Mon-Fri; 9am-11pm Sat; 9am-9pm Sun.
In a town where dining options are limited, the Chocolate Mirror is a shining beacon – especially for East Anglia's estimated 200,000 Portuguese migrants. They'll feel at home in this busy, lively café, where owner Guilherme serves Portuguese cakes, pastries and snacks, along with more substantial dishes and excellent coffee.

NORFOLK

Places to visit

Church Farm Rare Breeds Centre
*Stow Estate Trust, Home Farm, Stow Bardolph,
PE34 3HU (01366 382162, www.churchfarm
stowbardolph.co.uk). Open Mar-Oct 10am-5pm daily.
Nov-Feb 10am-5pm Thur-Sun. Admission £6.50;
£5.50 reductions; £22 family.*
A clean, well-tended farm where all the animals
(including super-cute piglets, sheep, goats, horses
and a donkey), look like happy cartoon ones. The
chickens and giant rabbits in the petting pen, in
particular, look as if they're straight from the pages
of *Alice in Wonderland*. There are also trampolines,
an indoor treehouse, tractor rides and other outdoor
activities to keep children happy for hours.

Denver Mill
*Sluice Road, Denver, PE38 0EG (01366 384009).
Open 10am-4pm daily. Admission £2; £1-£1.50
reductions; £5 family.*
Three generations of milling – wind, steam and electric
– are visible at this wonderfully pungent, fascinating
and still-working windmill, dating from 1835. Work up
an appetite by climbing to the very top of the mill and
wending your way precariously back down the ladders;
the process makes a lot more sense if you do it in
this direction. When you reach ground level, recover
in the mill yard's tearoom with a Denver Doorstep
Sandwich, made using your choice of bread from
the mill's bakery.

Downham Market Heritage Centre
*Downham Market Town Hall, Bridge Road, Downham
Market, PE38 9JS (01366 383355, www.downham
heritage.org.uk). Open 9.30-11.30am Tue; 10am-noon
Fri, Sat. Admission free.*
The Downham Market & District Heritage Society was
formed in 1995, but was homeless until 2002, when
the council offered the town hall's internal balcony as
a home. Pop in if you're interested in the history and
development of the town and, more intriguingly, the
surrounding Fens, all told through a series of panels
and more than 2,000 donated items (fortunately, not
all on show on the groaning balcony).

St Mary, Barton Bendish
*Broughton Long Road, Barton Bendish, PE33 9DP
(www.visitchurches.org.uk). Open by arrangement only.*
Now cared for by the Churches Conservation Trust,
the tiny, thatch-roofed church of St Mary is a real
delight. It's on the outskirts of the village; take the
road to Broughton and it's down the first left-hand
track, hidden by trees. You'll need to get the key from
the big house opposite the entrance. Through the
Norman doorway (deemed by Pevsner to be the finest
in England), you enter a sparse space decorated with
a 14th-century wall painting, a collection of ancient
carved pieces, including a stunning table, and pure
white light. It may not sound like much, but sometimes
less is definitely more.

WWT Welney Wetland Centre
*Hundred Foot Bank, Welney, PE14 9TN (01353
860711, www.wwt.org.uk). Open Nov-Feb 10am-
5pm Mon-Wed; 10am-8pm Thur-Sun. Mar-Oct*
*9.30am-5pm daily. Admission £6.30; £3.10-£4.75
reductions; £16.90 family.*
The Ouse Washes, a strip of land between two
drainage channels starting at the Denver Sluice and
ending at Earith in Cambridgeshire, is deliberately
flooded every winter to prevent unintended flooding of
the Fenland fields, creating a 13-mile long ecological
goldmine that's home, in part, to the Welney Wetland
Centre. With heated observatories, a lovely, light-filled
café, small hides and a number of trails, it's possible
to spend hours here marvelling at all manner of rare
and unusual water plants, fish, insects and butterflies,
and, of course, the huge number and array of birds
who visit and breed here. In the main observatory you
can train a CCTV camera on the lagoons and banks to
get terrific, close-up views of the birds. Binoculars can
be rented for £5.

Big Fish Walk
*Narborough Trout Lakes, Main Road, Narborough,
PE32 1TE (01760 338005, www.narfish.co.uk).
Open 10.30am-4pm daily (weather permitting).
Admission £5; £3.50-£4.50 reductions; £15 family.
No credit cards.*
Set in 27 acres of meadows in the Nar Valley, this trout
farm offers a short but lovely nature trail following the
river that flows through the site. There are benches for
quietly watching for kingfishers, dragonflies and other
insects detailed on the trail boards. On arrival you'll be
given some fish food and directed to one of the ponds:
stand well back to watch a feeding frenzy that children
will love – the trout are huge and go utterly crazy.

Grimes Graves

St Peter & St Paul. See p154.

Castle Acre Castle
Castle Acre, PE32 2XD (www.english-heritage.org.uk/ castleacre). Open dawn-dusk daily. Admission free.
There's not much left of the 11th-century castle itself, built by the baronial Warennes family (who were responsible for the whole of Castle Acre including the town and priory), but the mighty ditched earthworks are still very impressive. The main entrance, the Bailey Gate, still stands in the village.

Castle Acre Priory ★
Castle Acre, PE32 2XD (01760 755394, www.english-heritage.org.uk/castleacrepriory). Open July, Aug 10am-6pm daily. Apr-June, Sept 10am-5pm daily. Oct-Mar 10am-4pm Mon, Thur-Sun. Admission £5; £2.50-£4.30 reductions; £12.50 family.
Bah, another pile of ancient religious ruins, you might think. You'd be wrong. Castle Acre is one of England's best preserved monastic sites, with Cluniac decoration that looks way way younger than its 700-plus years. It's a delight to ramble around, up and down. Don't miss the prior's personal quarters, a space that manages (along with the excellent audio guide) to give a very real sense of history and medieval monastic life.

Dad's Army Museum & Trail
Cage Lane, Thetford, IP24 2DS (01842 751975, www.dadsarmythetford.org.uk). Open Mar-June, Sept-Nov 10am-2pm Sat. July, Aug 10am-2pm Tue, Sat. Admission free.

From 1968 to 1977, Thetford doubled for Walmington-on-Sea, home town of TV's *Dad's Army*. Thousands now come to pay homage to the popular wartime-set sitcom at this recently enlarged museum, which tells the story of the show's links with Thetford, as well as the history of the town's real Home Guard. To discover which locations were used during filming, follow the Dad's Army Trail via a leaflet that includes plenty of information and a quiz – you can download it from the website. There are occasional group tours or you can book your own guide online.

Gooderstone Water Gardens
The Street, Gooderstone, PE33 9BP (01603 712913, www.gooderstonewatergardens.co.uk). Open Summer 10am-5.30pm daily. Winter 10am-dusk daily. Admission Summer £4.75; £4.25 reductions. Winter £3.75; £3.25 reductions. No credit cards.
Coral Hoyos restored these beautiful gardens in memory of her parents Billy and Florence Knights, who had turned a series of boggy grazing pastures into a six-acre water garden filled with ponds, a trout stream, 13 lovely wooden bridges (discreetly numbered for easy orienteering) and an nature trail with a kingfisher hide. A small wooden tearoom completes the idyll.

Grimes Graves
Seven miles north-west of Thetford, off A134, IP26 5DE (01842 810656, www.english-heritage.org.uk/ grimesgraves). Open July, Aug 10am-6pm daily.

NORFOLK

Places to visit

Apr, June, Sept 10am-5pm daily. Mar, Oct, Nov 10am-5pm Mon, Thur-Sat. Admission £3; £1.50-£2.60 reductions; £7.50 family.
Everyone describes this Neolithic flint mining complex near Thetford as a lunar landscape, and so it is (give or take some scrubby grass and grazing sheep). It's the terrain that's moon-like; more than 400 shafts, pits, craters and spoil dumps are scattered around the site, where 5,000 years ago prehistoric miners dug with deer antlers for floorstone, a black flint that was ideal for making axes and other tools. It's a great spot to explore, and that's before you descend via a 30ft ladder into a mine shaft to view the ancient underground workings.

Iceni Village
Cockley Cley, PE37 8AG (01760 724588, www.iceni village.com). Open July, Aug 10am-5.30pm daily. Apr, June, Sept-Nov 11am-5.30pm daily. Admission £5; free-£4 reductions.
Taking its cue from the fact that the nearby village of Cockley Cley has its orgins in the Iron Age, this reconstruction of an Iceni village is fun for both children and adults. With a canny eye to expansion, the complex also includes a nature trail, a tiny ruined Norman church, a 17th-century cottage and assorted 18th-century farm buildings containing an array of antique carts, carriages and tools.

Narborough Hall ★
Narborough, PE32 1TE (01760 338827, www.narboroughhallgardens.com). Open Apr-Sept 10am-4pm Wed, Sun. Admission £4; free-£3 reductions.
Surrounded by ancient parkland, lakes and woods, these award-winning gardens created by owner Joanne Merrison are utterly enchanting. Wild flowers and natural landscapes are mixed in with more formal designs, and there's a series of lovely walks. If you're lucky, there'll be an exhibition inside the 16th-century, wisteria-clad house too: Cork Street gallerista Robert Merison has curated shows here of work by Barry Flanagan, Bridget Riley and Andy Warhol. The café is a charmer, with teas and vegetarian lunches that use produce from the kitchen garden.

Oxburgh Hall ★
Oxborough, PE33 9PS. (01366 328258, www.nationaltrust.org.uk/oxburghhall). Open House & Gardens Aug 11am-5pm daily. Mid Mar-July, Sept, Oct 11am-5pm Mon-Wed, Sat, Sun. House Late Feb-mid Mar 11am-5pm Sat, Sun. Gardens Feb-mid Mar, Nov-Jan 11am-4pm Sat, Sun. Admission House & Gardens £6.75; £3.45 reductions; £17.85 family. Gardens only £3.45; £2 reductions.
You'll gasp as you come through the entrance and see the gorgeous proportions and setting of this 15th-century moated house. From the French parterre and impressive medieval brick gatehouse to the house itself, where 16th-century needlework panels created by Mary, Queen of Scots and Bess of Hardwick deservedly draw crowds, Oxburgh Hall is a real winner. Do take a walk along the battlements; the roof and chimneys are masterpieces of craftsmanship, and the views are marvellous. You can also see the priest hole, used to hide Catholic priests during Elizabeth I's reign.

St Mary, Houghton-on-the-Hill
Houghton-on-the-Hill, between North Pickenham & South Pickenham (01760 440470, www.hoh.org.uk). Open 2-4pm daily. Admission free.
An ivy-covered ruin in the early 1990s, this tiny flint church was saved from dereliction mainly due to the hard work of local churchwarden Bob Davey. In the course of restoration, a series of rare Romanesque wall paintings (dating from 1090 and among the finest in Europe) were discovered, and St Mary is now one of the most famous and most-visited churches in Norfolk. It's a serene and lovely space, and the paintings are stunning.

St Peter & St Paul, Swaffham
Market Place, Swaffham, PE37 7AB (01760 721373, www.swaffham.churchnorfolk.com). Open Summer 9am-4pm Mon-Fri. Winter 9am-3pm Mon-Fri. Admission free.
This grand church contains much of note. There's the marvellous medieval double-hammerbeam roof covered in carved angels, and impressive stained-glass windows, including some by William Morris & Co commemorating World War I. The elegant, early 16th-century tower was funded by churchwarden John Chapman, who, according to local legend, was the famous Pedlar of Swaffham; his carved figure, plus dog, adorn one of the pews (and he also appears on the town sign). The church is also open on Saturday mornings for tea and cake.

Swaffham Museum
4 London Street, Swaffham, PE37 7DQ (01760 721230, www.swaffhammuseum.co.uk). Open Mid Feb-Dec 10am-4pm Tue-Sat. Admission £2.50; £1-£1.50 reductions; £6 family. No credit cards.
A small social history museum, housed in a grand Georgian town house next to the market square. As well as Stone Age, Roman and Saxon artefacts, there's a gallery devoted to the discovery of the tomb of Tutankhamun by Swaffham-born Howard Carter.

Thetford Forest
01842 815434, www.forestry.gov.uk/england. Spread across some 80 square miles, Thetford Forest is the largest lowland pine forest in Britain, and a joy to explore. The carefully managed woodlands are home to all sorts of rare breeds, including red squirrels, bats and woodlark, some of them visible from the vast network of trails that criss-cross the forest. Head for the High Lodge Forest Centre for maps, activity sheets and suggested trails. See also p297.

West Acre Gardens
West Acre, PE32 1UJ (01760 755989, www.west-acre.co.uk/gardens.html). Open Feb-Nov 10am-5pm daily. Admission free.
Located a mile outside West Acre, this garden centre doesn't feel like a garden centre at all. A notice in the potting shed says 'please ring the bell if you want to buy something'; otherwise, you're left to wander round the walled domain of this old Norfolk manor house. The orchards offer rich pickings for those happy to battle the wasps for windfalls, and the display gardens are a delight, with mixed borders, shrubs, roses, bamboo, Mediterranean beds and even a shade garden.

NORFOLK

Swaffham Market. See p150.

SWAFFHAM

NORFOLK

Church Gate Tea Room & B&B ★

Willow Cottage, Stocks Green, Castle Acre, PE32 2AE (01760 755551, www.churchgatecastleacre.co.uk). Open Summer 10.30am-5pm Tue-Sun. Winter 10.30am-4pm Wed-Sun.

Rambling roses and wrought-iron tables outside and beamed ceilings inside combine to make this a lovely spot for lunch or tea. It helps that the service is friendly and the food delicious – the own-made soups, cakes and puddings are particularly good. You can also stay here: the four bedrooms (£65 double incl breakfast) are comfortable, and owners Sheila and Frank Moister are especially considerate of ramblers' and cyclists' needs, happy to arrange clothes-drying facilities and luggage transfers.

Market Cross Café Bar

15A Market Place, Swaffham, PE37 7AB (01760 336671). Open 10am-6pm Mon-Wed; 10am-11pm Thur-Sat; 10am-6pm Sun.

This licensed café is a nice alternative to Swaffham's plethora of pubs. Typical dishes include beef stroganoff, sea bass or coconut curry, all served by amiable staff in a small, warm and welcoming space.

Ostrich Inn ★

Stocks Green, Castle Acre, PE32 2AE (01760 755398, www.ostrichcastleacre.com). Open 10am-11.30pm daily. Lunch served noon-2.30pm daily. Dinner served 6.30-8.30pm Mon-Sat.

In a perfect spot opposite a perfect green in a perfect Norfolk village, the 16th-century Ostrich Inn is a great eating and sleeping spot. New owners arrived in 2009 and have been gradually renovating the five rooms (£90 double incl breakfast) with tasteful touches, such as gilded handmade wallpaper by Jasper Conran. The landscaped garden has an enclosed play area complete with sand pit and beach hut. Inside, it's all warm woodwork and copper and gold hues, and the food (starters such as potted shrimps and sourdough toast, mains such as fish stew or Houghton Hall venison stew with dumplings) is delicious.

TEN NORFOLK CLIMBS

Appleton Water Tower
Sleep in an octagonal Victorian water tower near Sandringham, courtesy of the Landmark Trust. *See p29.*

Beacon's Hill
Norfolk's highest point, a whopping 338ft above sea level. *See p67.*

Cathedral Church of St John the Baptist
Take a tower tour for a breathtaking view of Norwich, the surrounding countryside and, on a clear day, the sea. *See p86.*

Cathedral of the Broads
Climb the 100ft tower of St Helen's Church, Ranworth, and see the Broads the way the birds do. *See p113.*

Denver Mill
Four floors of flour-filled fun at this working 1830s mill. *See p152.*

The dunes at Winterton-on-Sea
Exhilarating fun in the sand on the north-east Norfolk coast. *See p95.*

Grimes Graves
Exercise your knees on a neolithic lunar landscape near Thetford Forest. *See p153.*

Happisburgh Lighthouse
This candy-striped lighthouse, the oldest working lighthouse in East Anglia, is deemed to be one of Norfolk's seven wonders. *See p98.*

Old Hunstanton cliffs
Clamber up millennia of rock, but don't let anyone catch you at it. Better still (for conservation reasons – erosion here is a big problem), take the path to the top and admire the view. *See p32.*

Oxburgh Hall
Climb the circular staircase to the priest's hole and battlements in this 15th-century moated manor house. *See p154.*

Where to stay

Plenty of choice in all styles and price brackets means you should find the accommodation you want in this area.

There are country hotels such as Greenbanks (01362 687742, www.greenbankshotel.co.uk) in Wendling; Great Danes (01366 328443, www.countryinns.co.uk) in Beachamwell; and Brovey Lair restaurant and hotel (*see p151*) near Thetford. Superior B&Bs include Castle Acre's Coppers (01760 755487, www.the-coppers.co.uk), housed in the old police house, and Church Gate Tea Room & B&B (*see above*); and Narborough's Mill View Rooms B&B (01760 338005, www.millview bandb.co.uk) at Narborough Trout Lakes. Fans of pubs with rooms might prefer the Ostrich Inn (*see above*) in Castle Acre or the Bedingfield Arms (01366 328300) in Oxborough, perfectly sited opposite Oxburgh Hall.

Self-caterers could consider the two cottages in Narborough run by Church Farm Holiday Homes (07801 641570, www.churchfarmholidayhomes. com). And if you really want to go to town – and

Thetford. See p151.

KING STREET

TEN NORFOLK BREWERIES

Beeston Brewery
Fransham Road Farm, Beeston, PE32 2LZ (01328 700844, www.beeston brewery.co.uk). Open phone for times.
This small craft brewer in west Norfolk set up only in 2007, but has already won a handful of awards, including Overall Champion Beer at the 2007 Norwich Beer Festival and Bestselling Beer at the 2008 East Anglian Beer Festival.

Fat Cat Brewery
98-100 Lawson Road, Norwich, NR3 4LF (01603 788508, www. fatcatbrewery.co.uk).
Norwich's much loved Fat Cat pub (*see p92*) expanded to include a cask ale brewery in 2005. Beers include Fat Cat Bitter, which mixes speciality malts from the continent with classic English pale malts, Stout Cat, Top Cat, Wild Cat and Marmalade Cat.

Fox Brewery
22 Station Road, Heacham, PE31 7EX (01485 570345, www.foxbrewery.co.uk). Open Pub noon-11.30pm daily. Tours by arrangement only. Admission free.
Based at the Fox & Hounds pub in Heacham, near Hunstanton, the Fox has up to 20 beers ranging across all styles and strengths, including fruit beers and seasonal ales. The light Heacham Gold was its first ale and remains a firm favourite for its sweetish malty taste with citrus undertones. Also popular is Branthill Best, a red amber beer with a malty and very nutty aroma.

Humpty Dumpty Brewery
Church Road, Reedham, NR13 3TZ (01493 701818, http://humptydumpty. typepad.com). Open Shop Easter-Oct noon-5pm daily. Tours by arrangement only. Admission free.
This charming brewery and off-licence sells its own award-winning cask- and bottle-conditioned beers (East Anglia Pale Ale and Broadland Sunrise among them) plus beers from around the world, including a specialist Belgian collection.

Iceni Brewery & Hop Garden
Foulden Road, Ickburgh, Mundford, IP26 5HB (01842 878922, www.iceni brewery.co.uk). Open Shop 8.30am-4.30pm Mon-Fri; 9am-3pm Sat. Tours by arrangement only.
Brendan Moore makes more than 30 cask- and bottle-conditioned ales, lagers and stouts at his brewery on the edge of Thetford Forest. Try the Raspberry Wheat for a lively fruit beer or the macho Men of Norfolk if you prefer a heavy, dark brew with a liquorice finish, but don't miss Iceni's original beer, the Boadicea Chariot Ale. Phone to arrange a brewery tour.

there are 18 people in the party – Cliff Barns (0870 850 5468, www.cliffbarns.com) in Narborough is a cross between a private house and a hotel, decorated in a rumbustious style described as 'Rancho-Deluxe – an irresistible mix of Mexican hacienda and American hunting lodge'.

Best Western George Hotel
Station Street, Swaffham, PE37 7LJ (01760 721238, www.bw-georgeswaffham.co.uk). Rates £75 double incl breakfast.
This elegant building just off Swaffham's market square may be a chain, but don't discount it as a possible sleeping option. Rooms are sizeable and the public areas comfortable, with free Wi-Fi and good amenities in both.

Horse & Groom
40 Lynn Road, Swaffham, PE37 7AX (01760 721567, www.horseandgroomswaffham.co.uk). Rates £80 double incl breakfast.
It might not be terribly inspiring from the outside, but the interior of this above-standard pub is welcoming and warm. There are eight refurbished bedrooms and three dining spaces, offering a two-course lunch menu for a wallet-friendly £8.95, an à la carte menu in the evenings, and, best of all, a good Sunday roast.

Pentney Park Caravan & Camping Park
Pentney, PE32 1HU (01760 337479, www.pentney-park.co.uk). Rates Camping £16.50-£18.50. Lodges £118-£488 3-4 nights.
If you like the idea of camping, but hate the faff of tents, Pentney Park has the solution with a selection of wooden lodges and mobile homes, with prices so keen that a two-room lodge for a week is cheaper than many hotel rooms for one night. Not convinced? The site also contains a year-round indoor pool, spa, sauna and gym, a heated outdoor pool in the summer, a licensed café and a Spar supermarket.

And if you do want to camp, the woodland pitches are spacious and the facilities excellent.

Repton House
Oaks Drive, Swaffham, PE37 7ER (01760 336399, www.reptonhouse.com). Rates £60 double incl breakfast.
Bright, modern rooms are the selling point of this pretty B&B with its own wooded garden. It's on the edge of town, which means you can wake to the sound of the free-range chickens that supply the breakfast eggs, rather than the sound of traffic. Two of the three rooms have en suite showers; the third has a large bathroom across the hall.

Strattons Hotel ★
4 Ash Close, Swaffham, PE37 7NH (01760 723845, www.strattons-hotel.co.uk). Rates £150 double.
The pick of the crop in Swaffham, this flamboyantly decorated boutique hotel is stuffed to the gills with sumptuous touches: lush velvet drapes, Persian rugs, overstuffed armchairs, rococo gilt mirrors and bright, bold colours everywhere – anyone for shocking pink handmade wallpaper? The award-winning Modern European restaurant makes everything on the premises, from bread to after-dinner chocolates, and is admirably conscientious about supporting small local businesses. Although prices for both food and rooms (five doubles, five suites) are high, a meal or stay here makes for a memorable event.

Vines B&B ★
The Street, Great Cressingham, IP25 6NL (01760 756303, www.thevinesbedandbreakfast.co.uk). Rates £59-£69 double incl breakfast.
On the easternmost edge of the Brecks, this lovely cottage B&B is supplemented by a good village pub, the Olde Windmill Inn, and a very attractive location. Parts of the building date back to the 15th century – check out the dining room for original beams and warming log fire – and the well-appointed rooms overlook a large garden.

Strattons Hotel

Spectrum Brewery
Unit 11, Wellington Road, Tharston, NR15 2PE (07949 254383, www.spectrumbrewery.co.uk).
Around ten draught and bottled ales are produced by East Anglia's only totally organic brewery. The range is varied – from Light Fantastic bitter to full-flavoured and vegan Black Buffle (named after the brewer's cat).

Wagtail Brewery
New Barn Farm, Old Buckenham, NR17 1PF (01953 887133, www.wagtailbrewery.com).
This specialist in bottle-conditioned beers uses only vegetable-based finings, so is that rare thing, a supplier of wholly vegan beers. Lovely old-style labels hark back to days of yore, and the beers are equally traditional, from popular English Ale to Black Beauty porter made using Fairtrade coffee. Outlets include the Real Ale Shop (*see p43*) near Wells.

Why Not Brewery
17 Cavalier Close, Dussindale, Thorpe St Andrew, Norwich, NR7 0TE (01603 300786, www.thewhynotbrewery.co.uk). Open phone to check times.
Colin Emms set up his tiny brewery in his back garden on the outskirts of Norwich in 2005, and now produces six beers, among them the smooth, full and malty Chocolate Nutter. Unsurprisingly, it has a nutty bitter chocolate and roasted grain in its aftertaste.

Woodforde's
Broadland Brewery, Woodbastwick, NR13 6SW (01603 720353, 01603 722218 shop, www.woodfordes.co.uk). Open Shop & visitor centre 10am-4.30pm Mon-Fri; 11am-4.30pm Sat, Sun.
Norfolk's most famous brewery keeps things small and simple, producing just six ales and one barley wine from its rural setting north-east of Norwich. Wherry is the populist one, with a floral aroma and fruity flavour; Admiral's Reserve is most complex, providing a rich and rounded taste with subtle fruit undertones.

And if you don't like beer...

Whin Hill Cider
The Stables, Stearman's Yard, Wells-next-the-Sea, NR23 1BW (01328 711033, www.whinhillcider.co.uk). Open Shop July, Aug 10.30am-5.30pm Tue-Sun. Easter-June, Sept, Oct 10.30am-5.30pm Sat, Sun.
This appealing cider producer grows apples on its orchard at Stanhoe, ten miles south-west of Wells, which are then pressed into golden nectar in an 18th-century barn and outbuildings off the main car park in Wells. Single-variety apple juices, ciders (standard and sparkling) and perry are for sale.

Suffolk

Woodbridge Tide Mill. See p235.

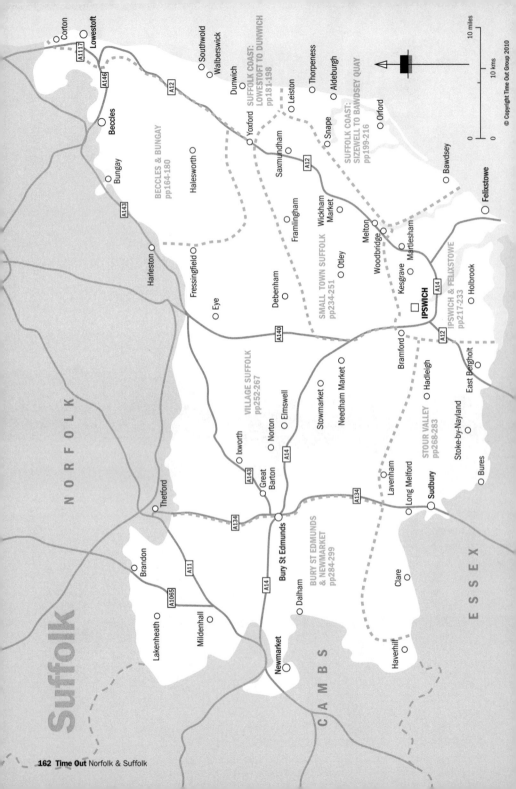

Suffolk

NORFOLK

CAMBS

ESSEX

Corton
Lowestoft
A117
A146
Beccles
A12
Southwold
Walberswick
Dunwich
SUFFOLK COAST:
LOWESTOFT TO DUNWICH
pp181-198
Yoxford
Leiston
Thorpeness
Aldeburgh
Snape
Orford
SUFFOLK COAST:
SIZEWELL TO BAWDSEY QUAY
pp199-216
Bawdsey
Felixstowe

Bungay
A143
Harleston
Halesworth
Saxmundham
Wickham Market
A12
Melton
Woodbridge
Martlesham
Kesgrave
A14
Holbrook

BECCLES & BUNGAY
pp164-180

Fressingfield
Eye
Framlingham
Debenham
Otley
SMALL TOWN SUFFOLK
pp234-251
IPSWICH
IPSWICH & FELIXSTOWE
pp217-233
East Bergholt
A12

A140
Bramford
A14
Hadleigh

Ixworth
Norton
Elmswell
Stowmarket
Needham Market
VILLAGE SUFFOLK
pp252-267
A143
Great Barton
A14
STOUR VALLEY
pp268-283
Lavenham
Long Melford
Sudbury
Stoke-by-Nayland
Bures

Thetford
A134
Bury St Edmunds
A134
BURY ST EDMUNDS
& NEWMARKET
pp284-299
Clare

Brandon
A11
A1065
Lakenheath
Mildenhall
A14
Dalham
Newmarket
Haverhill

10 miles
10 kms
© Copyright Time Out Group 2010

Cavendish. See p277.

Suffolk

Beccles & Bungay

This area of Suffolk is particularly independently minded. It's one of those places where each generation stays close to the one before. Local characters are famous for miles around and everyone knows everything about each other. The strong sense of community has helped people pull together in the many fights over the last few decades to stop supermarket chains building out-of-town sites. Consequently, Bungay, Halesworth and Harleston (just over the border in Norfolk) retain not just the architectural charm of classic British market towns, but also the tradition of family businesses run with local knowledge and passion. The area doesn't attract many tourists away from the focal point of the River Waveney, and there's a sense that the inhabitants like it this way. But Bungay is a lovely little town well worth a day's visit, and Beccles and Halesworth are also very pleasant. The surrounding countryside is mostly flat agricultural land interrupted by farms, smallholdings, hamlets and villages. But it's not flat in the way the Fens are flat. Ridges and folds in the land, stands of trees, larger copses, hedgerows and heathland make this landscape much more friendly and intimate.

SOMERLEYTON & BECCLES

This area is part of the Broads, which lie mostly in Norfolk. Oulton Broad is the widest expanse of water on the Suffolk side of the county boundary and there are numerous marshes and water meadows here. Because the boundary runs along the River Waveney, which curves and doubles back dramatically, most of the land between Somerleyton and Beccles is in Norfolk, and there are some lovely circular walks to be found starting in the Millennium Garden at Aldeby, to the north of Beccles, just on the other side of the River Waveney. Look out for the Pathways In Stone, seven standing stones set up in 2000 to celebrate the tradition of parish boundary markers.

Somerleyton ★ & Fritton

Somerleyton is one of the most northerly points in Suffolk. It's cut off from the rest of the county by Lowestoft and the River Waveney and sits in a beautifully isolated marshy spot. Incredibly, Somerleyton's rail station survived Beeching's cuts, so you can still get here by train. The focal point of the village is the beautiful Tudor and Jacobean Somerleyton Hall (see p174), which lies in the middle of open countryside. The quaint Tudor houses in the village itself are pastoral fakes, built in the 19th century by Sir Morton Peto, the man who renovated the Hall before bankrupting himself. The estate now belongs to the Crossley family, who also own the incredibly popular Duke's Head pub (see p169) and Fritton Lake (see p174), where families gather for old-fashioned fun at weekends and in the holidays.

Like nearby Belton and St Olaves, the actual village of Fritton, a couple of miles north-west of Somerleyton, was in Suffolk for centuries, until, in the 1970s, it was decided to drop the county

boundary down to Fritton Lake, so that Great Yarmouth's southern sprawl was in the same county as its town centre. This meant Suffolk losing a pretty little village and one of East Anglia's few prized Norman round-towered churches – Fritton's St Edmund church. Inside, the 20th-century stained-glass windows depicting Suffolk saints are beautiful, as are the medieval wall paintings in the chancel. Just down the road at St Olaves are the remains of an Augustinian priory, now preserved by English Heritage.

Beccles ★

Beccles is a sleepy market town that was once at the frontier of East Anglia's Saxon boom, but then the Waveney silted up and what was a thriving port became just another small inland town next to a river. Beccles is full of pretty streets with red-brick Georgian town houses, and older medieval buildings with first-storey overhangs. There are also several former Victorian maltings that are very handsome. The town's north-westerly edge sits on a ridge overlooking the Waveney and its surrounding water meadows. The view from the tower of St Michael's

> ### Across the border
>
> **Waveney River Centre**
> Just inside Norfolk on the north bank of the Waveney at Burgh St Peter is the Waveney River Centre (Staithe Road, 01502 677343, www.waveneyrivercentre.co.uk, open Easter-Oct 8am-5pm daily). There's self-catering accommodation in wooden chalets and cottages, a campsite, a marina and a boatyard, but you can also just hire a boat for a few hours. Choose from motor cruisers, canoes or rowing dinghies and follow the Waveney to Beccles or Somerleyton.

The Little Green Wholefood Shop. See p172.

Church is extraordinary. You can clamber up the rickety wooden spiral stairs, clutching on to a rope that's not entirely free of pigeon poo, past the bells at the top (which are still rung on Wednesdays and Sundays) and walk on to the roof.

Unusually, the bell tower is not attached to the church, but sits separately to the south-east of the main building. Why? Because the western end of the church is near the edge of the ridge dropping down into the valley, and the townspeople were afraid the tower might pull the church over the edge.

There's not much of note to look at inside the church itself, as most of the medieval interior was lost in a fire, but the two-storey medieval porch is very handsome. Incidentally, Horatio Nelson's parents were married here.

Walk up Ballygate and you'll find the town's museum (*see p174*), which used to be the local school. There's also the Upstairs Gallery (01502 717191, www.theupstairsgallery.co.uk, closed Mon, Sun) above Lloyds Bank on Exchange Square. It has 15 rooms of arts, crafts and exhibitions and

SUFFOLK

Bungay. See p172.

there's always work by professional local artists. Tesco finally managed to build a store in Beccles a few years ago, despite local protests, which means food shopping in the town centre isn't as interesting as in nearby towns such as Bungay and Halesworth (Tesco is gunning for a store in Halesworth too). Bailey's Delicatessen (*see right*), is a good source of olives, cheese, bread and wine, and there are two butchers and a greengrocer, but the only baker in town is a branch of underwhelming chain Greggs.

Beccles's former port is now a beautiful rural stretch of water, popular with the sailing fraternity, but it's a shame to let them have it all to themselves. Although the Waveney links with the Norfolk Broads, it's one of the least crowded waterways around these parts. Mature trees overhang the water's edge and there's a stillness to the place that makes it feel as if history is trapped in the very air itself. The huge skies reflected in the water are exquisite.

There are lovely walks along the banks. Take the path from Beccles Quay to Geldeston a couple of miles away and you can have lunch in the Locks Inn (*see right*). Or set off in the opposite direction and follow the Marsh Trail (the marsh was given to the town by Elizabeth I in 1584), where there's plenty of birdlife, including kingfishers. Those who don't want to walk can take a river trip on the Big Dog Ferry. There's also an outdoor swimming pool (01502 714911, www.becclesopenair pool.org.uk) near Waveney Meadow – funds permitting, it's open in summer.

Around Beccles

The tiny village of Westhall, around eight miles south of Beccles, holds more medieval treasure.

St Andrew's Church is down a small lane and sits within a lovely canopy of trees. Inside is a very rare example of a medieval font that has retained much of its original paintwork. This quiet backwater church also has a stunning rood screen with depictions of the saints painted on its panels, and some medieval paintings on the walls. At Sotterley, a few miles north-east on the other side of the A145, there's an unusual octagonal chapel that often holds fundraising garden produce markets in summer.

Where to eat & drink

There's a good range of options in and around Beccles, whatever your needs. Twyfords (Exchange Square, 01502 710614, closed Sun) is a favourite for breakfast, lunch and coffee. Its prominent position on the market place and glass frontage provide great opportunities for watching the rest of Beccles pass by. The food is good, but expensive for this part of the world. For a more serious lunch or dinner, head to the Swan House (*see p170*) in the shadow of the church tower. Those seeking a decent pint should head for the Bear & Bells at 11 Old Market opposite the bus station. It serves Adnams and Greene King, plus a range of guest beers, and has a large bar and two separate dining areas.

Just outside Beccles, there's an unlikely-sounding gem on the Ellough Industrial Estate: the Posh Pigs Café (01502 717596) serves great cooked breakfasts that are amazing value. For something a little more rural, head to the Duke's Head on the Somerleyton Estate or the Locks Inn at Geldeston (for both, *see right*).

Bailey's Delicatessen

2 Hungate, Beccles, NR34 9TL (01502 710609,
www.baileyswines.com). Open/food served 9am-5pm
Mon-Thur, Sun; 9am-10.30pm Fri, Sat.
If you're staying in self-catering accommodation and need
to stock up on edibles, Bailey's offers a good selection of
breads, meats, cheeses and olives at the deli counter
downstairs – don't miss the wines at the back. The café
upstairs serves light meals, with options listed on a
blackboard. It's an airy space, and there's a box of toys and
books for children. The food, from moussaka to cheese to
tunisian orange cake, is excellent, and there's also a full
selection of delicious Mövenpick ice-creams. It's just a shame
such a promising business is staffed by surly teenagers who
react to every request with a sigh.

Duke's Head ★

Slug's Lane, Somerleyton, NR32 5QR (01502 730281,
www.somerleyton.co.uk/dukeshead). Open 11am-11pm
Mon-Sat; noon-10.30pm Sun. Lunch served noon-3pm
Mon-Sat; noon-4pm Sun. Dinner served 6.30-9pm
Mon-Sat.
This red-brick pub occupies an isolated position on one of
the quiet lanes around Somerleyton village. The views from
the garden tables overlook the Waveney. The setting may
be tranquil, but the pub is incredibly popular so you won't
be dining alone. The tiny kitchen manages to deliver
excellent food; ingredients are first class, with many coming
from the Somerleyton Estate's own farms. A simple fish pie
was gourmet fare, with huge chunks of cod and salmon
sitting under a buttery mash topping. There are real ales at
the bar and live music in the garden in summer. Wednesday
night is quiz night, and every three weeks Club Uniquity
comes to the newly renovated barn, and local performers
take turns entertaining the crowd.

Locks Inn

Locks Lane, Geldeston, NR34 0HW (01508 518414,
www.geldestonlocks.co.uk). Open Summer noon-11pm
Mon-Sat; noon-10.30pm Sun. Winter 5-11pm Wed,
Thur; noon-11pm Fri, Sat; noon-7pm Sun. Food served
Summer noon-2.30pm, 6-8.30pm Mon-Sat; noon-
2.30pm Sun. Winter noon-2.30pm, 6-8.30pm Fri,
Sat; noon-2.30pm Sun.
Just over the border in Norfolk, this friendly local pub is a
good destination to aim for on the charming riverside walk
from Beccles. It used to be owned by an anarchist, then had
a stint as a squat, but now is just a regular pub, albeit with
a strong community flavour. Local musicians often turn up
for an open jam on summer weekends, but there's live music
all year round on Thursday nights and Sunday afternoons.
The bar has an unpolished rustic charm and the large grassy
garden bang next to the Waveney has plenty of tables for
alfresco imbibing. You'll find Green Jack Beers from the
Lowestoft Microbrewery and simple old-fashioned pub grub
(Friday is curry night).

Holy Trinity Church. See p173.

SUFFOLK

St Peter's Hall & Brewery. See p176.

Swan House

Beccles, NR34 9HE (01502 713474, www.swan-house.com). Open 11am-11pm Mon-Sat; noon-10.30pm Sun. Lunch served noon-2.15pm, dinner served 6.45-9.30pm daily.

This restaurant was a tavern for hundreds of years and now serves Modern British food in an intimate and cosy restaurant. The kitchen uses vegetables, fruit and herbs from its own garden, and sources meat and fish locally. In the summer, you can have afternoon tea outside on the terrace overlooking St Michael's Church tower, or in the tiny courtyard. The art on the walls forms a monthly changing exhibition, and there are regular music evenings.

Where to stay

Church Farmhouse

Uggeshall, NR34 8BD (01502 578532, www. uggeshall.fsnet.co.uk). Rates £80 double incl breakfast. No credit cards.

This Elizabethan farmhouse is in a peaceful spot between Halesworth and Southwold, south of Beccles just off the A145. Views from the windows of the three double bedrooms take in rolling fields where red poll cattle graze contentedly. Breakfasts are served around a large table in the lovely beamed dining room and include local meat and eggs, own-made marmalade and Fairtrade coffee.

Fritton House ★

Church Lane, Fritton, NR31 9HA (01493 484008, http://hotels.adnams.co.uk/fritton-house). Rates £120 double incl breakfast.

Adnams runs this friendly restaurant with rooms, set in bucolic Fritton Lake. Most of the nine bedrooms are cosy nooks up in the eaves, so it might be wise to check the ceiling height if you're particularly tall. The rooms aren't huge, but everything is stylishly fitted out, and hearty breakfasts full of local fare are served in the restaurant (which is run by Lee Knight, who used to work at the excellent Crown Hotel in Southwold). There's also a sitting room, with deep sofas, newspapers, board games and a fire on cold days.

1 Barracks Cottages

Henstead (01502 722717, www.suffolk-secrets.co.uk). Rates £220-£350 per week.

Just outside the village of Henstead, around five miles east of Beccles, the pink-painted Barracks Cottage is a spacious place for two people to have a quiet getaway. There's an inglenook fireplace (with wood-burning stove), wood panelling and lots of oak beams, but the furniture and decor is brightly modern.

Saltgate House

5 Saltgate, Beccles, NR34 9AN (01502 710889, www.saltgatehouse.co.uk). Rates £65-£70 double incl breakfast. No credit cards.

SUFFOLK

A blue Georgian-fronted house with five B&B rooms. The decor is a little dated (although plain, not fussy), but hosts Carol and Steve are very welcoming and do a fine breakfast full of tasty local produce. Saltgate House is right in the middle of Beccles, so handy for its cafés, pubs, shops and riverside walks.

Springlake
Siding Road, Barnby, NR34 7QP (01502 476742, www.springlake-suffolk.co.uk). Rates £325-£575 per week.
Two modern wooden chalets sit in the five-acre grounds of the owners' home. Both have open-plan living areas, outdoor seating and sleep four in two bedrooms. The shared gardens are lovely, and there's also a shared indoor heated pool and a games room with a full-size snooker table, table tennis and table football. With so much to do, the danger is you'll never leave the gates of the property and explore the local area.

Waveney House Hotel
Puddingmoor, Beccles, NR34 9PL (01502 712270, www.waveneyhousehotel.co.uk). £98-£110 double incl breakfast.
A large, very pretty old hotel that makes the most of Beccles' position on the river. The restaurant is right on the waterfront, with a conservatory extension that offers lovely views. All 12 bedrooms are en suite, and the rooms on the second floor have vaulted oak-beamed ceilings; decor is

PRODUCE AT THE GATE

Maybe it's that stubborn streak of independence in the Suffolk mindset, but the big supermarkets have a battle on their hands when it comes to opening stores here: you're much more likely to find a small Co-op on a high street than an out-of-town supermarket. Tesco has been trying its hardest, but residents across the county have campaigned against the chain, and wars are still being fought from Halesworth to Hadleigh.

At the same time, Suffolk has a strong culture of supporting fresh local produce. Many people grow their own food, so there's an unusual number of roadside stalls selling all kinds of edible goods. You'll find seasonal fruit and vegetables everywhere; signs offer everything from asparagus and strawberries in early summer to apples and wet walnuts in autumn. There are also plenty of opportunities to buy newly laid eggs, home-made jams and chutneys, and even fresh meat from various farm doors. The honesty box (often just a jam jar or plastic pot) next to the produce on display says it all... you are my neighbour, and I trust you.

soothingly simple and neutral. It's a peaceful place to stay, but only five minutes' walk from the town centre.

Woodland Lodges ★
Church Lane, Fritton, NR31 9HA (01493 488666, www.somerleyton.co.uk). Rates £353-£1,060 per week.
There are 44 delightful, eco-friendly lodges on the 5,000-acre Somerleyton Estate, dotted around the woods and banks of Fritton Lake. There's a choice of one-, two- and three-bed lodges, all with solid wood floors, open-plan living areas and top-of-the-range fittings, including Bosch kitchen appliances and a TV and DVD player. You're close to all the amenities of the lake and Somerleyton Hall and grounds, but have your own little den of woodland privacy.

BUNGAY & THE SAINTS
The further inland from the coast you go, the less likely you are to see other holidaymakers. Bungay gets its share of visitors because, like Beccles, it's on the River Waveney, but the villages south of the A143 are little explored and consequently a very peaceful spot to head for a walk or cycle ride.

Bungay ★
Bungay is little known outside Suffolk, and gets bypassed by tourists heading to the coast or the better known delights of the Norfolk Broads, but it's a thriving little town and a lovely place for a day out. Tucked in a loop in the Waveney River in the last reaches of the Suffolk Broads, it's a picturesque

place with an air of cultured gentility – but there's also a sense of firm Suffolk independence. This is the only place left in the UK that still upholds the Saxon tradition of a Town Reeve and Feoffees (trustees). Together, they look after the lands and buildings left to the town by rich benefactors. In 2001, the town also bought back the disused Georgian theatre for its population. It's now called the Fisher Theatre (10 Broad Street, 01986 897130, www.fishertheatre.org) and offers a robust programme of arts, talks and cinema screenings.

There has been a weekly market in Bungay for 700 years (now held on Thursday), and the residents' healthy disdain for chain stores – Boots only managed to get a foothold here after years of struggle – means the shops have a strong local character. Take draper and furniture shop Wightmans (2A Trinity Street, 01986 892889, closed Wed, Sun), a Bungay institution that's been in the hands of the Wightman family for several generations. It may look old-fashioned both outside and in, and chaotic to boot, but the staff really know what they're talking about and can put their hands on anything in seconds.

Earsham Street is lined with inviting independent shops and is great for browsing. The Little Green Wholefood Shop (nos.39-41, 01986 894555, closed Sun) sells meat and meals prepared on a nearby farm, fresh bread and cakes, fruit and vegetables, as well as pulses, nuts, grains, cosmetics and environmentally friendly household

products. The Cork Brick gallery and antiques shop (no.6, 01986 894873, closed Mon, Sun) has some unusual treasures, plus work by artists living on the Suffolk/Norfolk border. Potter Clive Davies makes and sells his pots in Ramms Yard (no.25, 01986 892685, closed Sun). There are plenty of places to find refreshments here too. Head through Market Place and into St Mary's Street, where 4Nel Jewellers (no.44, 01986 894827, closed Wed, Sat afternoon) specialises in silver and amber (the owners have family ties to the Amber Shop in Southwold, *see p187*).

Three churches sit in close proximity on Trinity Street. Holy Trinity is the oldest – its round tower supposedly dates from the tenth century – but it's not the most beautiful. The exterior of St Mary's is much prettier, with its decorative flintwork, handsome tower and evocative remains of a former priory in the churchyard. The medieval interior was destroyed in a 17th-century fire that started in a nearby bakery; the fire wiped out many of the town's older buildings, but made space for the lovely Georgian houses visible around Bungay today.

The church is also renowned for being visited in 1577 by the legendary black dog of Bungay (the dog is everywhere, featuring on the weather vane in the market square, the town's shield, and in the name of the town's football club). This mythical hell hound is said to have rampaged through the church during a thunderstorm, attacking the congregation. St Mary's is no longer used as a place of worship, and is in the care of the Churches Conservation Trust (www.visitchurches.org.uk)

The third church, St Edmund's, is Roman Catholic and unusually showy for Suffolk. There are wood-panelled walls, opulent stained-glass windows and decorative giltwork in the sanctuary. There's also a large octagonal baptistery that houses an incredibly ornate font carved out of coloured marble.

Around the corner, through the little passage opposite the Butter Cross in the Market Place (next to the White Swan pub) is Bungay Castle. Like Beccles, there was a thriving settlement at Bungay since Saxon times, but it really began to flourish in the Norman era, with Baron Hugh Bigod building the castle in the last decades of the 12th century. All that's left now are the remains of crumbling walls and turrets, but you can walk to the top of Castle Hills to get a good view of the ruins and the marshes beyond the town. There's also a visitor centre with a café. On Broad Street, above the Waveney District Council offices, is a small local history museum (01986 892176, closed Sat, Sun).

Falcon Meadow, beside the River Waveney, is one of Bungay's most beautiful spots. Take the footpath from the bridge at the bottom of Bridge Street for lovely views across the meadow and the backs of handsome houses on the opposite bank. This is one of the spots mentioned in Roger Deakin's *Waterlog*, a book that recounted his adventures swimming in Britain's rivers, ponds and tarns – so bring your costume if you're feeling brave.

Suffolk Apple Juice & Cider Place. See p176.

One of the best ways of seeing Bungay is to follow the Bigod Way, a series of walks of varying lengths around the town; the Bath Hills route towards Ditchingham is particularly lovely. Guides are available from the Kings Head pub in the Market Place and the Café @ The Castle in Earsham Street.

Don't miss one eccentric local attraction, the 'Chicken Roundabout' between Bungay and Ditchingham on the A143. Several dozen chickens have gone native and made the middle of the roundabout their home – the locals are so fond of them that they dodge the traffic to feed them.

The Saints

If you want to step back in time, look no further than the Saints: a collection of 12 neighbouring hamlets and villages to the south of Bungay, each with the word 'saint' in their names. To outward appearances, little has changed here in centuries. Take a day to walk or cycle through the area's network of footpaths and narrow roads; it's quite possible you won't meet anyone for hours, except, perhaps, some children whose day just got that much more exciting because they saw someone they didn't know. You're more likely to

Places to visit

SOMERLEYTON & BECCLES

Beccles Museum
Leman House, Ballygate, Beccles NR34 9ND (01502 715722, www.becclesmuseum.org.uk). Open Apr-Nov 2.15-5pm Tue-Sun. Admission free.
Attractive Leman House, with its flint and brick frontage and pretty Gothic windows, is now home to the town museum. Established as a Free School in the 15th century, the building continued to function as a school until the turn of the 20th century. The museum entrance is at the back, taking you past the lovely garden with views over the River Waveney. Inside, displays chart the history of the school, and the town of Beccles. Possibly there hasn't been enough judicious editing of artefacts and material, but there's plenty to keep you interested.

Fritton Lake ★
Beccles Road, Fritton, NR31 9HA (01493 488288, www.somerleyton.co.uk). Open varies; check website for details. Admission £6; free-£4 reductions.
Part of the Somerleyton Estate, Fritton Lake is a beautiful and well-equipped country park with a large expanse of water at its centre. It's very popular with families, especially in the school holidays. The walks and trails around the lake and surrounding woodland are lovely, and there are tons of activities for children of all ages. The adventure playground has an enormous wooden fort for climbing, as well an assault course, aerial slides for older children, and a large bouncy pillow. Or you can take a rowing boat out on the lake, try the putting green or perhaps a spot of fishing. There are also self-catering lodges to rent (*see p172*).

Moo Play Farm
Low Farm, Locks Road, Brampton, NR34 8DX (01502 575841, www.mooplayfarm.co.uk). Open 10am-5pm daily. Admission £1 adult; £3.75-£4.75 child; £7.50-£9.50 family.
Moo Play Farm, around five miles south of Beccles on the A145, runs petting and grooming sessions with pigs, horses and other animals. There are tractor rides and nature rambles around the farm and plenty of climbing equipment indoors and out (the indoor playframe has superslides for bigger children). A café serves coffee for the adults and good children's meals. The farm also runs regular mother and toddler groups.

Somerleyton Hall ★
Somerleyton, NR32 5QQ (01502 734901, www.somerleyton.co.uk). Open July-Sept 10am-5pm
Tue-Thur, Sun. Apr-June 10am-5pm Thur, Sun. Admission £8.25; £4.35-£7.25 reductions; £23 family.
This magnificent Tudor-Jacobean house (still home to the Crossley family, who have owned it since the 1860s) is awesome enough from the outside with its numerous windows and mutiple chimney pots. The inside is even better. The imposing entrance hall is clad in oak and has a stained-glass ceiling dome; the ballroom is done out in a startling crimson damask; the library is hung with oil paintings. But for many, it's the gardens that are the real draw. There's a fantastic yew maze to get lost in; when you finally make it to the middle, you can climb the mound and enjoy the view from the benches. The iron and glass greenhouses were designed by Crystal Palace architect Joseph Paxton. There are tunnels, a small museum hidden in one of the outhouses, and some wonderfully mature trees set in extensive lawns. Note the splendid clock, designed as a small-scale prototype for the Palace of Westminster by clockmaker Benjamin Lewis Vulliamy. The design wasn't used in the end, and Big Ben was built in its place. There are plenty of picnic spots around the grounds and the café has a wonderful setting inside the Loggia, overlooking the formal Winter Gardens.

HALESWORTH & AROUND

Oasis Camel Centre
Cratfield Road, Linstead, IP19 0DT (07836 734748, www.oasiscamelcentre.co.uk). Open Apr-Oct 10.30am-5pm daily. Admission £6.95; £5.95-£6.45 reductions. £23.50 family.
The entry fee may seem expensive for this part of the world, but it's worth it: a trip to the Oasis Camel Centre is a whole morning or afternoon out for the family. The group of smug-looking camels near the entrance gives the place its name, but all sorts of animals live here, from horses to donkeys and pigs to goats and sheep. Children love indulging them with the bags of feed sold in the shop. They also love the petting shed, where they can hold Flossie the white rabbit, Cheese and Pickle the ferrets, or one of the guinea pigs. Then there's all the play equipment: the bouncy castle and the zip-wire in the playground are favourites, as are the peddle tractors on the grassy fields between the enclosures. The shop sells coffee, cream teas and ice-creams (the seating area could be spruced up). The centre is just off the B1123, near Linstead, around three miles west of Halesworth.

Somerleyton Hall

startle some wildlife, though – a hare in a hedgerow, or a stork on a pond that will take to the huge Suffolk skies in annoyance at your interruption. Much of this area is open arable land dotted with small farms, so the only sounds are the odd whirr of farm machinery and the occasional distant pop of farmers' guns.

The Saints are Suffolk's Bermuda Triangle, so specific locations are quite difficult to find, but St Peter's Hall at St Peter South Elmham is a lovely spot if you make it. It dates from the 13th century, although much of the building was added later, using reclaimed materials from Flixton Priory following its dissolution. The Hall is now a bar and restaurant (see right) and there's a shop too, selling local produce as well as the whole range of excellent beer from adjacent St Peter's Brewery (see p179), which is owned by the same company. Tours of the brewery are available; the owners are very friendly and knowledgeable about the local area as well as their beer.

Stop at the church at St Margaret South Elmham for some quiet meditation (don't miss the old village stocks inside the porch). You might also stumble upon South Elmham Hall (01986 782526, www.southelmham.co.uk), the former summer retreat of the Bishops of Norwich, which is now run as a traditional mixed farm and B&B. The hall contains what are probably the earliest domestic wall paintings in Suffolk; tours can be arranged with Invitation To View (www.invitationtoview.co.uk). It's a popular place to come all year round because of the marked walks that lead through its fields, ancient woods and water meadows. A café (open May-Sept Thur, Fri, Sun; Oct-Mar Sun) serves food straight from the farm. A highlight of any walk here is to come across the quiet and atmospheric remains of South Elmham Minster. Historians remain unsure about what the ruins represent; it seems likely that they were a chapel rather than a larger religious building.

The only main (not to mention straight) road through the Saints is Stone Street (A144), going directly from Bungay to Halesworth. As you travel south to Halesworth, look carefully in the hedgerow just before the Ilketshall St Lawrence turn-off on the left. A small faded board covered by undergrowth announces the Suffolk Apple Juice & Cider Place (see p291).

This is an example of cottage industry at its most chaotic. Behind the hedge is a ramshackle collection of sheds, barrels and bottles and a man called Jonathan (you may have to bang on all the doors and shout loudly to make yourself heard). Jonathan buys apples from local smallholders whose harvests are too small for large commercial companies. The choice of apple juices is unusually varied and most of it is delicious.

Just to the west of the Saints, Mendham is a straggling village with a mix of old and new buildings and a strong community spirit. It was the birthplace of the respected Edwardian painter Sir Alfred Munnings, hence the Sir Alfred Munnings pub, which hosts friendly outdoor busker sessions on summer Sundays. The village hosted its first farmers' market in the grounds of the church in July 2009 and plans to hold one every third Saturday of the month in summer. Stalls have great-value baked goods, home-grown fruit, vegetables, plants and herbs; and there are tables and chairs for those who want to eat their purchases then and there, with a cup of tea or coffee.

Where to eat & drink

If you like real ale, head to the Green Dragon in Bungay (29 Broad Street, 01986 892281), which brews its own around the back. The pub is ferociously proud of its old-world, back-to-basics approach and usually serves two different types of mild, as well as its Chaucer Ale and Bridge Street Bitter. Wednesday is curry night. There's another small brewery at the Queen's Head (Station Road, 01986 892623) in nearby Earsham, producing three real ales and one-off specials.

For old-fashioned fish and chips and some local gossip, head into Norfolk to Monty's fish and chip shop (7 Redenhall Road, 01379 852669) in Harleston. It only fries on Wednesday lunchtimes and Wednesday, Friday and Saturday evenings, but the chips are cooked in beef dripping and the fish is really fresh.

Artichoke ★
162 Yarmouth Road, Broome, NR35 2NZ (01986 893325, http://home.btconnect.com/theartichoke atbroome). Open noon-11pm Tue-Thur, Sun; noon-midnight Fri, Sat. Lunch served noon-2.30pm, dinner served 6.30-9pm Tue-Sat. Meals served noon-4.30pm Sun.
Despite its Suffolk postcode, the Artichoke was CAMRA's Norfolk Pub of the Year 2009. It's at Broome, just across the Waveney from Bungay, and is a delight: cosy and warm inside, with flagstones and scrubbed floorboards and a large inglenook fireplace. At the back is a secluded beer garden. Up to eight real ales are on tap: Elgoods Black Dog Mild and Adnams Southwold are always available; guest beers come chiefly from craft brewers. A separate dining room serves good gastropub-style food, eschewing the fancy in favour of old favourites such as pies and pan-fried fish.

Castle Inn ★
35 Earsham Street, Bungay, NR35 1AF (01986 892283, www.thecastleinn.net). Open/food served noon-11pm Mon-Sat; noon-4pm Sun.
Its powder blue exterior may make the Castle Inn look a bit too much like a doll's house, but inside it's more convivial. There are cosy rooms front and back that feel more like a restaurant than a pub, and the kitchen serves soup and sandwiches all day if you miss the lunchtime slot. The menu is full of locally sourced food and the small back garden is pleasant on a warm day. Upstairs are four comfortable B&B rooms (£85 double).

Earsham Street Café ★
13 Earsham Street, Bungay, NR35 1AE (01986 893103). Open 9.30am-4.30pm Mon-Sat.
This well-loved café is always busy. You can have anything from a cup of coffee or glass of wine to one of the well-conceived main courses, such as pan-fried calves' liver with

bacon bubble and squeak or confit of duck with mustard mash. The café sometimes provides evening meals at the weekends and run the occasional jazz night.

St Peter's Hall ★
St Peter South Elmham, NR35 1NQ (01986 782288, www.stpetershallsuffolk.co.uk). Lunch served noon-3pm Tue-Sat; noon-4pm Sun. Dinner served 6-9.30pm Tue-Sat.
The great hall inside this eccentric building is wonderful (children love the peephole upstairs that lets you spy on the proceedings below), though it's often out of bounds as the rooms is used for functions. Still, you can always find space in the bar/restaurant, which serves the whole range of beer from the adjacent St Peter's Brewery plus an excellent gastropub menu. The moated gardens are a peaceful place to sit and enjoy a very quiet pint; the views across open fields are delightful.

Waveney Farm Shop Café
High Road Wortwell, Harleston, IP20 0HG (01986 788609, www.waveneyfarmshop.co.uk). Open 9am-4.30pm daily.
This café serves homely meals and offers free Wi-Fi. All-day breakfasts are hearty and popular, as are the pasta dishes, but the specials board is worth checking out too. Coffee and tea is Fairtrade, and meals are served on checked tablecloths in an area screened off from the shop (there's also seating outside if you don't mind the hum of traffic on the A143). The shop stocks fruit and veg from neighbouring farms, a range of local juices and beers, Goulborns tasty tarts and cakes and delicious Lane Farm ham, bacon and salami; there's a butcher's van outside selling Barnhall Village Meats too.

Where to stay
The Castle Inn (*see left*) has four B&B rooms on one of Bungay's loveliest streets. They're pleasant if fairly plain, comfortable rather than luxurious, but it's worth coming here just for the breakfasts (the restaurant downstairs is one of the best in Bungay). Two of the double rooms have sofa beds that can be used for children.

Buckland House
Halesworth Road, Ilketshall St Lawrence, NR34 8LB (01986 781413, www.buckland-house.co.uk). Rates £75 double incl breakfast.
This medieval former chapel lies in Ilketshall St Lawrence, which is on the A144 about halfway between Bungay and Halesworth. The presence of the main road means it's not one of the quietest of the Saints. The three bedrooms are simply furnished, and breakfasts include own-made muesli, French toast with fruit compote and a full English, featuring local sausages and eggs cooked any way you like them.

Old Rectory ★
Abbey Road, Flixton, NR35 1NL (01986 893133, www.oldrectorycottagesflixton.co.uk). Rates £250-£440 per week for 2 people.
Four outbuildings have been converted into simple, one-bedroom self-catering accommodation in the grounds of a handsome former rectory in this village just outside Bungay. Perhaps the best thing about staying here is that it's also

the home of the Humble Cake, a cottage industry selling fantastic baked goods. The owners can provide evening meals and cakes straight to your cottage.

HALESWORTH & AROUND

Halesworth
Halesworth is another small Suffolk town with a strong identity. The railway station is in the middle of town (Halesworth is on the Ipswich to Lowestoft line), with the town museum in the old station building. The main street, the Thoroughfare, is lined with a wonderful collection of Georgian and Victorian buildings as well as a few curios from other centuries. A town trail starts from the Angel Hotel (*see p180*); pick up a leaflet inside or from the library. Little brass ducks sunk into the pavements note places of interest.

The Italianate terracotta front of the building opposite the Angel Hotel is unusually ornate for such a small place, but it's evidence that Halesworth was once one of the fastest growing places in East Anglia. At the main roundabout at the top of Bridge Street is Hooker House, once home to botanist William Hooker, who became the first director of Kew Gardens. Quay Street got its name from the bustling quay that was here in the 18th century, when the River Blyth was navigable all the way to the town. Nowadays, the waterway is used mainly for leisure activities, and there are gorgeous walks along the banks in both directions.

The buildings on the Thoroughfare house small independent concerns selling antiques, furnishings, organic food and local produce. There are also two good bookshops; Halesworth Books (no.42, 01986 873840, closed Sun) and excellent second-hand emporium James Hayward (no.20, 01986 874447, closed Mon, Thur, Sun). Tesco is still trying to build an out-of-town store here, but locals have been protesting for years. Shops around the Market Place – Wednesday is market day – include Allen's the butchers (01986 872132, closed Sun), which makes 20 different types of sausages and also has a great cheese counter, and the Market Place Wine Shop (01986 872563, closed Sun), which stocks a large variety of Suffolk and Norfolk beers.

Halesworth also has a thriving cultural scene. On Market Place is the Little Gallery (01986 875367, closed Mon, Sun), run by local artist Mary Gundry and photographer Colin Huggins. The Halesworth Gallery (Steeple End, 01986 873064, www.halesworthgallery.co.uk), larger and more established and located in the beautiful ex-almshouses opposite St Mary's Church, mounts shows of modern painting and sculpture, often by artists with local connections. The Cut Arts Centre (box office 0845 6732123) occupies the former maltings buildings on New Cut and is a strong focus for community activities, running workshops and classes as well as presenting theatre, cinema, music and comedy performances; there's a good café/bar too. It also organises the annual Halesworth Arts Festival.

FIVE SUFFOLK
BOTTLED BEERS

Suffolk is one of the best regions in the world to grow malted barley (as with hops, the soil has an effect on the final flavour) and, as a result, is prime beer-making territory. Here are a few of our favourite brews.

Adnams Broadside
Sole Bay Brewery, East Green, Southwold, IP18 6JW (01502 727200, www.adnams.co.uk). Open Brewery tours 2.15pm Mon, Wed, Fri; 10am Sat, Sun. Admission £10.
Adnams' most popular bottled beer packs a punch at 6.7% ABV, and won the 2009 International Beer Challenge Gold Medal in the strong ale category.
Tasting notes Only one hop variety is used in brewing Broadside, which provides its distinctive marmalade and fruitcake overtones. Excellent served with cheese.

Comrade Bill Bartrams Egalitarian Anti Imperialist Soviet Stout
Rougham Estate, Ipswich Road, Rougham, IP30 9LZ (01449 737655, www.bartramsbrewery.co.uk).
Bartrams is a microbrewery based at Rougham Airfield just outside Bury St Edmunds (it's waiting for permission to open a shop on the premises). The titles and labels may be eccentric, but the beer is excellent. This particular stout (6.9% ABV) won gold at the 2007 Society of Independent Brewers awards and was pronounced 'the best bottled beer in the country'.
Tasting notes A smooth texture with bitter chocolate and peppery notes.

Around Halesworth

The villages near Halesworth are prettier than the somewhat bleak and mystifying acreage around the Saints to the north. These are the inner reaches of the Blyth Valley, which leads all the way to Southwold on the coast.

Bramfield, a couple of miles south of Halesworth on the A144, certainly fits the bill (even its bus stop is thatched). Pop into the Queen's Head (*see 180*) for lunch, and then explore the unusual church of St Andrew's. It has painted white walls and a thatched roof and is the only church in Suffolk to have a round tower that is separate from the main building. The tower's flint walls are over a yard thick. Take a look at the little carved faces on the exterior window arches. Inside the church, the painted rood screen is a showstopper and there are some interesting memorials, particularly the one describing the death of Bridgett Applethwaite, who was struck by an 'Apopleptick dart' in 1737.

The village parson used to run an abattoir in the village, but now there's just KW Clarke the butcher's, which cures its own meat – its red poll beef is hung for at least two weeks. Horse fanciers might like to explore the surrounding countryside on a hack; contact the North Manor Equestrian Centre in the village (01986 784552, closed Mon, Tue).

Nearby Wenhaston has a particular boast. Its church is home to one of the few medieval 'doom' paintings (paintings of the Last Judgement) to survive the Reformation. It was whitewashed over for centuries, and then left out in the churchyard during a late 19th-century renovation. A night of rain revealed the bright painting underneath and it now has pride of place inside the church once again. Wenhaston is a beautiful village with plenty of common heathland around its edges, criss-crossed with footpaths.

Walpole, on the other side of the A144 from Wenhaston, is a pretty cluster of houses with a post office and what was once a corner shop that looks as if it's been closed and empty for decades – odd items left in the windows seem like ghosts from a bygone era. The estate of Heveningham Hall seems to own most of the land around here and the roads are atypical of Suffolk, bordered by a uniform fencing that allows good views of the sheep grazing in the fields and the managed woodlands beyond.

Heveningham and Huntingfield villages, both a little way along the B1117 from Walpole (Heveningham is on the road; the turn-off for Huntingfield is shortly before it) have collections of aesthetically pleasing houses lining their streets, but proximity to the Heveningham Estate lends something of an odd atmosphere. The Huntingfield Arms (*see right*) is a freehouse that looks very pretty sitting on the village green, while the church has an extraordinarily garish painted ceiling, with angels protruding from the walls.

Cratfield – a couple of miles further along country lanes from Huntingfield – is also remote and pretty, but continuing in the same direction from Cratfield to Fressingfield brings a landscape of mostly fairly flat arable land, broken up by farms and smallholdings. Just north-east of Fressingfield, Metfield has a well-stocked shop owned and run by the community.

Laxfield

It's worth stopping for a walk around Laxfield, south-west of Halesworth, for the sheer variety of house fronts on the main street. The old Guildhall, with its timber frame and ornate Tudor brickwork houses a museum about the domestic and working life of the village and surrounding area, but it's only open at weekends and bank holidays. Opposite is the church. All Saints has no central aisle and most of it is very plain, with white walls, plain glass and a utilitarian wooden ceiling. It's unusual still to see box pews, but several remain here (the large banked sets were built for the local school children). But the medieval font isn't plain at all; it's survived with most of its carving intact. You can enjoy pleasant views of both the church and the Guildhall while sitting in the afternoon sun in front of the Royal Oak freehouse. Through the churchyard and over the stream is Laxfield Low House, also known as the King's Head (*see below*).

Where to eat & drink

Halesworth has a lot going for it for such a small town, but unfortunately there isn't a huge choice of restaurants and bars. Your best bet is to head to one of the local pubs. The Angel Hotel (*see p180*) has a popular bar and a well-regarded Italian restaurant, Cleone's (01986 873365, www.cleones.co.uk). The White Swan (01986 872273, www.halesworthwhiteswan.co.uk) serves Adnams and is a local hub, with regular darts and pool nights, and poker sessions on Wednesday nights and Sunday afternoons. The Triple Plea (01986 874750, www.thetripleplea.co.uk) has a short menu of locally sourced food in its restaurant, while the cosy, old-fashioned bar dispenses at least three real ales.

Pubs in the surrounding villages often serve excellent food. Sadly the characterful Bell Inn in Bramfield is up for sale, but there are still plenty of eccentric pubs with real local flavour. Take the Huntingfield Arms (01986 798320, www.stmarys huntingfield.org.uk), which keeps a good Adnams and serves well-executed home cooking, and the Cratfield Poacher (01986 798206), which has occasional live music. The Buck at Rumburgh (01986 785257), near the Saints, offers fantastic Sunday roasts and fine beer, while the Fox at Shadingfield (01502 575100, www.shadingfield fox.co.uk) has gained a good reputation for its food and Adnams and Woodfordes beers.

King's Head ★

Gorams Mill Lane, Laxfield, IP13 8DW (01986 798395, http://laxfield-kingshead.co.uk). Open Summer noon-11pm Mon-Thur; noon-midnight Fri, Sat; noon-10.30pm Sun. Winter noon-3pm, 6-11pm Mon-Thur; noon-3pm, 6-midnight Fri, Sat; noon-4pm, 7-10.30pm Sun. Food served Summer noon-9pm daily. Winter noon-2pm, 7-9pm daily.

Mauldons Silver Adder

Black Adder Brewery, 13 Church Field Road, Subdury, CO10 2YA (01787 311055, www.mauldons.co.uk).
Mauldons has been brewing beer in Sudbury since 1795 (although it had a period of management under Greene King) and still creates fine bitters using traditional methods. Silver Adder is a light-coloured, 4.2% ABV brew that is fizzier than many bitters – so you get a refreshing finish without the gaseous effects of most lagers.
Tasting notes A hoppy, malted taste with bitter orange notes and a crisp finish.

Nethergate Old Growler

Growler Brewery, Pentlow, CO10 7JJ (01787 283220, www.nethergate.co.uk).
The Nethergate Brewery sits on the River Stour near Sudbury, right on the Suffolk/Essex border. The multi award-winning Old Growler porter, with its British bulldog logo, is its most famous beer, though we're also very fond of the summery, coriander-laced Umbel Ale too.
Tasting notes Malty and fruity, with powerfully hoppy overtones and a hint of liquorice.

St Peter's Best Bitter

St Peter's Hall, St Peter South Elmham, NR35 1NQ (01986 782322, www.stpetersbrewery.co.uk). Open Brewery tours Apr-Dec 11am-3pm daily. Admission £4.50.
St Peter's Brewery is hidden away in the depths of the Saints. Their Cream Stout, Grapefruit Beer and Old Style Porter have won several awards apiece, but the Best Bitter is our personal favourite.
Tasting notes A full-bodied ale with fruity caramel notes, which slips down a treat without making things too heady (it's 3.7% ABV).

This gorgeous 16th-century thatched inn just beyond the churchyard is an Adnams pub. One room is dominated by huge high-backed bench seats for drinkers, the other is dedicated to diners, and it has a good reputation for its own-cooked food. What's really unusual is that there's no bar; instead staff have to amble down to the tap room and pour pints straight from the casks. There's an arbour and small pavilion in the garden for sheltered evening drinking. Accommodation comes in the form of three rooms (£60-£70 incl breakfast) and a self-contained flat (£70).

New Round House

Thorington, IP17 3RE (01502 478220, www.new roundhouse.co.uk). Food served 10am-5pm Tue-Sat; noon-2.30pm Sun. Dinner served 7-9.30pm Fri, Sat.

The unusual keeper's cottage on the Thorington Hall Estate is now the setting for a small-scale everyday bistro that turns more serious at weekends (when you need to book). During the week, father-and-son team John and Jonathan Dean serve morning coffee, light lunches, and afternoon teas with own-baked cakes. Come the weekend, the menu is full of British classics with Mediterranean touches and uses local ingredients wherever possible.

Queen's Head (Blyford) ★

Southwold Road, Blyford, IP19 9JY (01502 478404, www.queensheadblyford.co.uk). Open Summer noon-3pm, 5.30-11pm daily. Winter 5.30-11pm Tue; noon-3pm, 5.30-11pm Wed-Sun. Food served Summer noon-2.30pm, 5.30-11pm daily. Winter 5.30-11pm Tue; noon-2.30pm, 5.30-11pm Wed-Sun. No credit cards.

A pretty thatched Adnams pub, with a menu that foregrounds the best of Suffolk's produce with a particular focus on game in season. Head chef Paul Freeman took over in 2009 and runs his own smallholding with chickens, pigs bees, fruit trees and vegetable beds to help stock his kitchen. The menu changes according to the season but expect the unexpected. Pike fish cakes, anyone?

Queen's Head (Bramfield) ★

The Street, Bramfield, IP19 9HT (01986 784214, www.queensheadbramfield.co.uk). Open 11.45am-2.30pm, 6.30-11pm Mon-Sat; noon-3pm, 7-10.30pm Sun. Lunch served noon-2pm daily. Dinner served 6.30-9.15pm Mon-Fri; 6.30-10pm Sat; 7-9pm Sun.

This lovely pub has been run by the same couple for more than a decade; they're keen supporters of the local and organic food movement in Suffolk. The menu is full of meat, fruit and veg from local farms and fish from the nearby coast, and there's Adnams beer on tap. The bars and lounge have large open fires and scrubbed pine tables, and the large enclosed garden is great for active children.

Where to stay

Angel Hotel

Thoroughfare, Halesworth, IP19 8AH (01986 873365, www.angel-halesworth.co.uk). Rates £69 double incl breakfast.

A small hotel in the middle of town, with seven en suite bedrooms – ask if you can have one of the large bedrooms at the front as the back rooms are much smaller and a bit dark. Interiors are dated throughout, but the staff are ultra-

friendly and helpful, and the on-site Italian restaurant is decent. The town trail starts from the hotel's front door.

Brights Farm

Bramfield , IP19 9AG (01986 784212, www.brights farm.co.uk). Rates £70-£80 double incl breakfast. No credit cards.

This working organic farm has four homely B&B bedrooms, plus a sitting room with a TV, DVD and lots of books. Breakfasts are served in the garden room overlooking the pond and use produce from the farm, including eggs and own-made bread and jams. The best thing, however, are the 12 miles of walks through ancient meadows and woods that start right outside the farmhouse door.

Duke House B&B

Beccles Road, Upper Holton, IP19 8NN (01986 873259, www.halesworth.ws/dukehouse). Rates £60-£65 double incl breakfast. No credit cards.

A former coaching inn set in tranquil gardens, with a meadow and orchard, close to Halesworth. Breakfasts full of tasty local ingredients are served in the conservatory, which overlooks fields. The three double rooms (all en suite) are comfortable and modishly chintzy. There are wonderful country walks in the neighbourhood.

Grove Farm ★

Bramfield, IP19 9AG (07751 268180, www.holiday farmhouse.co.uk). Rates £625-£725 per week for 4 people; £2,100-£2,250 per week for 13 people. No credit cards.

There are three self-catering properties on this farm a mile outside Bramfield. Nicely spaced from one another, each has been renovated to make the most of the buildings' historic features while providing a stylish, modern vibe. The Granary has lovely beams in the vaulted ceilings of the bedrooms upstairs and an open-plan living area. The Milking Parlour has a separate living room, but otherwise offers much the same accommodation as the Granary; both sleep four. The main farmhouse (with six bedrooms sleeping up to 13) has two sitting rooms, a large kitchen and a games room.

Hall Farm B&B

Wenhaston, IP19 9HE (01502 478742, www. wenhaston.net/hallfarm). Rates £70 double incl breakfast. No credit cards.

Hall Farm is set in a lovely secluded spot in the middle of pretty meadows – great for walks or cycle rides. The 17th-century farmhouse has bags of character. Both bedrooms are bright and airy, and one has a roll-top bath. A guests' sitting room has a collection of books about Suffolk to browse through. Breakfasts are cooked on the Aga and include organic eggs from the farm.

Roslyn House

Church Farm Lane, Halesworth (07947 366858, www.roslyn-house.yolasite.com). Rates £210-£390 per week. No credit cards.

Down a quiet lane two minutes walk from the centre of Halesworth, this charming house sleeps four (one double, one twin). Decor is modern but homely; there's a lovely kitchen-dining room, a separate living room with TV and DVD player, and a small, south-facing patio garden with table and chairs for alfresco dining.

SUFFOLK

Suffolk Coast: Lowestoft to Dunwich

The northern stretch of the Suffolk coast has the county's only traditional English seaside resort. Sitting on the border with Norfolk, Lowestoft has the amusement arcades, donkey rides and acres of white sand that just aren't typical of the rest of the county. It's a bit tacky, but in a good way. The rest of the coast consists of crumbling sandy cliffs, marshy fields, shingle-dominated beaches, and settlements that are falling into the sea; most of Dunwich, once one of the largest towns in Britain, is already under the waves, a village drowned. Walberswick and Southwold are very popular with middle-class holidaymakers looking for a taste of the simple life, but both have retained a strong sense of identity despite the influx of visitors. Walberswick is a small village known for its crab fishing, while larger Southwold has many genteel attractions including an unusually tasteful pier with a wonderfully eccentric amusement arcade. The whole stretch of coast south of Kessingland is designated as an Area of Outstanding Natural Beauty and begs to be explored on foot.

LOWESTOFT & AROUND

A few miles south of Great Yarmouth lies the coastal border of Norfolk and Suffolk. Corton is now the first settlement on the Suffolk side; south from here to Kessingland is Suffolk's only stretch of classically tacky seaside attractions. Corton had one of the first designated naturist beaches in England, but it was closed at the end of 2009 because erosion had reduced the beach significantly from its glory days.

Lowestoft

Lowestoft is the second largest town in Suffolk, and can claim to contain the most easterly piece of land in the British Isles (at Ness Point), but it isn't what you'd call quaint or pretty. The pedestrianised town centre is full of chain stores that could place you anywhere in England if it weren't for the seagulls overhead, and it's hard to catch a glimpse of the sea because the harbour area is boxed in by industrial buildings used by the once considerable Lowestoft fishing fleet. There's a good bookshop, Panda Books (117 High Street, 01502 574515), and a regular market – though the stalls are located next to the unlovely 1980s Britten Shopping Centre. Even the town's Marina Theatre (01502 533200 www.marinatheatre.co.uk) is hidden down an unappealing backstreet; it doubles as a cinema when there's nothing on stage.

If you're interested in Lowestoft's fishing heritage, pop aboard the *Mincarlo* (*see p188*), the last remaining fishing trawler to be built in the town: from Easter to October it flits between the yacht harbour and Great Yarmouth. If you'd prefer to sample the wares, head for the Old Smokehouse

(37 Raglan Street, 01502 581929, closed Sun), which sells traditionally smoked Lowestoft fish, or the World Of Fish (6 Cooke Road, 01502 517171, www.world-of-fish.co.uk, closed Mon, Sun) in the town's industrial estate, but worth the trip.

To be fair, there is a nice side to Lowestoft. Coach parties of retirees and cars loaded with families head to the sandy beaches located south of the harbour and across the bascule bridge for a classic British seaside day out. The further south you go, the more pleasant it gets, with seafront public gardens, beach huts, Victorian villas facing the sea (Benjamin Britten lived at 21 Kirkley Cliff Road as a child – the building, like many of the neighbouring houses, is now a B&B), and the Claremont pier; although you can no longer walk along the pier, it has amusements at the shore end and is a dramatic landmark.

The other pier, South Pier, was incorporated into the harbour and also has amusement arcades at its shore end. The all-glass East Point Pavilion houses the tourist information office (Royal Plain, 01502 533600, www.visit-lowestoft.co.uk). Kids can splash around in the new play fountains outside; for inclement days, there's the indoor play area Mayhem next door. For bigger thrills, head for Pleasurewood Hills (Leisure Way, NR32 5DZ, 01502 586000, www.pleasurewoodhills. com, open June-Oct). It's north of town, just off the A12 on the way to Corton. Unlike giant theme parks such as Thorpe Park, this is good for families with young children: it's relatively small-scale and there are plenty of rides for the shorter thrill-seeker. The place could do with a bit of TLC, but at least the queues aren't huge all year round.

Oulton Broad

On Lowestoft's western fringes lies Oulton Broad. It's known as the southern gateway to the Norfolk Broads, but is also a good point from which to explore the lesser-known Suffolk Broads along the River Waveney. There's a large grass car park at Oulton Broad village (since the 1950s, really just a suburb of Lowestoft) from where you can walk through Nicholas Everitt Park, past the playground and dinky old-fashioned amusement park, to the southern banks of the water. There you can enjoy the peaceful tacking and jibing of boats from the Waveney & Oulton Broad Yacht Club, although it's also popular with far less tranquil motorboats.

If you want to take to the water, head around the corner to Mutford Lock, where Waveney River Tours (01502 574903) runs trips several times daily from April to October (do check first that all advertised trips are running, especially outside school holidays).

Oulton Broad is not what you'd call a foodie mecca, so it's best to take a picnic. There's a selection of cafés facing the lock, but all offer a similar litany of fried food. The park café does at least have pleasant views from its terrace (and brass bands on summer Sundays), but the food and decor are straight out of the 1970s. Near the café is the Lowestoft Museum. It's housed inside a pretty and unusual flint building, but there's not much inside for the general browser except perhaps some paintings of Lowestoft docks in their pomp. Much more fun is the open-air East Anglia Transport Museum (see p188) in nearby Carlton Colville.

Kessingland

Kessingland is a relatively large village, but is only notable for its extensive holiday park (0871 664 9749, www.kessinglandbeach.org.uk) right next to the beach, where you can rent static caravans or pitch a tent; its car boot sale every Sunday from February to December; and nearby wildlife park Africa Alive (see p188). There's no coast road along this whole stretch (or indeed anywhere much else along the Suffolk shoreline) thanks to the uncertain terrain of saltmarshes and crumbling coastline. The best way to explore the landscape is on foot. Experience the drama of the eroding coast a few miles away at Covehithe. By the size of the original church walls (a smaller thatched church now sits within the ruins of the larger building), the village was clearly once a parish to be reckoned with. From the church, take the road to the sea. It ends abruptly, but you can ignore the signs claiming there is no public right of way. This is a permissive footpath and a popular route – though do keep back from the clifftop as a few more feet of land tumble into the sea each year. A bit further north, the trail joins the Suffolk Coast & Heaths Path, which turns back inland.

If all this walking has developed a thirst, swing by the Real Ale Shop on Priory Farm (01502 676031, closed Mon) in nearby Wrentham. The farmyard looks unpromising, until you see the newly converted barn. What used to be full of animal feed is now stocked to the rafters with local bottled beers (plus a few brews from Cornwall); they even stock a selection brewed by a local hospital anaesthetist in his garage. Staff are very keen to advise on the best buys and you'll probably come away with an armful of Brandon, Elveden, Oulton and Nethergate beers.

Keen hikers can get from Kessingland (start at the Sailor's Home pub) to Southwold in about three hours. Follow the clifftop path or, at low tide, walk along the shore: take in the large Suffolk skies, wonderful sense of isolation and the undisturbed landscape. The knowledge that it all might not be here in a few years' time adds a certain wistfulness to the experience. Just before Southwold, take a look at the house that's teetering on the cliff, just yards from the sea. It's owned by local pensioner Peter Boggis, who has been trying to build up the coastal defences by dumping soil along the shore, but his efforts can only stave off the inevitable for so long.

Where to eat & drink

A picnic is the best choice for a day on Lowestoft beach. Otherwise, options include Flying Fifteens (19A Esplanade, 01502 581188, closed Mon-Fri May, all Oct-Apr), which serves a world-class bacon buttie as well as Cromer crab, great ham and good soup and salads. It also has probably the largest choice of teas in Suffolk. The café/restaurant inside East Point Pavilion isn't bad either, offering fish and chips and other seaside classics. For a decent pint, head to the friendly Triangle Tavern (29 St Peter's Street, 01502 582 711, www.thetriangletavern. co.uk) in the Triangle Market Place on St Peter's Street. It brews its own Green Jack Ales, and bands play every Thursday and Friday in the front bar, where there's a roaring fire in winter. The back bar has a pool table and a jukebox.

Where to stay

As you'd expect, Lowestoft has plenty of B&Bs, but nothing in the area exceeds seaside resort expectations, with the exception of the Ivy House below.

Ivy House Country Hotel

Ivy Lane, Oulton Broad, NR33 8HY (01502 501353, www.ivyhousecountryhotel.co.uk). Rates £115-£170 double incl breakfast.

Not all the bedrooms are up to boutique hotel design standards, but this is a gorgeous spot with gardens leading on to Oulton Broad shore, where you can stroll by the water or take a boat trip. The restaurant, in an old beamed, thatched barn, does sterling breakfasts and dinners that focus on local seasonal ingredients.

SOUTHWOLD ★

There's a certain sort of Londoner who knows this stretch of British coastline very well and has carved a well-worn groove up the A12. It's unspoilt, serenely beautiful, culturally well mannered and offers fantastic opportunities for the walker,

Southwold. See p183.

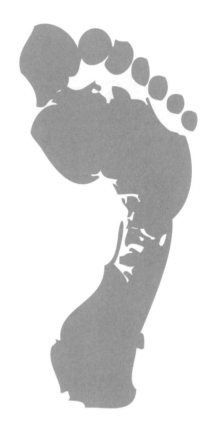

Whatever your carbon footprint, we can reduce it

For over a decade we've been leading the way in carbon offsetting and carbon management.

In that time we've purchased carbon credits from over 200 projects spread across 6 continents. We work with over 300 major commercial clients and thousands of small and medium sized businesses, which rely upon our market-leading quality assurance programme, our experience and absolute commitment to deliver the right solution for each client.

Why not give us a call?

T: London (020) 7833 6000

www.CarbonNeutral.com

birdwatcher and urban weekender in search of a perfectly groomed rural experience. Southwold, in particular, is so popular with out-of-towners that second homes make up more than 60 per cent of the town's housing. The influence of the capital is evident in the chichi clothes in the town's boutiques and the food on offer in both restaurants and shops (the Black Olive Deli on the High Street even sells sausage rolls from renowned Marylebone butcher Ginger Pig). So what's the appeal?

Basically, Southwold is the sort of small town sophisticated city types dream of moving to for a simpler life. It's picture-postcard idyllic, with sandy beaches, a classy promenade, charming, higgledy-piggledy streets and verdant greens. What's more, there's absolutely no urban sprawl, thanks to the town being bounded to the south by the River Blyth, to the east by the North Sea and to the north by Buss Creek. It's almost an island, and has behaved accordingly for many centuries.

As in much of the rest of north Suffolk, the town's planners have resolutely steered away from out-of-town supermarkets. There is a small Somerfield on Market Place, but the smaller independent shops along the High Street and surrounding streets thrive. There's a butcher, a greengrocer, a fishmonger, several delis, a bakery, and the Adnams Wine Shop on Pinkney's Lane. There's even an old-fashioned sweet shop on St James's Green, which sells chewing nuts, lemon bonbons and sucking mints by the quarter, as well as sugar mice and fudge. Southwold brewery Adnams supplies all the local pubs with barrels of its irresistible brews, and also runs a small café in its Cellar & Kitchen Shop (4 Drayman Square, Victoria Street, 01502 727244, http://cellarand kitchen.adnams.co.uk). There are also a couple of bookshops: Bookthrift (10 Market Place, 01502 724999) and the Orwell Book Shop (64 High Street, 01502 724370). Market days are Monday and Thursday, and antiques and arts and crafts sales often appear in the lovely little Town Hall on the High Street.

The town punches above its weight for culture too. Museums include the Southwold Museum (see p188) and Britain's only Amber Museum, which is in the Amber Shop on the High Street (15 Market Place, 01502 723394, www.amber shop.co.uk). Michael Palin opened the Electric Picture Palace cinema in 2002 (Blackmill Road, 07815 769565, www.exploresouthwold.co.uk/ cinema); it has a tiny Wurlitzer organ, and runs an interesting and varied schedule of films. Jill Freud (widow of Clement) runs the Southwold summer theatre season (www.southwoldtheatre. org) and has been curating a varied programme for adults and children for over two decades. In short, the pleasures and entertainments of Southwold are genteel. None more so than the delightful Sailors' Reading Room (see p188) on East Cliff – every town should have one.

Southwold's churches run from the magnificent flint beauty of St Edmund's (like a lot of churches along the coast, it's vast compared to the size of the town today) to the eccentricity of the Sacred Heart Catholic church and its mock Tudor presbytery, to the simplicity of the Wesleyan Chapel (no longer a place of worship).

The skyline is dominated by Southwold Lighthouse (see p188), which nestles among the houses and still acts as a crucial beacon warning passing ships of the coast's treacherous sandbanks. Developments in technology have seen the bulbs shrink from the size of a man's head to three tiny 90-watt Osram Halostar lamps. With cunning refraction, this trio of pinpricks can be seen from a distance of 12 nautical miles.

The seafront

Southwold's beaches are glorious, with wide stretches of golden sand where you can set up camp and sit for whole days at a time. Colourful beach huts are available to hire (£130-£180 per week) but you'll have to plan well in advance; bookings are taken more than a year ahead – contact HA Adnams Estate Agent on 01502 723292.

Southwold Pier is a key landmark (North Parade, 01502 722105, www.southwoldpier.co.uk). To get to it, there's a large car park just next to the shore end, or you can take a 15-minute walk along the seafront clifftop from the centre of town, passing town houses that sell for almost £1 million and pastel-hued beach huts below. The pier was refurbished in 2001 to much acclaim; in line with the rest of Southwold, it's significantly more tasteful than the average seaside pier. It's open all year round (except Christmas Day).

On the pier itself, neat white buildings along the bleached wooden boardwalk house various eateries, and shops selling trinkets, clothes and toys. Also here is the Under the Pier Show, probably the most eccentric amusement arcade in the land, as well as a family-friendly alternative with two penny push machines, bowling and air hockey tables. The Under the Pier Show has 'games' and 'rides' customised by mechanical artist and humourist Tim Hunkin (who also made the wonderfully offbeat and witty performing clocks both on the pier and at London Zoo). Enjoy a Mobility Masterclass, a trip in the Bathyscape, or a session in the Expressive Photobooth, which will give you an amusing memento of your visit. New in summer 2009 was Whack A Banker – according to pier owner Stephen Bourne, it's been so popular and played with such feeling that the mallets have to be frequently replaced.

As well as the amusements on offer, the sea end is a good spot to try line fishing for cod, plaice, mackerel and bass (you can pick up bait and tackle from the Southwold Angling Centre on Station Road, 01502 722085). Just opposite the shore end of the pier is the pitch and putt mini golf course and model boat pond where regular regattas are held (see p193). In summer, a Punch and Judy show is held six times a day, just beside the pier on the beach.

The Harbour

Across the sedate greens south of Queen Street, past the cannons resting on Gun Hill

Places to visit

Holy Trinity Church, Blythburgh

LOWESTOFT & AROUND

Africa Alive
White's Lane, Kessingland, NR33 7TF (01502 740291, www.africa-alive.co.uk). Open 10am-4pm daily. Admission £9.50; free-£8.50 reductions.
A little bit of Africa in Suffolk. See rhinos, giraffes, lions and cheetahs from the Safari Roadtrain, enjoy the birds of prey displays or watch the animals during feeding time. It's not cheap, but is a hit with families all year round. There's also a farmyard corner where children can get a bit closer to some four-legged friends, and an adventure playground.

East Anglia Transport Museum
Chapel Road, Carlton Colville, NR33 8BL (01502 518459, www.eatm.org.uk). Open Apr-Sept times vary, phone for details. Admission £6.50; £4.50-£5.50 reductions.
An outdoor museum with a bustling 1930s street scene, which offers the chance to ride on trams, trolleybuses and various models of bus. The East Suffolk Light Railway chuffs around the site and there's a tearoom if you want to make an afternoon of it. This and the museum are staffed by volunteers, so service is not always what it could be.

Mincarlo Fishing Trawler
Heritage Quay, South Pier, Lowestoft, NR33 0AP (01502 565234, www.lydiaeva.org.uk). Open Easter-Oct 10am-3pm daily. Admission free.
Visit the last surviving fishing vessel from Lowestoft's once mighty fleet. Built and fitted in the town, the *Mincarlo* spends the summer flitting between Great Yarmouth and Lowestoft. Visitors can tour the ship and learn about the history of the local fishing industry.

SOUTHWOLD

Sailors' Reading Room ★
East Cliff, IP18 6EL (01502 723812). Open Summer 9am-5pm daily. Winter 9am-3.30pm daily. Admission free.
This lovely, high-ceilinged reading room was built in 1864 to encourage local sailors and fishermen to stay out of nearby pubs. Local women would read to those who didn't have the skill themselves. Today, anyone can go in and peruse the newspapers at the large wooden tables or curl up in an armchair with a novel while listening to the sea crashing on the shore outside. Model boats and mementoes of Southwold's seafaring history adorn the walls.

Southwold Lighthouse
Shadbroke Road, IP18 6LU (01502 722576, www.trinityhouse.co.uk). Open Apr-Nov times vary, check website for details. Admission £3; £2 reductions; £8 family.
Southwold's lighthouse is open to the public on weekends, bank holidays and occasional weekdays – check the website for exact timings. Tours take 20-30 minutes and include a steep climb – 92 steps – to the lamp room at the top for sterling views to Lowestoft in the north and Sizewell in the south.

Southwold Museum ★
9-11 Victoria Street, IP18 6HZ (01502 726097, www.southwoldmuseum.org). Open Aug 10.30am-noon, 2-4pm daily. Easter-July, Sept, Oct 2-4pm daily. Admission free.
This delightful small social history museum explains how Southwold emerged as a favourite holiday resort in the 18th century, when the harbour proved unreliable

thanks to the changing coastline. Following a total refurb in 2007, the imaginative displays are a joy. Memorable exhibits include Southwold at War and copies of sections of the Walberswick Scroll, a 66ft-long panorama of Walberswick village (building by building, shack by shack) by Camden Town Group artist John Doman Turner. Children should head for the small red cabinet holding different objects in its many compartments. Each prompts a story when placed on a touch-sensitive screen.

WALBERSWICK TO SIZEWELL

Dunwich Museum
St James Street, Dunwich, IP17 3DT (01728 648796, www.dunwichmuseum.org.uk). Open Apr-Sept 11.30am-4.30pm daily; Oct noon-4pm daily; Mar 2-4.30pm Sat, Sun. Admission free.
A small but very informative museum, with a 3D model showing what lies under the sea, and an interesting set of timeline displays about the gradual disappearance of the once mighty Dunwich.

Holy Trinity Church, Blythburgh
Church Road, Blythburgh (www.holytrinityblythburgh.org.uk).
A stunning church, inside and out. The brick floors and plain walls suit modern minimalist tastes, and the tie-beam roof is magnificent, with its faded original paintwork and characterful angels (all have unique faces and are placed, unusually, in the middle of the ceiling rather than at the sides). Legend has it that the scorch marks on the north door are the paw marks of the devil, who took the form of a black dog, Old Shuck, in August 1577 and ran down the nave killing two parishioners before toppling the steeple on his way out. More prosaically, the rings in the pillars nearby were probably used for tethering horses. The carvings on the bench ends in the nave and fronting the choir stalls are also worth a closer look. Above the porch is a small priests' room, which you can access via a tiny and disconcertingly uneven spiral staircase to the left of the main door.

RSPB Minsmere ★
Westleton, IP17 3BY (01728 648281, www.rspb.org. uk/minsmere). Open 9am-dusk daily. Admission £5; £1.50-£3 reductions.
Minsmere has been a nature reserve for more than 60 years and in that time has expanded bit by bit to cover 2,500 acres. It has been pivotal in encouraging avocets back to Britain after an absence of over a century, but you don't have to be a bird lover to enjoy the walks around the reedbeds, along the sand dunes and through woodland. That said, it's best to bring a pair of binoculars (or hire some from the visitor's centre). Bird hides dotted around the reserve offer close-up views over the reedbeds and ponds but just standing out in the open, you'll see plenty of birds flying overhead. There's a range of guided walks to make the most of a visit. In spring they might take you to see the avocets, bitterns and marsh harriers and in autumn there are 'migration watch' walks that locate the waders, ducks and geese visiting the reserve. There are plenty of organised activities for children and a visitor's centre with a shop and tearoom.

SUFFOLK

(to commemorate the Battle of Sole Bay between the English and the French in 1672) and about half a mile south along the dunes lies Southwold Harbour. Small and pretty, it has a timeless and informal villagey feel. Just past the popular caravan and campsite run by Waveney Borough Council (Ferry Road, 01502 722486, www.waveney.gov.uk) is the Alfred Corry Museum (Ferry Road, 01502 723200, http://freespace.virgin.net/david.cragie), housed in a Cromer lifeboat shed brought here in 1998. It charts the history of Southwold's Lifeboat Crews from 1893 to 1918. As you walk up Blackshore, heading inland, there are families crabbing in all but the most inhospitable of weathers. Sailing and fishing boats line the shore and you can buy that day's catch from the Sole Bay Fish Company (*see p190*). There's also a chandlery, and a variety of refreshment options, including a wonderfully unpretentious tearoom. A tiny rowboat ferry (Apr-Oct) takes pedestrians, dogs and the odd bicycle and pram to Walberswick. You can also walk to Walberswick by going a mile up the Blyth estuary to cross at the Bailey Bridge to the other side.

Where to eat & drink

There's an abundance of good food in Southwold, although eating out can be expensive. Real ale drinkers should be happy, thanks to Adnams' monopoly on the town's beer pumps. Adnams also runs a number of pub-hotels in town, including the longstanding Swan (*see p193*), which is right next to the brewery and offers food in both bar and restaurant. Cooking is Modern European in style, and uses plenty of local fish.

For a cheaper bite, Adnams also has a café in its Cellar & Kitchen shop (*see p187*), serving baked potatos, paninis and sandwiches. There's seating inside and out. The Lord Nelson (*see p193*) is deservedly popular in high season, but you can avoid the queues by heading instead to the good-value Red Lion (2 South Green, 01502 722385). Down on the pier, you can get takeaway fish and chips, sandwiches and deliciously creamy ice-creams at the daytime-only Promenade café, or simple family-friendly food at the Boardwalk (01502 722105, open Nov-Apr Fri & Sat only, May-Oct daily), which has a more sophisticated menu for evening diners.

More options await at the harbour end. The fabulous café next to the Chandlery on Blackshore serves excellent own-made pies and quiches, baked potatoes with imaginative salads, and top-notch cakes – all at very reasonable prices. There's even a pack of cards, in case it's raining. Pick up fish and chips and seafood at Christina Cara's takeaway hut or take your own bread and wine to accompany a huge and varied seafood platter at the Sole Bay Fish Company (Shed 22E, Blackshore, 01502 724241, www.solebayfishco.co.uk). Further up Blackshore, the bustling Harbour Inn (01502 722381) is a favourite for large portions of fish and chips, plenty of outdoor seating beside the River Blyth, and the friendly lifeboatman landlord.

CULTURAL CONNECTIONS

● Charles Dickens came to stay with Lowestoft entrepreneur Samuel Morton Peto in the 1880s, and set *David Copperfield* in Lowestoft's beach village and nearby Blundeston.
● Damien Hirst studied in Southwold under the tuition of resident artist Margaret Mellis.
● The Southwold Harbour estuary is pivotal in the plot of Peter Greenaway's film *Drowning by Numbers*.
● Julie Myerson set her murder story *Something Might Happen* in the sleepy seaside town of Southwold, which she had visited as a child and returned to after having her own children.
● Walberswick is renamed Steerborough in Esther Freud's novel *The Sea House*, but the village, with its hidden houses, marshes and beautiful seascape, is an unmistakeable backdrop to the narrative.
● Henry James and Jerome K Jerome both stayed in Ship Cottage in Dunwich (still available to rent) while dreaming up plots for assorted novels.

Harbour Camping & Caravan Park. See p193.

Dunwich. See p196.

Crown

High Street, Southwold, IP18 6DP (01502 722186, http://hotels.adnams.co.uk/the-crown). Open noon-3pm, 5.30-11.30pm Mon-Sat; noon-4pm, 7-10.30pm Sun. Lunch served noon-2.30pm (2pm winter) Mon-Sat; noon-3pm Sun. Dinner served Summer 5.30-9.30pm Mon-Sat; 7-9pm Sun. Winter 6.30-9pm Mon-Fri; 6-9.30pm Sat; 7-9pm Sun.

This Adnams hotel may look offputtingly sanitised from the outside, but its weathered charm remains intact inside. The beamed main bar has mismatched tables and chairs that have no doubt heard many a salty tale shared over a pint of Broadside, while the smaller, oak-panelled locals' bar at the rear is friendly and informal. Local ingredients (Lowestoft cod, Cromer crab cakes, Suffolk lamb) figure large. Arrive early as you can't book. The 14 bedrooms (£145-£165 double incl breakfast) have a pleasingly contemporary feel.

Lord Nelson ★

East Street, IP18 6EJ (01502 722079, www.the lordnelsonsouthwold.co.uk). Open 10.30am-11pm daily. Lunch served noon-2pm, dinner served 7-9pm daily.

A homely and perenially popular pub, located bang on the seafront and just round the corner from the Sailors' Reading Room. There's seating in a courtyard garden, as well as the main bar and two small side rooms. Staff are good-natured, even when the place is heaving – a frequent occurrence in summer. They pour a lovely pint of Adnams and serve classic pub grub; the huge portions of cod and chips are hard to resist.

Sutherland House

56 High Street, IP18 6DN, 01502 724544, www.sutherlandhouse.co.uk). Apr-Nov Lunch served noon-2.30pm, dinner served 7-9pm daily. Dec-Mar Lunch served noon-2.30pm Tue-Sun. Dinner served 7-9pm Tue-Sat.

Modern European dishes using plenty of local, seasonal ingredients, including pork from Blythburgh, fish from Southwold's fishermen and vegetables from the hotel's allotment are what you'll find at this smart but not offputting restaurant and hotel. The handsome building is medieval, but the rooms have been tastefully brought up-to-date (doubles from £140).

Tilly's

51A High Street, IP18 6DJ (01502 725677, www.tillys ofsouthwold.co.uk). Open 9am-7pm daily.

There are several tearooms in Southwold, but Tilly's is the best, dispensing traditional English breakfasts, light lunches and tiered teas inside or out in the walled garden. Cakes are freshly made classics and the ice-cream sundaes something special. It's not quite as characterful as when it was Sarah's, with a gift shop attached, but there's more space now the tearoom has taken over entirely. Staff are very friendly and accommodating, though we (and probably they) could do without the period-costume uniforms.

Where to stay

If you're relectant to leave urban glamour behind, stay at Sutherland House (*see above*), particularly the top-floor John Sutherland suite.

Things to do

SOUTHWOLD

Coastal Voyager Boat trips

Stage S35, Southwold Harbour, IP18 6TA (07887 525082, www.coastalvoyager.co.uk). Open by arrangement only. Rates from £20; £10 reductions; £54 family.

Coastal Voyager, based on a New Zealand Coastguard vessel, has 12 seats, and a deep V-hull to ensure a smooth ride even in heavy seas. Take a high-octane whizz around Sole Bay for half an hour and annoy the fishermen, or a longer cruise around the coast to say hello to the seals at Scroby Sands and view a nearby windfarm. There's also a three-and-a-half-hour round trip up the River Blyth with a stop for lunch. Ingeniously, Coastal Voyager run a Walker One Way service, which means you can have both a good walk and a boat trip.

Model boat sailing

Opposite Southwold Pier (01315 527146, www.exploresouthwold.co.uk/smyr). Phone or check website for details.

Several regattas are held each year (and were first established as far back as 1894) on the model boat pond next to the boating lake, which lies opposite the shore end of Southwold Pier. If you fancy trying your hand at racing a model boat (no radio-controlled vessels allowed), there are always some available to be borrowed or bought on the day.

Harbour Camping & Caravan Park

Ferry Road, IP18 6ND (01502 722486, www.waveney.gov.uk). Open Apr-Oct. Rates £15 for 2 people.

This council-run campsite at the end of Ferry Road, just before the harbour, offers fabulous, no-frills camping in a sheltered site. The sea is a short scramble over the dunes, and the unfettered sunset views are amazing.

Palm House

Cautley Road, IP18 6DD (01502 722717, www.suffolk-secrets.co.uk/cottage-details/PLM). Rates £942-£1,600 per week.

For upmarket self-catering, book into this three-storey Edwardian family home, set in a quiet road a few minutes from both the beach and the centre of town. Decorated to an elegant standard, it sleeps eight adults and two children (there's even a separate kids' sitting room with a TV, games and books).

Swan ★

Market Place, IP18 6EG (01502 722186, http://hotels.adnams.co.uk/the-swan). Rates £95-£210 double incl breakfast.

Stay in the main hotel buildings for traditional bedrooms overlooking the town and the sea (two suites in particular offer spectacular views) or in the refurbished (summer 2009) Lighthouse Rooms. These 'chalets' are now elegantly furnished, in line with the rest of the hotel: there are 16 rooms, all facing the garden and with their own patio area – great for winding down after a long day on the beach.

Looking south from Minsmere towards Sizewell

WALBERSWICK TO SIZEWELL

Walberswick & Blythburgh

Just across the Blyth estuary from Southwold is Walberswick, a very pretty village protected by the dunes from the sea. In fact, it's so good-looking that artists have flocked here for years to capture its beauty. Charles Rennie Mackintosh had a house in Walberswick, and Philip Wilson Steer made it the centre for his circle of English Impressionists in the 1880s. Although some find the village's determined celebration of the past, with its chocolate-box houses and pristine village green, a little forced, it's undoubtedly a lovely place to visit and a great starting point for a gentle stroll or a series of longer walks inland or along the coast. The Anchor pub (see p198) is worth a detour too. Footpaths criss-cross the mud flats, which are home to a wide variety of birds. If you're visiting in August, don't miss the British Open Crabbing Championships.

Like Southwold, Walberswick has its share of famous admirers. If Southwold has Michael Palin, Walberswick has the Freuds. Clement made this his family's home, and his widow Jill still lives here, while their daughter Emma and her partner Richard Curtis, have a house here too. Clement's niece Esther Freud may have rebelled and bought a second home in Southwold, but her novel *The Sea House* is set in Walberswick.

HARD AS FLINT

Suffolk is built on chalk, clay and sand, so locating large amounts of stone is tricky. The most readily available hard building material around here is flint, and so it's no surprise there are flint walls everywhere, on houses, barns and churches, and defining the boundaries of gardens and churchyards across the county. Much of what you see in domestic buildings are field flints, picked off the land. But mined and knapped flints are often used in grander buildings, presenting a flat, shiny face to the outside world and used for decorative work, as on the beautiful St Mary's church in Woodbridge (see p235). Stone was so scarce in Suffolk that when Leiston Abbey (see p242) was built in 1363, most of the stone was dragged over from a former abbey at Minsmere, while the flint walls were covered with plaster in order to make them look like stone. Flints vary widely in colour, and some archaeologists could tell you exactly where they were in East Anglia just from the flints on the nearest building.

A few miles inland from Walberswick lies Blythburgh. It's bisected by the busy A12, which rather spoils its charms, but it's worth visiting to see the huge Holy Trinity Church (see p189). Nicknamed the 'Cathedral of the Marshes', it's a wonderful building; even atheists will get a spiritual lift once inside. The light streams in through the clerestory windows and produces a gauzy glow around the simple nave. It's almost more impressive at night, when it's floodlit. A little way down the road, the White Hart pub (see p198) has the full range of Adnams' ales and is a good spot for lunch.

Elsewhere in Blythburgh, there's a delightfully low-key village hall built on the remains of the old priory, and the 18th-century Bulcamp Workhouse, known locally as the 'death trap' for the high mortality rate among inmates. Later turned into a hospital, it was converted into private dwellings in 1994. The marshes spreading around the Blyth estuary are prime birdwatching territory and a wonderful place for a walk; the light bounces off the stretches of water in a way that makes you think of Turner's masterpieces. Footpaths lead the three miles to Walberswick, where you can continue along the shore for a longer walk.

Dunwich ★

Further down the coast is one of Suffolk's must-see villages, Dunwich. The central paradox of this tiny seaside settlement is that its appeal lies in what it no longer has to offer. In the 13th century it was the sixth most important town in England: a thriving port and major hub of the wool and corn trade, with 18 parish churches, its own mint and two representatives in parliament.

But for more than 2,000 years the town has been steadily consumed by the sea. Now all that's left is a pebble beach with a car park and the Flora Tea Rooms (see p198), and about ten lonely buildings. Dunwich folklore runs parallel to the already colourful truth. Legend has it that on certain nights, you can hear the distant toll of the church bells rising from the sea. The only way to get a sense of the town's former glories is to walk through the ruins of Greyfriars monastery, itself perilously close to a watery grave and looking wistfully out to sea. There's a palpable sense of loss and gloom to the whole place, and it's no wonder both Turner and Constable were keen to commit it to canvas. The full story of the town is told at Dunwich Museum (see p189). Dunwich's only pub, the Ship (see p198), is next to the museum.

The shingle beach is not the easiest of walking surfaces and it's a case of two steps forward, one step back. Even so, it's a pleasant hour's walk to the RSPB reserve at Minsmere (see p189). On the way you'll pass children throwing stones into the water, the occasional hardy swimmer, and fishermen hunkered down in the pebbles near the water's edge. Dunwich is renowned for sea bass in summer; in winter, cod rise to the bait. The day's catch can be supplemented at the produce stall just inside one of the private gardens on the way from the beach car park to James Street.

Dunwich Heath

The desolate shingle beach backs on to a heath teeming with wildlife, two of the largest reedbeds in Britain and a woodland where red stags can be heard rutting in autumn. The narrow roads in between are great for cycling and there are many footpaths through the woods and heathland. The Heath is run by the National Trust, and is a major draw for nature lovers. It's a beautiful patch, glowing with bright purple heather in the summer when butterflies, bees and dragonflies patrol the air, while adders, slow worms and grass snakes can occasionally be spotted slithering away from

the paths. The birdlife is various and plentiful, although the best sightings are at neighbouring reserve RSPB Minsmere.

Westleton to Eastbridge

Westleton is a typically attractive Suffolk village with a large open green lined by small cottages, and lanes leading off to a duck pond, an art gallery, an unusual thatched and towerless church and a handsome village hall with a blue clockface. The ex-Methodist chapel is now a second-hand bookshop, the post office doubles as a general store and the village supports two pubs (see p198).

There are a couple of good farm shops nearby. Towards Darsham, Emmerdale Farm Shop (Westleton Road, 01728 668648, www.emmerdalefarmshop.co.uk) has a chilled fruit and vegetable room, shelves full of local meat from butcher KW Clarke, preserves, baked goods of every description, cheese, wine and beer. And in Middleton – look out for the quirky rusty sculptures on your way through the village – Reckford Farm (01728 648253) sells its own fruit and veg as well as goods from small-scale local producers, such as fish from Orford, organic beef from Theberton, and cheese and bread from Friston.

Theberton itself is a tiny spot, three miles from Westleton, famous for having a German Zeppelin crash-land in the fields of Holly Tree Farm in 1917 after being shot down. It was a clear night and the burning hull could be seen from 50 miles away. Incredibly, a few survivors emerged from the wreckage, and local lore has it that when an injured German crew member was taken to a nearby farmhouse to be looked after until the proper authorities arrived, the owner replied: 'Not likely. Lock the bugger in the shed.' There's a memorial to the dead crew in Theberton churchyard extension (just over the road from the main churchyard), which reads: 'Who art thou that judges another man's servant'.

Just over a mile from here is Eastbridge, where you can hire bikes from the Eel's Foot Inn (see p198) or sit in the pub garden and enjoy views over the marshes. Suffolk 'Squit' nights take place on Thursdays, when folk music and monologues are performed at the pub (musicians are welcome to join in). The piano room also holds a dartboard.

Just around the corner, Eastbridge Farm has a very basic back-to-nature campsite (01728 830729, open Apr-Sept) that's great for people who like atmospheric walks along an unpopulated coastline in the evenings.

Where to eat & drink

For a small village, Walberswick punches above its weight for food and drink. Down near the harbour, there's Adnams' pub the Bell (Ferry Road, 01502 723109, http://hotels.adnams.co.uk/the-bell). It's a homely spot, with flagstone floors, open fires and little nooks to sit in and enjoy the great fish and chips, thick-cut sandwiches and

RSPB Minsmere. See p189.

West Scrape hides
Reedbed hides

Visitor Centre
Toilets & car park

North Hide
East Hide

Canopy Hide

locally sourced specials. There's also the Anchor (*see below*). On the green are two good cafés: the Parish Lantern (which serves unusual cakes) and the Potter's Wheel.

At Dunwich Heath, the National Trust tearoom in the old coastguards' cottages overlooking the sea is a lovely place to sit for a cuppa and some cake. The food is more individual than in many NT eateries and hosts occasional 'Food Glorious Food' meal events celebrating the best of the season's local produce. The café at Bridge Nurseries (01728 648850, www.bridgenurseries.co.uk) is good too.

The Westleton Crown (*see below*) is a simple but stylish setting (wooden floors and tables, bare-brick walls) for dishes that range from traditional, such as beer-battered haddock and chips, to fancier fare such as rabbit and ham hock terrine with poached figs. It's also one of those rare places in Suffolk that serves food all day, starting with breakfast. Westleton's other pub, the White Horse (Darsham Road, 01728 648222, www.westleton-whitehorse.co.uk), tucked away behind the green, offers a simpler menu of crowd-pleasers such as gammon with fried egg. It's an Adnams pub, so you can be sure of the beer, and also has rooms.

Anchor ★
Main Street, Walberswick, IP18 6UA (01502 722112, www.anchoratwalberswick.com). Open 11am-11pm daily. Lunch served noon-3pm, dinner served 6-9pm daily.
A pleasantly airy series of bar rooms in neutral colours lead to a large open terrace at the back that offers unfettered views of those large Suffolk skies (there's a choice of seating out front and at the side too). Licensee Mark Dorber used to run the acclaimed White Horse in Parsons Green, and the beer here is good. Service to teenagers lacks grace, but the food is excellent. A dish of skate wing with new potatoes and samphire looked simple but was just-so, while small children were wowed by the spaghetti bolognese.

Flora Tea Rooms
Beach Car Park, Dunwich, IP17 3EN (01728 648433). Open 11am-4pm daily (11am-5pm school summer hols).
This large wooden hut serves freshly cooked fish and chips to the walkers, anglers, families and coach-trippers who flood here. Order and pay at the counter and soon your brimming plateful is delivered by friendly and efficient servers. There's no fuss or frills: the green and yellow walls, green leatherette chairs, and utilitarian green crockery give the large room a comforting retro feel. Children will love the large ice-cream sundae selection. The Flora is busy whatever the season, but turnover is swift.

White Hart
London Road, Blythburgh, IP19 9LQ (01502 478217, www.blythburgh-whitehart.co.uk). Open 11am-2pm, 6-11pm Mon-Fri; 11am-11pm Sat, Sun. Lunch served noon-2.30pm, dinner served 6-9pm daily.
This former courthouse dates from the 16th century (check out the huge inglenook fireplace and carved oak beams) and offers a promising list of gastropub dishes, as well as board games, a dartboard and a great grassy bank with fantastic views over the marshes. It also operates a little farm shop from the shed to the side of the main building, which

Prince Charles praised as a great way for a pub to become a communal hub. There are also four en suite rooms (£80 double incl breakfast).

Where to stay
Hotels and B&Bs are thin on the ground in this part of the county; most people self-cater. The Eel's Foot Inn (01728 830154, www.theeelsfootinn.co.uk) in Eastbridge is an easy-going place with simple food and six B&B rooms.

Elm Gables
Main Street, Walberswick, IP18 6UY (www. walberswickcottage.co.uk). Rates £600-£1,250 per week. No credit cards.
Live the rural dream with a stay in this old rectory next to the church. The house sleeps eight, has been furnished tastefully and comfortably, and has a large, mature garden. On arrival expect fresh bread, eggs and a home-made cake.

Scotts Hall Cottage
Minsmere, IP17 3BY (01502 722717, www.suffolk-secrets.co.uk). Rates £436-£801 per week.
A self-catering cottage owned by the RSPB and situated right in the middle of the Minsmere nature reserve. Inside it's all stylish comfort, cosy bedrooms and mod cons; outside, you couldn't get more at one with the natural world if you tried. The cottage sleeps six people in two doubles and two singles, but there's also a sofa bed in the snug.

Ship
St James's Street, Dunwich, IP17 3DT (01728 648219, www.shipatdunwich.co.uk). Rates £95-£105 double.
There are ten recently refurbished rooms in Dunwich's only pub. All have a simple uncluttered feel, typified by the classic iron bedsteads, and are en suite. Ask for a room with views over the sea and the marshes. Downstairs, the pub has several cosy bars, a conservatory and a large back garden. The kitchen does fish and chips at around the same price as the Flora Tea Rooms.

Ship Cottage
St James's Street, Dunwich, IP17 3DT (01728 638962, www.bestofsuffolk.co.uk). Rates £498-£1,310 for 5 people per week.
Henry James and Jerome K Jerome have both stayed at Ship Cottage. Backing on to marshland and the beach beyond, with great views of Walberswick to the north, the large red-brick house is prettily decorated, full of charm and character, and has a decent-sized garden.

Westleton Crown
The Street, Westleton, IP17 3AD (01728 648777, www.westletoncrown.co.uk). Rates £115-£180 double incl breakfast.
From the front, the Westleton Crown looks like a modest red-brick house that's been turned into a pub. But it's deceptively large, with 25 stylish bedrooms in the main building and in converted stables and cottages. The rooms are categorised as 'good', 'better' and 'best'; the last have rolltop baths big enough for two in the bedrooms (some of which also have four-posters). The food is good, and the place is very popular, especially at weekends. There's also a conservatory, and a lovely garden.

SUFFOLK

Suffolk Coast: Sizewell to Bawdsey Quay

There is only one significant town along this stretch of Suffolk coastline, and that's the genteel resort of Aldeburgh. The rest is all about quiet treasures and simple pleasures; shingle beaches, marshland, reedbeds and forests. Apart from Aldeburgh, the only place tourists flock to in significant numbers is Snape Maltings, a large converted former brewery famous for hosting the annual Aldeburgh music festival. The Maltings has also hosted the Aldeburgh Food & Drink Festival for the last few years, celebrating the abundance of excellent local produce found in this area. The region is very proud of its small-scale food producers, and most of the pubs, restaurants and cafés support them when sourcing ingredients, so menus are full of the likes of Red Poll beef, Butley Creek oysters and Orford smoked fish. Visitors leave with memories, not just of the atmospheric landscape, but also of fine food served at affordable prices. Adnams oversees many of the pubs in the area, and has a commitment to celebrating individuality and quality.

SIZEWELL & THORPENESS

Sizewell

The white dome of Sizewell B, the UK's only pressurised water nuclear reactor, is visible on the horizon for miles around. Which is odd, because when you get down to the beach itself, the dome seems completely dwarfed by the grey hulk of the now defunct Sizewell A. This is the place to come for a seaside day out with eerie menace thrown in for free. The nuclear plant is huge and the few small houses and collection of blackened fishermen's huts look vulnerable beside it. The landscape will change again when French owners EDF begin building the planned third reactor here. There used to be a visitor centre and scheduled public tours of the plant, but both stopped after 9/11.

Sizewell beach is a place people come to brood on their own or with their dog; if you go in May there's the most stunning display of wild lupins on the seashore. Next to the car park is a café, on the dunes, serving greasy-spoon breakfasts, light meals and ice-creams, plus tea and cakes in the afternoon. Looking towards Aldeburgh, you can see the Tudor chimneys of Sizewell Hall (now a Christian conference centre and closed to the public); to the north, you can make out Southwold Lighthouse.

Thorpeness

A few miles south of Sizewell is Thorpeness. An anachronistic treasure, like something out of Enid Blyton, this peculiar village was dreamed up by Edwardian barrister and businessman Glencairn Stuart Ogilvie. He wanted to create a seaside resort to which he could invite his friends and colleagues and their families. The streets, lanes and houses are endearingly higgledy-piggledy, and though most of it was built in the early decades of the 20th century, it takes its inspiration from Jacobean and Tudor architectural styles. The lanes all lead down to the shingle beach.

At the centre of the village is Thorpeness Country Club, where mere mortals can watch members larking about on the tennis courts from the lanes behind the club building. Membership is available on a weekly basis for those staying nearby (01728 452176, £127 for a family of four). The club also has several self-catering apartments to rent (see p205). Next to the only pub, the Dolphin Inn (see p201), the village store stocks fresh fruit and vegetables, newspapers, newly baked bread and cakes, Suffolk apple juice, milk, deli goods and a small range of top-end cooking ingredients and general groceries. The brownies are heavenly.

The sea isn't the only water feature in Thorpeness; families flock to the large, shallow, man-made lake, the Meare, dug out by local workmen for Ogilvie. You can hire boats – it's a wonderfully evocative place for a spot of rowing – and there are several cafés. The regatta in August features races in the daytime and fireworks at night.

The Thorpeness Hotel & Golf Club (see p205) is on the side of the Meare. The golf course was part of Ogilvie's original scheme and is renowned for being playable even in winter, thanks to it being laid on sand (good drainage). At least one of the players in each group must have a handicap.

From pretty much anywhere in Thorpeness, you can see the weather-boarded eccentricity of the House in the Clouds. Built by Ogilvie as an enormous water tower to service the resort, it's now available for holiday lets. Opposite sits the

SUFFOLK

tiny windmill that used to pump water from the tank on top of the tower; built in the 19th century for grinding corn, it was moved and converted to service Ogilvie's growing resort. The curious can venture inside at weekends from Easter to September and every day in July and August.

Thorpeness wasn't designed with cars in mind, so bring a bike or walk. Electric bikes (www.electric bikehire.co.uk, 0845 602 6652) can be hired from the Thorpeness Hotel or the Dolphin Inn. The Haven nature reserve, with its wild flowers and nesting birds in season, lies to the south between Thorpeness and Aldeburgh – it's a lovely walk between the two.

Where to eat & drink

Down by the Meare, the café next to the boat hire does a good trade in decent cakes, light meals and Bennett's ice-creams. Over the road, the Beach House (01728 454639, closed Mon-Wed winter) serves breakfasts, lunches and dinners amid rooms full of antiques and bric-a-brac for sale, with outdoor seating in fine weather. Dining options at the Thorpeness Hotel run from snacks to full meals. The dining room overlooks the third tee; the terrace is a lovely place to watch people rowing past on the Meare.

Dolphin Inn
Peace Place, IP16 4NA (01728 454994,
www.thorpenessdolphin.com). Lunch served noon-
2.30pm Tue-Sun. Dinner served 6.30-9pm Tue-Sat.
A cottagey-looking building surrounded by a large lawn scattered with tables, this is the Mrs Tiggy-Winkle of village pubs. The interior is airy and modern, with huge floorboards stretching towards the bar. Choose from a blackboard list of gastropub dishes, such as a generous portion of dressed crab or salmon steak with crushed potatoes and salad. The one sour note on our visit was the price of a child's meal: plain pasta with a meagre amount of grated cheese cost £5.25.

Where to stay
Thorpeness has many quaint buildings for hire, including several wooden cottages, exemplified by the idyllic-looking holiday let at 1A Uplands Road (07711 612804, www.thorpenessholidayhome. co.uk). The Dolphin Inn (*see above*) has three simply decorated en suite rooms.

House in the Clouds ★
Thorpeness, IP16 4NQ (020 7224 3615, www.house
intheclouds.co.uk). Rates £2,030-£3,050 per week.
No credit cards.
This is the iconic place to stay in Thorpeness. There's room for a dozen guests, with five bedrooms, three bathrooms, a

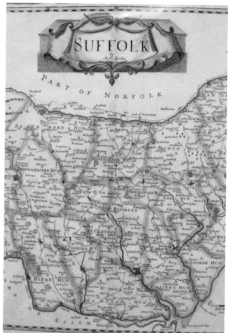

Snape Maltings. See p209.

Bags packed, milk cancelled, house raised on stilts.

You've packed the suntan lotion, the snorkel set, the stay-pressed shirts. Just one more thing left to do – your bit for climate change. In some of the world's poorest countries, changing weather patterns are destroying lives.

You can help people to deal with the extreme effects of climate change. Raising houses in flood-prone regions is just one life-saving solution.

Climate change costs lives.
Give £5 and let's sort it *Here & Now*

www.oxfam.org.uk/climate-change

Be Humankind Ⓧ **Oxfam**

dining room and a drawing room arranged over the upper floors of this extraordinary folly – once the water tower for the resort. The top-most chamber used to house the water tank; now it's a grand galleried games room with spectacular views over the countryside and the sea. There's a one-acre garden too. You'll need to book well in advance, and note that credit cards aren't accepted.

1 & 3 Ogilvie Lodge
Thorpeness Country Club, IP16 4NH (01728 452176, www.suffolkcoastapartments.co.uk). Rates 1 Ogilvie £300-£890 per week. 3 Ogilvie £330-£980 per week.
There are 11 self-catering apartments and houses in and around the grounds of the Country Club. Some are new, some occupy the original building, and most sleep four to six. The two in Ogilvie Lodge – no.1 on the ground floor, no.3 above it – are particularly popular, partly for the stunning sea views and proximity of the club's gardens and tennis courts, partly because of their attractive and comfortable furnishings. No.1 is particularly bright and sunny, all yellow, blue and white, with chunky striped sofas and an open-plan living area.

1 South Cottages
The Dunes, IP16 4NW (01728 638962, www.bestof suffolk.co.uk/south.asp). Rates £370-£690 per week.
A cute one-bedroom cottage situated close to the beach and the Meare boating lake. A guest annex for two extra people is also available, for a supplement of 30% of the main price.

Thorpeness Hotel & Golf Club
Lakeside Avenue, IP16 4NH (01728 452176, www.thorpeness.co.uk). Rates £92-£122 double.
You don't have to play golf to enjoy this hotel. With bright airy rooms and a lovely secluded position on the side of the Meare, with access up a small road, it's a relaxing spot to stay in. Sister hotel of the Swan in Lavenham, it has a slightly corporate feel, but is very pleasant nonetheless.

Valetta
Aldeburgh Road, IP16 4NR, (01728 638962, www.bestofsuffolk.co.uk/valetta.asp). Rates £780-£1,790 per week.
This oversized, single-storey beach hut (which sleeps six people) was once a fisherman's home – though it's hard to believe given the swish decor and superior fittings. There are windows on three sides, and the living area opens straight on to the beach.

ALDEBURGH ★
Like most towns on the Suffolk coastline, Aldeburgh was once a thriving port and shipbuilding centre. Francis Drake's *Golden Hind* was built here. But the Alde silted up, as did the natural harbours in neighbouring coastal towns, and left Aldeburgh surviving mainly on fishing for a living. These days, tourism is the biggest industry, a trend that started with the arrival of the railway in 1860, but one which has had its ups and downs. Cultural commentator Jonathan Meades once said that Aldeburgh would never slough off its somewhat down-at-heel identity, but, in fact, gentrification has been gently creeping up on the place for decades. Sure, parties of pensioners still file off tour coaches and straight

into the town's chippies for a parcel to take to the beach. And there are still corners where peeling paint and sea-battered neglect are allowed to remain, but they are few and far between.

These days the High Street feels positively well-to-do and the town just oozes culture. The main venue for the Aldeburgh Festival in June is at nearby Snape Maltings, but many concerts are also held in the town itself. The Red House (*see p210*), down the gravel bumps of Golf Lane (off the B1122 to Leiston) was where Benjamin Britten and Peter Pears lived for several decades. The couple originally lived on the seafront at Crag House, 4 Crabbe Street, but became sick of fans staring through the windows. Also on Crabbe Street is the Jubilee Hall, which is used for concerts and performances and is the Aldeburgh venue for Jill Freud's summer theatre season, which is based primarily at Southwold.

Parking isn't allowed in the town centre for more than an hour, so head for the pay car park on Thorpe Road to the north, or the free one at Slaughden Quay to the south. You can also park on the seafront, but it's tricky finding a space during high season.

The seafront
The shingle beach makes walking a real workout, so head for the promenade if it's too tough-going. Along the beach towards Thorpeness is Maggi Hambling's controversial sculptural tribute to Benjamin Britten, the town's most famous resident and founder of the annual music festival. The sculpture sits on the shingle and cleverly looks like the upturned hull of a wrecked boat from a distance. Up close, it's a large metal scallop shell with Britten's words from opera *Peter Grimes* punched out of the metal along the top edge: 'I hear those voices that will not be drowned.'

On the walk back towards town, there are fishermen's huts selling whatever features in the day's catch. There's a small and very popular boating pond, and the Moot Hall, sitting isolated on the seafront. It was never meant to be this close to the shore; when it was built, it would have been significantly further inland, but much of Aldeburgh has slipped into the sea, including the old market cross. The hall now houses the Aldeburgh Museum (01728 454666, www.aldeburghmuseum.org.uk), which tells the story of the town's fortunes as sea, silt and railway affected trade and tourism.

The High Street
Aldeburgh has good browsing opportunities, pretty much all on the long High Street. The Aldeburgh Book Shop (no.42 High Street, 01728 452389, www.aldeburghbookshop.co.uk) is a great independent bookshop, and the owners run the annual Aldeburgh Literary Festival. The unusual Aldeburgh Cinema opposite (no.51, 01728 452996, www.aldeburghcinema.co.uk) has been in business since 1924 when the auditorium was built behind an existing shopfront. It still has a Bechstein grand piano and hosts a children's film festival in October and a documentary festival in November.

SUFFOLK

There are also various delis and a couple of wine merchants. Lawson's Deli stocks plenty of Suffolk specialities, although prices aren't always competitive; Salters the butcher (who promise that all their meat comes from within a 30-mile radius) sells the same local apple juice at a cheaper price. Still, Lawson's did win the award for Best Pie at the 2009 Aldeburgh Food & Drink Festival. There's also a Co-op for basics. Art galleries, gift and homeware shops and several 'lifestyle' clothing outlets complete the picture. The street tapers out to the south, where there are some pretty candy-striped houses – look out for the Old Custom House, whose steps have been worn down by centuries of use.

Slaughden Quay

At the southern edge of Aldeburgh, a Martello tower sits by itself on the cliff. It used to be part of the settlement of Slaughden, which was gradually eaten away by the sea over the course of the 20th century. Before the railway arrived in Leiston in 1859, Slaughden Quay was where the Garretts Works offloaded ships from Staffordshire and Northumberland carrying large amounts of iron and coal for the Leiston Works. Now, you can stay in the tower (it's owned by the Landmark Trust), and the quay is the site of Slaughden Sailing Club, whose anchored boats rise in formation to the will of wind and tide. Races are held on a Wednesday evening from April to the beginning of September. Geographically, it's possible to access Orford Ness from Slaughden Quay, but a gate bars entrance, and the National Trust, which manages the large shingle-spit nature reserve, has erected a notice politely turning walkers back. The only way on to the Ness is by boat from Orford.

Where to eat & drink

There's plenty of choice at this thriving resort. The first port of call for many people is either the Golden Galleon (01728 454685) or Aldeburgh Fish & Chips

Things to do

Suffolk Coast & Heaths Path

01394 384948, www.suffolkcoastandheaths.org.
There are miles of footpaths to enjoy along this coastal stretch. Challenge yourself with a whole day's hike along the Coast & Heaths Path, which runs between Lowestoft and Felixstowe, or the Sandlings Path, another long-distance route that takes in Rendlesham Forest and the remains of the Sandlings heathland. Both lead through areas of outstanding natural beauty – and you'll often find yourself gloriously alone.

THORPENESS

Thorpeness Meare

01728 832523, www.themeareatthorpeness.com.
Open Mar-Oct 8.30am-dusk daily. Boat hire from £6; £3 reductions.
A lovely spot for messing about in a boat. The man-made lake covers 40 acres of water and is no more than three feet deep throughout, so very safe for children. They love the mystery of rowing down various channels and discovering the small islands and landing spots created for a pleasurable afternoon on the water. Many locations are named after characters and places in JM Barrie's *Peter Pan* (he was a friend of the resort's creator, Glencairn Stuart Ogilvie). More than 100 boats are for hire, including rowing boats, kayaks, punts, sailing boats and canoes. Allow at least an hour to explore the lake.

SNAPE

Snape Maltings Concert Hall ★

Snape, IP17 1SP (01728 687110, www.aldeburgh. co.uk). Open Box office Summer 10am-4.30pm Mon-Sat. Winter 10am-1pm, 2-4pm Mon-Sat. Tickets £10-£50.
The world-famous Aldeburgh Festival takes place in and around Snape Maltings in June, but there's so much more to the Maltings' music programme than one month of glory. The Snape Proms every August offers folk, poetry and jazz as well as classical concerts, and the Britten-Pears Young Artist Programme from April to

Snape Maltings Concert Hall

October attracts top young performers from around the globe. For something a little different, try the International Academy of String Quartets in September. Course directors Isabel Charisius and Ilan Gronich run masterclasses with young but established string quartets, which are open to the public for a bargain £3. To see Charisius in action as she dissects every nuance of a quartet's performance and internal dynamic is pure theatre. You don't have to be musical to appreciate the difference in the playing at the beginning and end of the masterclass as Charisius brings all of life to bear on her acute understanding of the situation in front of her.

SUFFOLK

House in the Clouds. See p201.

Orford Ness. See p211.

(01728 454685) – at opposite ends of the High Street but under the same ownership – for splendid portions of glistening fish and chips; expect long queues at peak times. The Golden Galleon also has a first-floor restaurant.

For a decent pint, head to the small White Hart Inn next to Aldeburgh Fish & Chips. Munchies café (01728 454566) serves good coffee and crab sandwiches, but service is lacklustre; Aldeburgh Market deli (01728 452520) sells fresh fish and samphire, and also has a few tables where you can eat simple dishes such as fish pie. For a more upmarket meal, 152 (152 High Street, 01728 454594) is worth considering.

Lighthouse
77 High Street, IP16 5AU (01728 453377, www. lighthouserestaurant.co.uk). Lunch served noon-2pm Mon-Fri; noon-2.30pm Sat, Sun. Dinner served 6.30-10pm daily.
The efficient and knowledgable waiting staff are a bonus (bored teenagers are the norm in Suffolk), but it's the food that keeps people coming back. The decor has splashes of the same bright blue and yellow you see all around Aldeburgh. The wooden tables in the front room are left bare, while the back room has tablecloths. The rooms are connected but also partially divided, which makes the place airy and intimate at the same time, and good for conversation. Fish is the star: Aldeburgh dover sole, bouillabaisse and salmon niçoise.

Regatta
171 High Street, IP15 1AN (01728 452011, www. regattaaldeburgh.com). Lunch served noon-2pm, dinner served 6-10pm daily (closed dinner Sun Nov-Mar).
This long-standing restaurant majors in fish and seafood, much of it caught in local waters; it even has its own smokehouse. It's not cheap, but has a lively atmosphere and a notably child-friendly attitude, with a dining area set aside for families with very young kids. Regular gourmet evenings focus on international cuisine or regional specialities.

Where to stay
Hotel options in Aldeburgh are limited, but there are various B&Bs and plenty of self-catering cottages and town houses.

Brudenell Hotel
The Parade, IP15 5BU (01728 452071, www.brudenellhotel.co.uk). Rates £126-£140 double.
A large hotel bang on the seafront with 42 rooms, many of which have wonderful sea views, though the place has never quite lived up to its original promise. At the time of writing, the rather tired bedrooms were being refurbished.

14 Market Cross Place
14 Market Cross Place, IP15 5BJ (01728 638962, www.bestofsuffolk.co.uk/marketcross.asp). Rates £750-£1,710 per week.
This Georgian house spreads over three floors. It sleeps eight people in two doubles and two twins, and has an eat-in kitchen and two living rooms overlooking the sea. Decor is bright and smart, with plenty of comfortable armchairs to curl up in. There's only a small patio garden, but who needs grass when the beach is right outside?

Laurel House B&B
23 Lee Road, IP15 5EY (01728 452775, www. laurel-house.net). Rates £85 double incl breakfast. No credit cards.
A few minutes' walk from the seafront, this beautifully restored Victorian town house is owned by Cristina di Paolo and Damian Risdon. The two en suite bedrooms (one double, one twin) are light, modern and uncluttered. Guests can borrow mountain bikes; Damian is a keen rider and can recommend routes.

Martello Tower ★
Slaughden Road, IP15 5DE (01628 825925, www.landmarktrust.org.uk). Rates £830-£1,716 per week.
This sea-facing, quatrefoil-shaped brick monolith, built to keep out Napoleon, is the most striking place to stay in Aldeburgh. The Landmark Trust building's lofty, vaulted interior, with sail-like canopies overhead, has a teak floor and two bedrooms screened but not completely separate from the main living space.

Old Cookery School
84 High Street, IP15 5AU (01728 638962, www.bestofsuffolk.co.uk/oldcookeryschool.asp). Rates £445-£910 per week.
There are two double bedrooms in this self-catering Georgian house on the High Street, each with a standalone roll-top bath for a relaxing soak before bedtime. It's a cheery place, with plenty of white and pale blue paintwork, polished floorboards and original (working) fireplaces.

SNAPE ★
Snape itself is a small backwater village, and although not technically on the coast, it's connected to the sea by the Alde estuary and was a busy port when the Victorian maltings (built by Newson Garrett for malting barley for beer-making) were in full swing. The breeze is salty and sea-fresh as it rolls across the marshes, and walks in the vicinity are wonderfully atmospheric in all weathers. The village wouldn't be famous at all if it weren't for Benjamin Britten's Aldeburgh Festival moving its base here in the 1960s when the vast maltings site just south of Snape bridge finally closed down.

Over the intervening decades, Snape Maltings (www.snapemaltings.co.uk) has developed slowly and organically into a whole complex of shops, cafés, art galleries and concert halls. It's still expanding – there are plans for new artists' studios and a public space in other dilapidated buildings. From April to October, boat trips from the quay take passengers down the Alde to St Botolph's Church in Iken. Alternatively, walk there along the riverside path through reedbeds (on raised wooden walkways) and low-lying fields, with arresting views of the beautiful countryside. St Botolph's, founded in 654, is a small, wonderfully simple church with a thatched roof and flint walls.

Snape Maltings can easily fill a day of mooching. It's at its busiest in June during the Aldeburgh

SUFFOLK

Places to visit

ALDEBURGH

Red House
Golf Lane, Aldeburgh, IP15 5PZ (01728 451700, www.brittenpears.org). Open Guided tours June-Sept 2.30pm Tue-Sat. Admission £7; free reductions.
The home of Benjamin Britten and Peter Pears – where they planned the Aldeburgh Festival and played host to numerous creative friends – has remained largely unchanged since their deaths. They lived first on the seafront, but swapped houses with artist Mary Potter; the arrangement offered more privacy for them and sea views for her. Containing the couple's art collection and eclectic pieces of furniture, the house is strongly reminiscent in atmosphere to Kettle's Yard in Cambridge. The library houses their book collection and Britten's grand piano. It was extended by the Britten-Pears Foundation in the 1990s to include a reading room and a large exhibition space, which features a changing display of items from the foundation's archive. Only ten people are admitted on house tours at any one time, so it's essential to book.

ORFORD TO BAWDSEY QUAY

Bawdsey Manor
Bawdsey, IP12 3AZ (01206 573948, www.bawdsey manor.co.uk). Tours by arrangement. Admission House & Gardens £15. House, Gardens & Exhibition £22.50 incl lunch.
Bawdsey Manor, located at the mouth of the Deben facing the North Sea, caters for B&B, private and corporate functions and runs a holiday school, but it's also the place where the MoD developed radar between the two world wars. Invitation to View (www.invitationtoview.co.uk) organises occasional tours of the house throughout the year with owner Ann Toettcher, who takes visitors around this sprawling architectural curiosity. Built by the eccentric William Cuthbert Quilter in the late 19th century, with no particular overall plan and following no single architectural style, it's a very unusual building. The fake cliffs, grottos and tunnels on the seaward side were Lady Quilter's idea, but she had 40 gardeners

at her disposal, so outré landscaping presented no obstacle. Quilter was MP for Sudbury for many years, but only made two speeches in Parliament. The first was against inheritance tax; the second proposed an act to protect the quality of real ale (he owned a large house and several breweries – spot the link?). Quilter was notorious for having a very high opinion of himself, so it's no surprise that the motto above the main door reads *Plutot mourir que changer* – 'Rather die than change'. The MoD bought the house in 1936 when the threat of war necessitated a new radar research establishment. By 1937, Bawdsey was the first fully operational (and top-secret) radar station in the world.

Bawdsey Radar
Bawdsey, IP12 3AZ (07821 162879, www.bawdsey radar.org.uk). Open 12.30-4.30pm occasional Sun & bank hol Mon Apr-Sept. Admission £3; free reductions.
The concrete bunker round the corner from Bawdsey Manor housing the old transmitter block is now a museum. Run by a committee of locals whose chair Mary Wain is a product of a liaison formed at Bawdsey during its wartime heyday, it provides a comprehensive history of the development of radar and the crucial role it played in the Allies' victory over Germany. The museum is open only on selected days – check the website for details.

Havergate Island
01394 450732, www.rspb.org.uk. Open Apr-Aug 1st & 3rd Sat, Sun of mth. Sept-Mar 1st Sat of mth. Admission £7; £3 reductions.
The only way on to the island, a nature reserve run by the RPSB, is by boat from Orford Quay, which leaves at 10am on designated days and returns at 3pm. The island is a haven for numerous birds (avocets, spotted redshanks, terns, owls, ducks and many varieties of waders), wild flowers, butterflies and hares, and you can sometimes spot seals in the River Ore. Advance booking is essential, and don't forget the picnic.

Orford Castle
Orford, IP12 2ND (01394 450472, www.english-heritage.org.uk/orfordcastle). Open July, Aug

Festival (*see p214*) – though there are concerts, masterclasses and workshops all year round – and the increasingly popular Aldeburgh Food & Drink Festival (*see p214*) in September.
Before the A12 was built, Snape bridge was on the main route from London to the coastal towns of Suffolk and Norfolk and a key point for smugglers to pass. Legend has it that the south-facing dormer window in the Crown pub was used to signal the all-clear when the guards were safely downing pints in the bar downstairs.

Where to eat & drink
The Maltings has two cafés, run by different companies; the food is better at the Metfield Café. During concert season, the Oyster Bar & Restaurant (supplied by the Metfield) is also open. Opposite the Maltings is the large Plough & Sail pub; a bit soulless, it serves old-fashioned pub grub.

Snape village has two pubs worth stopping at. On Priory Road, the Golden Key (01728 688510, www.snape-golden-key.co.uk) was named Adnams Pub of the Year 2009 and has a menu of enticing local specialities. Larger than it looks from the outside, it has real fires in winter and two terraces. More atmospheric is the Crown Inn, just around the corner on the main road.
A warm welcome, good beer, hearty home cooking and B&B accommodation in wooden chalets is available at the Ship Inn (01728 688316, www.blaxhallshipinn.co.uk) in Blaxhall, a couple of miles from Snape. A long-standing folk music venue, it still has regular music and singing sessions.

Crown Inn
Bridge Road, IP17 1SL (01728 688324). Open 11.30am-3pm, 6-11pm Mon-Fri; 11.30am-3.30pm, 6-11pm Sat; noon-3.30pm, 6-10.30pm Sun. Lunch

Orford Castle

because much is known about the use of particular rooms and chambers. The best way to get a full appreciation is with the hour-long audio tour. See the small but beautifully designed chapel with its dual-aspect windows, providing more light than elsewhere in the castle. Step into the large left-hand fireplace in the kitchen, then look up to see the sky. Appreciate the clever design of the latrines, and the small hole at hip height near the bed chamber reserved for the most important guests. It was put here for male guests caught short in the night. The Orford Museum in the upper hall houses historic artefacts, maps, documents and photos. Local legends include the story of the merman who was caught by fishermen in 1167 and kept and tortured by the townspeople on suspicion of being in league with the devil.

Orford Ness ★
Quay Office, Orford Quay, Orford, IP12 2NU (01728 648024, www.nationaltrust.org.uk/orfordness). Open July-Sept 10am-5pm Tue-Sat. Apr, June, Oct 10am-5pm Sat. Admission £6.90 incl ferry; free-£3.45 reductions.
About ten miles in length, Orford Ness is the largest vegetated shingle spit in Europe and a National Trust-run nature reserve. It's a mighty strange-looking reserve, though, because it was used as a secret military test site and research station from 1913 until the mid 1980s, which has left a legacy of peculiar, eerie structures such as the Bomb Ballistics Building, the Black Beacon and the distinctive Pagodas (some of these are accessible on guided tours). It was here in the mid '30s that Robert Watson-Watt's experiments led to the development of radar once the team had moved to nearby Bawdsey Manor (*see p210*). It looks as if you should be able to get reach Orford Ness via the tiny neck connecting it to the mainland at Slaughden Quay, but access isn't permitted there. The only route is by ferry from Orford Quay across the Ore. Once on the spit, visitors can walk the five-mile Red Trail through grazing marsh, mud and shingle, and feel the menace of the Ness's past life. A children's quiz and trail leaflet is available from the Quay Office.

10am-6pm daily. Apr, June, Sept 10am-5pm daily. Oct-Mar 10am-4pm Mon, Thur-Sun. Admission £5; £2.50-£4.30 reductions; £12.50 family.
Orford Castle was built by Henry II in the 12th century to keep an eye on the powerful Bigods at Framlingham Castle. Only the keep survives, but it's one of the best preserved examples from the period and has an unusual 18-sided design. It's a fascinating place, partly

served noon-2.30pm Mon-Fri; noon-3pm Sat, Sun. Dinner served 6-9pm Mon-Fri, Sun; 6-9.30pm Sat.
Much nicer than the rather plain exterior suggests, with characterful curved and high-backed wooden benches carving out a cosy horseshoe niche in the bar. Eating takes place in the surrounding rooms, where diners fall on the feasts set down at their tables. The pub grows its own vegetables, rears its own livestock, sources local fish and forages for wild seasonal ingredients for its menu.

Metfield Café & Deli
Snape Maltings, IP17 1SR (01728 688303, http://snape.metfieldbakery.com). Open 10am-5pm daily.
The Metfield Bakery opened its first café at Snape Maltings in 2008. The word 'café' suggests something casual, but this place takes its food very seriously indeed. Chef/owner Stuart Oetzman is famed for his award-winning meat pies, as well as his knowledge of old British dishes. The café is in an airy mezzanine space overlooking the well-stocked kitchen shop, and always has an interesting specials board.

Where to stay
Two B&B options in Snape sit next door to each other. Five rooms are available at Albion House (01728 687612, www.albionhouse-bandb.co.uk), though only one is en suite. The Old Mill Snape (01728 687906, www.oldmillsnape.co.uk) has two sweet self-contained cottages: the Miller's Cottage (one double, one twin) and the two-person Garden Cottage.

Admiral Cottage
Rectory Road, Blaxhall, IP12 2DP (07802 878172, www.snapecottages.co.uk). Rates £420-£675 per week.
For a real rural hideaway, this 200-year-old cottage in the hamlet of Blaxhall is just the thing. It's only two miles from the attractions at Snape, sleeps four in two bedrooms (plus a sofa bed) and is a bright, welcoming space with yellow paintwork and a log-burning stove. Weekend and midweek breaks are possible even in high season. Other

SUFFOLK

options in the village include Nelson Studio (sleeping two) and, new for 2010, Waterloo Cottage (sleeping four).

Holidays at Snape Matlings

Snape Maltings, IP17 1SR (01728 688303, www.holidaysatsnapemaltings.co.uk). Rates £385-£765 per week.
Many of the former Maltings buildings have been converted into residential homes. Most are privately owned, but two apartments – nos.4 & 11 The Courtyard – are available for holiday lets. Both are wonderful and stylish spaces with two bedrooms, private roof terraces, loft-style living rooms and top-notch fittings. There's also the use of the courtyard around which the buildings sit.

ORFORD TO BAWDSEY QUAY

Orford ★

Like many of its near neighbours on the Suffolk coast, Orford was once a town of major significance and political clout before coastline changes eroded its raison d'être. Back in the 12th century, when Orford's shingle spit was a fraction of a fraction of what it is now (it grows by 50 feet every year), it was not only a thriving port, but also a strategically important defensive point. Henry II built a castle (*see p210*) here, the keep of which still stands on the western edge of the town. As the harbour silted up and the huge shingle spit of Orford Ness grew to almost block the town from the sea, Orford moved into obscurity. These days, the place has had a renaissance, albeit for gastronomic rather than political reasons.

One day isn't really enough to experience Orford's considerable charms. Its network of wide streets and narrow alleys lead to numerous footpaths and rewarding walks at any time of the year. Cattle graze contentedly in marshy fields, the boats on the River Ore bob in the breeze and the castle stands sentinel over the town and history itself. Down at the quay, boat trips are available, as well as a simple café and a hut selling fresh fish. You can take a boat to the RSPB reserve at Havergate Island (*see p210*) or explore the river on a small wooden launch (01394 450169, www.orfordrivertrips.co.uk).

Orford Quay

A ferry carries foot passengers to Orford Ness (*see p211*), where they can explore the weird, wonderful (and defunct) heart of the area's recent military past. It's now a visually distinctive nature reserve run by the National Trust.

St Bartholemew's Church off Market Hill was enlarged in the 14th century to accommodate the rising population and the resulting wide nave is

Admiral Cottage. See p211.

SUFFOLK

perfect for the concerts that are held here during the Aldeburgh Festival. Since tourism is now its main industry, Orford has much in the way of holiday accommodation. The cumulative influence of the Adnams brewery, which owns two pubs here; the highly rated Butley Orford Oysterage (see p216); and Ruth Watson, star of TV shows *The Hotel Inspector* and *Country House Rescue* and owner of the Crown & Castle Hotel (see p216), means that food-lovers come in droves.

South to Bawdsey Quay

Tourists make a beeline for the musical highlights of Snape and the foodie mecca of Orford, but the rest of the area is very quiet. Heading south doesn't really lead anywhere… unless you count the small ferry to Felixstowe at Bawdsey Quay.

Inland are Tunstall and Rendlesham Forests, large, peaceful tracts of managed woodland run by the Forestry Commission. Pick up a map from the main Forest Centre (0845 3673787, www.forestry.gov.uk/rendlesham) in Rendlesham Wood, which is also the site of the largest car park. There are plenty of walking and cycling trails, and also a UFO trail; for it was at Rendlesham that Britain had its Roswell moment. In 1980, an American serviceman at the local RAF base reported seeing a strange

metallic object hovering overhead. The day after, one of his commanders found indentations in the ground and a strange red light pulsing through the forest. Spookiness aside, the forest is a good place to find mushrooms in season, while August brings a whole month of theatre performances (see p214) in the evenings.

The mystery deepens at the Bentwaters Cold War Museum (Building 134, Bentwaters Parks, 07588 460355, www.bcwm.org.uk) in Rendlesham village, which tells the story of the units and squadrons based over the years at RAF Bentwaters and RAF Woodbridge. It's open on the first and third Sundays of the month from Easter to mid October, and is probably best suited to Cold War enthusiasts.

Nearby is the small village of Butley, home to the wonderful Butley Priory (see p216) – an upmarket B&B occupying the sole remnant of a once-extensive priory – a plain but attractive church, a decent pub and a collection of barns with artists' studios and a pottery. The Butley River is the source of the succulent oysters that are sold at the Butley Orford Oysterage in Orford. A mile away is the ancient woodland of Staverton Thicks, containing some of the oldest oaks and tallest holly trees in the country.

South of Orford Ness lie the tiny dead-end hamlets of Shingle Street and Bawdsey Quay. You can walk

ANNUAL FESTIVALS

Aldeburgh Literary Festival ★
*01728 452389, www.aldeburgh
bookshop.co.uk. Date early Mar.*
Organised by the owners of the Aldeburgh
Bookshop, this weekend event is held at
the Jubilee Hall on Crabbe Street. There's
room for only 200 people, so if you're
lucky enough to snaffle a ticket, you can
see top names in a village hall setting.
Writers at the 2009 festival included
Margaret Drabble and Sebastian Faulks.

Aldeburgh Festival ★
*01728 687100, www.aldeburgh.co.uk.
Date June.*
The big one. The festival was launched
in 1948 by Benjamin Britten, Peter Pears
and Eric Crozier, moved inland to Snape
Maltings in the 1960s and has continued
to expand ever since. Lasting two weeks,
it attracts top performers from around the
world, and fills the area's churches and
public halls with a fantastic variety of
music, poetry, literature, drama and more.

Theatre in the Forest
*01473 288886, www.redrosechain.com.
Date Aug.*
Theatre and film company Red Rose
Chain holds performances in Rendlesham
Forest throughout the month. In 2009
they celebrated ten years of the event by
staging *The Winter's Tale* and a wild bear
hoax. Picnic hampers can be pre-ordered.

Aldeburgh Food & Drink Festival
*01728 688303, www.aldeburghfood
anddrink.co.uk. Date late Sept.*
The first weekend of this ten-day gourmet
fest sees 70 local producers selling their
wares at Snape Maltings, plus workshops,
talks, tastings, RSPB walks, activities for
children and river trips. Fringe events the
following week, in neighbouring towns,
include cookery demos and farm walks.

Aldeburgh Poetry Festival
*01986 835950, www.thepoetrytrust.org.
Date early Nov.*
A weekend celebration of contemporary
poetry that takes place at various venues
around Aldeburgh. Readings, workshops,
discussions and the odd quiz help to
make it a lively event for all ages. In
2009, there were sessions with John
Hegley, Tom Paulin and Maureen Duffy.

Aldeburgh Documentary Festival
*01728 452996, www.aldeburgh
cinema.co.uk. Date Nov.*
Attracting names such as Paul
Greengrass, Hugh Fearnley-Whittingstall,
Adam Nicolson, Sarah Raven and Sue
Bourne to feature in its discussions
about contemporary documentary-making,
this is a small festival with clout. No
wonder... its programmer is none other
than satirist and writer Craig Brown.

between the two on the Suffolk Coast & Heaths
Path, a long-distance trail from Felixstowe and
Lowestoft – but do get an up-to-date OS map,
because the path can be diverted or closed as
the coastline changes shape.

Shingle Street is a ghostly little place whose
inhabitants were forcibly evacuated on 22
June 1940 by the government, who then laid a
minefield along the beach in case of a German
invasion. Later in the war, the buildings were
used as target practice for bombing trials –
which did for the hamlet's only pub. By the
time the village was passed as safe to inhabit
again, the houses were dilapidated and, anyway,
most residents had settled elsewhere. The
place never recovered its population and
most buildings are now holiday homes.

Nearby Hollesley Bay has a large open prison,
and is also home to the Suffolk Punch Trust
& Stud (01473 612639, www.suffolkpunchtrust.
org). This is where the mighty chestnut-coloured
Suffolk Punch workhorse is bred and protected
in an attempt to arrest the decline of an
endangered species. Check the website
for occasional open days.

The road runs out at Bawdsey Quay, at the
mouth of the River Deben. You'll find a great
café, excellent crabbing (as long as you've
remembered your bacon-loaded line) and the
simple pleasure of watching boats bobbing
on the water. The tiny foot-ferry to Felixstowe
(01394 282173) runs 10am to 6pm daily from
May to September, with some weekend crossings
in April and October. The skipper is usually on
the opposite bank, so you have to wave the
'bat' to call him over (although regulars say
he'll come quicker if you don't bother).

It's hard to imagine now, but Bawdsey was
once a very busy place when the RAF and Britain's
pioneering radar development team were stationed
at Bawdsey Manor (*see p210*) between the wars.
The Ministry of Defence still has a base in nearby
Rendlesham Forest.

Just inland, next to the Deben, is Ramsholt,
which isn't marked on most road maps. In
medieval times, this was a bustling village with
its own ferry crossing; now, it's hard to spot the
place at all. Take the dead-end road with a sign
to the 'Ramsholt Arms' and park in the first grass
car park (unless you're planning on visiting the
pub). The tranquility at this very secluded spot
settles around the skin and bones like a balm;
out of season, it's perfect for a moody evening
stroll, though it can be heaving on a hot summer's
day. The riverbank is full of wading birds and
seagulls, sailing boats rest quietly on their
anchors and there's a footpath that leads inland
through marsh grass and patches of woodland.

You can take a detour to All Saints', one of
Suffolk's prized round-tower churches (it looks
square from a distance, thanks to the buttressing).
It stands gracefully alone in a small churchyard;
inside, the silence really is silent and the stillness
is utterly still. As a place for meditation, it's
hard to beat.

Butley Orford Oysterage. See p216.

Where to eat & drink

Orford has quite a range of food options. From the fish stall at the quay, and the Sole Bay Cheese stall in the garden of the Jolly Sailor Pub, to the smokehouse behind the Butley Orford Oysterage, you'll find delicacies in the most unlikely corners. The café at the quay serves full breakfasts until noon and delicious own-made cakes at any time of day – save room for the cream tea. For a special occasion, head to the Trinity restaurant at the Crown & Castle Hotel (*see right*). Just around the corner on Front Street is the King's Head Inn (01394 450271, www.thekingsheadorford.co.uk), run by Susan and Adrian Searing, who serve interesting takes on pub classics using locally sourced ingredients.

The Bawdsey Boat House Café (07900 811826, www.boathousecafe.co.uk, closed Mon-Thur Nov, all Dec-Feb) perches above the sailing club at Bawdsey Quay and serves simple but great basic dishes. You can sit on the wooden balcony and enjoy the beautiful views over the Deben, and watch the small ferry go back and forth. Also on the banks of the Deben is the Ramsholt Arms (Dock Road, 01394 411229); it's a choice place for a pint and serves local seafood and game in season.

In Butley, the Oyster Inn (Woodbridge Road, 01394 450790, closed Mon) has a larger bar area than most, making it a great place for an old-fashioned pint of Adnams.

Butley Orford Oysterage ★

Market Square, Orford, IP12 2LH (01394 450277, www.butleyorfordoysterage.co.uk). Lunch served noon-2.15pm daily. Dinner served Summer 6.30-9pm Mon-Fri, Sun; 6-9pm Sat. Easter 6.30-9pm Wed-Fri; 6-9pm Sat. Winter 6.30-9pm Fri; 6-9pm Sat.

A restaurant, shop and smokehouse, all supplied by its own small fishing fleet. The premises are basic, but the food lures diners from miles around. Smoked fish – cod roe, sardines, trout, mackerel – and a few smoked meat dishes are listed alongside fresh fish and oysters.

Froize Inn

Chillesford, IP12 3PU (01394 450282, www.froize.co.uk). Lunch served noon-2pm Tue-Sun. Dinner served 7-8.15pm Thur-Sat.

The Suffolk Coast & Heaths Path goes right by the door of the Froize Inn, and the friars who used to walk along the path from Butley Priory to the monastery at Dunwich give the pub its unusual name. It's a freehouse presided over by chef/owner David Grimwood, who serves locally sourced main courses from a buffet station with bonhomie and generosity. He's absolutely happy to give you a mound of Jimmy Butler's free-range pork with crackling, as well as a stuffed breast of guinea fowl with ten types of vegetables. Save room for the extraordinary puddings. The upside-down ginger and pear cake is worth crossing the county for.

Jolly Sailor

Quay Street, Orford, IP12 2NU (01394 450243, www.thejollysailor.net). Open 11am-3pm, 6-11pm Mon-Fri; 11am-11pm Sat, Sun. Lunch served noon-3pm, dinner served 6-9pm daily.

A wonderful 16th-century pub with several small, eccentric bar rooms with fires to warm your toes on cold, misty days. There's Scrabble and Trivial Pursuits, a large garden with a children's play area, a good selection of Adnams ales, and a cheese stall run by the Sole Bay Cheese Company; you can even camp here. The four guest rooms (£75-£85 double incl breakfast) have been recently refurbished in a simple but stylish way. The menu features fish straight from the quay; fish and chips and moules with frites are recommended.

Where to stay

The Old Butcher's Shop B&B (01394 450517, www.oldbutchers-orford.co.uk) has three bedrooms in an 1830 brick building in the middle of Orford. The pretty garden and great breakfasts – local bacon and sausages, plenty of fresh fruit – make up for the slightly cramped sleeping quarters. The King's Head Inn (*see left*) also has four smart, simply furnished B&B rooms.

Butley Priory ★

Butley, IP12 3NR (01394 450046, www.butleypriory. co.uk). Rates £90-£165 double incl breakfast. Cottage from £500 per week.

All that remains of Butley's 12th-century Augustinian priory is this ornate gatehouse, remodelled in the 18th century and now a sumptuous, romantic and unique B&B with spectacular fan-vaulting, log fires and masses of antiques. There are four rooms in the main house, plus the lovely, white-painted Garden Cottage in the grounds (sleeps four).

Crown & Castle Hotel ★

Market Square, Orford, IP12 2LJ (01394 450205, www.crownandcastle.co.uk). Rates £115-£155 double.

Ruth Watson owns this hotel, and the 19 rooms have the sort of attention to detail you would expect from *The Hotel Inspector*. The understated decor is fresh and modern, and the views from the main building and the ten garden rooms (each with its own secluded terrace) are wonderful. The hotel's Trinity Restaurant has a Michelin Bib Gourmand to recommend it; come for a casual lunch (eggs benedict, steak and kidney pie, treacle tart) or splash out on the smarter and pricier evening meals.

Quay View

Quay Street, Orford, IP12 2NU (01394 412304, http://suffolkcottageholidays.com). Rates £485-£700 per week.

Occupying one wing of a large traditional house, this is a homely place full of old-fashioned comforts, sleeping four. The setting is idyllic, right next to the quay, with a front terrace that overlooks the River Ore and Orford Ness – you couldn't get much closer to the water.

Well Cottage

Crown Lane, Orford, IP12 2NB (01728 638962, www.bestofsuffolk.co.uk/well.asp). Rates £435-£830 per week.

A timber-framed cottage with an award-winning, glass-walled, curved extension and simple, tasteful decoration that's packed with individual touches. It's homely and stylish at the same time, and sleeps five.

Ipswich & Felixstowe

Ipswich is Suffolk's largest town – in fact, it's larger than many cities – but you don't often hear people mention it when they discuss their Suffolk holiday itinerary. Despite an attractive medieval centre, for years it didn't make the best of itself. Now, pedestrianisation has made it easier to enjoy the half-timbered shopfronts; there are fantastic museums and compelling shops; and the redevelopment of the Waterfront is making a decayed industrial zone appealing to visitors.

The coastal town of Felixstowe is another destination largely ignored by modern holidaymakers. Faded today, it was once on everybody's must-visit list – Queen Victoria, the Empress of Germany and Wallis Simpson all sampled its pleasures – and, even if the pier has been lopped, it still has a lovely Georgian seafront promenade and some good shops. A different kind of pleasure is to be had watching the cargo ships load and unload in Felixstowe docks.

To the south, the Shotley peninsula has been designated an Area of Outstanding Natural Beauty. Tranquil and with real back-of-beyond rural appeal, the peninsula's roads take their time meandering along the estuaries – forcing you to calm down and do the same.

IPSWICH ★

Say the word 'Ipswich' and what springs to mind? Perhaps the town's football club (winners of the UEFA Cup in 1981 and the only professional team in Suffolk), but otherwise most people struggle for a concrete image. Visit the town, however, and there are almost constant reminders of a more illustrious past. Even beyond the medieval centre, the riverside zone now known as the Waterfront, almost entirely deserted by the shipbuilding industry, is beginning to thrive as a tourist attraction after extensive regeneration has created a marina and waterside cafés and restaurants. The first phase of development of a new university, as well as bringing an influx of young people, should have a good effect on the artistic scene too. Best of all for visitors, the most handsome parts of town are squeezed into a very compact area: once you're in the centre, nothing is much more than a 15-minute walk away.

The medieval centre

Originally the Anglo-Saxon town of Gippeswyk, Ipswich was already an important place in 1200, when it received its royal charter. The town grew rich on the pottery and wool trade and much of its existing street plan dates from the Middle Ages, when it rivalled London and York in significance and size. There are 600 listed buildings in Ipswich, so there's plenty to see: just look up above the modern shopfronts in the pedestrianised centre and you'll find many timber-framed buildings and highly decorative merchants' houses. The finest of these is the Ancient House, on the corner of St Stephen's Lane and Butter Market, which is now leased by kitchenware chain Lakeland. The magnificent pargeting (thoroughly restored in the last few years) dates from the mid 17th century, with each of the four window panels depicting the known continents at that time: Europe, Africa, Asia and America (Australasia was still to be 'discovered'). The timber-framed Oak House on Northgate Street looks like it has always been there (it may have been founded as early as the 1400s), although recent historians have suggested it was built mainly with found sections from other timber houses around the town.

Another must-see structure is the red-brick Wolsey's Gate, just next to St Peter's Church on College Street. Cardinal Wolsey was Ipswich's most famous son, one of the few men without noble blood (his father was a butcher and cattle dealer) to rise to power during the Tudor period. For a while he was Henry VIII's right-hand man, but inevitably fell out of favour with the capricious king. The even older, half-timbered Pykenham's Gateway is on Northgate Street, not far from Oak House. For something more modern, look for the rotund bronze statue of Giles's Grandma, armed with a fierce umbrella. The much-loved *Daily Express* cartoonist used to work in the buildings opposite.

Ipswich is also well endowed with square-towered medieval churches. Something had to be done with them as the population grew steadily more secular; six of the 12 were retained for worship, while the others are mostly being put to good civic use. St Stephen's became the Ipswich tourist information centre (St Stephen's Lane, 01473 258070, www.visit-ipswich.com), and tickets for boat tours, plays and museums can be bought here. Themed walking tours around the town centre are run every Tuesday at 2.15pm, from May to September.

St Lawrence Church on Dial Lane is now a community-run café, but its tower still houses the

oldest ring of bells in Christendom (cast in the mid 15th century, they were used for the first time in 25 years in September 2009). After many years of disuse, St Peter's Church has been converted into a concert venue and rebranded St Peter's by the Waterfront (St Stephen College Street, 01473 225269, www.stpetersbythewaterfront.com). It also houses the Charter Hangings, eight wonderful tapestries depicting the history of Ipswich that were designed by Isabel Clover for the Millennium – they can be viewed on Wednesdays, from April to September. St Mary at the Quay on Key Street is an artist-led space that sometimes puts on shows, while St Nicholas on Cutler Street is a more regular performance venue – and the place where Wolsey was baptised.

The prettiest of Ipswich's churches, however, is still used for worship: head to Christchurch Park (formerly the site of an Augustinian priory) to admire the fine double-hammerbeam roof of St Margaret's.

The Waterfront

Ipswich was once one of the most important ports in Britain, and famous for its shipbuilding industry. Its place at the head of the River Orwell ensured it retained national importance until the size of ships outgrew the harbour. During the latter decades of the 20th century, the riverside area was dismal and neglected. Since this was partly due to the short-sightedness of mid 20th-century town planners, who had cut the riverside off from the town with an inner ring road, it is oddly appropriate that ten years of piecemeal redevelopment by local entrepreneurs should have reversed the process.

The short walk here from the town still needs tidying up, but the riverside is now a thriving leisure attraction – there's even some luxury boat-building going on (the yacht used in *Casino Royale* was made here). The Marina is bustling and smart, cafés and restaurants gather at the water's edge, and cranes hover around the new university building (the first phase of a larger development). Dance East has its headquarters in the love-it-or-hate-it Jerwood DanceHouse, a white, 23-storey monolith designed by John Lyall Architects, which towers over the rest of low-rise Ipswich.

Several boats offer trips from the docks; Victor (01621 857567, www.top-sail.co.uk), one of the oldest London barges still in active use, was built in Ipswich Docks and makes occasional cruises and birdwatching trips. There's also the Orwell Lady (*see p225*), a 118-seater vessel with an open top deck.

The parks

Before Henry VIII got a hankering for a new wife, there were several priories in Ipswich. Christchurch Mansion (*see p228*), which lies outside the old medieval town, is built over the top of an Augustinian priory. The red-brick Tudor beauty was given to the people of Ipswich in 1892 by local brewer and philanthropist Felix Thornley Cobbold, who stopped Victorian developers tearing it down to build terraced houses. The grounds he saved, still dotted with ancient oaks and chestnuts, are now a much-loved public park. Recent restoration

has invigorated the planting and generally spruced things up, as well as providing a new pavilion, bird reserve, benches and seats. The Mansion itself was made into a museum in 1896, housing a fantastic collection of objects that tell their own idiosyncratic story of Ipswich.

Christchurch Park contains a playground, but the redeveloped Holywells Park, near the docks, has rather overshadowed it. Play facilities here include a large new adventure playground with a bird's-nest swing, play fountains and a galleon theme. Hollywells also has its own canal and waterway system. If you want a proper swim rather than mucking about by the water, Crown Pools on Crown Street has eight 25m lanes and, for family fun, a beach area, wave machine and water fountains.

Culture & shopping

Ipswich has a bustling arts scene. There are several theatres in the centre of town: the Regent Theatre is the largest seated venue in East Anglia, and numerous smaller alternatives include the Corn Exchange, the New Wolsey Theatre, the Sir John Mills Theatre and, due to open in 2010 near the Waterfront, Red Rose Chain's Witchbottle Theatre. Also on the docks, the new headquarters of Dance East (Foundry Lane, 01473 295230, www.dance east.co.uk) opened in autumn 2009, with several dance studios offering a full programme of events, as well as a theatre space. If you're after a film, there are two choices: the multi-screen cinema at Cardinal Park for Hollywood blockbusters or the Corn Exchange's Film Theatre for independent and world movies.

When it comes to shopping, you'll find the familiar range of global-brand chain stores, but also plenty of independents. The Busy Fingers knitting shop, Memorable Cheeses, Mr Simms Olde Sweet Shop and traditional family butcher Proctors, which makes speciality sausages, are all in the centre. There's also a busy market on Cornhill four days a week (Tuesday and Thursday to Saturday) with fruit and veg, a fishmonger and hot food stalls, as well as clothes and other bits and bobs. The imposing classical edifice of the Town Hall, which dominates the market square, houses galleries showing and selling vibrant work by local arts and craft makers.

The two modern shopping centres built within the medieval town are unfortunate, especially the Buttermarket Centre – the dismal interior lighting makes you want to scuttle for the exits. Tower Ramparts, north of Tavern Street, is better, but still unimaginative and a wasted opportunity.

Where to eat & drink

If you're after a quiet drink, head to the Fat Cat (288 Spring Road, 01473 726524, www.fatcat ipswich.co.uk), a pub that cares how it keeps its beer and favours conversation rather than the racket of gaming machines or background music. Breweries nationwide are represented in addition to local Adnams and Woodforde's, and there are plenty of Belgian bottled beers. Bar snacks include cornish pasties, scotch eggs and pork pies, with

Felixstowe. See p226.

baguettes at lunchtime. Just around the corner from Christchurch Park and Mansion, the Woolpack (1 Tuddenham Road, 01473 253059) has the feel of a country pub, even though it's just outside the town centre. A tiny snug at the front gives way to a larger lounge bar that has a roaring fire in the winter. The decor is a bit tired, but the simple, own-cooked food is tasty.

For a pint on the Waterfront, the Isaac Lord (7 Wherry Quay, 01473 259952, www.isaac lord.org) is situated in one of the Cobbold brewery's former malt warehouses. It has a large courtyard area overlooking the Marina, as well as roomy timbered bars inside, and serves a small menu of pub grub favourites at reasonable prices. The Greyhound (9 Henley Road, 01473 252862, www.greyhound-ipswich.com) is a serious real ale pub, while Felaw Street's Steamboat Tavern (01473 601902, www.thesteamboat.co.uk) is good for bands.

Restaurants include smart chains such as Loch Fyne (1 Duke Street, 01473 269810, www.lochfyne.com) and Galley (25 St Nicholas Street, IP1 1TW, 01473 281131, www.galley. uk.com, closed Sun), sister to the restaurant of the same name in Woodbridge. For something a bit different, try Keralam (26 St Helens Street, 01473 288599), a fine, reasonably priced South Indian restaurant.

If you want dinner at the Waterfront, with its numerous cafés and restaurants, do book: the whole stretch gets very busy. The restaurant inside the smart Salthouse Harbour Hotel (see p224) has just doubled in size. Local seasonal ingredients are put to good use in its Mediterranan-slanted menu, served from 11am to 10pm. Another former salt warehouse contains the Bistro on the Quay (3 Wherry Quay, 01473 286677, www.bistro onthequay.co.uk), which offers good-value set menus in an airy interior.

On the eastern outskirts of Ipswich, Kesgrave Hall (see p224), a stylish boutique hotel with a bistro-style restaurant, is a welcome newcomer. It's an informal place with a huge outdoor terrace, open kitchen and plenty of jolly banter between regulars and staff. The food is Modern British, peppered with regional ingredients such as local pork and smoked mackerel, and Lane Farm sausages. Although you can't book, it's open all day – unlike many restaurants in Suffolk.

Arlingtons

13 Museum Street, IP1 1HE (01473 230293, www.arlingtonsbrasserie.co.uk). Open 8am-10pm daily.
When the Ipswich Museum moved to its current premises on the High Street, its former home was converted into a huge restaurant. The large and light central space features a mezzanine level that now includes a platform for a grand piano. The restaurant's atmosphere and menu are reminiscent of the Brown's brasserie chain, but Arlingtons is independently run and the quality of the cooking a cut above. This is comfort food done well, with hearty classics such as lamb pudding with vegetables, or steak, mushroom and ale pie. The café downstairs serves a range of moreish sandwiches.

FIVE SUFFOLK GOLF COURSES

Aldeburgh Golf Club
Saxmundham Road, Aldeburgh, IP15 5PE (01728 452890, www.aldeburgh golfclub.co.uk).
Old-school but excellent, Aldeburgh is a tough test and not one for the casual player. You'll be picking the ball out of the gorse on a regular basis if you haven't got to grips with your game.

Ipswich Golf Club
Purdis Heath, Bucklesham Road, Ipswich, IP3 8UQ (01473 728941, www.ipswichgolfclub.com).
A heathland course at Purdis Heath on the outskirts of Ipswich, and a cracking test of golf. Similar dress code requirements to Woodbridge.

Southwold Golf Club
The Common, Southwold, IP18 6TB (01502 723234, www.southwold golfclub.co.uk).
A well-cared-for nine-hole course, with a good atmosphere.

Thorpeness Hotel & Golf Club
Thorpeness, IP16 4NH (01728 452176).
An attractive heathland golf course, five minutes from the sea, combined with a modern hotel (see p205). Visitors are encouraged to play here, and there are plenty of deals available (many including rooms in the hotel).

Woodbridge Golf Club
Bromeswell Heath, Woodbridge, IP12 2PF (01394 382038, www.woodbridgegolfclub.co.uk).
The setting is Suffolk heathland, the atmosphere formal – check the website for details of the dress code.

SUFFOLK

Dove
76 St Helens Street, IP4 2LA (01473 211270, www.dovestreetinn.co.uk). Open/food served noon-midnight Mon-Sat; noon-11pm Sun (last entry 10.45pm daily).
Winner of numerous CAMRA awards, this is a pub for serious beer-heads. There's a staggering and ever-changing array of real ales on offer, on hand pump and in the tap room, plus foreign brews (in bottles and barrels) and ciders. Keep hangovers at bay with cheap, hearty dishes such as vegetarian curry or beef and ale stew.

Mariners ★
Neptune Quay, IP4 1AX (01473 289748, www.ilpunto. co.uk). Lunch served noon-2.30pm, dinner served 7-9.30pm Tue-Sat.
Renamed Mariners in 2009, the former Il Punto is still run by Regis and Martine Crepy, the people behind the highly regarded Maison Bleue (*see p287*) in Bury St Edmunds and the Great House (*see p283*) in Lavenham. The setting is an ex- Belgian gunboat – all gleaming wood and brasswork – that also saw service as a Red Cross hospital ship and a party boat, before ending up moored in the Marina between the Salthouse Hotel and the Old Custom House. It serves traditional French cuisine to a very high standard, but there's also a £5.95 snack menu for those who aren't interested in the full à la carte experience.

Where to stay
There are, of course, plenty of chain options in a town the size of Ipswich, but the boutique hotel concept hasn't taken hold here yet, with the exception of the Salthouse (*see right*).

Hintlesham Hall
Hintlesham, IP8 3NS (01473 652334, www.hintlesham hall.co.uk). Rates £160-£210 double incl breakfast.
This 16th-century manor house, four miles west of Ipswich, owes its resurgence partly to Ruth Watson (now at the Crown & Castle in Orford; *see p216*), its owner for six years. The current management continue to make the most of the historic setting with grand reception rooms decorated in conservative, formal style. A gym, a heated outdoor pool, a tennis court, ESPA treatment rooms and a golf course in the grounds lend a more contemporary appeal, and visitors can enjoy country walks straight from the grounds without having to get out their car keys.

Kesgrave Hall ★
Hall Road, Kesgrave, IP5 2PU (01473 333741, www.milsomhotels.com). Rates £108-£191 double.
The company that runs the seriously successful Maison Talbooth and Milsoms hotel in Dedham, just over the border in Essex, opened their first Suffolk outpost in 2008. Kesgrave Hall is a lovely Georgian mansion, hidden at the end of a sweeping gravel driveway a few miles east of Ipswich. Built for a former MP, it was requisitioned as a USAF base during World War II. The Hall has been renovated using the best of the building's elegant traditional features, but with touches of modern glamour. There are 23 rooms; the three 'principal' rooms are the most luxurious, with roll-top baths, walk-in showers and zebra-print sofas. It's also got a restaurant and bar, with a terrace that overlooks a huge green carpet of lawn.

Salthouse Harbour Hotel ★
Neptune Quay, IP4 1AX (01473 226789, www.salthouseharbour.co.uk). Rates £110-£250 double incl breakfast.
Converted from a large warehouse, this boutique hotel has been so successful that the owners added a vast modern extension at the end of 2009, doubling the hotel's size. Many of the rooms have great views over the Marina, and the penthouses on the sixth floor offer unparalled vistas. Carved headboards and unusual, individual pieces of retro furniture give the rooms character, and the restaurant overlooking the water – also popular with non-residents – puts Suffolk meat and fish at the heart of its menu. The Salthouse is sister to the Angel Hotel (*see p289*) in Bury St Edmunds.

IPSWICH TO FELIXSTOWE
Thanks to the A14, which circumnavigates Ipswich before heading down to the docks in Felixstowe, this peninsula isn't as quiet as Shotley to the south, but there are plenty of peaceful and lovely corners to discover. Just outside Ipswich, Orwell Country Park, covering 200 acres of ancient woodland, recreational heathland (locally referred to as 'The Lairs') and natural wetland, offers great opportunities for seeing wildlife – once you've found the park in the first place. If there are any signposts on the A14, they are easily missed; access is to the north of the park, from the final junction with the Nacton Road before the Orwell Bridge. There are car parks at Pipers Vale and Bridge Wood.

The eastern side of the peninsula has such attractive spots as Waldringfield (on Regional Cycle Route 41). On the banks of the River Deben, the beer garden of the Maybush pub (Cliff Road, 01473 736215, www.debeninns.co.uk) is a lovely place to sit and watch the flowing water. Walk along the riverbank in either direction for gorgeous views across the estuary. From April to September, you can take a two-hour cruise (01473 736260, www.waldringfieldboatyard.co.uk) up the river to Woodbridge and back.

A short distance south in the hamlet of Hemley, several footpaths lead from the little red-brick church, while Newbourne provides two opportunities to buy fresh produce: the first is a small shed on the roadside with an honesty box; the second is Newbourne Farm Shop (26 Mill Road, 01473 736407, www.newbournefarmshop.co.uk, closed Mon). A decidedly larger concern, it sells local meat (try Revett's sausages), dairy and baked goods, and some very tempting seasonal fruit and vegetables that are all labelled either 'grown on site' or 'grown in Suffolk'. When the café hut is open, you can buy soup and bread, plus tea, coffee and cakes. Kirton and Falkenham largely consist of post-war housing built for the dockworkers.

On the west side of the peninsula, the Stour & Orwell Walk leads 42 miles from Felixstowe all the way to Manningtree in Essex (for maps, visit www.ldwa.org.uk). The Ship pub (*see p226*) in Levington is a choice spot for refreshments. At Nacton, there's a small car park beside the river, with a grassy picnic area that offers good views towards the Felixstowe docks.

Things to do

IPSWICH

Orwell Lady ★

*Orwell Quay, Haven Marina, Ipswich Wet Dock, IP3
0ED (01473 836680, www.orwellrivercruises.co.uk).
Tours July, Aug 2pm Wed, Fri-Sun. Easter-June, Sept
2pm Wed, Sat, Sun. Tickets £13; £7-£11 reductions.
No credit cards.*

Tour the River Orwell aboard this cruise boat, with an
open top for sightseeing and an enclosed lower deck.
A guide describes the history of the river and significant
landmarks, including Freston Tower and Orwell Park
House, home of the puritanical Admiral Vernon, who
earned the nickname 'Old Grog' for watering down the
men's rum ration. Lucky day-trippers might see the
river's resident seal or the peregrine falcon who lives
under the concrete mass of Orwell Bridge. Longer
cruises get as far as the Felixstowe and Harwich docks.

Suffolk Leisure Park

*Bourne Hill, Wherstead, IP2 8NQ (01473 602347,
www.suffolkleisurepark.co.uk). Open Winter 10am-
10pm Mon-Fri; 10am-6pm Sat, Sun. Summer 1-9pm
Tue, Thur, Fri; 10am-6pm Wed, Sat, Sun. Admission
varies; check website for details.*

Learning to ski might not be your first objective when
visiting Suffolk, but that doesn't mean you shouldn't
give it a try when the opportunity presents itself.
The dry slopes here are categorised red, blue and
beginners (the last of which is new), and each slope
has a ski lift to get you to the top (the main slope is
590-feet long (180 metres)). There's also a climbing
centre, with various walls and high rope-walks to
master. Whichever way you choose to work up an
appetite, you can retire to the Lodge afterwards for
the likes of cajun cod fish cakes and ribeye steak
– not especially cheap, but hearty.

Orwell Bridge

SUFFOLK

FIVE SUFFOLK ICE-CREAMS

Suffolk isn't renowned for its ice-cream, but many small independent makers have started up in the last decade or so, making fantastic, old-fashioned ice-cream.

Alder Tree Ice-cream
Alder Carr Farm, Needham Market, IP6 8LX (01449 721220/01449 720820, www.alder-tree.co.uk). Open Farm shop Summer 9am-5.30pm Tue-Sat; 10am-4pm Sun. Winter 9am-4.30pm Tue-Sat; 10am-4pm Sun.
Made with the fruit you see growing on Alder Carr Farm, this ice-cream tastes of what it's supposed to: cream and fruit. Food writer Nigel Slater put it well when he said there is something refreshingly clean and pure about the Alder Carr range. And what a range it is… the irresistible flavours include tayberry, elderflower and gooseberry, stem ginger and rhubarb, and summer fruits.

Criterion Ices
The Manor Farm Creamery, Bird Green, Thurston, IP31 3QJ (01359 230208, www.criterion-ices.co.uk).
A small family-run business that was started in London by an Italian family 80 years ago, but moved to Suffolk in the intervening decades. Flavours veer towards the exotic – vintage marmalade, brown bread, maple walnut, brandy and orange – and contain no artificial colourings or flavourings.

Little Ice-cream Company
59-61 Undercliff Road West, Felixstowe, IP11 2AD (01394 670500, www.little icecream.co.uk). Open 10.30am-5pm Mon-Fri; 10am-6pm Sat, Sun.
Made on Adams Farm, not far from the Little Ice-cream Company's parlour in Felixstowe (see p231). No artificial flavourings or colourings are used in the selection of 60 different flavours; we like the pistachio version, topped with salted nuts. Even the cones are above average.

Suffolk Meadow Ice-cream
Marybelle Dairy, The Clink, Walpole, IP19 9AU (01986 784658, www.marybelle.co.uk).
The original recipes came from Belgium, but the milk is fresh from Suffolk cows. The wide variety of flavours ranges from vanilla to lemon and ginger, turkish delight and the Indian-style kulfi. Sorbets too.

Vitalina's Ice-cream
Unit 23B Fysh, House Farm, Cuckoo Hill, Bures, CO8 5LD (01787 229029, www.vitalinasicecream.co.uk).
This brand is named after the proprietor's Italian mother and comes in classic Italian flavours such as stracciatella, bacio (chocolate and hazelnut) and pistachio.

Where to eat & drink

The Fox (01473 736307, www.debeninns.co.uk) in Newbourne is a cottagey pub, painted Suffolk Pink. There are tables outside, and a cosy, low-ceilinged interior, full of beams, with views over the gardens. Daily specials include soup, pâtés and interesting main dishes, alongside pub staples such as fish and chips or steak and ale pie.

The Ship
Church Lane, Levington, IP10 0LQ (01473 659573). Lunch served noon-2pm Mon-Sat; noon-3pm Sun. Dinner served 6.30-9.30pm Mon-Sat; 6.30-9pm Sun.
The Ship is a thatched pub with several small and cosy bar rooms, full of inviting crannies. Prints and photos of boats adorn the walls, and large beams and slate floors lend a rural air. Blackboard specials are updated daily and include plenty of fresh fish and seafood, while drinkers choose from cask ales and wines (many available by the glass). There are views of the estuary from the patio, but you might prefer to work up an appetite with a walk along the Orwell – footpaths follow the riverbank in both directions. Children aren't allowed in the Ship, so it's a refuge for adults in search of a quiet weekend lunch.

Where to stay

Quayside Cottage & the Boathouse
The Quay, Waldringfield, IP12 4QZ (01473 736724, www.quaysidecottage.com). Rates £385-£585 per week.
These two properties – both sleeping two – are wonderful places for couples to stay, right next to the Deben river. Both are havens from the bustle of modern life, with all details attended to – right down to books, CDs and DVDs for guests to enjoy in the evening or on rainy days.

Windy Bank ★
The Quay, Waldringfield, IP12 4QZ (020 7274 1183). Rates £350-£520 per week. No credit cards.
A small wooden house overlooking the Deben, Windy Bank has all sorts of individualistic touches in an appealing interior. Floor-to-ceiling windows on the river side let you appreciate the landscape in all weathers, and there's a garden too. It sleeps up to four people.

FELIXSTOWE ★

Nowadays, Felixstowe doesn't register highly as a tourist destination, but there was a time when it was a very well-to-do resort. Victoria, Empress of Germany (daughter of Queen Victoria) started the town's good fortunes when she stayed for a month-long summer holiday in 1891. The arrival of the railway in 1898 was another boon, and when the water trickling out of Felixstowe's cliffs was declared as fine a curative as the waters of Harrogate and Bath, its future seemed secure: a 1902 act of parliament granted Felixstowe new status as a spa town. Paddle steamers ran from London and back, dropping off hordes of passengers on a pier that was so long (at 903 yards, it was the third-longest in the country) it had a tram to transport people to the shore.

Kesgrave Hall. See p224.

Along a seafront promenade that stretched for miles, genteel Edwardian streets were built to house upper-class guests. During the abdication crisis of 1936, Wallis Simpson stayed here for six weeks. Once she had gained the residential status she needed to divorce her husband, legal proceedings went ahead in Ipswich.

The seafront

At its centre, Felixstowe is still a very handsome small town. Despite falling out of favour with Londoners, the seafront remains popular with locals. You can begin a hearty walk from the car park at Felixstowe Ferry (the foot ferry to Bawdsey sails from here during the season). The first of Felixstowe's several Martello towers is to the north, and colourful beach huts line the top of the cliff; among them, the Dip Kiosk (closed Feb) serves mugs of tasty ground coffee and Bennetts ice-cream at a few outside tables on dry days. Head south-west on the seafront path to the Spa Pavilion (01394 282126, www.thespapavilion.org), a glamorous music venue in Felixstowe's heyday that was bombed to smithereens in World War II. The current 1950s building isn't at all glamorous: the café has unloved plastic tablecloths and a musty smell, but there are shows for children and adults all through the year. The gardens are typical of English seaside resorts, tidy, colourful and pleasant, and there's a little waterfall right by the Pavilion. Nearby is the tourist information office (91 Undercliff Road West, 01394 276770, www. suffolkcoastal.gov.uk/tourism/, closed Sun winter).

The stretch between the Pavilion and the pier has changed little since Edwardian times. There's no

tacky seafront clutter and, if you're lucky, you might catch a man playing sea shanties on an accordion in the little shelter halfway along. The pier is very family-friendly: an amusement arcade of the old-fashioned sort offers tuppenny falls, basic slot machines and claw grabs, and there are stalls selling fish and chips, candyfloss and beach toys. Of more interest to adults is the hut selling freshly caught fish. If it's raining, the swimming pool, fun pool and indoor play centre at Felixstowe Leisure Centre (01394 670411, www.felixstoweleisure centre.co.uk) should keep children occupied.

It's a great pity that you can no longer walk along the pier itself. Already a fraction of the length it once was, there are rumours it will be pulled down and the seafront buildings redeveloped – a great shame, since it would rob the seafront of its most significant landmark. Across the road from the pier are several cafés, ice-cream parlours and chippies from which you can ponder its demise. Beyond the pier, the town begins to get tattier, but there are several more amusement arcades up Sea Road.

The town centre

Perched on the cliff, the grid of large Victorian and Edwardian villas gives the town a genteel air, and several shops are worth a browse. Hamilton Road is the main shopping street. Be sure to peek into Fabric8 (nos.3-5). Recently rebranded after 65 years as the Remnant Shop, it sells a colourful array of fabric, wool and buttons, and is an essential stop for fans of sewing and knitting. Miss Magpie's Emporium (no.28) is an upmarket children's toys and clothes shop, while Magpie Books (no.36) is a well-stocked independent. The Deben Butcher

SUFFOLK

Places to visit

IPSWICH

Christchurch Mansion ★

*Soane Street, IP4 2BE (01473 433554, www.
colchestermuseums.org.uk). Open Summer 10am-
5pm daily. Winter 10am-dusk daily. Admission free.*
A stunning red-brick Tudor edifice in Christchurch Park,
this house has hosted such royal visitors as Charles
II and Elizabeth I – although no one is sure whether
the Virgin Queen stayed the night or just popped by for
tea. The museum now occupying 31 of the mansion's
rooms is a wonderful showcase of art, furniture, pottery
and curios. Many people visit just to see the fine
collection of paintings and drawings by Gainsborough
and Constable, but there is much more to see.

It's worth lingering over John Cleveley the Elder's
intricate paintings of Ipswich and the Orwell, but other
delights include a primitive exercise machine (built to
mimic the action of riding a horse) and the backwards
reading chair, both found in the library. You can also
tease out details from the Hawstead Panels, painted
in the early 1600s for the puritanical Lady Drury after
her only child had died. She was an early advocate
of abolishing the slave trade: one of the many Latin
slogans on the panels proclaims 'All People are Equal'.
A more eccentric treat is the Manor doll's house,
made by Violet Ellington of Felixstowe to raise funds
for the Red Cross during World War II: most of the
house and its furniture were created from Winston
Churchill's cigar boxes.

For refreshments, the tearoom just off the old
Tudor Kitchen serves sandwiches, cakes, tea and
coffee when the museum is open. Free tours take
place on Wednesday afternoon during the summer.

Ipswich Museum

*High Street, IP1 3QH (01473 433550, www.ipswich.
gov.uk). Open 10am-5pm Tue-Sat. Admission free.*
The first stop here should be the incredibly ornate,
galleried Victorian Natural History Room. As well as

old-fashioned displays of birds and fossils, it houses
a woolly mammoth, a rhino and a giraffe. Further
exhibits cover Roman and Anglo-Saxon Suffolk,
and explore the region's geology. Despite the local
emphasis, the museum has artefacts from as far
away as Africa and Asia.

Ipswich Transport Museum ★

*Old Trolley Bus Depot, Cobham Road, IP3 9JD
(01473 715666, www.ipswichtransportmuseum.
co.uk). Open 11am-4pm Sun; 1-4pm Mon-Fri in
school hols. Admission £4; £2.40-£3.50 reductions;
£12 family.*
Ipswich's former trolley bus depot is now stuffed full
of vehicles that were either made or used in Ipswich.
The 1904 electric tram – a reminder of how beautiful
everyday transport used to be – is one of a number
of recently renovated items. The museum also has
the oldest complete trolley bus in the world, and the
first mobile crane to have been built anywhere. Only
130 Trident cars were ever made, and one is here.
Why? Because it was manufactured nearby. On the
first weekend of October, the museum hosts a self-
explanatory and thoroughly enjoyable 'Come and Ride
on Our Buses' event. The volunteer-run café serves
hot drinks and own-made cakes.

Jimmy's Farm

*Pannington Hall Lane, IP9 2AR (08444 938088,
www.jimmysfarm.com). Open Summer 9.30am-
5.30pm daily. Winter 9am-4pm Mon-Fri, Sun;
9am-5pm Sat. Admission free.*
Jimmy's done pretty well out of being a childhood friend
of Jamie Oliver. The celebrated chef gave him a loan
to start a farming business, and the TV cameras duly
followed the money in 2002. Since then, Jimmy's Farm
has become much more than just a haven for rare-
breed pigs. It's a family attraction that's open year-
round, well equipped with a nature trail, adventure
playground, butterfly house, wildlife ponds, a café,

Alton Water

produce and plant shops, and an on-site butcher. There's a farmers' market on the first Saturday of the month (10am-2pm), and the farm hosted its first festival in autumn 2009 (www.harvestatjimmys.com).

IPSWICH TO FELIXSTOWE

Martlesham Heath Control Tower Museum
Off Eagle Way, Marltesham, IP5 3UZ (01473 624510, www.mhas.org.uk). Open Apr-Oct 2-5pm Sun, or by arrangement. Admission free.
Suffolk's first control tower was built on the heath in 1917. The displays relay stories about the aerodrome's significance in the early history of aviation, as well as its importance during World War II.

FELIXSTOWE

Felixstowe Museum
Viewpoint Road, IP11 7JG (01394 675355, www.felixstowe-museum.co.uk). Open June-Sept 1-5pm Wed, Sun. Easter-May, Oct 1-5pm Sun. Admission £1; free-50p reductions. No credit cards.
Situated next to the Landguard Fort, Felixstowe Museum is housed in the fort's old submarine mining building. The dozen rooms describe the town's social history, beginning with its importance as a Roman settlement. The exhibits take in the prominence of Henry VIII's fort, Felixstowe's boom years as a seaside tourist resort in the late 19th and early 20th centuries, and the story of how the present-day docks came into being. Using photos, models, maps and colourful artefacts, it brings the people and institutions of Felixstowe into neat focus, with friendly volunteers always on hand to embellish the source material. The café (instant coffee, builders' tea and biscuits) is full of local history books to browse.

Landguard Fort
Viewpoint Road, IP11 3TW (07749 695523, www.landguard.com, www.english-heritage.org.uk/
landguardfort). *Open Apr-Oct 10am-5pm daily. Admission £3.50; £1-£2.50 reductions. No credit cards.*
Henry VIII commissioned the first fort on Landguard Point, which remained strategically significant for many centuries. Indeed, the military only left the place in 1971. Today, it's well run by by English Heritage, with lots to enjoy. The audio tour goes on a bit, but does provide insight into the everyday lives of the men who were posted here, as well as details of the various scrapes they got into. The labyrinthine ammunition chambers, soldiers' wash rooms and seaward defence quarters are all powerfully atmospheric. A hint of privations suffered by the fort's personnel is given by the fact there is still no running water here. For refreshments, just walk around to the dockside seafront, where you'll find Felixstowe Museum's small café.

SHOTLEY PENINSULA

Alton Water ★
Holbrook Road, Stutton, IP9 2RY (01473 328408, www.altonwater.co.uk). Open Apr-Sept 10am-8pm Mon-Fri; 10am-6pm Sat, Sun. Oct 10am-7pm Mon-Fri; 10am-6pm Sat, Sun. Nov-Mar 10am-4pm daily. Admission Reservoir free. Activities vary; see website for details.
This reservoir is the largest area of inland water in Suffolk and a popular leisure spot. There are bird hides, walks and cycle trails, bream and pike for fishing, and a large watersports centre where 60 coaches teach sailing, windsurfing and other watersports. The centre is at the main car park (signposted from Stutton); it also has a café with tables overlooking the reservoir, and you can hire bikes. If you're seeking to enjoy the quieter pleasures of Alton Water – perhaps hoping to spot a skylark, sand martin or kingfisher, maybe hear a nightingale – it's better to start from one of the smaller car parks on the perimeter.

SUFFOLK

Alex

(no.120) sells game in season – it's not often you see wood pigeon, partridge and pheasant for sale on the high street – and Good Food (no.82) is a baker and deli. Where Cobbold Road crosses Hamilton Road, you'll find the Palace Cinema and bingo hall. A block further, we particularly enjoyed poking our nose into Poor Richard's second-hand bookshop at 17 Orwell Road. For craft items, home-made cakes and preserves, try the country market, held on Fridays at the Trades & Labour Club on High Road West.

The docks

Felixstowe's docks are a couple of miles south of the town centre, just around the corner from Landguard Point, far enough away for the cranes to look like majestic sculptures rather than engines of heavy industry. There is also something fascinating about watching large ships come into dock: for a close-up view, follow signs to Landguard Fort (*see p229*), a site of military and historic interest run by English Heritage. Just to the right of the fort, where the broad River Orwell meets the North Sea, a viewing area overlooks the container docks and estuary. You can see sailing boats on the Orwell and the workings at Harwich on the far side. A kiosk serves tea, coffee and ice-cream. Between the fort and the viewing area, the Felixstowe Museum (*see p229*) is situated in an old mine store.

Where to eat & drink

There's a really good range of places to eat in Felixstowe. Right on the clifftop, Ruby's Kitchen (1 Bent Hill, 01394 276627, www.rubys-kitchen) is a friendly establishment that bakes cakes fresh every day and serves seasonally inspired breakfasts and lunches. Ruby's coffee, available to take away, is blended and roasted in Suffolk. At Felixstowe Ferry, the Ferry Boat (01394 284203) is a 17th-century pub with bags of historic charm. It serves good food, including lots of fresh fish, at reasonable prices. The position is lovely, between the golf course and the banks of the Deben. It changed hands at the end of 2008, to the approval of its many regulars.

The pier has plenty of ice-cream parlours. You could try Rossi's Ice Cream or Joe Crowley's American Ice Cream Bar, with its soda fountain, but we liked the Little Ice-Cream Company (*see p226*) best. On Crescent Road, a short distance inland, the Oaks Tea Room (01394 273444, closed Mon, Sun) is a choice spot when everywhere near the seafront is heaving. It serves porridge until 10.45am, soups and deep-filled sandwiches for lunch, and own-made cakes all day.

Alex

123 Undercliff Road West, IP11 2AF (01394 282958, www.alexcafebar.co.uk). Open Café-bar 9.30am-9.30pm daily. Restaurant Lunch served noon-2pm Mon-Sat; noon-3pm Sun. Dinner served 6-9.30pm Mon-Sat.
The Alex is the best place for a meal on the seafront, and very popular. The informal café-bar downstairs serves breakfasts until noon and has a lengthy kids' menu. Dishes

for adults (with the exception of the steak) come in at under a tenner. The upstairs restaurant, with its deep-blue walls, produces food that is slightly more bistro than pub, but still reasonably priced. Huge picture windows on both floors provide great views of the sea.

Bonnet's Café ★

1B Hamilton Road, IP11 7AX (01394 282310, www.bonnetcafe.co.uk). Open Summer 9am-5pm Mon-Thur, Sun; 9am-5pm, 7-11pm Fri, Sat. Winter 10am-4pm Mon-Thur, Sun; 10am-5pm Fri; 9am-5pm Sat.
There has been a Bonnet's Café here since 1926, when a Swiss chocolate-making family arrived during Felixstowe's boom years. Subsequent owners – who kept the café's lovely antique sign, now part of an exquisite window display – haven't altered the successful formula of selling hand-made chocolates, coffees and teas to take away from downstairs, while running a restaurant in the airy room upstairs. The restaurant is terribly genteel and the waiting staff don't come up as often as they should, but there are a few tables downstairs where the atmosphere is more bustling. Breakfast is served until 11.30am, when the menu gives way to thick-cut sandwiches and hearty lunches. Save room for one of the incredibly moist traditional cakes.

Little Ice-Cream Company

59-61 Undercliff Road West, IP11 2AD (01394 670500, www.littleicecream.co.uk). Open 10.30am-5pm Mon-Fri; 10am-6pm Sat, Sun.
This pier-side parlour makes its own ice-cream at nearby Adams Farm; there's only one other outlet, in Colchester. The place buzzes whatever the season, with children tucking into sundaes and parents sighing over coffee. Flavours are regularly rotated to keep return customers guessing, but whatever's on offer will be good: topping pistachio ice-cream with salted nuts was puzzling, for example, but it worked.

Where to stay

The accommodation scene in Felixstowe hasn't yet matched the revival in food. There are plenty of hotels in lovely Edwardian buildings, but the decor and service tend to be a bit tired. The best of them is the Hotel Elizabeth Orwell (Hamilton Road, 01394 285511). Although some bedrooms could do with sprucing up, the bar, dining room and reading room retain much of the charm of their glory days, and the breakfasts are a bit more imaginative than the norm. It's cheaper and often better to stay in a guesthouse, or to self-cater.

Mariners Lodge

Ferry Road, Felixstowe Ferry, IP11 9RZ (0845 2680760, www.cottages4you.co.uk). Rates £557-£912 per week.
A light and spacious self-catering house, the Mariners is a bit outside the town centre at Felixstowe Ferry, but has views of the sea from the first-floor living room and a small patio garden at the rear. There are great options for walks right outside the door, and plenty of books, CDs and games for when the weather's wet. It sleeps up to seven people.

Norfolk Guest House

1-3 Holland Road, IP11 2BA (01394 283160, www.thenorfolk.com). Rates £65-£70 double incl breakfast. No credit cards.

SUFFOLK

Rob and Dee Northcut run this guesthouse, which is close to the town centre and the seafront. The design isn't what you'd call modish, but it's very comfortable and clean. A nice touch are the towels, folded into the shape of swans at the end of the beds, with a wrapped chocolate nestling between their wings. Breakfasts use local ingredients wherever possible, providing a choice of fresh fruit and yoghurt, a full English or smoked salmon and scrambled eggs.

SHOTLEY PENINSULA

Cyclists and weekend day-trippers love the small lanes and picturesque estuary views from this whale's tail of land between the Orwell and Stour rivers. If the Romans ever made it here, they certainly didn't build any of the roads. Just try finding Harkstead from the minor roads off the B1456: they wiggle and wind and double-back until a driver has no earthly sense of which direction the car is pointed, and the 30mph speed-limit seems pretty much beside the point when it's hard to drive above 20mph. Those that do make it to Harkstead will find a farmers' market at the village hall on the third Saturday of every month, with local farmers selling meat, local ladies selling cakes, local gardeners selling plants, and all sorts of other homespun crafts and foodstuffs sold by all sorts of other characters. You can park on the village green opposite, and there's a children's playground.

Down at Shotley Gate, at the tip of peninsula, things are a little more down-at-heel. Retirees stroll beside the Orwell rivermouth watching container ships at Felixstowe docks on one side, Harwich cruiseliners on the other. Some spectators have binoculars, some have notepads, some have both. The few lone canoeists provide a contrast with the boom of cranes, and the clang of metal striking metal echoes across the water.

At one time Shotley Gate didn't just look on passively as the hectic business of trade was conducted across the water. It had a huge training centre for Navy cadets, who first occupied the decommissioned, teak-hulled boat HMS *Ganges* and then purpose-built units on the shore. The site has fallen into disrepair since closing in 1976, though the local council has plans to build 400 retirement homes here. The small HMS Ganges Museum, next to the entrance to the Marina, is short on narrative and big on group photos, but it has the cumulative charm of a silent movie, the faces, clothes and kit on display together telling a story without words.

On the north coast of the peninsula, off a small road from unremarkable Chelmondiston, is the riverside hamlet of Pin Mill. Arthur Ransome moored his yacht, the *Nancy Blackett*, here and the child-heroes of his novel *We Didn't Mean to Go to Sea* sailed, by accident, from Pin Mill to Holland. It was also the site of Britain's last recorded outbreak of the bubonic plague.

The National Trust manage an 80-acre chunk of woodland around the cluster of buildings on the shore, so it's a good spot for a walk. Either set off from the picnic area adjacent to car park or from the Butt & Oyster pub, turning left before reaching Harry

King & Sons boatbuilders. The path leads round the back of the boatyard (where men of various ages are always messing around with boats), past a series of gardens and out into open countryside.

Walkers and boaters alike lunch at the Butt & Oyster (*see p233*), perhaps the only boozer in the country where sailors can get a pint without stepping off their vessel – when the tide is high enough, customers on the river are served through the windows. Next door is the Pin Mill Studio (01473 780130, www.thepinmillstudio.com), with its painted concrete floors and bright, airy exhibition space. It combines art and photography shows with shelves of books and gifts, and also has a few tables indoors and out for those in need of refreshment. The filter coffee is good, the cakes excellent and the welcome warm.

Heading south, Holbrook is notable for the Royal Hospital School, a vast independent boarding school that moved here from Greenwich in the 1930s. The road west towards Brantham leads through some of the school's stylish and immaculately tended buildings – it feels as if you've driven into an English version of *The Truman Show*. The school has strong connections to the Navy, and its pupils learn to sail on nearby Alton Water.

Where to eat & drink

Entering the Shotley peninsula from the north on the B1456, you can't miss the huge Suffolk Food Hall (01473 786610, www.suffolkfoodhall.co.uk). As well as the Samford Restaurant (*see p233*), there's an extensive range of indoor stalls selling Suffolk delicacies: notable among them are butcher

Suffolk Food Hall

Gerard King (who sets local ladies' hearts aflutter), Dave the fishmonger, baker Helena Doy and Hamish Johnston, the deli man. There's also a garden. Make an afternoon of it by combining a visit with a walk around the neighbouring country lanes (maps of two circular walks of different lengths are available inside the Food Hall).

Pubs offering good food include the Baker's Arms (01473 328595, closed Mon) in Harkstead, and the White Horse (01473 328060, www.whitehorse tattingstone.co.uk) in Tattingstone, where the menu is largely gluten-free.

Butt & Oyster
Pin Mill, IP9 1JW (01473 780764, www.debeninns. co.uk). Open 11am-11pm Mon-Sat; noon-10.30pm Sun. Food served noon-9pm daily.
This 16th-century hostelry is blessed with an incredible location, mere steps from the Orwell, with indoor and outdoor seating from which to enjoy the fantastic river views. That, coupled with its monopoly on pub trade at Pin Mill, means it doesn't have to try hard to win customers: staff border on rude, and men seem to get priority service over women at the bar. Although the menu features fresh regional fare such as own-cooked Suffolk ham and local beef and fish, dishes are served with little flair – undressed salad, tasteless bread rolls.

Samford Restaurant ★
Suffolk Food Hall, nr Wherstead, IP9 2AB (01473 786616, www.suffolkfoodhall.co.uk). Open/food served 9am-6pm Mon-Sat; 10.30am-4.30pm Sun.
The Pauls have farmed around the Shotley peninsula for generations. In 2007 two of the younger scions of the family, cousins Oliver and Robert, set up Suffolk Food Hall to foster a stronger relationship between local food producers and consumers. The centre's Samford Restaurant serves a simple seasonal menu that might include dressed Cromer crab, summer vegetable risotto or a chicken caesar salad, using meat from the butcher located below. Prices are lower than you might expect for the quality, and the premises are large and airy, with solid wooden tables and great river views through the glass wall at the far end.

Where to stay

Charlie's Cottage
Main Road, Chelmondiston, IP9 1DX (01502 578278, www.heritagehideaways.com). Rates £350-£585 per week.
With just one bedroom and a bathroom at the top of a cast-iron spiral staircase, this self-catering Victorian terraced cottage is a lovely little hideaway, not far from the Butt & Oyster. There's a coal fire for cosy nights in, and plenty of interesting maritime bits and bobs.

Freston Tower ★
Freston, IP9 1AD (01628 825925, www.landmark trust.org.uk). Rates £679-£1,348 per week.
No one is quite sure why this 16th-century red-brick folly was built, though it's been suggested, with little warrant, that young heiress Ellen de Freston insisted on the curious design so that she could enjoy a different view with each lesson of the day, culminating with astronomy at the top. Now owned by the Landmar Trust, the tower has 26 windows over its six floors, and the views over the River Orwell and surrounding area are certainly impressive. With just one room per floor, the place sleeps up to four people.

Small Town Suffolk

In the east of the county, between the coast and the flat agricultural lands of north Suffolk, lies this pretty stretch of countryside peppered with interesting market towns. Like the coast, it's an area full of potential for walking, cycling and eating great local food, but it's much quieter. Woodbridge and Framlingham are the largest and most characterful of the small towns. Both are good bases for a holiday as they're only a short drive from the coast and have many attractions within striking distance, as well as a plethora of small independent shops that make for a great day's browsing. Wickham Market is the smallest settlement and not technically even a town; Saxmundham and Leiston are less genteel than their neighbours, but both have things to offer. As elsewhere in Suffolk there's a noticeable lack of out-of-town supermarkets and, consequently, more family butchers and local food producers.

WOODBRIDGE ★

The town

Woodbridge is exactly the sort of place conjured up by the words 'market town'. Its higgledy-piggledy streets and lanes are full of beautiful houses built across the last five centuries; there's a pretty market square (although, sadly, the market itself relocated to the car park behind Budgens several years ago), independent shops, cafés and galleries, a gorgeous river and a handsome church. But it's not preserved in aspic in the way that Lavenham is; it's quite sizeable, has post-war housing on its outskirts and feels like a living, breathing, proper town.

It also has more of a contemporary buzz than other towns nearby (and, indeed, most of Suffolk); there's a good mix of young and old, artsy and boaty types, workers and retired folk, those who are Suffolk born and bred, and newcomers. The streets – particularly the Thoroughfare, Market Hill and Church Street – are full of intriguing boutiques, pleasant tearooms, good restaurants and lively pubs.

Independent food retailers include Woodbridge Good Food Company (2A New Street, 01394 610000, www.woodbridgefinefoodcompany.co.uk, closed Sun) for fabulous pork pies, and the family-run Cake Shop (21 Thoroughfare, 01394 382515, closed Sun), with its specialist rustic breads displayed in the window. For excellent bookshops, try Browsers (60 Thoroughfare, 01394 388890, www.browsersbookshop.com), which also has a café, and Woodbridge Books (66 Thoroughfare, 01394 382382, closed Sun). There's even a violin shop on the market square with a workshop in the large front windows for all to see. St Mary's Church, just by the market square, is worth a detour. It has rare square flintwork, and the decorative stone patterns laid into the base of the external walls are unusual and strikingly beautiful.

There are two museums in the market square. Housed in the handsome Elizabethan Shire Hall, the Suffolk Horse Museum (01394 380643, www.suffolkhorsesociety.org.uk/the-museum, open Easter-Sept 2-5pm Tue, Thur, Sat) is dedicated to the Suffolk Punch horse, the oldest breed of heavy horse in Britain. Woodbridge Museum (5 Market Hill, 01394 380502, www.visitwoodbridge.co.uk/museum.htm, closed Mon-Wed except school hols, all Nov-Easter) deals with the history of the town. However, its presentation is unimaginative and overly focused on the town's rich historical benefactors, the Seckfords. There's also some information on Sutton Hoo (*see p240*) – the famous Anglo-Saxon burial mounds just outside town, and Woodbridge's main attraction – that feels paltry to anyone who has been to the very well-staged exhibition at the site itself. More culture can be found at the Seckford Theatre (Burkitt Road, 01394 615015, www.seckfordtheatre.org), in the grounds of Woodbridge school, which offers a mix of amateur and professional performances.

The riverside

The town faces inward and doesn't make much of its former role as a busy port and shipbuilding hub, mainly because it's now cut off from the banks of the River Deben (pronounced 'Dee-ben') by the railway line. The handsome Tide Mill (closed Oct-Apr), containing a rather dull exhibition and some local artworks, is on the river side of the tracks, as are a couple of cafés. The mill's huge water wheel is currently out of action; £35,000 is being raised to get it going again, though it's only for show – the flour sold here comes from Pakenham Water Mill.

Nearby, the Woodbridge Art Club (15 Tide Mill Way, www.woodbridgeartclub.co.uk) hosts regular exhibitions of paintings, pottery and crafts by local artists. Also near are the Riverside Restaurant & Theatre (01394 382587, www.theriverside.co.uk), which also shows films in its wonderfully retro auditorium; the town's swimming pool and the tourist information centre (Station Buildings, 01394 382240, closed Sun winter). There are

Waterfront Café. See p239.

THE WATERFRONT CAFÉ

"THE FINEST SPOT IN TOWN"
BINKY SMITH WOODBRIDGE
OPEN 7 DAYS
FOOD SERVED ALL DAY
BOOKINGS WELCOME
DOGS & WELL BEHAVED
CHILDREN, WELCOME

Tide Mill. See p235.

River Deben. See p235.

Cafe

Discover the best of rural Britain

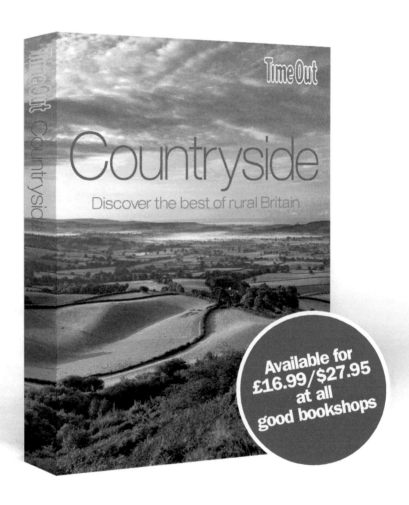

Available for
£16.99/$27.95
at all
good bookshops

lovely riverside walks in both directions; head south-west on the Fynn Valley Walk, or north-east along the narrower stretch of the Deben.

Where to eat & drink

There's plenty of choice in Woodbridge. Along the Thoroughfare are the Georgian and Frangipani coffee houses, and there are also cafés inside Jars of Clay pottery-painting shop and the excellent Browsers bookshop. Of the several pubs, Ye Olde Bell & Steelyard (103 New Street) is probably the best for sheer historic character, while you can be sure of a good pint at the Kings Head Inn (17 Market Hill), an Adnams-run pub. The Angel pub on Theatre Street, which recently reopened under new management after a refurb, looks promising.

For a special occasion, head to the Galley (21 Market Hill, 01394 380055, www.galley.uk. com) or the Modern European restaurant in the relaunched Crown (see p239). At the station is the homely Whistlestop café; on the waterfront are the Riverside Restaurant & Theatre (see p235) with its bistro menu and own-made bread and pasta, and the jaunty Caravan Café with its colourful outside tables, strong tea and proper bacon rolls.

Spice ★

17 Thoroughfare, IP12 1AA (01394 382557, www.spicewoodbridge.com). Lunch served noon-3pm, dinner served 7-11pm daily.
This restaurant might be behind a door that's as heavy and unwelcoming as a bank vault's, but once inside, the decor (orange walls, jute carpets, wooden tables) and cheerful staff make for a welcoming atmosphere, and it deserves its popularity. From the globe-trotting menu, Java beef curry, and honey and cinnamon brûlée were tip-top.

Waterfront Café

The Granary, Tide Mill Way, IP12 1BY (01394 610333, www.woodbridgefinefoodcompany.co.uk). Open Summer 9.30am-6pm daily. Winter 10am-4pm daily.
The setting is wonderful: in the 300-year-old granary buildings adjacent to the Tide Mill, with outdoor seating overlooking the Deben. Local fish dishes are the thing to order, and there's game in season too.

Wild Strawberry Café

19A Market Hill, IP12 4LX (01394 388881, www.wild strawberrycafe.co.uk). Food served 8am-2.30pm Mon-Fri; 9am-3pm Sat.
This diminutive café (with free Wi-Fi) does great sandwiches and baguettes. Fillings include sausage from Wickham Market butcher Revett's, Suffolk ham, potted shrimps, Sutton Hoo chicken, and houmous and veg. The own-made cakes are delicious too. There are a few tables on the pavement outside, and some on the quiet market square opposite.

Where to stay

Crown ★

Thoroughfare, IP12 1AD (01394 384242, www.the crownatwoodbridge.co.uk). Rates £140-£180 double incl breakfast.

After an extensive makeover, the Crown is the most chi-chi place in town – locals call it 'flash for Woodbridge' – with a glass frieze and deep red walls in the chic restaurant, and ten very contemporary bedrooms styled in grey and white. It shares owners with the Swan at Lavenham (see p283) and the Brudenell Hotel in Aldeburgh (see p209), but has more 'boutique' credentials.

Hill House

30 Market Hill, IP12 4LU (01394 383890, www.hill housewoodbridge.com). Rates £75-£90 double incl breakfast. No credit cards.
The Georgian façade is misleading; immediately behind is a 14th-century Wealden hall, one of the oldest buildings in this part of Woodbridge, with original beams, Tudor wall paintings and large brick fireplaces. The four characterful rooms are full of ancient detail. Breakfasts use organic ingredients wherever possible.

Old Granary Cottage

Tide Mill Way, IP12 1BY (01394 383793, www.the oldgranarycottage.co.uk). Rates from £90 double incl breakfast.
A lovely B&B set in an 18th-century clapboard building next to the Tide Mill. There are gorgeous views across the River Deben (it's practically surrounded by water) and magazine-worthy interiors. Two double bedrooms are available, and you can also rent the whole place by the week.

Seckford Hall Hotel

Woodbridge, IP13 6NU (01394 385678, www.seckford. co.uk). Rates £124 double incl breakfast.
A mile outside Woodbridge, what was the Tudor manorial seat of the mighty Seckford family has been a hotel (with 32 rooms) run by the Bunn family since the 1950s. The decor is a bit dated, especially the blue and gold in the Great Hall, but there are so many individual historical details of interest, plus a good restaurant and beautiful gardens, that it's hard not to enjoy it for what it is.

WICKHAM MARKET & AROUND

Five miles north-east of Woodbridge, just off the A12, lies Wickham Market. It feels more like an overgrown village than a town, with its dainty market square and handful of shops – most strikingly, well-stocked lingerie store Sweet Dreams (Market Hill, 01728 748171, www.sweetdreams-lingerie. co.uk, closed Sun). There has been a settlement here for a long time: in 2009 a local man found a huge cache of Iron Age coins buried in a pottery jar. These days, most people come for the meat at Revett's (see p246), a locally revered butcher that makes excellent sausages and always has a queue snaking along the pavement before opening time (rather quaintly, it still shuts for an hour at lunchtime). It also sells Orford smoked fish, a small selection of fruit and vegetables, a large range of cakes, and other delicatessen goodies. Just across the road is Quilter's Haven (68 High Street, 01728 746275, www.quilters-haven.co.uk, closed Sun), a marvellous haberdashery and workshop. Also on the square is antiques shop Vintage 46 (46 High Street, 01728 746642, www.vintagefortysix.co.uk) next to the Teapot Tearooms (see p245).

Places to visit

WOODBRIDGE

Sutton Hoo ★
Tranmer House, Sutton Hoo, IP12 3DJ (01394 389700, www.nationaltrust.org.uk/suttonhoo). Open all year; times vary, check website for details. Admission £6.50; £3.40 reductions; £16.45 family.
Just before World War II, Edith Pretty decided to excavate some of the large burial mounds she could see from the windows of her home, Tranmer House, so she invited local archaeologist Basil Brown to start digging. While she watched from a wicker chair, Brown found some rusting, crumbling rivets that turned out to be the remains of a 90ft-long Anglo-Saxon royal burial ship with hoards of treasure alongside. Now run by the National Trust, Sutton Hoo (hoo means 'spur of a hill') is a beautiful spot, lying on a rise above the River Deben and Woodbridge. Early morning is the best time to visit, when the mist clings to the mounds and it's easy to imagine some woad-painted warrior setting off to hunt game. Those who prefer an expert to guide them around the site can join a tour (bookable on the day), which lasts just under two hours. The exhibition hall tells the story of Sutton Hoo and the discovery with an imaginative short film and lively displays. It's a nice touch to have Brown describing the find in his laconic Suffolk drawl on the audio-guides. The café has a large wooden terrace with fantastic views.

WICKHAM MARKET & AROUND

Easton Farm Park ★
Easton, IP13 0EQ (01728 746475, www.eastonfarm park.co.uk). Open Mar-Sept 10.30am-6pm daily; other times may vary, check website for details. Admission £7.25; £6-£6.75 reductions; £25 family.
The huge car park is a warning of Easton Farm Park's popularity, especially in summer when it's packed with families. Set in 35 acres of peaceful countryside, it's modelled on a Victorian farm, with vintage machinery, a Victorian dairy and displays about the Suffolk Punch horse. There are free pony rides, pig racing, egg collecting and lots of animal petting and feeding opportunities. Regular workshops show what skills are required to be a blacksmith, a wheelwright or a picture framer. Make a day of it with a walk along the River Deben and a picnic. Too lazy for that? The Riverside Café serves jacket potatoes, sandwiches, soup, cream teas and own-made cakes. A farmers' market is held here every fourth Saturday of the month (9am-1pm).

Helmingham Hall Gardens
Helmingham, IP14 6EF (01473 890799, www.helmingham.com). Open May-Sept noon-5pm Tue-Thur, Sun. Admission £6; £3 reductions.
As you enter between two elaborate gatehouses, look out for a herd of deer wandering nonchalantly across the tree-lined driveway. The wonderful Hall – which lies across the moat, accessible by two drawbridges that are pulled up every night to keep out unwanted visitors – has been owned by the Tollemarche family for several centuries and has had many a royal visitor. Sadly, it's not open to the public, but the spectacular gardens are. There's a parterre, a knot garden, a rose garden, a meadow full of wild flowers and a series of marvellous borders, plus a tea room and shop.

Otley Hall
Hall Lane, Otley, IP6 9PA (01473 890264, www.otleyhall.co.uk). Open House by arrangement only. Gardens Summer noon-5pm Wed. Admission House £7.50. Gardens £5.50. No credit cards.
In 1606, Bartholomew Gosnold of Otley Hall set off to found Jamestown, the first English-speaking settlement in the US. He named Martha's Vineyard after his daughter. The ten acres of gardens, including a moat walk and knot garden, are lovely, but the 16th-century house with its impressive Great Hall and Linenfold Parlour is even more memorable. It's only accessible on private guided tours, though you can join a pre-booked tour run by Invitation to View (www.invitationtoview.co.uk) followed by lunch or afternoon tea.

FRAMLINGHAM

Framlingham Castle ★
Framlingham, IP13 9BP (01728 724189, www.english-heritage.org.uk/framlingham). Open July, Aug 10am-6pm daily. Apr-June, Sept-Nov 10am-5pm daily. Nov-Mar 10am-4pm Mon, Thur-Sun. Admission £6; £3-£5.10 reductions; £15 family.
Proceed from the ticket hut across the bridge above the deep empty moat and enter another age. Roger Bigod built Framlingham Castle in 1189, shoring up defences against 'Bad' King John. Bigod was a very powerful landowner, and his son Hugh was one of the barons responsible for having a bow and arrow pointed at King John's head while he was forced to sign the Magna Carta. The castle was later owned by Thomas Howard, who was close Henry VIII, procuring two of his own nieces, Anne Boleyn and Catherine Howard, as the king's wives. Needless to say, he eventually fell out of favour: his tomb is inside Framlingham's church. Mary Tudor also lived in the castle just before she became Queen of England. Poor-lad-made-good Robert Hitcham purchased the castle in 1635; after his death, as he had instructed, the inner buildings were demolished and a poorhouse built instead.
Vistors can walk around the top of the castle's curtain walls (an early example of this style) and enjoy the history plaques or the spectacular views over the town, Framlingham College and the countryside. Below are two museums. The one next to the shop inside the former poorhouse presents an imaginative and amusing animated history of the castle, and an exhibition about the castle's time as a poorhouse. The other is the Lanman Museum, with rather dusty, old-fashioned displays about local trades, although it does have some lovely prints and watercolours of the town and castle. There are picnic tables on the lawns within the walls, and a large outdoor chess set.

Shawsgate Vineyard
Badingham Road, IP13 9HZ (01728 724060, www.shawsgate.co.uk). Open Apr-Sept 10am-5pm Mon-Sat. Admission free.
Just outside Framlingham, this established vineyard runs free tasting and tours from April to September. You can also just pop in and follow a DIY trail, which takes you on a lovely walk around the vineyard. ▶

Framlingham Castle

Places to visit

Leiston Abbey

Abbey Road, Leiston, IP16 4TD (01728 832500, www.english-heritage.org.uk/leiston, www.leiston abbey.co.uk). Open 24hrs daily. Admission free.
Just north of Leiston, on the B1122, this ruined 14th-century abbey is permanently open. An atmospheric time to visit is dusk, when you can imagine the friars making their rounds between refectory, church and dormitory. Stone was hard to come by in this sandy, marshy part of Suffolk, so much of the building material came from a former abbey at Minsmere; the rest was constructed with brick and flint, then plastered over to give the appearance of stone. A viewing platform looks into the large refectory, while drawings indicate the vast size of the original church. One section was rebuilt as a farmhouse and is now occupied by the Pro Corda chamber music academy (01728 831354, www.procorda.com) – though the plastic windows facing the abbey ruins do marr the historic site. On the plus side, the academy presents a summer concert series and other performances throughout the year.

Long Shop Museum ★

Main Street, Leiston, IP16 4ES (01728 832189, www.longshop.care4free.net). Open Apr-Oct 10am-5pm Mon-Sat; 11am-5pm Sun. Admission £5; free-£4.50 reductions; £12 family.

This is one of those unexpected pleasures: an absolute treasure of a local museum. It's housed in the Leiston Works buildings just off the High Street and serves as a history of the Garrett family (who founded the Works), the business and the town itself. In the Long Shop building – constructed to house the first assembly line in the world, to keep up with orders from the 1851 Great Exhibition at Crystal Palace – are many examples of the Works' machines and a history of some of the women employed here during both world wars. Up the uneven stairs, the gallery tells the story of the development of steam power, from its first days to its modern application in nuclear power reactors (with a model of how nearby Sizewell B operates). But visitors don't have to be interested in the industrial revolution to enjoy the museum. The panels on Newson Garrett and his offspring are universally appealing, telling the story of his pioneering daughters, Elizabeth Garrett Andersen (the first woman in Britain to qualify as a doctor, in 1865), and Millicent Garrett Fawcett (who was at the forefront of the suffragist movement and educational reform and went on to found Newnham College for women at Cambridge). The oral histories from townsfolk are also fascinating, painting a picture of a thriving and lively Leiston – very different to the town we see today. There's a small picnic area and plenty of hands-on activities for children, including colouring stations, puzzles and brass rubbing.

Long Shop Museum

E.W. REVETT & SON

Revett's. See p246.

Along with rows of pretty painted cottages, there are several larger houses to appreciate. Overlooking the market square, 52 Hill House is an imposing dwelling with a front balcony and a crinkle-crankle wall in the back garden. Past Wickham Place – a charming house with espaliered trees marking the border of the front garden – is All Saints' Church. The exterior is unusual (the tower is to one side, and the belfry roof is covered with chevron-shaped tiles), but the interior is heavily Victorianised and further darkened by deep blue carpets. The two mills on the north side of town are owned by Rackham's, which stopped milling flour here in 1970 and now sells coal, animal feed and turf.

Train travellers should note that Wickham Market rail station is actually in the village of Campsea Ashe, two miles away on the other side of the A12. Campsea Ashe is also the site of Abbotts' Monday auctions (01728 746323, www.abbotts auctionrooms.co.uk), which deal in everything from antiques and household bric-a-brac to dead rabbits, live chickens and garden furniture. Even if you're not interested in buying anything, it's a great place to see a piece of vanishing Suffolk. Characters with broad Suffolk accents carry on like it was the 1950s, albeit trading in decimal coinage rather than the pounds, shillings and pence they'd prefer. There's a tearoom and local produce stalls on site too.

In nearby Ufford, the Ufford Produce & Provision Co (Loudham Lane, 01394 460813, www.suffolk-produce.co.uk) sells local foodstuffs and operates a handy delivery service.

West to Needham Market

Heading west from Wickham Market, the area bounded by the A12 and the A1120 is pretty, typical rolling Suffolk countryside. It's also quiet, so perfect for walking or cycling (National Cycle Route 1 comes down via Framlingham and wiggles through here on its way to Woodbridge). The single-lane roads that wind and wend through Easton, Hoo, Monewden and on towards Otley are generally car-free and provide classic countryside views around every bend. Take care in autumn, when pheasants are everywhere, and can easily startle a cyclist off a bike.

Easton is relatively well known for being the site of Easton Farm Park (*see p240*), one of Suffolk's prize-winning tourist attractions, and also has an impressively long crinkle-crankle wall. Just north of Otley is Otley Hall (*see p240*), described by architectural historian Nikolaus Pevsner as 'one of the most interesting 15th- and early 16th-century houses in Suffolk'. A couple of miles north is the red-brick Tudor majesty and glorious gardens of Helmingham Hall (*see p240*).

From Helmingham, the B1077 leads to Ashbocking, home of James White apple juice (*see p291*); you can buy juices at the processing plant on the right-hand side of the road as you enter the village. Further along the same road, the Crockery Barn (01473 890123, www.the crockerybarn.co.uk, closed Sun winter) offers racks of white porcelain as well as Emma Bridgewater and other colourful pottery ranges, a small selection of gifts and a coffee shop.

Quilter's Haven. See p239.

Turn right on to the B1078 to reach Coddenham, one of those serene, picturesque villages found all over Suffolk, which sits quietly unremarked upon, but could absorb an artist for several days. From there, it's a few miles to Needham Market (see p262).

Where to eat & drink

Decent fish and chips are available at Wickham Market's Eat Inn (73 High Street, 01728 746361, closed Sun), which also does takeaways.

You can't miss the Dog (The Green, 01473 735267, www.grundisburghdog.co.uk) in Grundisburgh, its exterior a striking Suffolk Pink. The award-winning menu – cooked by two brothers – consists of well-sourced local ingredients; expect game in season, pork, hearty roasts and well-filled sandwiches. There's a good range of local ales to wash it all down with. The village itself is pretty, with a green and a shop. In Easton, the White Horse Inn (01728 746456, http://whitehorse easton.com) is a pleasant pub (painted pink) with two bar rooms, open fires, an attractive garden and decent food that also features plenty of East Anglian produce: Revett's sausages, Brancaster mussels, Orford smoked trout.

The Moon & Mushroom (01473 785320, http://themoonandmushroom.co.uk) at Swilland is a characterful country pub with an array of local cask ales and a homely dining room. The pub-grub menu often features local game, and occasional music evenings are held on Sundays.

Farmcafé & Foodmarket

Main Road, Marlesford, IP13 0AG (01728 747717, www.farmcafe.co.uk). Open Café Summer 7am-5pm Mon-Sat; 8am-5pm Sun. Winter 7am-4pm Mon-Sat; 8am-4pm Sun. Shop Summer 7am-6pm Mon-Sat; 8am-6pm Sun. Winter 7am-5pm Mon-Sat; 8am-5pm Sun.

A couple of miles north of Wickham Market on the A12, this very popular roadside eaterie has bucolic views from the back over meadows of grazing cows. In summer the transparent tarpaulin walls are drawn up to let in the air. You can get all-day breakfasts using the best piggy ingredients, alongside Orford kippers, baguettes and heartier fare such as wild rabbit pie and muntjac deer and haricot bean casserole, and cakes, cream teas and fairtrade coffee for an afternoon pick-me-up. There are occasional glitches – stale bread with dull soup on our last visit – but it remains a local favourite. The shop sells a wide range of local provisions.

Teapot Tearooms

46 High Street, IP13 0QS (01728 748079). Open 9am-5pm Mon-Sat. No credit cards.

Come for tasty savouries and moist cakes and tarts (the warm treacle tart with custard is superb). The tearoom is cosy, carpeted and inviting, and there's also a cluster of wrought-iron tables and chairs on the gravel terrace overlooking the square. Staff are friendly to locals, less so to people they don't recognise – but then, that's often the way in Suffolk.

Where to stay

Dameron's Farm

Henley, IP6 0RU (01473 832454, www.damerons farmholidays.co.uk). Rates £270-£675 per week.

Five modern cottages (sleeping two to six), converted from the farm's former milking parlour and granary buildings, sit around a courtyard. Each has its own patio, and there's a games room with pool table, table tennis, table football, skittles and lots of board games. The shared grassy picnic area also has some play equipment for kids.

Easton Farm Park ★

Easton, IP13 0EQ (01728 746475, www.easton farmpark.co.uk). Rates £500-£1,100 per week.

Three self-catering cottages (sleeping five to six) are available in the grounds of this popular farm attraction (see p240). It's a great place for families to stay, as the farm has plenty of child-friendly activities, an adventure playground and an indoor play centre. Another cottage is in Easton village itself, opposite the White Horse Inn.

Flindor Cottage

The Street, Framsden, IP14 6HG (01473 890058, www.flindorcottage.co.uk). Rates £100 double incl breakfast. No credit cards.

A double bedroom is available in a converted barn adjoining this 17th-century timber-framed house – one of only five Wolsey Lodges (www.wolseylodges.com) in Suffolk. Expect tea and own-made cakes and biscuits on arrival and a tasty breakfast in the main house in the morning. The Victorian cast-iron roll-top bath and exposed beams add to the characterful feel. Framsden is about nine miles north-west of Wickham Market.

Old Rectory

Campsea Ashe, IP13 0PU (01728 746524, www.theoldrectorysuffolk.com). Rates £95-£140 double incl breakfast.

Mike and Sally Ball run this thoroughly updated former rectory. B&B accommodation consists of seven elegantly furnished en suite double rooms, five in the main house and two in a converted coach house and garden cottage. Breakfasts use Suffolk sausages, eggs from the house's chickens and home-made jams. Dinner is also available, but must be pre-booked.

Orchard Campsite

28 Spring Lane, IP13 0SJ (01728 746170, www.orchardcampsite.co.uk). Rates £15-£20 per pitch. No credit cards.

A lively, fun campsite that's popular with families and groups. Tents dominate, fires are allowed, there's a good shop and the friendly owners hire bikes and organise activities such as rounders matches. Best of all is the small observatory with sliding roof and telescope.

FRAMLINGHAM ★

Framlingham – 'Fram' to locals – is larger and wealthier than the area's other small towns (bar Woodbridge), with some extremely good-looking houses and much less in the way of unsympathetic restoration than elsewhere. The place comes alive on Tuesday and Saturday mornings when the

FIVE SUFFOLK SAUSAGES

Powters
Wellington Street, Newmarket, CB8 0HT (01638 662418, www.powters.co.uk). Open 8am-5pm Mon-Fri; 7am-4pm Sat.
Some of the best sausages known to man (and woman). Two families, the Musk's and the Powters, claim to make the famed Newmarket sausage, but we think Powters is the one to go for. Not even locals know the special secret ingredient, although some have guessed at samphire.

Revett's
81 High Street, Wickham Market (01728 746263). Open 7.30am-1pm Mon, Wed, Sat; 7.30am-1pm, 2-4.30pm Tue, Thur; 7.30am-1pm, 2-5pm Fri. No credit cards.
There's usually a queue at opening time, both in the morning and after the hour-long lunch break, at this established and highly regarded family butcher. The sausages don't look like much raw, being an undramatic, quite anaemic pink, but cooked they're the closest thing to a Newmarket sausage this side of the A14.

Richardson's Smokehouse
Baker's Lane, Orford, IP12 2LH (01394 450103, www.richardsons smokehouse.co.uk). Open Summer 10am-4.30pm daily. Winter 10am-4pm Mon-Fri, Sun; 10am-4.30pm Sat.
The Richardson family has been smoking food for generations. The smokehouse is down a lane at the back of Orford's famous fish restaurant, the Butley Orford Oysterage (*see p216*). The smoked sausages are unusual and tasty; options are pork and venison, pork and garlic, pork and apple, old English, and chorizo.

Salters Family Butchers
107-109 High Street, Aldeburgh, IP15 5AR (01728 452758, www.salters familybutchers.co.uk). Open 7am-1pm Mon, Wed; 7am-5pm Tue, Thur, Fri; 7am-4pm Sat.
This Aldeburgh butcher promises to sell meat from no further afield than 30 miles, and that it's free of preservatives and flavourings. Choose from plain pork, pork and leek, and pork and herb; all are delicious. Meaty, solid and with no trace of grease, these are great bangers.

KB Stannard & Sons
8 High Street, Saxmundham, IP17 1DD (01728 602081). Open 8am-5pm Mon-Fri; 8am-3pm Sat.
A really lovely family butcher that produces some fabulous sausages. Both the pork, and the pork and herb versions are excellent; if pushed, we'd probably choose the latter.

market is in full swing in the town square, Market Hill. Piles of fresh fruit and veg are lined up alongside stalls selling local fish and meat. There are also wholefoods, own-made cakes, household goods, plants, antiques and more. Fram bustles on non-market days too – it's one of those towns where everyone knows everyone else's names, addresses and life stories.

The market square is home to old-fashioned pharmacy Coopers, upmarket Italian deli Leo's, homeware shop Bridges & Garrods, and Polly Pringle, which sells statement jewellery at affordable prices. Second-hand book lovers should visit Framlingham Books. There's no longer a butcher in the town centre (although there is a butchery outlet on the tiny industrial estate on the south side of town) – if it's not market day, most locals head to nearby Revett's in Wickham Market or John Hutton's in Earl Soham for their meat. There's good wine to be had at Shawsgate Vineyard (*see p240*) on the B1120 just outside town.

For a view of traditional England that is hardly touched by modernity, take a stroll down Double Street in the town centre. The houses are a gorgeous jumble of architectural styles from Tudor to Georgian to Victorian, and range from grand to cottagey in size. The large street-level windows suggest many had former lives as shops. On adjacent Church Street is stately St Michael's Church. The exterior has lovely proportions, while its interior houses several items of historical interest. There are two organs: the Thamar Organ, a serious piece of kit at the foot of the nave, was built in 1674 and has decorative painted pipes (its only equal in age and majesty is in Gloucester Cathedral). The much smaller 18th-century chamber organ is inside the chancel, where you'll also find the tombs of the Howard family, a dynasty of the Earls of Surrey and Dukes of Norfolk. The tomb of Thomas Howard, the 3rd Duke of Norfolk, is on the right-hand side at the end, and is one of the best preserved examples of 16th-century monumental sculpture in Europe, with fine carvings of the 12 apostles around its sides. Look up at the ceiling at this point; there's an ancient ceremonial helmet perched on one of the ceiling timbers.

The Town Trail (a map, leaflet and audio guide are all downloadable from www.framlingham.com) takes you on a circular walk, marked by metal plaques, around Fram's main sights. Most famous are the remains of 12th-century Framlingham Castle (*see p240*), which lie a short stroll from the church. It was from here that Henry VIII's daughter Mary Tudor rode to London in 1553 to claim the throne from her rival Lady Jane Grey, her brother Edward's preferred successor as monarch. The castle walls are still standing, albeit having crumbled here and there; the site is run by English Heritage, and well worth a visit. After an imaginative leap back into history, it's a pleasure to follow wooded paths into the valley and walk around the perimeter of the mere, now a nature reserve teeming with birdlife. There's no café on site, but the Lion's Den ice-cream parlour sits just opposite the castle's entrance.

Where to eat & drink

Framlingham has half a dozen pubs, assorted cafés and a handful of restaurants. The Crown Hotel (*see below*) on the main square has a solid bistro menu, but it's not as good or as reasonably priced as the Station Hotel. Also on the square is the Prince of India (01728 724275), a perfectly decent if not very exciting Indian restaurant, as well as the best of Framlingham's cafés: the daytime-only Dancing Goat Café (01728 621434, closed Sun), which has an attractive interior and sells fresh cakes and own-made light snacks.

Station Hotel ★
Station Road, IP13 9EE (01728 621018, www.the stationhotel.net). Lunch served noon-2pm Mon-Sat; noon-4pm Sun. Dinner served 7-9pm Mon-Thur; 7-9.30pm Fri, Sat.
The Station's location isn't much, but don't be put off. There's a cracking chef in the kitchen, transforming what might be an unprepossessing edge-of-town tavern into a genuinely impressive yet unpretentious gastropub. Decor is pleasantly woody, service politely po-faced in traditional Suffolk style, and there's a good range of beer from the nearby Earl Soham Brewery. But it's the food that does it for us. Pies, pastas and roast pork belly, plus locally sourced game in season and shellfish from the Suffolk coast, are typical, substantial, simple and delicious – and all cost much less than you might expect for food of this quality. A range of own-made desserts, and an excellent cheeseboard, complete the picture.

Where to stay

Crown Hotel
Market Hill, Framlingham, IP13 9AN (01728 723521, www.framlinghamcrown.co.uk). Rates £130 double incl breakfast.
The Crown Hotel has been refurbished recently, and although the decor of the 14 en suite rooms isn't always subtle, the antique pieces and spanking new bathrooms give the accommodation its own identity. This 16th-century coaching inn fronts Framlingham's market square, so the location couldn't be more central.

Garden View
Parham Hall, Parham, IP13 9AB (01502 722717, www.suffolk-secrets.co.uk). Rates £245-£381 per week.
The one-bedroom flat in this lovely old hall three miles south of Framlingham is a good self-catering hideaway, with windows overlooking the large mature garden (hence the name). The flat has an open-plan living room/kitchen, a private area of the garden to sit in, and use of the all-weather tennis court by prior arrangement.

Tarka Cottage
Kettleburgh, IP13 7JS (01394 412304, www.suffolk cottageholidays.com). Rates £474-£745 per week.
Just outside Framlingham in the village of Kettleburgh, this dinky two-bedroom thatched cottage is carved out of a medieval hall. Sparrow Cottage next door is available to rent too, if you have a party of ten. The master bedroom has a super-kingsize bed, and there's a conservatory and barbecue to help you enjoy the garden.

PIGGY BUSINESS

Visitors touring Suffolk will notice a lot of semi-circular tin shelters lined up in fields. That'll be for the pigs, then. Suffolk has a respected tradition of outdoor pig farming, especially around the coast, where the sandy soil is ideal terrain for little trotters.

And where there's pigs there's pork... the county is famous for its high-quality ham, bacon and sausages (*see left*). And the pork pies found in many a local butcher's shove Melton Mowbray into the shadows.

If you want to get close to a live squealer, visit Baylham House Rare Breeds Farm (*see p265*) near Needham Market, where you can come face to face with Large Blacks, Middle Whites and Kune Kunes; or Jimmy's Farm (*see p228*) south of Ipswich, which breeds Gloucester Old Spots and Saddlebacks – and where you can also stock up on top-quality pork products at the farm shop, including artisan dry-cured bacon and air-dried hams.

The livestock parade at the Suffolk Show, held in Ipswich in May or June, is also a top draw for swine enthusiasts.

SUFFOLK

SAXMUNDHAM, LEISTON & YOXFORD

Saxmundham

Saxmundham is old-fashioned, but not in a particularly quaint way; it feels like a place still waiting for its revival. The High Street is handsome, though too many of the businesses seem to have lost focus and there are a number of empty premises.

More lively-looking shops include the very well-equipped modern haberdasher's Elizabeth (whose influence is more Stitch 'n Bitch than Patons), upmarket interiors shop Cotton Tree and fabulous butcher's KB Stannard (see p246). There's also Darren Smith's fish stall (open Tuesday, Wednesday and Friday) at the back of the White Hart pub. The Wednesday market is tiny – just three stalls, selling fruit and veg, sweets and dry goods – but there are two farm shops just outside Saxmundham. South of town, the Railway Farm Shop (Benhall Green, 01728 605793, closed Sun) sells fruit, vegetables, milk, bread and firewood from a small black wooden hut. Much larger is the Friday Street Farm Shop (Friday Street, 01728 604554) on the turn-off to Aldeburgh from the A12. It has fruit and veg (as well as PYO in season), local meat, cheese, fish and all sorts of dry goods, plus a thriving café.

Saxmundham Museum (49 High Street, closed Sun, all Oct-Mar) – open mornings only – is small but delightful. It's full of life and clearly blessed with an imaginative curator. Look out for the story of John Shipp, born in Saxmundham in 1785, and the man who inspired Bernard Cornwell's 'Sharpe' stories. Shipp signed up for the boy soldier regiment penniless and illiterate, and rose to become highly influential in political and military circles. The cinema in the middle room – a small-scale re-creation of the defunct Saxmundham Playhouse – plays an archive film about the East Anglian railways, while in the next room, you can hear the story of a local man who was caught having a liaison with the dyer's wife (he ended up being thrown in a vat of dye). It's a chance to hear the genuine Suffolk accent and dialect, one that's dying out with the younger generation – and is usually misrepresented on TV by a West Country burr.

Just outside town, on the other side of the A12, is the Walled Garden (01728 602510, www.the walledgarden.co.uk, closed Mon), a plant nursery with free entry to a two-acre garden. On Sunday afternoons (Mar-Oct) tea and own-made cakes are served on the lawn by the pond.

Leiston

Head west from Saxmundham to Leiston and the landscape is flat and drably agricultural; the roads zigzag along the boundaries of square fields through the villages of Knodishall, Coldfair Green and Aldringham. In the early 19th century, this unremarkable area would have been extremely busy, thanks to the 'Leiston Works' – as Richard Garrett & Sons, makers of steam tractors, cast

White Horse Inn. See p245.

SUFFOLK

Orchard Campsite. See p245.

Long Shop Museum. See p242.

metal products, and munitions in both world wars, was commonly known. It turned Leiston village into a town – the church had to be significantly enlarged to cope with the extra souls in the parish – and was the reason for bringing the branch railway line through from Saxmundham (the line was then extended to Aldeburgh, speeding the latter's popularity as a seaside resort).

Nowadays, the town is one of the poorest in the area, and the house prices some of the cheapest. It has suffered a double whammy of localised recession: Sizewell nuclear power station was built next to its nearest beach in the 1960s, scuppering the town's chances of ever becoming a tourist resort, and then the Leiston Works closed in 1980. Much of the land where the factory stood was taken over by cheap, ugly modern development. The High Street supports what is still a large town, but clearly there's little money around.

It's difficult to understand Leiston without some knowledge of the Works, and the best way to do

that is to visit the fantastic Long Shop Museum (see p242). Also worth visiting is Volga Linen (01728 635020, www.volgalinen.co.uk), currently trading its exquisite linen clothes and bedding from Leiston's industrial estate – check before you visit, as they may return to premises in Saxmundham. A small cinema shows one film a week, with a daily screening at 7.30pm. And the huge ruins of Leiston Abbey (see p242) lie off a small back road between the town and Saxmundham.

One final Leiston fact – it's the home of Summerhill, the famous alternative school founded by AS Neill in 1921 and still thriving.

Yoxford

Yoxford village is on the A1120, the scenic route from the A14 to the A12, so gets a lot of passing trade. Known locally as 'the garden of Suffolk', it looks to the cultured sophistication of the coast for inspiration and keeps its back to the agricultural heartland of the north. There are several galleries and antiques shops along the main street, and the post office doubles as a health and wholefood shop. Even the general store sells local sausages and chicken. There are three pubs – though one is a victim of Britain's great pub decline and was for sale at the time of writing.

The church, St Peter, is unremarkable apart from its large collection of brasses, and the unusually low windows offering worshippers mullioned views over the churchyard on one side and the village on the other. Adjacent to the main street, a sweet little walled garden serves as a picnic area, and footpaths lead from the village past Cockfield Hall, a red-brick beauty of a stately home in need of a bit of TLC. On the way to Peasenhall, just off the A1120, is Yoxford Antiques Centre (01728 668844, www.yoxfordantiques.com, closed Tue), a large establishment with extensive gardens and three resident alpacas. It also sells second-hand books.

Where to eat & drink

In Saxmundham, the Bell Hotel (31 High Street, 01728 602331, www.bellhotel-saxmundham.co.uk, closed Mon, Sun) offers Anglo-French meals in a formal setting. Budget diners either fish and chips should choose the Trawler's Catch on the High Street over the Golden Fish Bar on the south edge of town. There's also a café inside Waitrose on Church Street. Three miles out of town at Great Glenham, the Crown pub (The Street, 01728 663693, closed Mon) offers an appealing mix of real ales, no-nonsense food and log fires.

In Leiston, Simply Delicious on the High Street is really the only place worth considering sitting down in, but even this well-stocked health food shop and café has a wilted air. The white plastic tablecloths are unfortunate, and the salads and cakes look like they've seen better days, but the freshly ground coffee is good and a total bargain. At the Engineers' Arms on Main Street, opposite the old Works, the landlord used to set up row upon row of pints as the end of each shift approached. Today, it's the best place for a beer (Adnams), and also has a pool table, dartboard and enclosed garden.

Bistro at the Deli ★
26A High Street, Saxmundham, IP17 1AJ (01728 605607, www.thedeli.biz). Food served 9am-5pm Mon-Fri; 9am-2pm Sat.
A buzzy little place that serves really great coffee. The bright orange walls and colourful oil paintings make for a slightly dark interior, but service is noticeably cheerful and food is available all day. Try the local Dingley Dell pork pies, the delicious own-made cakes and soups, or one of the 'black slates', which are piled high with tasty tapas-style morsels. Or go all out at one of the occasional gourmet evenings. The deli offers sandwiches, an impressive selection of cheeses and its own-label salad dressings.

Main's ★
26 High Street, Yoxford, IP17 3EU (01728 668882). Lunch served noon-2.30pm, dinner served 7-11pm Tue-Sat.

With a flagstone floor, deep pinky-red walls, and paintings of kitchen crockery, Main's manages to feel both homely and modern. The restaurant attracts locals and holidaymakers in equal measure with its simple menu of fresh local fare. There are around six options for each course: perhaps braised lamb, sea bass or dover sole with lemon butter sauce for mains and chocolate tart or raspberry cranachan for pudding.

Where to stay

Saxmundham's Bell Hotel (*see left*) has ten rooms, and there are some B&Bs, but in general self-catering is the way to go round here.

Albion Mill ★
Rendham Road, Saxmundham, IP17 1BJ (01502 722717, www.suffolk-secrets.co.uk). Rates £338-£691 per week.
The round tower of this 19th-century windmill has been converted into a wonderful open kitchen/dining room, with a mezzanine living room above. The two bedrooms and bathroom are in a ground-floor wing leading off the tower, and designed with an architect's eye.

Beech House Gite
Yoxford, IP17 3JJ (01728 638962, www.bestofsuffolk. co.uk/gite.asp). Rates £690 per week.
A stylish, French-influenced retreat for two, with a small but beautifully designed south-facing courtyard garden. The interior features some iconic designer furniture, such as the 'Barcelona' chair designed by Mies van der Rohe. A lovely spot from which to explore the Suffolk coast.

Sans Souci B&B
Main Road, Yoxford, IP17 3EX (01728 668827, www.sanssoucibandb.co.uk). Rates £75-£80 double incl breakfast.
This Suffolk Pink-painted house has three B&B rooms (two doubles, one twin), each with their own distinctive look. There's free Wi-Fi, and a smart breakfast room.

School Cottage
Yoxford, IP17 3EU (01728 638962, www.bestofsuffolk. co.uk/school.asp). Rates £315-£490 per week.
The one-bedroom cottage just off Yoxford's High Street is small but charming, with pale yellow walls, a wood-burning stove and a small back patio. Blythburgh Cottage next door (sleeping two) is also available.

Thurstons
Rendham, Saxmundham, IP17 2AR (01728 663485, www.thurstonsbarn.com). Open Easter-Oct. Rates £70 double incl breakfast. No credit cards.
This former farm has two twin bedrooms (with tiled floors and colourful bedspreads). It's a peaceful spot and right beside National Cycle Route 1. Breakfasts use local ingredients where possible.

Yewtrees
Aldringham, IP16 4PW (01728 638962, www.bestof suffolk.co.uk/yewtrees.asp). Rates £375-£690 per week.
Set on the outskirts of Leiston, this semi-detached Victorian house sleeps five. It has a large garden and conservatory, and an open fire in the spacious living room.

Village Suffolk

Suffolk is all about villages rather than towns, and this is nowhere more evident than when travelling through the swathe of countryside either side of the A14. In High Suffolk, along the north-western side, Eye is the only place with sufficient chutzpah to describe itself as a town, and yet it's considerably smaller than some Suffolk villages. It's much the same story in the agricultural heartland south-west of the A14: there are towns in the Gipping Valley, but you wouldn't describe them as tourist attractions. Instead, it's village after village after village, quaint almost to the point of cliché – so get out of your car and explore the region on foot or pedal. The roads here are perfect for cyclists: since they don't run in straight lines, they never became main roads, and although it's easy to get lost, you'll find yourself bowling along for sizeable stretches without being disturbed by another soul. Suddenly the subtle charm of this rural patch begins to make itself felt.

FRESSINGFIELD, DEBENHAM & EYE

Fressingfield & around

Relatively large, but compact rather than strung out along a single road, the village of Fressingfield is a pleasure to stroll around. Its lanes and pathways always seem to lead somewhere interesting, but any navigation is likely to begin – and almost certain to end – at the 16th-century Fox & Goose pub (*see p258*), right at the centre of the village. It's easiest to see the timber frame beneath the pub's plasterwork from the churchyard next door. The St Peter & St Paul Church makes pleasant viewing too, with unusual square flintwork on the outside of the entrance porch and a carved wooden ceiling. On the other side of the churchyard, the Fox has a rival. The Swan's looks (*see p257*) lack the charm of the Fox, but it's still a popular place to eat and drink.

The village also has a pottery and a village shop, which, in addition to the usual groceries, sells everything from local meat and artisan bread to locally baked savoury goods and freshly made sandwiches. Fressingfield is relatively lively and community-focused, with numerous and various events going on at the village hall and church: there's even a Fressingfield Music Festival (www.fressingfield.suffolk.gov.uk) in September.

Long and winding roads

After Fressingfield, enjoy a meander between villages. Apart from the Barns (Church Road, 01379 384505, www.wingfieldbarns.com, closed Mon, Sun), a lovely space for exhibitions, workshops and performances, there isn't much to detain you at Wingfield, but bustling Stradbroke is more substantial. There's an unusual business centre at the edge of the village that is made entirely of black timber and glass. From a distance it looks like a collection of modernist barns – an effective ruse to blend it in with the rest of Stradbroke's buildings. A farmers' market on the first Saturday of the

month, a small bakery and deli, a butcher and a Spar keep villagers stocked with essentials, while a swimming pool, a Victorian library and a community centre that has occasional movie screenings cater for less quotidian needs. The Queen's Head freehouse is dated in appearance and atmosphere, but the Grade II-listed White Hart on Church Street, due to reopen under new management as we went to press, has lovely, airy rooms oozing with history and character.

Hoxne (pronounced 'Hoxen') is famous in archaeological circles for two major finds. The first came in 1797 when Cambridge graduate John Frere was travelling between his family home and Eye and noticed unusual flints uncovered by Hoxne mud-builders. The depth at which the flints – clearly man-made tools – were buried led Frere to make the suggestion, radical at the time, that human civilisation dated far further back than had been imagined. The second major discovery was in 1992, when a huge hoard of Roman coins, jewellery and tableware was found in a field by retired local gardener Eric Lawes; the collection is now in the British Museum.

The diminutive Hoxne museum, in the north aisle of the church at the top of the hill, recounts the legend of the martyrdom of St Edmund, patron saint of East Anglia. Most historians believe Edmund was killed here; a monument, situated in fields between the two main sections of the village, marks the spot. An oak tree used to stand here: it's said that when it finally fell, an ancient arrowhead was found embedded in its trunk. Before heading to the lovely Swan Inn (*see p258*) for lunch, walk around the village and Brakey Wood, a 17-acre site planted to mark the millennium, where a ten-foot-tall sculpture of Hoxne Man commemorates Frere's find.

Further south, Brundish is odd in that its church and village hall are cloaked by woods, seemingly hiding the village entirely – until you realise the residential areas and pub are a good distance from their community and spiritual gathering places.

Brundish is home to Lane Farm (01379 384593, www.lanefarm.co.uk), which makes Suffolk salami, an air-dried sausage that's growing in reputation – you'll find it in many farm shops hereabouts, but check www.suffolksalami.co.uk for a full list of local suppliers. Foodies might also want to divert to the nearby village of Kenton, from where delicious Suffolk Apple Juice comes.

Debenham ★

Although it's smaller and hasn't quite such grand buildings, Debenham is almost as pretty and historically rich as Lavenham (*see p282*). The large ground-floor windows and names of the houses along the main street suggest many of them were once shops, but enough businesses remain to cater to village needs: there's a newsagent, post office, greengrocer, bakehouse and vet, stores for homewares, antiques and bathroom fittings, a fish and chip shop that opens on Wednesday, Friday and Saturday evenings, and the plain-looking Neaves of Debenham (21 Cross Green, 01728 860240, www.feneave.co.uk, closed Sun), primarily a master butcher and producer of smoked and cured meats, but also the village deli. Carters Teapot Pottery (Low Road, 01728 860475, www.cartersteapots.com, closed Sun) sells its distinctive, individually crafted china just around the corner from the High Street: if you want a teapot in the shape of a mantelpiece and roaring grate, this is where to come. Those who are feeling creative can take part in a ceramics painting session.

Debenham's wealth was built in medieval times on dairy exports to London and elsewhere, and its long history has left buildings that are full of architectural curiosities and mismatches. It's a delightful place for a stroll, from the Toll House at the north end of the village past the antiquated timber-frame houses on Gracechurch Street – Merchant House is a highlight – to Old Bakery Row, which has had its entire roof lifted and a row of 20th-century windows added, allowing yourself to be seduced by little lanes and footpaths along the way. There are several circular walks around the village or into the surrounding countryside.

Eye

Eye was once clearly very prosperous, as demonstrated by many big houses, several civic buildings and an impressively large church. Until 1974, it was a borough in its own right – albeit the smallest in the United Kingdom – but it is now a backwater that few people outside Suffolk have heard of. Don't let that deter you: head to the church to pick up the town trail leaflet, which includes a map and details of interesting buildings.

Approaching from the east, the first thing you see is the great tower of St Peter & St Paul's Church. Described by Pevsner as 'one of the wonders of Suffolk', it took 25 years to build and, compared to most Suffolk churches, the decorative flint and stonework seem terribly smart. Peek inside for an intricately carved rood screen with blue and gold patterned paintwork and a series of carved figures. Next door, the Tudor Guildhall has good examples

of carved period woodwork: look out for the Angel Gabriel on the front corner post. The remains of Eye Castle are in the centre of the village, though the ruins you see on top of the mound are from a later construction. Steps up to a platform give visitors fantastic views over the town and the countryside – perhaps painter Cavendish Morton, who lived in Stanley House on Castle Street, was inspired to paint one of his famous Suffolk landscapes from here. To the north of the village, you'll find one of Suffolk's characteristic curving 'crinkle-crankle' walls.

Many of Eye's historic buildings still bear indications of having been pubs. Back in 1850, there were 14 pubs in Eye and two breweries, but only one pub remains – and even then, only just. The Queen's Head had closed and was 'To Let' at the time of writing. In fact, there were several signs of hard times. The Assembly Room (which can be glimpsed through the arch by White Lion House, a former coaching inn) was the cultural heart of Eye for several centuries, but its latest incarnation as a theatre ended in 2005: check out the family-run second-hand bookshop (01379 870190, closed Mon, Sun) on the site. Despite several businesses displaying closed signs, the butcher, baker and ironmonger remain – as well as a pair of Co-ops within spitting distance of each other – and there are some decent places to eat. Note that most shops and businesses close on Monday.

Eye to Ixworth

After the relative architectural sophistication of Eye, the surrounding villages can seem a bit insubstantial and lacking in interest, but Thornham Magna has pretty cottages, the brilliant Thornham Walks (*see p264*) and the Four Horseshoes pub (*see p257*), founded in the 12th century. Nearby Thornham Parva contains a small, sweet church, St Mary's (*see p264*), which also has a wonderful medieval retable and wall paintings. There are more wall paintings at St Mary's, Troston (just outside Ixworth), as well as in lovely Wissington Church (*see p263*), right on the Essex border.

Cyclists should ignore the road through the unremarkable trio of Finningham, Wyverstone and Long Thurlow, and take the more picturesque route through pretty Walsham-le-Willows, Hunston and Stowlangtoft. Walsham dates back to medieval times and is full of character. You can get picnic provisions from Rolfes traditional butcher and deli (01359 259225, www.rolfesbutchers.co.uk, closed Sun), and a drink at either the thatched Six Bells (Summer Road, 01359 259726), which can rustle up a sandwich on request, or the Blue Boar freehouse (01359 258533). It's less handsome than the Bells, but has a full menu, pool table and jukebox. Henry Watson's Potteries (01359 251239, www.henrywatson.com) in nearby Wattisfield, has been in operation for more than 200 years, although potters have been exploiting the area's clay-rich soil for much longer: two dozen Roman kilns have been uncovered in the vicinity. You can buy Watson's kitchenware from the gift shop or refuel in the café.

Eye Castle

'Crinkle-crankle' wall

St Peter & St Paul's Church, Eye. See p254.

Located on the River Thet, Ixworth has some handsome streets lined with historic buildings, a scattering of shops, a post office and two slightly intimidating pubs. Behind the High Street, St Mary's church is much modernised, but does have a good second-hand bookshop inside. Just outside Ixworth, Wyken Hall has been transformed by Carla Carlisle (who married into the fourth generation of Carlisles to own the hall) into a thriving vineyard with award-winning gardens (*see p265*), the Leaping Hare eaterie (*see p258*) and a gift shop.

Where to eat & drink

Fressingfield's other pub, the Swan (Harleston Road, 01379 586280, www.fressingfield swan.co.uk, closed Mon, lunch Tue) has plenty of outdoor seating and Suffolk nosh on the menu. In Wingfield, the De La Pole Arms (Church Road, 01379 384545, closed Mon) offers a small menu of well-prepared British food and decently kept beer.

Unless the pleasant-looking Angel Inn reopens, drinkers in Debenham only have the single-room Woolpack (49 High Street, 01728 860516), but there are several cafés for sustenance. Anyone with pollen allergies will have to avoid the Garden of Deben (6 High Street, 01728 860190, www. gardenofdeben.co.uk, closed Sun), since it's in the middle of the flower shop, but the Vanilla Bakehouse & Café (7A High Street, 01728 861582, closed Tue, Sun, Sat afternoon) is just opposite and serves own-made cakes, tea and coffee. There's another café in Carters Teapot Pottery (*see p254*) at the other end of the village.

You'll find a couple of good pubs between Eye and Ixworth. At Thornham Magna, the rambling Four Horseshoes (Wickham Road, 01379 678777, www.greenekinginns.co.uk) has been serving ale since about 1150, and also offers a wide range of own-cooked food in the bar and restaurant; while Market Weston's Mill (Bury Road, 01359 221018) provides beer from the village's Old Chimneys brewery, cider from local farms and top-notch, locally sourced food. In Thurston, enjoy freshly made lunch dishes and superior cakes at the airy Orchard Room (Great Green, 01359 233363, www.theorchardroom.co.uk, closed Mon-Wed, Sun), right in the middle of Harveys plant nursery.

Auberge

Ipswich Road, Yaxley, IP23 8BZ (01379 783604, www.the-auberge.co.uk). Lunch served noon-2pm Tue-Fri. Dinner served 7-9.30pm Tue-Sat.
Long thought of as 'a restaurant with rooms', this small, family-run business opened seven more bedrooms in 2009 to bring the total to 11, but the restaurant remains key. The menu covers local favourites such as slow-cooked belly of Norfolk pork, as well as dishes with a more international flavour, perhaps chicken tagine with pine nut, raisin and harissa couscous. The classic puddings come with a twist: stem ginger crème brûlée, treacle sponge with crème fraîche, apricot bread and butter pudding. Prices are reasonable for quality, especially if you take advantage of the £24.95 three-course dinner deal (not available on Saturdays).

Leaping Hare

wall-hangings give the space a welcoming air. A pair of wood-burning stoves keep the place cosy in winter, and large sash windows let in plenty of light all through the year. Owner Carla Carlisle's transatlantic roots come through in the menu. Carefully sourced local dishes – Red Poll beef, Stowlangtoft lamb, plus an excellent selection of vegetables, some of which come from the hall's garden – are punctuated by American classics such as eggs benedict, key lime pie and chocolate brownies. Everything is prepared with the exquisite attention to detail you'd expect of a kitchen that has been awarded the Michelin Bib Gourmand two years running.

Lindsay House Restaurant
16 Broad Street, Eye, IP23 7AF (01379 870122). Lunch served noon-3pm Fri-Sun. Dinner served 6.30-9pm Wed-Sat.
Polished pine tables, leather chairs and fireplaces provide an informal, homely setting for some good, seasonally led cooking at this small restaurant in the middle of Eye. Look our for midweek set meal deals.

Swan Inn ★
Low Street, Hoxne, IP21 5AS (01379 668275, www.hoxneswan.co.uk). Open 11.30am-3pm, 6-11pm Mon-Sat; noon-10.30pm Sun. Lunch served noon-2pm Mon-Sat; noon-3.30pm Sun. Dinner served 6.30-9pm daily.
In winter, the Swan is never-want-to-go-home cosy, with its deep-red walls, low lights and several log fires; in summer, the picnic benches in the huge back garden get all the attention. Don't expect much deviation from pub classics, but do expect them to be done really well – even the simple lasagne is packed with flavour. The lengthy vegetarian menu has the most surprises, including an appealing savoury cheese and pickle bread and butter pudding, and carrot, courgette and walnut roulade.

Beards
39 Church Street, Eye, IP23 7BD (01379 870383). Open 8.30am-6pm Mon, Wed-Sat.
This licensed café is set in an atmospheric timbered room in Grade II-listed premises (the outside loo is quaintly marked 'shelter'). The friendly owners are knowledgeable and attentive, putting care into their own-made soups, sandwiches and light bites. There are locally made fruit ice-creams for hot days, and generous slices of cake if a serious energy-boost is required. The attached deli sells Suffolk produce and other artisan labels, as well as cakes, pastries, cheese and wine.

Fox & Goose ★
Church Road, Fressingfield, IP21 5PB (01379 586247, www.foxandgoose.net). Open noon-3.30pm, 6.30-11pm Tue-Sun. Lunch served noon-2pm, dinner served 6.30-9pm Tue-Sun.
Occupying the show-stopping, multi-beamed former Guildhall in the middle of Fressingfield, the Fox serves a menu of irresistible seasonal Suffolk classics, running from Metfield pork belly to asparagus and line-caught fish. The kitchen also makes its own ice-creams and sorbets. The food is fancier than most pub fare, the menu peppered with foams, jus and tuile from the how-to book of fine dining. Guests can sit in the restaurant or more informal bar, while drinkers have a few tables outside next to the pond and churchyard. Set lunch deals bring the prices down if you're on a budget.

Leaping Hare ★
Wyken Vineyards, Wyken Road, Stanton, IP31 2DW (01359 250287, www.wykenvineyards.co.uk). Open/ food served 10am-6pm Mon-Thur, Sun; 10am-6pm, 7-9pm Fri, Sat.
Under the steepling roof of an ancient, timber-framed barn on the Wyken Hall estate, the Leaping Hare is both café and restaurant, with the two separated by a picket fence. Frames and wood trims are painted in Farrow & Ball greens, and the sisal matting, wicker chairs and patchwork

Where to stay
Eight rooms (£65 double incl breakfast) are available at Thornham Magna's atmospheric Four Horseshoes pub (*see p257*).

Camomile Cottage & Chobbs Barn ★
Brome Avenue, Eye, IP23 7HW (01379 873528, www.camomilecottage.co.uk). Rates Camomile Cottage £90 double incl breakfast. Chobbs Barn £250 double, minimum 2 nights.
Camomile Cottage is, in reality, more of a house, but the two oak-beamed bedrooms are lovely. Discreetly run by Tim and Aly Kahane, who live a distance away, you'll get plenty of own-baked treats and local produce for breakfast, as well plenty of time and space to yourselves. For self-catering couples, there's also Chobbs Barn. A new, oak-framed cottage in the grounds, it has an open-plan living space with modish decor and all mod-cons, including a large flatscreen TV, Bose iPod sound system and en suite wet room. Doors open on to a patio that overlooks fields and is shaded by a walnut tree.

Gables Farm
Wingfield, IP21 5RH (01379 586355, www.gables farm.co.uk). Rates £65 double incl breakfast. No credit cards.

Things to do

FRESSINGFIELD, DEBENHAM & EYE

Mid Suffolk Light Railway ★
Brockford Station, Wetheringsett, IP14 5PW (01449 766899, www.mslr.org.uk). Open Easter-July, Sept 11am-5pm Sun, bank hol Mon; Aug 11am-5pm Wed, Sun, bank hol Mon. Admission £5; £2.50-£4 reductions; £12.50 family.
A visit to this volunteer-run museum is a fantastic outing for all the family. Park in a field just across the road from the museum and head over to find guards and drivers – all dressed in the railway's 'Middy' uniforms – and a gleaming steam train. On our visit, there seemed to be no limit to how many times you could ride the train, with swaps between first- and third-class carriages keeping things interesting. The museum tells the history of the Edwardian line, which never turned a profit. Next to the souvenir shop there's a café, which serves own-made cakes and Alder Carr ice-cream, while adult refreshment can be had in pints from the Middy Ale Carriage. Event days (check website for dates) often include a parade of vintage cars and displays of model trains.

YOXFORD TO STOWMARKET

Suffolk Owl Sanctuary
Stonham Barns, Pettaugh Road, Stonham Aspal, IP14 6AT (01449 711425, www.the-owl-barn.com). Open 10am-4pm daily. Admission £6.50; £4 reductions.
SOS is popular with families, not least because of the regular flying displays in summer. The entry fee gives you access to the bird hide, red squirrel colony and adventure playground. There's also a nine-hole golf course and putting green, as well as several shops selling furniture, bags, pets, gifts and cards. The wooden toys are a particular delight, but the gorgeous doll's-houses, furniture kits and tea sets don't come cheap. The restaurant has outdoor seating, plenty of highchairs and space for pushchairs, but the food served is disappointing stuff.

Mid Suffolk Light Railway

Michael and Sue Harvey let three timbered rooms (two doubles, one twin, all en suite) in this 16th-century moated farmhouse. Fresh fruit and flowers are placed in the bedrooms, and breakfasts use local produce wherever possible – very local when it comes to the eggs, produced by the Harvey's own chickens.

Old Rectory
Hopton, IP22 2QX (01953 688135, www.theold rectoryhopton.com). Rates £100 double incl breakfast. No credit cards.
The Old Rectory is part of the Wolsey Lodge consortium, a group of well over 100 private houses that promise high-quality accommodation and hosts who will welcome you like an old friend of the family. At this 14th-century, Georgian-adapted mansion, Bobby and Sarah Llewellyn are fine exponents of the rather genteel Wolsey Lodge approach. Expect own-baked cakes, a delicious supper if you decide to eat in, and friendly conversation around the dining table.

Rokeby Old Hall
Wilby, IP21 (01728 638962, www.bestofsuffolk.co.uk). Rates £720-£1,505 per week.
Ever felt like pretending you own a 15th-century country farmhouse? This could be the perfect opportunity. Situated at the end of a mile-long track in large private gardens, tranquillity is a given at Rokeby. The building even has the lovely, slightly sagging roof of all old farms, looking as if it has just emitted a resigned sigh. There are beautiful timber frames throughout, and if the design has some old-fashioned touches, most of the rooms are simply decorated, bright and fresh. It sleeps eight.

Thornham Hall
Thornham Magna, IP23 8HA (01379 783314, www.thornhamhall.com). Rates £110 double incl breakfast.
Three rooms are available to let at Thornham Hall, the seat of the Henniker family. The current building dates from the mid 20th century, after a fire destroyed the original, but there are family portraits in the dining room, open fires and rooms blessed with wonderful views over the gardens. Watch the peacocks roam and listen for horses neighing, or explore the terrific Thornham Walks (*see p264*). Lady Lesley is your host: as well as a friendly welcome, she provides food that combines seasonal local dishes (when available, game is a speciality) with more exotic touches gathered during her extensive travels. Breakfast is communal in style, with guests gathered around a large dining-room table.

YOXFORD TO STOWMARKET
Although the A1120 is an official tourist route, most people use it only to reach the coast, briefly admiring pretty villages and stand-out buildings as they flash past, perhaps stopping for provisions, but rarely exploring this part of Suffolk in any depth. Yet any of the villages would make a good base for circular walks, with plenty of good food to be found when you've worked up an appetite: grab Ordnance Survey Explorer maps 231, 212 or 211 and work out a route to suit your fitness level and time limitations.

Lindsay House Restaurant. See p258.

At Peasenhall, weathered brick and timber-framed cottages sit on the small green, and freshly made scones are piled on a wire rack at the entrance to the tea shop. The river runs alongside the main street, which has a general store, post office, furniture shop and upmarket wine and artisan food shop Emmett's (01728 660 250, www.emmettsham.co.uk, closed Sun), just the place for own-cured hams and bacon.

Further west, the popular Queen's Head (*see p260*) in Dennington is a good start and finish point for a circular walk to Framlingham (*see p245*). The delightful Post Mill (01728 685789, www.english-heritage.org.uk/saxteadgreen, closed Mon-Thur, Sun, all Nov-Mar) at Saxtead Green was still grinding corn during World War II. A little further west, at Earl Soham, deli-cum-café Eat Anglia (*see p261*) competes with local stalwart John Hutton (01728 685259, closed Sun) – not just a butcher, but also a grocer, selling cheese, fish, bread, fruit and veg, pies made with hand-raised pork, posh condiments and preserved food. All Hutton's meat is free of growth hormones and antibiotics, and there's usually a queue of locals stocking their larders. Opposite the village green, the Earl Soham Brewery (01728 684097, www.earlsohambrewery. co.uk) has been making ale since the mid 1980s.

On the A1120 just before the ugly outskirts of Stowmarket is the popular, family-friendly Suffolk Owl Sanctuary (see p259). From here, it's a small diversion down the A140 to Suffolk Farmhouse Cheeses (01449 710458, www.suffolkcheese. co.uk). On Thursday mornings or Friday and Saturday afternoons, buy Suffolk Gold and Suffolk Blue cheese straight from the farm shop, which also sells its own milk, cream and meat.

Where to eat & drink

The menu at Sibton's White Horse (Halesworth Road, 01728 660337, www.sibtonwhitehorse inn.co.uk) is full of local ingredients and the guest ales change every week. The Queen's Head (The Square, 01728 638241) in Dennington is ideal if you have children, thanks to its family room, kids' menu and position right by the village playground. The serious-minded Shepherd & Dog (01449 711361, www.theshepherdanddog.com, closed Mon, dinner Sun) in Forward Green attempts cosmopolitan, restaurant-quality food, including two- and three-course lunch deals midweek, but also has a pub grub menu of sandwiches, sausages and chips.

Eat Anglia

The Street, Earl Soham, IP13 7RT (01728 685557, www.eatanglia.co.uk). Open 8am-6pm Mon-Fri; 8.30am-5pm Sat; 9.30am-4pm Sun.
This deli-cum-café is run by friendly London escapee Maria Johnson. Her idea of having all the seats arranged round one large table gives the café an intimate air that perhaps goes down better with second-homers and holidaymakers than locals. There's a large range of local and artisanal produce to draw on, as well as a good selection of wine and beer.

Victoria

Earl Soham, IP13 7RL (01728 685758, www.earlsoham brewery.co.uk). Open 11.30am-3pm, 6-11pm Mon-Sat; noon-3pm, 7-10pm Sun. Lunch served noon-2pm, dinner served 7-10pm daily.
This was the first pub to serve Earl Soham Brewery ale. In fact, ESB brewed all its beer from the chicken shed at the rear until it moved to new premises opposite the village

green in 2001. The food and decor are simple, while the interior is friendly and cosy; the perfect spot in which to sup a pint of Victoria Bitter or Albert Ale. The brewery also runs the Station Hotel (*see p247*) in Framlingham.

Where to stay

High End, Low End & the Cottage

New Inn, Peasenhall, IP17 2JE (01628 825925, www.landmarktrust.org.uk). Rates £417-£1,009 per cottage per week.
In the middle of these three connected buildings, renovated and divided into holiday lets by the Landmark Trust, is a double-height 15th-century hall, complete with grand hearth and oriel window. The rooms of High End and Low End lead directly off the hall, but access to it is also shared with the Cottage, a 19th-century addition to the original inn. All three properties sleep up to four people, with High End the largest and Low End blessed with an open fire.

Sheep Cottages

Bruise Yard Road, Peasenhall, IP17 (01728 638962, www.sheepcottages.co.uk). Rates White Sheep Cottage £620-£946 per week. Black Sheep Cottage £420-£740 per week.
Thoroughly but sensitively modernised, these adjoining 16th-century cottages still have many of their original features – including open fires, exposed oak beams and lime plaster throughout – but otherwise the owners have left the decor refreshingly plain. The cottage kitchens are fully equipped, there's wireless internet and DVD players, and the sheets are made of Egyptian cotton. White Sheep Cottage sleeps six, Black Sheep four – or they can be rented together.

SUFFOLK

Workshop ★

Lime Tree Farm, Badingham, IP13 8LU (01728 638962, www.contemporarysuffolk.co.uk). Rates £796-£820 per week.

This converted Victorian stable (sleeping two) is a rare and successful 21st-century incursion into the Suffolk countryside. Kitted out with design-classic furniture and top-end appliances, it's ultra-contemporary to the point of being sparse, but kept cosy by a natty suspended fireplace at one end of the main kitchen/lounge space. Opposite the large flatscreen TV, huge sliding glass doors open on to a large decked area, surrounded by meadows.

THE GIPPING VALLEY

Neither of the main towns on the River Gipping – Stowmarket and Needham Market – are tourist attractions, with even inhabitants of other parts of Suffolk liable to turn up their noses when they're mentioned. It doesn't help that the busy A14 passes within a short distance of both town centres: visitors will find it hard to get away from the roar of traffic. Historically, this has been a comparatively poor part of the county, where unemployment remains high and post-war town planning less than kind – this has made Stowmarket especially unappealing. Needham Market is, in fact, nicer than its reputation, great for an untouristy day out.

Stowmarket

Much of Stowmarket was destroyed by a gun-cotton factory explosion in 1871 and what remained suffered further indignity at the hands of short-sighted town planners, but the town's reputation as another Haverhill isn't entirely deserved. The centre has managed to keep some historic character, and on Station Road West, the fifth generation of the Palmers bakery (01449 613088, closed Sun) continues to bake bread and numerous varieties of cake in traditional brick ovens, much as it has been doing since 1869. There's also a market on Thursday and Saturday, as well as a farmers' market every first Friday of the month

at the largest tourist attraction in Stowmarket, the Museum of East Anglian Life (*see p265*). The museum sprawls over 70 acres around Abbott Hall, which was left in trust to the town in the first half of the 20th century by the spinster sisters who lived there; the hall has received Heritage Lottery funding and should soon undergo renovations. The church of St Peter & St Mary isn't especially old, but it does have one of the few spires in Suffolk. The old churchyard is now a public garden.

Needham Market ★

Needham Market doesn't really feature in most guides to Suffolk, usually finding itself grouped with Stowmarket under 'not much of interest here'. But this little market town is a delight to explore. The High Street isn't unlike fêted Long Melford, but the place is a lot less touristy. The town built its riches on the cloth trade and, before the A14 was built, lay on the main route from Ipswich to Bury St Edmunds. Disembark from a train at the handsome red-brick station (closed by Beeching in 1961, but reopened in 1971 thanks to public outcry) or your car in the car park by Needham Lake on the south side of town, and you can follow a circular route that takes in the landmarks, running up the High Street and back along the banks of the River Gipping.

At the height of its medieval prosperity, Needham Market was hit so hard by the plague that chains were placed across the roads at either end of the town to stop people entering or leaving. Chainhouse Farm to the south of the town and Chain Bridge to the north both get their name from the incident.

Buildings in all manner of architectural styles (most of them timber-framed underneath) line the High Street and there are several appealing shops. RJ Smith the butcher makes its own sausages and pork pies, and sells Blythburgh Pork and other meats of good provenance, and there's also Bretts the baker and the Sweet & Savoury Deli.

Joseph Priestley, who discovered oxygen, was a minister here in 1755. The church he presided over was replaced by the Congregrational chapel opposite the town hall. More visually impressive

Workshop

is medieval St John the Baptist. It has one of the best examples of a double-hammerbeam roof in England – look out for the pagan figure of Jack the Green carved into one of the beams, and a row of high-altitude windows. Unusually, the clock is over the porch rather than in the tower, and there's no graveyard.

Music lovers can check out the Barrandov Opera programme, performed in a beautiful converted barn at Kennels Farm on Barking Road (01449 720796, www.barrandov.co.uk). Bargain hunters should come on Wednesday and Saturday mornings, when there's a car boot sale on Coddenham Road.

At the north end of town, turn right up Hawksmill Street and past the imposing red brick watermill to complete the circular walk via the riverbank. A brief detour leads up the drive of Alder Carr Farm, where there's a great café (see p266) and a very well-stocked farm shop. It has a chart of seasonal vegetables and fruit on the wall, and another showing how many miles the produce has travelled: 30 is the maximum. The shop sells Alder Carr's excellent fruit ice-creams, baked goods and meat, plus top-end deli goods from other local producers. A farmers' market is held here on the third Saturday of the month.

Continue the walk back at the river, taking in the views of gardens on the opposite bank. It's very tranquil, disturbed only by the distant hum of the A14. Your stroll can extend to the footpaths of the Wildwood nature reserve or across the bridge and around Needham Lake. Both are good sites for birdwatchers, who will definitely see ducks, geese and the usual waterfowl, but perhaps also green woodpeckers, kestrels overhead and various barely distinguishable warblers in the undergrowth.

Woolpit

Locals used to talk of the 'Woolpit Whiff', the smell from a nearby pig farm; now the only whiff dominating the village, located six miles north-west of Stowmarket, comes from the fish and chip shop in the main square. Otherwise, Woolpit's genteel streets are full of amiable, half-timbered buildings, including a bakery, two pubs, a tea shop, a grocer and the Woolpit Village Museum (http://woolpit.org/museum), the self-proclaimed smallest museum in Suffolk. Open on weekend afternoons, it explains how the village used to make its distinctive white bricks, once a commodity exported across the world. There's a car boot sale every Sunday, and on Thursday from May to September. Just east of Woolpit, you can buy meat, eggs and a few groceries from the butcher and small shop on Green Road at pretty Grange Farm (01359 241467, closed Sun).

Where to eat & drink

In Stowmarket, either grab a snack from Palmers or head to the Bistro & Tea Room (see p266) at the Museum of East Anglian Life. Needham Market is good for ice-cream – either the town's own Alder Carr brand, or Bennett's, available at Woodwards Tea Room, opposite St John the Baptist on the

TEN SUFFOLK CHURCHES

All Saints, Ramsholt
A church without a village, or that's how it appears. Very little is left of isolated Ramsholt, so All Saints, sitting on a ridge above the River Deben, has a serene if slightly mournful atmosphere. See p214.

Holy Trinity, Blythburgh
Known as the 'Cathedral of the Marshes', this church has wonderful light, thanks to its clerestory windows. Look out for the footprints of the devil on the north door. See p189.

Holy Trinity, Long Melford
Riches from the wool trade paid for the glories of Holy Trinity, which sits hidden behind Long Melford's famously large green. It has one of the best collections of medieval glass in Suffolk. See p277.

St Edmund, Southwold
Another of Suffolk's majestic, ship-like coastal churches. Look out for the rare medieval rood screen, with depictions of Jesus' disciples. See p187.

St James' Chapel, Lindsey
This small place of worship is easily missed, but it's an unusual example of an early church without the adornments of later centuries. See p281.

St Mary, Badley
Surely one of the country's most isolated churches, St Mary's sits on a track a mile or two from the nearest road. Birds sing in the churchyard, sunlight slowly bleaches the pews inside and nothing much moves from one decade to the next. See p267.

St Mary, Dalham
You reach Dalham's church by walking through a kissing gate and along a sweeping avenue of chestnut trees. It's a beautiful, quintessentially English scene, unchanged for centuries, and the view from the top of the ridge takes in some gorgeous countryside. See p292.

St Mary, East Bergholt
Another lavishly commissioned wool church. It's worth a visit for the medieval bell cage: a wooden construction in the graveyard that survived because the church tower was never built. See p269.

St Mary, Wissington
In an idyllic spot by the River Stour, this church exudes a palpable sense of history, with some fine early wall paintings, and, rather sweetly, an ad-hoc second-hand bookstall in the porch. See p254.

St Mary, Woodbridge
Sitting just behind the picturesque market square in the handsome town of Woodbridge, St Mary's has some unusual flint flushwork to boast about. See p235.

Places to visit

Wyken Vineyards

FRESSINGFIELD, DEBENHAM & EYE

Mechanical Music Museum
Blacksmith Road, Cotton, IP14 4QN (01449 613876).
Open June-Sept 2.30-5.30pm Sun. Admission £5;
£1 reductions. No credit cards.
Worth a detour on a summer Sunday afternoon, this
wonderful array of organs (including a Wurlitzer), street
pianos and pianolas is brought to musical life. As you
listen, let your eyes wander around rafters hung with
records and walls plastered with unusual memorabilia.

Pakenham Water Mill ★
Mill Road, Pakenham, IP31 2NB (01284 724075,
www.pakenhamwatermill.co.uk). Open Apr-Oct
10am-4pm Thur; 1.30-5pm Sat, Sun. Admission
£3; £1-£2.50 reductions. No credit cards.
Pakenham is the only parish in Britain to have both a
working windmill and a working watermill. The former is
owned by a farmer and open by appointment only. The
watermill is run as a museum and opens three days a
week during the season. If you want to see the mill in
action, visit between 10am and 11am on a Thursday:
this is when volunteers produce the stoneground flour
sold in the museum shop. The 90-minute guided tour is
both fascinating and funny. Our guide Syd explained how
the clay-bottomed mill pond works; why stoneground
flour retains more vitamins than flour ground on metal
rollers; why medieval teeth had become stumps by the
time their owners reached adulthood; and how the
Napoleonic Wars were briefly halted by a gentlemen's
agreement so that England could get enough new
grindstones from Europe to feed its boys. A charming
tearoom opened in 2009 in the Miller's House next
door, serving lunches on Thursdays and cakes and
scones (made with Pakenham flour) at weekends.

St Mary's
Thornham Parva. Open dawn-dusk daily.
Admission free.
Saxon in origin, but mainly Norman in style, St Mary's
is small and simple, with a thatched roof and squat
square tower. Inside, behind protective glass, is the
beautiful, highly coloured Thornham Retable, thought
to be part of a larger altarpiece from Thetford Priory
that was broken up in 1538, during the Dissolution
of the Monasteries. It was hidden in a barn at nearby
Thornham Hall for several centuries before being
rediscovered, coated in grime. The church also
has some very rare examples of 14th-century wall
paintings, depicting the childhood of Jesus on one
side and the martyrdom of St Edmund on the other.
Look out too for the lovely etched glass windows
by Lawrence Whistler. Basil Spence, architect of
Coventry Cathedral, is buried in the graveyard.

Thornham Walks
Thornham Magna, IP23 8HA (01379 788345,
www.thornham.org.uk). Open Apr-Oct 9am-6pm
daily. Nov-Mar 9am-4pm daily. Admission free.
On the Thornham Estate, 12 miles of paths lead
visitors through rows of lime and linden trees to the
walled garden, where they can stroll under the apple
and quince trees. In season, try to find the Lady
Henniker cooking apple trees (named after a former
lady of the house): look for large, angular fruit that's
yellow, except when it has been touched by the sun
to leave a red blush. Also watch out for Mrs Perkins,
the garden's cat. The nuttery is lovely in spring, when
wild flowers poke through the grass beneath the hazel
trees. In fact, the only disappointment is the café
by the car park – serving soup that might have come
straight from the can, sliced white bread, chips and

salads of little but iceberg lettuce – so bring a picnic instead or try your luck at the Old Coach House restaurant near the walled garden. It looks a bit old-fashioned, but at least promises food that's freshly made. Other amenities include a photographer's gallery, a jewellery shop and a small gift shop.

Wyken Vineyards
Wyken Hall, Wyken Road, Stanton, IP31 2DW (01359 252372, www.wykenvineyards.co.uk). Open Shop, Vineyards & Wood 10am-6pm daily. Garden Easter-Sept 2-6pm Mon-Fri, Sun. Admission Gardens £3.50; free-£3 reductions.
This is so much more than a place that grows grapes. Visitors can walk to the seven-acre vineyards through beautiful Wyken Wood, or visit the farmers' market held here every Saturday. The Country Store is basically a fancy gift shop, but does stock some beautiful things for adults, children and the home. It also sells the vineyards' wine, with the award-winning Bacchus our favourite – fruity, but very dry. Next to the shop, the Leaping Hare restaurant and café (*see p258*) is housed in a converted barn. You have to pay to go into the four acres of gardens that surround the Elizabethan Wyken Hall, but it's worth the money: the gardens have been completely redesigned over the last three decades and are full of imaginative corners and interesting plants. There's a knot garden, herb garden, copper beech maze, English kitchen garden and a nuttery.

THE GIPPING VALLEY

Baylham House Rare Breeds Farm
Mill Lane, Baylham, IP6 8LG (01473 830264, www.baylham-house-farm.co.uk). Open Feb-Oct 11am-5pm daily. Admission £5; free-£4 reductions.

South of Needham Market, Baylham Farm provides plenty of opportunities for children to meet animals at close quarters. There's the lamb tunnel in early spring, shearing demonstrations in June, and plenty of unusual cows, pigs and goats to get friendly with all through the year. You can also take the children along a riverside walk or follow the old Roman road through the paddocks, then visit the café.

Museum of East Anglian Life ★
Stowmarket, IP14 1DL (01449 612229, www.eastanglianlife.org.uk). Open Mar-Oct 10am-5pm Mon-Sat; 11am-5pm Sun. Admission £6.50; £3.50-£5.50 reductions; £17.50 family.
In an unlikely looking spot behind the Asda car park lies this extensive social history museum. In fact, it's much more than a museum: it's also a farm, nature reserve and working craft centre rolled into one. Many of the historic buildings housing exhibits have been moved here from elsewhere in Suffolk – Edgar's Farmhouse, showing how a typical farm would have looked in medieval times, is from the nearby village of Combs, while FJ Crapnell's smithy is from Grundisburgh. The timber-clad Boby building contains installations about traditional crafts such as basket-weaving, coopering, clockmaking and printing (there are workshop sessions to bring these old trades to life), and the Bone building tells the story of Ransome, maker of agricultural machinery. You'll also find a tin tabernacle, a wind pump, a working watermill and a fine collection of steam-powered vehicles that are brought out for the fortnightly steam days. Sheep and red poll cows roam the fields, and there are some extremely rare Suffolk Black pigs and Tyson, a majestic Suffolk Punch horse – a breed more endangered than the panda.

Museum of East Anglian Life

SUFFOLK

SUFFOLK

PINK IS THE COLOUR
These days, as you make your way around Suffolk, the most fashionable colour for its cottages seems to be one of the various yellows from the Farrow & Ball range, set off by woodwork in complementary greens. But there's still a lot of 'Suffolk Pink' around, traditionally accompanied by crisp white woodwork. The county has always been famous for its pig-rearing and it's said that, before the likes of Dulux and Crown appeared, Suffolk folk mixed pigs' blood into their whitewash to give it a pinkish hue. Admittedly, most historians believe red ochre or sloe berries were the more likely secret ingredient, but that doesn't make for such a good story. The tradition is probably no older than the early 20th century (before then, most houses would have been painted a variation of off-white), but in the 1970s Suffolk Pink was marketed by the large commercial paint companies, which successfully sold the idea back to East Anglian home owners.

High Street. North of Stowmarket, decent pub grub is available at the Kings Arms in Haughley (3 Old Street, 01449 614462), which has games in the bar and a family-friendly garden; and in Tostock at the Gardeners Arms (Church Road, 01359 270460), which also has a garden as well as a pool table, cribbage and darts. In Woolpit, daytime snacks and hot drinks are available at the Elm Tree gift shop and the old-fashioned tearoom next to the baker.

Alder Carr Farm Café ★
Creeting St Mary, IP6 8LX (01449 721215, www.aldercarrfarm.co.uk). Open 10am-2.30pm Tue; 10am-4pm Wed-Sun.
Inside a lovely, airy, timber-framed converted barn, this café serves loose-leaf tea in proper pots, tasty coffee and delicious cakes. One customer, on receiving her scone, noted its heft: 'Yes, that is a bit mighty,' the waitress concurred. In truth, all the cakes are pretty mighty, from a fresh-cream swiss roll the size of a barrel to a Victoria sponge almost as tall as the diminutive queen herself.

Bistro & Tea Room
Museum of East Anglian Life, Stowmarket, IP14 1DL (01449 612229, www.eastanglianlife.org.uk). Open 10am-5pm (3.30pm winter) daily.
Caterers Gilberts serve hearty pies, soups and sandwiches, cakes in huge slabs, hot drinks and excellent Ronaldo's ice-cream in a long, wood-panelled hut. The teenaged serving staff could do with some lessons in manners (the occasional smile wouldn't hurt, for starters), but otherwise this is a lovely spot, with a grassy garden and picnic tables outside. There's also a small shop selling local produce.

Swan Inn
The Street, Woolpit, IP30 9QN (01359 240482, www.woolpitswan.co.uk). Open 11.30am-3pm, 6-11pm Mon-Thur; 11.30am-3pm, 6pm-midnight Fri, Sat; 10am-3.30pm Sun. Lunch served noon-2.30pm daily. Dinner served 6.30-9pm Mon-Sat.
Originally a coaching inn, the Swan has seen some changes over the years, including its 19th-century red-brick exterior, made by the Woolpit Brick Co. As well as good beer, you can enjoy a daily changing menu (chalked up on boards) that features locally caught fish and meat from a nearby family butcher. There are also four rooms in the former stables (£65 double with breakfast).

Where to stay

Burnt House Cottage
Darmsden, Needham Market, IP6 8RA (0845 268 1458, www.cottageselection.co.uk). Rates £409-£1,096 per week.
This lovely thatched cottage (sleeping eight) has uninterrupted views over the surrounding countryside. It is decorated in a simple style with wood and brick floors, and scattered rugs and cushions. In one of the sitting rooms, there's a wood-burning stove in the inglenook fireplace.

Haughley House
Haughley, IP14 3NS (01449 673398, www.haughley house.co.uk). Rates £90 double incl breakfast.

This medieval manor house with Georgian additions has three en suite bedrooms, a three-acre garden and a beautiful fire to enjoy in winter. Your hosts are the Lord and Lady of the Manor, Jeffrey and Caroline Bowden, who make the most of their surrounding land when cooking meals for guests, serving fresh vegetables from the garden, eggs from their chickens and, during shooting season, local pheasants.

WEST OF THE A14

The area bounded by the A14 and the A1141 is bleak, with flat expanses of agricultural land where there's very little to see. Traditionally one of the poorer areas of Suffolk, it can blur into a succession of small villages. You can, however, make an enchanting little loop from Needham Market that takes in the home of late DJ John Peel.

Head towards Barking on the B1078 and turn right towards Battisford and Little Finborough. In the former, a very unusual tower graces St Mary's Church, its stepped brick-and-flint base sat under a wooden belfry. Great Finborough is one of the prettiest villages in the area, famous to some as the location of the thatched cottage that John Peel drily called 'Peel Acres'. He moved here with his wife Sheila in the 1970s, slowly filling up the outbuildings with his terrifyingly large record collection. His headstone is in Great Finborough's churchyard, inscribed with the words 'Teenage dreams so hard to beat', a line from his favourite record by the Undertones. The church is worth a look in its own right. Its spectacular and unusual octagonal spire is used as a geographical reference point from miles around (it's said the local squire built the church so his wife wouldn't get lost when out riding). The village green is lined with attractive cottages and the Chestnut Horse pub, the finishing point of the annual Race of the Bogmen at Easter.

Compared to some stretches of agricultural land around Mid-Suffolk, the area between Great Finborough, Rattlesden, Harleston and Onehouse (actually about six houses) is run through with footpaths, so it's a great area for quiet walks. Neighbouring Buxhall is almost as pretty as Great Finborough, with dramatic Tudor chimneys on some houses, while the thatched cottages and timber-framed buildings along the streets and the river make Rattlesden especially picturesque.

Nearby St Mary's, Badley is a very unusual church. Its uniqueness is partly its isolated position several miles up a track, with only a farmhouse for company, and partly a result of that isolation. Once you've walked to the church, sit and enjoy the solitude and birdsong from the open-sided porch or, if it's a weekend and the door is open, go in to absorb the sense of timeless peace. Thanks to its seclusion, the church was untouched by Victorian renovation and remains simplicity itself: just white walls, sun-bleached wooden pews and simple floor tiles. It's now in the care of the Churches Conservation Trust (www.visit churches.org.uk). You'll find the track on the B1113 from Stowmarket to Needham Market, on the right just after the sign for Badley village.

Where to eat & drink

There are several good pubs hereabouts, although none of them have quite the gastronomic reputation of the Bildeston Crown (see below). The beamed lounge bars at the Brewers Arms (Lower Road, 01449 736377, closed Mon) in Rattlesden lead to a main dining area with exposed old bread ovens. The Crown (Mill Road, 01449 736521, www.the buxhallcrown.co.uk, closed Mon) in Buxhall, once John Peel's local, is now a good, genteel food pub.

Bildeston Crown

High Street, Bildeston, IP7 7EB (01449 740510, www.thebildestoncrown.com). Open/food served 7-10am. noon-2.45pm, 7-9.45pm daily.
With its red walls, leather dining chairs and wine store on display in the restaurant, the award-winning Crown gives the impression of being serious about food. There's no doubting the quality of the raw ingredients, many of which come from owner James Buckle's farm around the corner. The prices are very high, though: we paid £11 for a starter that featured just a single scallop on the plate, when you get four (plus a more exciting accompanying sauce) at the nearby Great House (see p283) in Lavenham for the same price. Main courses are competently prepared, but come on fussy crockery and still don't justify the prices. Even the puddings are priced at £8: can any trifle be that good? Try the £20 midweek dinner menu, also available at lunchtime Monday to Saturday, to make up your own mind.

Where to stay

Applemount Farm B&B

Nr Thorpe Morieux, IP30 0NQ (0800 583 2583, www. applemount.co.uk). Rates from £85 double incl breakfast.
Applemount has two en suite doubles in the 19th-century farmhouse, but several more – including a self-contained studio – in sympathetically converted outbuildings. Make the most of a hearty Suffolk-sourced breakfast (or continental alternative) before heading to the indoor heated swimming pool, sauna or tennis court.

Minto House Cottages

Bildeston, IP7 7ED (0870 1921109, www.bookcottages. com). Rates Minto Mews £270-£576 per week. Minto Cottage £270-£576 per week. Minto End £297-£497 per week.
In the middle of the lovely village of Bildeston, Minto House offers three cottages to let. Minto End (sleeping four) and Minto Cottage (three) are part of a 15th-century hall, while Minto Mews (two) is a separate converted barn. The unfussy decor is mostly pale woods and bright whites, with wooden floors and simple furniture.

Ravenwood Hall

Rougham, IP30 9JA (01359 270345, www.ravenwood hall.co.uk). Rates £153-£199 double incl breakfast.
There are 14 ornate bedrooms in this former country mansion, apparently built for a local noble woman after she'd had an affair with the Abbot of Bury St Edmunds and needed to disappear for a while. The three rooms in the oldest part have the most character, but the interiors are generally a bit old-fashioned. The wood-panelled dining room attracts local non-guests with its meaty menu and good cellar.

Stour Valley

Along with the coast, this is perhaps the best-known area of Suffolk. The countryside surrounding the River Stour is prettier than the flatter agricultural tracts further north, and it doesn't hurt that nothing much has changed since Constable and Gainsborough idealised the landscape in their paintings. Cows still graze in water meadows; willows still weep prettily over rivers and ponds; thatched cottages lean and huddle in undisturbed hamlets; and pheasants startle out of cornfields and woods much as they have for centuries. As well as vistas of bucolic perfection, there are many handsome towns built on the riches of the wool trade. From the famous timber-framed streets of Lavenham to the high streets of Hadleigh and Long Melford, the area's former position as one of the richest in England means there's plenty of architectural drama to behold.

FLATFORD TO SUDBURY

Flatford

The most obvious place to begin when getting to know Stour country is the hamlet of Flatford, the home of John Constable's father and the inspiration for many of Constable's paintings. It's now run by the National Trust, though even NT members have to pay £2.50 for the 'private' car park, despite the fact that the trust owns 500 acres surrounding Constable's home. Drivers are cornered, though: there's nowhere else to park on the narrow one-way by-road loop from East Bergholt.

Walking from the car park to Flatford feels a bit like entering a theme park for retirees, as clots of aging art- and history-lovers search for something to see. The museum in Bridge Cottage contains a small display showing where in the hamlet Constable must have sat to paint his most famous works – the views are tidier than when the artist lived here, although they're still recognisable.

Willy Lott's Cottage and Flatford Mill are privately owned (and the Mill runs courses on natural history and art, so you'll often see groups of students painting in the fields around the village). The two short circular walks from Willy Lott's Cottage are unremarkable and face a row of pylons. It's much better to follow the riverbank on the other side of the bridge towards Manningtree or Dedham, where friesian cows graze in the meadows, rub their backs lazily against trees and wade into the Stour – just as in Constable's paintings (such as the famous *Haywain*, featuring the river and Flatford Mill).

Especially on a late afternoon in spring or autumn, when the air is gauzy and time seems to stop, Dedham Vale is stunning. Remember, however, that it's one of the stars of the English natural world, and its beauty and fame means there's little chance of solitude or even gentle reflection here. For a more peaceful appreciation, head across Fen Bridge and up the hill towards East Bergholt, where there's a magnificent view of the whole vale from the top, or take to a rowing boat, available for hire next to Bridge Cottage for £6 per hour.

East Bergholt & Dedham

Flatford visitors who aren't tempted by the National Trust café by Bridge House may be lured into the Fountain House Tea Room (01206 299955) along the pretty high street in nearby East Bergholt. There are also several pubs: the most promising is the King's Head (Burnt Oak, 01206 298190), with its beamed lounge and separate dining room. St Mary's Church has something you won't see anywhere else in England: a medieval bellcage built in 1531, when the planned church tower had to be scrapped due to lack of funds. The bells are rung on Sundays at 9.30am.

No tour of Constable country is complete without hopping over the border into Essex and visiting the handsome town of Dedham. It makes much more sense to take the two-mile walk here across the vale from Flatford if you have time, rather than driving: the road follows a much longer route that includes a short stretch on the busy A12. The footpath into Dedham from the river takes walkers past the village's majestic church (paid for by riches from the wool trade) and on to the High Street. The Sir Alfred Munnings Art Museum (01206 322127, www.siralfredmunnings.co.uk, open Apr-Sept), located in the equestrian painter's former home, Castle House, contains a large collection of Munnings' works. It's only open in the afternoon on certain days; check the website for details.

Nayland to Bures ★

The footpath that links Flatford and Dedham is part of the Stour Valley Path, which follows the River Stour from Cattawade, then forks north and arrives in Newmarket 60 miles later. It's worth coming off the path at Nayland, a pretty medieval village with timber-framed houses that haven't changed much for hundreds of years. Nayland's Anchor Inn (*see p273*) occupies a lovely spot on the river and is a good place to stop for refreshments. Just north of the village, on top of what, for Suffolk, passes as quite a hill, is Stoke-by-Nayland. Attractions include a village shop; Suffolk Black pork products, sold at the gate of Weylands Farm; and the Crown pub

Stoke-by-Clare. See p278.

(*see p274*), which opened a boutique hotel in 2008. The pub's large terrace has fine views over the countryside that drops away from the ridge.

In the valley, Polstead lies much as it has for centuries. It's a charming village, worth a stop to see the sole medieval stone church spire in Suffolk, at St Mary's; the views from the churchyard deserve a moment of contemplation too. Until recently, the church owned a 'Breeches Bible' containing records of the first wave of Suffolk villagers to emigrate to the New World, but it's now in the care of the cathedral in Bury St Edmunds. About seven miles west is the Arger Fen Nature Reserve (01473 890089, www.suffolkwildlifetrust.org), an ancient wood that's open all year round and is mapped with walking trails; entry is free. Keep an eye out for nightingales and grasshopper warblers.

Back on the Stour, the next settlement is marked Wissington on most maps, though the village sign says 'Wiston'. Whatever you call it, this spread-out sprinkling of houses is also home to St Mary the Virgin, a Norman church in a wonderfully peaceful location. Leave the door ajar when you enter, as the dark interior makes it difficult to see at first. Soon, though, your eyes will adjust, and some fabulous wall paintings will become apparent. Sketched in red ochre, they depict various biblical scenes and local legends. Near the chancel arch is a picture of

Places to visit

SUDBURY

Gainsborough's House ★
46 Gainsborough Street, CO10 2EU (01787 372958, www.gainsborough.org). Open 10am-5pm Mon-Sat. Admission £4.50; £2-£3.60 reductions; £10 family.
This handsome house, with its modest square rooms, was the Gainsborough family's home for many years. Thomas Gainsborough was born here, and the walls of the house are lined with his paintings, many of them portraits of the gentry. Perhaps the most exciting material to the modern eye are the prints and sketches the painter made of the local landscape, which are kept in the large, airy weaving room upstairs. This is a lively museum, with much going on; there are temporary exhibitions throughout the year, a programme of lectures held in the Education Centre, regular print workshops in the old coach house and a good café just by the ticket office. In summer, you can take refreshments out in the garden, and help yourself to fabulous mulberries from the 400-year-old tree in the middle of the lawn.

LONG MELFORD TO STOKE-BY-CLARE

Kentwell Hall ★
Long Melford, CO10 9BA (01787 310207, www.kentwell.co.uk). Open Feb-Oct times vary, check website for details. Admission House, Gardens & Farm £9.15; £5.90-£8.05 reductions. Gardens & Farm only £6.40; £4.50-£5.60 reductions.
The avenue of lime trees, planted in 1678, leads visitors up the long drive to this red-brick Tudor spectacular. Make sure you get some fish food at the ticket office, so that you can feed the enormous carp in the moat. The way they flash and flip and gape and grab is an amazing sight. There's so much to see and do here, it's worth arriving early. The house feels cosier than most stately homes, and that's because it's still lived in by the owners, who rescued it from ruin in the early 1970s. On event days, staff and volunteers dress up and perform demonstrations of medieval cookery using the grand kitchen ovens, as well as embarking on processions around the grounds flaunting music, dance and pageantry as they go. There's a rare-breeds farm at the old stables, a camera obscura, an ice house, imaginative topiary around the house, a sculpted tree trunk that looks like Enid Blyton's Faraway Tree, a wonderful walled garden with fruit

and vegetables, and dozens of other points of interest. The tearoom is unusually eccentric, and there are plenty of picnic tables on the lawns, so you can enjoy tea beneath a tree in the company of peacocks.

Melford Hall
Long Melford, CO10 9AA (01787 379228, www.nationaltrust.org.uk/melfordhall). Open May-Sept 1.30-5pm Wed-Sun. Oct 1.30-5pm Sat, Sun. Admission £6; £3 reductions; £15 family.
Originally this was a medieval hunting lodge, but Sir William Cordell turned it into the Tudor house we see today, with its six octagonal turrets and numerous towering chimney stacks. Cordell entertained Elizabeth I here in 1578. It's got more character than some National Trust properties because the Hyde Parker family (in residence since 1786) still uses it, but if you only have time to see one of Long Melford's Tudor houses, make it Kentwell Hall (*see left*) as its attractions are greater and more varied. Beatrix Potter was related to the Hyde Parkers and often visited, keeping her pets in the eaves during her stay; some of her sketchbooks are on display, as well as toys from the period. Access to the formal gardens is limited to the north lawn (which has croquet set out ready to play in summer) and the front lawn with its pond and large mulberry tree. A mile-long circular walk takes visitors through the surrounding parkland.

LAVENHAM

Lavenham Guildhall ★
Market Place, CO10 9QZ (01787 247646, www.nationaltrust.org.uk/lavenham). Open Apr-Oct 11am-5pm daily. Mar 11am-4pm Wed-Sun. Nov 11am-4pm Sat, Sun. Admission £3.80; £1.59 reductions; £9.20 family.
This handsome building was constructed in Lavenham's heyday, just before the Reformation. These days it's a museum run by the National Trust, with exhibits relaying the history of the town. The first room as you enter has a dressing-up box to get children into a medieval mood. Downstairs are displays on early settlers and the emergence of the town as a wool-trading centre. Upstairs, in a series of small rooms, are more particular exhibitions about the families that thrived in Lavenham, the specifics of the cloth trade, the now defunct railway line and other local stories.

St Francis feeding the birds; it's thought to be the earliest surviving representation of St Francis in English art. The highest row of paintings depicts the life of Christ; the huge dragon over the north door is said to be based on a local story about a dragon that killed sheep in neighbouring Bures.

To reach the church from the river, follow the path as it leads around the front of Wiston Hall. If you're driving, park in a designated spot before heading up the private road to the hall. In autumn, you'll be greeted by boxes of pumpkins balanced along the low church wall, each variety marked with cooking instructions. Year-round, the church's characterful timber and glass porch houses a

makeshift second-hand book stall. Both the books and pumpkins have honesty boxes alongside.

Bures, the next village along the Stour Valley Path, straddles the border between Suffolk and Essex. There's a weir and an old watermill; the village also has a tiny post office, a newsagent, a deli and three pubs, one of which, the Swan (*see p273*), hosts a farmers' market every second Saturday of the month. Next to the church is a castle mound that's thought to be of Norman origin; from the top, 30 feet above the ground, you can enjoy fantastic views over the Stour Valley in all directions. In June, Bures holds a Coracle Regatta, organised by the River Stour Trust (01787 313199, www.riverstourtrust.org).

Back on the Stour Valley Path, you'll pass the Cornard Mere Nature Reserve, also cared for by the Suffolk Wildlife Trust, before reaching Sudbury. High summer is the best time to visit; watch out for sand martins, dragonflies and reed warblers, who like its mix of open water and scrubby wetland.

Cavendish. See p277.

Where to eat & drink

East Bergholt has several pubs, of which the King's Head (see p269) is the most promising for lunch, offering a varied menu and well-kept beer.

Just a few miles away in Stoke-by-Nayland, the Crown is now a boutique hotel (see p274) but also has a vast dining area (in different rooms and on a large terrace outside) that serves local specialities, and is popular all year round. There's also the more homely Angel Inn (Polstead Street, 01206 263245, www.theangelinn.net) for classic pub grub done well; the dining room in the double-height medieval well room is a lovely place to eat. There's also B&B accommodation in six rooms. The Fleece (Broad Street, 01787 210247, closed Mon) in Boxford is friendly and serves own-made food, as does the Cock (The Green, 01206 263150) in Polstead.

In Bures, the Swan and the Eight Bells are on the Essex side of the village; the Three Horseshoes, with a garden on a raised bank away from the road, is on the Suffolk side. The Swan (01787 228121, www.buresswan.co.uk) serves mid-priced pub classics in its dining room and large enclosed garden, and, unusually these days, also has an old-fashioned bar just for drinkers. It holds a music night every second Thursday of the month.

Anchor Inn ★

26 Court Street, Nayland, CO6 4JL (01206 262313, www.anchornayland.co.uk). Open 11am-3pm, 5-11pm Mon-Fri; 11am-11pm Sat; 11am-10.30pm Sun. Lunch served noon-2pm Mon-Fri; noon-2.30pm Sat; noon-3pm Sun. Dinner served 6.30-9pm Mon-Fri; 6.30-9.30pm Sat; 5-8.30pm Sun.

This free house serves beers from Greene King, Adnams and Mauldons, but it's mostly taken over at meal times by diners, who enjoy the pub's commitment to local produce. The enterprise even has its own kitchen garden and heritage farm, where you can sometimes see Suffolk Punch horses working the land, plus a smokery and a vineyard to complete the gastronomic set. In sunny weather, the outdoor tables along the riverside really comes into their own.

Where to stay

Case Restaurant with Rooms

A134, Assington, CO10 5LD (01787 210483, www.thecaserestaurantwithrooms.co.uk). Rates £85-£135 double incl breakfast.

The seven en suite rooms aren't enormous, but everything is neat, crisp and modern in this recent accommodation extension to the Case Restaurant. Breakfasts use local produce wherever possible, and the restaurant, serving hearty, mainly British dishes, is on hand if you don't want to drive to any of the nearby towns in the evening.

Clare Priory. See p278.

Cobbs Cottage ★

Stoke-by-Nayland, CO6 4RP (01787 211115, www.grove-cottages.co.uk). Rates £525-£938 per week.

This sweet thatched cottage, painted primrose yellow and sleeping five, overlooks the Box Valley in a secluded position down a single-track lane. The rooms are quirky and full of nooks and crannies, but beware the low ceilings – it wasn't designed for comparatively strapping 21st-century humans.

Crown ★

Stoke-by-Nayland, CO6 4SE (01206 262001, www.crowninn.net). Rates £75-£200 double incl breakfast.

The Crown Inn added a boutique hotel to its assets in 2008. Locaed at the back of the pub, it has 11 en suite rooms decorated either in a smart contemporary style or in a more traditional and homely manner. The mouthwatering breakfast menu is extensive, with everything from egg-white omelettes via porridge to the full English.

Gladwins Farm ★

Harper's Hill, Nayland, CO6 4NU (01206 262261, www.gladwinsfarm.co.uk). Rates from £285-£630 per week for 2 people.

Nine self-catering cottages (sleeping from two to eight) in rolling countryside, with additional attractions such as a heated indoor swimming pool, a sauna, a hard tennis court, a children's playground and fishing facilities.

SUDBURY

A settlement has existed on what is now Sudbury since Anglo-Saxon days. You'll have to look past some unfortunate modern planning decisions to see what remains of this rich history, but it's there, and it's worth seeking out.

The church of St Peter on Market Hill is no longer used for worship, but it's a busy place, open on market days (Thursday and Saturday); for a monthly farmers' market (9.30am-1pm, last Friday of the month); and for concerts and other events. Outside

SUFFOLK

stands a statue of Thomas Gainsborough, one of the town's most famous sons; there's a museum (*see p272*) in the painter's former house on Gainsborough Street. Those that are inspired by the art can visit the occasional auctions run by Sworders at the Saleroom on Birkitts Lane (01787 880305, www.sworder.co.uk/olivers).

It's also worth visiting another of Sudbury's churches, St Gregory. This is where the townspeople keep the mummified head of Simon of Sudbury, the lord chancellor who pushed forward the poll tax that began the Peasants' Revolt in 1381. Simon's head was cut off and stuck on London Bridge before it was eventually brought back here without his body. If you want to make his acquaintance, you'll have to make a prior arrangement.

North Street is lined with over-familiar high-street names, but there's more appealing shopping elsewhere. On Market Hill, for instance, you'll find the Winch & Blatch department store (01787 373737, www.winchblatch.co.uk, closed Sun). And look out for the two silk weavers: Vanners on Weavers Lane (01787 313933/372396, www.vanners.com, open Thur, by arrangement other times) and Stephen Walters on Cornard Road (01787 466189, www.stephenwalters.co.uk, closed Mon, Sun). Both enterprises have been here since the 19th century.

Sudbury is cradled by a large curve in the Stour, which forms the town's borders to the south and west. The water meadows and marshes are unsuitable for development, which means you can walk straight out of the town centre into fantastic countryside in just a few minutes. Just off Friars Street – which houses the excellent Kesterel Bookshop (nos.10-12, 01787 372735, closed Sun – a walk down Quay Lane past Sudbury's tennis club, croquet lawn and cricket green takes you to the tiny quay, where walks go off in all directions: you could take the Valley Walk to Lavenham via the old railway line, say, or one of myriad paths around the riverside meadows. Boat trips (*see p276*) run from the Granary on selected days during tourist season. Also down here is the Quay Theatre (01787 374745, www.quaytheatre.org.uk), a lively little place staffed by volunteers with a delightful auditorium that doubles as an arts cinema. Back in town, you can hire bikes from Street Life (01787 310940, www.streetlifecycles. co.uk) next to the bus station.

Where to eat & drink

For a meal with a difference, head to the Mill Hotel (Walnut Tree Lane, 01787 375544, www.elizabethhotels.co.uk), a former watermill converted in the 1970s into a hotel with 56 bedrooms; the wheel is encased behind glass in the hotel's restaurant. There's a mummified cat displayed beneath the floor in the hotel foyer; apparently, every time it's been removed from the building, unfortunate things have happened to the hotel and its staff.

Elsewhere, the Angel (01787 882228) on Friars Street changed hands in 2009, but locals say it's

CULTURAL CONNECTIONS

● Ruth Rendell lived in the pretty village of Polstead before she became Baroness Rendell of Babergh in 1997. Several of her books are set in the Stour Valley, including *Gallowglass* (Sudbury), and *A Fatal Inversion* (Polstead and Nayland). She's also used other areas of Suffolk around Bury St Edmunds and the coast – she used to keep a place near Aldeburgh for several years.

● Tom Waits wrote 'Murder in the Red Barn', a song about William Corder and Maria Marten. The couple planned to elope, but instead Corder killed Maria and buried her in Polstead's Red Barn, where they had arranged to meet. He sent the family letters about Maria's good health, but her body was found and he was hanged in Market Hill in Bury St Edmunds, in 1828, in front of huge crowds. A rather grisly exhibit in Moyse's Hall Museum (*see p294*) is a written account of Corder's trial, bound in the murderer's own skin.

● Charles Dickens was sent to Sudbury in 1834 as a young reporter for the *Morning Chronicle* to get the lowdown on the corrupt dealings of the town councillors, who met at the Rose & Crown hotel. Dickens later wrote about Sudbury as Eatanswill in *The Pickwick Papers*.

● Legend has it that band leader Glen Miller spent a lot of time at the bar inside Lavenham's Swan Hotel after entertaining the local troops during World War II. It's also claimed that he had his last ever tipple there, before getting in the plane bound for France that went down in a storm.

pricey and service can be slow. The White Horse (01787 371063) on North Street does own-made burgers and fish and chips, and has music on alternate Saturday evenings. Most of the pubs in the area are owned by Greene King.

Brewery Tap ★

21 East Street, Sudbury, CO10 2TP (01787 370876, www.blackaddertap.co.uk). Open/food served 11am-11pm Mon-Thur; 11am-midnight Fri, Sat; noon-10.30pm Sun.
The only freehouse in town, the Brewery Tap sells up to eight beers brewed by the local firm of Mauldons. Other drinks include Aspall's cider; food runs to own-made scotch eggs, hearty salt beef or smoked gammon baps, and pork pies.

Secret Garden ★

21 Friars Street, Sudbury, CO10 2AA (01787 372030, www.thesecretgardentearoom.co.uk). Food served 9am-5pm Mon-Thur; 9am-5pm, 7-9.30pm Fri, Sat.
If the little flourishes on the capital letters and the uprights don't immediately give away the owners' French origins, the menu might: changed daily, it's mostly based on French home cooking, with gastronomic finery saved for Friday and Saturday nights. It's a friendly little place with an airy front

room, a smaller back room and a small garden; the owners are also the people serving. At lunchtime, the home-made soup is always good, and it's worth saving room for pudding.

Where to stay

Mill House B&B

Cross Street, Sudbury, CO10 2DS (01787 881173, www.millhouse-sudbury.co.uk). Rates £75 double incl breakfast.
This 500-year-old house has a lovely garden looking over water meadows. Owners Peter and Maria Mills let out two double bedrooms plus a very small single for a child. Breakfasts include home-made preserves and fresh fruit, cold meats, free-range eggs and smoked salmon or haddock.

LONG MELFORD TO STOKE-BY-CLARE

Long Melford ★

Sudbury is a couple of miles south of Long Melford, but the best way to reach the town is from the other

Things to do

River Stour boat trips

FLATFORD TO SUDBURY

Fleece Jazz

Stoke-by-Nayland Hotel, Golf Club & Spa, Keepers Lane, nr Leavenheath, CO6 4PZ (01787 211865, www.dovbear.co.uk). Shows 8pm Fri (occasional Sat). Tickets £15-£20.
This well-regarded jazz night used to be held at the Fleece pub (hence the name). It grew too big for the small village drinking den, so has moved to smarter digs at the Stoke-by-Nayland golf club, on the way to Leavenheath.

SUDBURY

Rancho Pavo Real

1 Peacock Hall Cottages, Little Cornard, CO10 0PE (01787 377490, www.paso-finos.co.uk).
Learn to ride like a Colombian, and find out about the history of South American *paso fino* horses at the same time. Riders with some experience can

go hacking in the surrounding Stour Valley countryside. If you'd rather stick to English riding, there are cobs and connemaras too.

River Stour boat trips ★

The Granary, Quay Lane, Sudbury, CO10 2AN (0845 803 5787, www.riverstourtrust.org). Trips Easter-Oct 2-5pm Wed, Sun, bank hols. Tickets £5-£12.50; £2.50-£5 reductions. No credit cards.
The River Stour Trust has been instrumental in keeping the Stour navigable. It has raised money for the restoration of locks at Flatford, Dedham and Great Cornard and has plans for more projects in the future. The Trust organises regular river activities and also runs trips on two electric boats during the tourist season.

LONG MELFORD TO STOKE-BY-CLARE

Clare Castle Country Park

Maltings Lane, Clare, CO10 8NW.
Once through the car park, the first thing you find is a disused railway station in a quiet riverside setting. This now houses the Clare Park Centre, a bitty series of exhibitions that jump from the history of the railway to the history of the castle to displays about the natural world. Entering the park, you can't miss the castle motte, rising 50ft above the grassy plain. A spiral footpath leads to the top, where the red-brick and flint wall remains are just enough to kickstart the mind into imagining what once sat here. The views take in Clare to the north and the country park and River Stour to the south. The park is a great place for a family picnic and has a small adventure playground that goes down well with children. In summer, a moving stall on the back of a trike serves coffee and cake to passers-by. There are also some lovely walks along the banks of the Stour (part of the Stour Valley Path), an old railway line walk and a signposted 3.5-mile circular walk around Clare.

Bell. See p279.

direction, from the north, where the driveways of the town's great Tudor mansions, Kentwell Hall (*see p272*) and Melford Hall (*see p272*), peel off at opposite ends of the large, handsome green. Play 'pick the house you'd live in' as you survey the line of character houses along the green's edge.

As if that weren't enough, this side is also home to Holy Trinity Church, a magnificent 15th-century building of elegant proportions and Perpendicular design that's also blessed with top-notch internal acoustics. Anyone with a head for gothic letters might be able to make out the names of the church's benefactors, which, unusually, are inscribed on the exterior. The Long Melford Music Society (www.longmelford.info/music.html) stages regular lunchtime and evening concerts here from May to September; they're free, although donations towards the restoration of the church's wonderful medieval stained-glass windows are appreciated.

Long Melford boomed during the medieval wool bonanza and again in Victorian times, when coconut matting and horse hair were big industries in the town. These days, its main source of wealth is upmarket tourism. There are six crinkle-crankle walls in the town and a multitude of handsome houses on Hall Street, the main thoroughfare. Many of the buildings have newer frontages that lie over the original timber frames; it's fun trying to spot the old houses behind the façades. The 50-plus independent businesses include galleries, pubs, hotels and shops selling antiques and books; in the final category sits Landers (01787

378957, www.landersbookshop.co.uk), a fine independent bookstore on Hall Street.

Glemsford to Stoke-by-Clare

To some people, Glemsford counts as another of Suffolk's picturesque villages, but while there are some interesting buildings along the high street, there's also some ugly infill, so you may as well head to neighbouring Cavendish for the real deal. You may, however, want to check out the Sunday car boot sale at the Old Filling Station on Lower Road between Febuary and December. Another pretty village worth making a detour for is Hartest, three miles or so to the north. Its large village green, lined with cottages in all sorts of different colours, is idyllic.

Now that the Sue Ryder Museum is closed (the charity was founded here in the 1950s), there's not much to actually visit in Cavendish. Strange to think this quiet place used to have a railway station, cinema, several schools and many more shops. Yet, it's such a pretty, quintessentially English village with a grand stretch of village green, thatched cottages and tree-lined avenues that many people still come for a walk and lunch. On one side of the green is the Five Bells, an old-fashioned drinkers' pub that was closed at the time of writing (although a campaign is in place to get it reopened). St Mary's Church, with its impressive white stone exterior, is across the road. The interior is full of light, thanks to many of the mullioned windows containing plain glass. The wooden ceiling has a beautiful painted section above the altar, but the most decorative art object is the 16th-century Flemish reredos and a relief sculpture showing the crucifixion scene. The Duck or Grouse newsagent must be one of the smallest shops in England; mind your head when you go through the door. There's still a Sue Ryder shop in the village, and a farm shop at Willow Tree Farm (between Glemsford and Cavendish) that sells fresh fish on Saturday mornings. Also just outside Cavendish, in Pentlow, is the Nethergate Brewery (01787 283220, www.nethergate.co.uk); book in advance if you want to pop in to buy some Old Growler, Umble or any of its other fine ales.

The small town of Clare ★ is one of those places in which it would be handy to install an elderly relative for occasional visits; there's more than enough to keep a family occupied for a day or two. Wander around its compact centre and visit the Ancient House Museum (01787 277572, www.clare-ancient-house-museum.co.uk, closed Mon-Wed, all Oct-Mar), where you can learn about the social and architectural history of the town – you can also stay here (see p280). Around the corner is the large flint church of St Peter & St Paul, which is also very light inside, because much of its medieval stained glass was destroyed during the Reformation.

Near the river is the green expanse of Clare Castle Country Park (see p276). Take the river path in the opposite direction and you'll find Clare Priory (01787 277326, www.clarepriory.org.uk), where a stroll around the grounds provokes a vivid sense of history. Step through the doorway of the ruined church nave, which now makes an unusual walled garden planted with fruit trees. Built in the 13th century, it was the first Augustinian priory to be established in England, until Henry VIII closed down the order during the Reformation. The Augustinians returned to the priory about 50 years ago, and now use the lovely pink house as accommodation. It's closed to the public, but you can wander into the shrine that's housed in a former barn. It's very simple inside and a good place for contemplation, whatever your religious views.

Stoke-by-Clare is another picture-postcard village along the Stour Valley. Its village green and pastel-hued, pargeting-covered cottages offer an eyeful of quiet English beauty. When the village shop and post office shut a few years ago, the community banded together to establish a community shop in the old stable block of the Lion pub (01787 277571). The resulting Stoke Stores (01787 279261) still has post office facilities, and sells freshly baked bread on Tuesday and Friday and a bit of everything else the rest of the week. The Lion also does a fish and chip takeaway service in the evenings.

PARGETING

One of the most common traditional adornments on Suffolk houses is pargeting: the raised plaster decoration you see on the external walls of cottages and houses across the county. Most of the best examples are in the Stour Valley – in Cavendish, Clare, Long Melford, Lavenham and the villages in between. This is because this was the richest area of the county, and pargeting was a popular way to show off personal wealth in medieval times. Traditionally, pargeters mixed horsehair and sand into a lime plaster (much more malleable than ordinary plaster), which allowed them to fashion animals, heraldic images and geometric designs into the plasterwork before it set. It's still a rarified craft, but there has been a resurgence of pargeting on new-builds over the last decade, as well as conservation work on fine historic examples of the art, such as on the Ancient House (see p217) in Ipswich, whose four panels represent the known continents at the time it was built.

Where to eat & drink

Long Melford provides a good range of choice. There's a café in Long Melford's Fine Foods & Deli (Dudley House, Hall Street, 01787 881361), and paninis, baguettes and cakes in the homely Lounge (Little Saint Mary's, 01787 379279). Unusually for Suffolk, you can also enjoy a range

Lavenham. See p282.

of global cuisines at Indian restaurant Melford Valley (01787 310079), Austrian restaurant Gappmaiers (Hall Street, 01787 319319, closed dinner Mon, Sun) and at the chippy, which also has a Chinese menu (Chips 'n' Chopstix, Hall Street, 01787 378776). Of the many pubs, the George & Dragon (Hall Street, 01787 371285) offers burgers, fish and chips and other pub favourites, while the Bull and the Black Lion have finer dining (for both, *see p280*).

In Hartest, the Crown (The Green, 01284 830250) is a good spot for lunch. Take time to look up at the ceiling beams near the fireplace, where each man from the village who went off to fight in World War I pinned a coin next to a lucky horseshoe. The

Countryside around Lavenham. See p282.

agreement was they would remove their coin when they returned – 25 remain, with only a few holes where coins were removed.

Currently, there are two operating pubs in Cavendish. The Adnams-owed Bull Inn (High Street, 01787 280245, www.thebullcavendish. co.uk) serves classic pub grub; for gastropub fare, head to the George (*see below*).

Clare is also well endowed with food options. A fish and chip shop and the Number One Deli cater for casual needs, while the town's pubs offer more hearty options. The Swan (High Street, 01787 278939) has recently changed hands and undergone a makeover, and has so far got a local thumbs-up. Its ancient pub sign is supposedly one of the oldest in England. The Cock Inn (Callis Street, 01787 277391) is an Adnams pub and was named the brewer's pub of the year in 2008. It has a pretty garden at the back and serves pub classics (fish and chips, steak and ale pie), as well as tapas. There's also a bar billiards table and occasional live music.

Bell ★

Market Hill, Clare, CO10 8NN (01787 277741, www.thebellhotel-clare.com). Open 8am-11pm Mon-Fri, Sun; 8am-midnight Sat. Lunch served noon-3pm daily. Dinner served 6-9pm Mon-Fri; 6-9.30pm Sat; 6-8.30pm Sun.

Another Suffolk pub with a long past – it's said that some of the building's beams came from Clare Priory, after it was dissolved by Henry VIII. Don't let the old-fashioned menu put you off, as the pub-grub dishes that arrive in enormous portions have the wonderful taste of great home cooking. There's a conservatory and small terraced garden out the back for diners, and staff are very amenable to families with children, bringing out crayons and paper and serving kid-sized portions of anything on the adult menu. There are also 15 bedrooms (£90-£100 double incl breakfast), should you wish to stay over.

George ★

The Green, Cavendish, CO10 8BA (01787 280248, www.thecavendishgeorge.co.uk). Lunch served noon-2pm Mon-Sat; noon-3pm Sun. Dinner served 6-9.30pm Mon-Sat.

The Farrow & Ball paintwork on this gloriously positioned gastropub (right on the village green) gives the game away that this is a modern-thinking establishment rather than a traditional boozer. Indeed, inside it's much more restaurant than pub, with hessian carpets, blond leather armchairs and modern art on the walls. The menu is a combination of gastro classics (loin of pork with mash and veg) and the odd surprise (chinese beef filo parcels with hoi sin sauce). Desserts, such as rice pudding with cardamom, are exquisite. The £10 two-course lunch deal is a bargain, and there's a large patio garden with a covered area for summer eating. The four double bedrooms (£75-£95 double, breakfast extra) were recently revamped.

Scutchers of Long Melford

Westgate Street, Long Melford, CO10 9DP (01787 310200, www.scutchers.com). Lunch served noon-2pm, dinner served 7-9.30pm Tue-Sat.
An efficient welcome awaits at this well-regarded spot, which takes its name from the flax workers who frequented the building when it was a pub. The tables and chairs sit beneath exposed beams in the nooks and crannies of what is a lovely old building. The Modern European food is good, though perhaps not as superb as the elevated prices might suggest (there are cheaper set menus too). That said, it's very popular.

Where to stay

The Bell (*see p279*) in Clare, and the George (*see p279*) in Cavendish also have accommodation.

Ancient House

26 High Street, Clare, CO10 8NY (01628 825925, www.landmarktrust.org.uk). Rates £233-£484 for 4 nights.
The date on the elaborate pargeting of one of Clare's most distinctive buildings reads 1473. In the 1930s, one buyer wanted to transport it timber by timber to the US, but a local farmer bought it and gave it to the parish council, who saved it for local citizens by establishing a museum inside (*see p278*). The Landmark Trust rents out a one-bedroom apartment in the building, which gives good views of the local church through its oriel windows.

Black Lion Hotel

The Green, Long Melford, CO10 9DN (01787 312356, www.blacklionhotel.net). Rates £153-£199 double incl breakfast.
The Black Lion's frontage commands lovely views across Long Melford's famous green. Each of the ten rooms is decorated in its own distinctive style; some would benefit from a freshen-up, but the hotel is a nice spot for a weekend away. Downstairs is a long oak bar, with cosy sofas and armchairs on one side and dining tables and chairs on the other. The food leans towards fine dining, but you can get filled rolls if you want to keep things simple.

Bull Hotel ★

Hall Street, Long Melford, CO10 9JG (01787 378494, www.thebull-hotel.com). Rates £90-£140 incl breakfast.
Built in 1450, this timber-framed building now has 25 bedrooms, all with en suite facilities. Furnishings

throughout are richly textured, and coloured to suit the old world charm of the place. The bars downstairs are cosy and full of character, and the restaurant serves decent food at reasonable prices. Guests should watch out for the resident ghost.

THE BRETT VALLEY

Hadleigh ★

Hadleigh is another of Suffolk's once-thriving wool towns, which achieved incredible prosperity during the 15th, 16th and 17th centuries. There are some 19th-century façades along the High Street, but most buildings have timber-framed origins beneath. Locals have been fighting the proposed opening of a Tesco for ten years (notice the 'Hands off Hadleigh' posters in many windows) – a sign of the town's strong community. The liveliest time to visit is on Friday or Saturday, when the market is in full swing.

The main commercial stretch, along the High Street and running into Benton Street, is good for an afternoon's browse. There's an Adnams Cellar & Kitchen shop, as well as old-fashioned ironmonger Partridges (in business since 1823); the latter also has a farm shop selling fruit and veg from the family farm, and general groceries. At the south end of the High Street is second-hand bookshop the Idler (01473 827752, closed Sun) and the Cooking Experience (01473 827568, www.cooking experience.co.uk), which holds one-day and residential cookery courses.

The most picturesque corner is around the churchyard just behind the High Street. To get there, walk up Queen Street or Church Street. Both are very handsome; the whole of Queen Street is Grade-II listed and would be the stuff of dreams for any location manager scouting for the BBC's costume drama department, apart from one small detail: the owner of the small white cottage in the corner of the churchyard has made the strange decision to paint the entire chimney tower cobalt blue.

St Mary's is one of the largest parish churches in East Anglia, and has a bell that has been in the same place since 1584. The interior was renovated in the 19th century, so lacks the historical resonance of some of Suffolk's churches, but its lead-covered tower is handsome. West of the church is the Deanery Tower, constructed in 1495 as an incredibly dramatic gatehouse to a new rectory that was never built. Behind the trees to the north you can spy Hadleigh Hall with its wonderfully decorative chimney stacks. On the south side, the Guildhall has been restored to its former medieval glory and is now home to the town council; rooms are also for hire for community-based events.

Duke Street leads to the 500-year-old Toppesfield Bridge over the River Brett – the oldest bridge in Suffolk still in use. For an enjoyable stroll, take the riverside path leading north through the narrow strip of woodland; the first path on the left takes you to Broom Hill, a small nature reserve (full of bluebells in spring) with a good view of the town and surrounding countryside. Several footpaths from here lead walkers on longer circular routes.

SUFFOLK

Angel Hotel. See p283.

Alternatively, there's a two-mile walk along the old railway line from Hadleigh to Raydon; signs on the former station building (now a private home) show the way. At the start of the path is a small wood known locally as the Fuzz, which is home to nightingales in early spring.

Nearby villages
The countryside around Hadleigh is very pretty, incredibly rural and sparsely populated. The single-lane roads are not kind to cars, and there are several marked cycle routes: South Suffolk Cycle Routes A1 and A2 both take in some gorgeous topography and rich architectural pickings.

Kersey ★, a couple of miles north-west of Hadleigh, is particularly lovely. If it were in Dorset, it would be overrun with olde tea shoppes, but in Suffolk, there's no fuss and no tourist car park – it's just another village. Ducks splash in the small ford in the middle of the village, and there are fine views from the hilltop churchyard at one end of the main street. The Bell pub (01473 823229) can provide a pint and a decent hot meal, and you can poke your nose in the charming Kersey Pottery & Gallery (01473 822092, www.kerseypottery.com, closed Mon), which exhibits and sells distinctive, brightly glazed stoneware.

Route A1 takes cyclists up a narrow lane that has an English Heritage site hidden just by its side. Look out for the small sign marking St James's Chapel. This simple thatched building was put up in the 13th century, used as a barn between the 16th century and about 1930, and is now a blissful place for quiet reflection.

A couple of miles north is Lindsey Tye, where the Lindsey Rose pub (see right) is a good place for a meal. On the other side of the A1141 is Chelsworth. The best time to visit is in June when the open gardens charity fête means lots of home-made produce to indulge in (visit www.chelsworth.co.uk for dates).

If you need provisions, Hollow Trees Farm Shop (01449 741247, www.hollowtrees.co.uk) in nearby Semer has the added appeal of a café and a farm

trail. Basic foodstuffs and newspapers are available at the community-run shop/post office in Monks Eleigh, next to the Swan Inn (see below).

Where to eat & drink
Post-war development means that Hadleigh is quite a sizeable town, but it has a surprising shortage of appealing places to eat and drink. Best by far is Crabtree's (66 High Street, 01473 828166), a licensed café in one of the town's most decorative buildings, although the Orangery tea shop in the Market Place does serve own-made cakes (01473 823600, closed Mon, Sun).

The Lindsey Rose pub (01449 741424, www.redroseinn.co.uk) in Lindsey Tye has been a drinking establishment for more than 500 years, and has recently become a reliable eaterie, selling local goodies such as Colchester oysters, venison salami and Cromer crab. It's the sister pub of the Bildeston Crown (see p267), but noticeably cheaper. Look for the resident alpacas in the rear beer garden.

Monks Eleigh's Swan Inn (The Street, 01449 741391. www.monkseleigh.com, closed Mon) also has a good reputation, serving local seasonal food and plenty of game in autumn. For an old-style boozer, head for the thatched Cock (01787 247371) at Brent Eleigh, where there's darts in the bar, and coal fires and casseroles in winter. The White Horse (Mill Green, 01787 211211, www.edwardstone whitehorse.co.uk) in Edwardstone is another traditional pub, but with various modern touches including a wind turbine to generate electricity. It serves simple, straightforward food, and beverages from its own microbrewery and cider press, as well as other Suffolk beers. There's a folk night every second Wednesday and a blues night every fourth Thursday, and you can even camp here in the summer months.

Where to stay

Grove Cottages ★
The Grove, Priory Green, Edwardstone, CO10 5PP (01787 211115, www.grove-cottages.co.uk). Rates £179-£438 for 2 nights.
There are six small renovated buildings – Gun Cottage, Snow Cottage, Rose Cottage, Orchard Cottage, Dons Barn and the Bakery – around the double quadrangle of Old Grove Farm. Each has been sympathetically converted into quirky accommodation that makes excellent use of the original space. All are lovely hideaways for a country retreat, especially for couples (most sleep only two). Guests can also hire canoes for a paddle down the Stour, make use of the bikes in the sheds or the herbs in the garden, and buy eggs and honey produced on site.

Milden Hall
Milden, CO10 9NY (01787 247235, www.thehall-milden.co.uk). Rates from £100 per person per weekend. No credit cards.
Self-catering groups of four to ten people can stay in the Cartlodge, but anyone looking for a space for a weekend

party should consider the amazing 95ft-long Tudor Barn, which sleeps 22. There's table tennis, table football, a dressing-up box and all the fun of the farm right outside the door. Guests who want a quiet night can opt for one of the three B&B rooms inside the hall itself (from £65 double).

Old Monkey
115 Benton Street, Hadleigh, IP7 5AR (01787 211115, www.grove-cottages.co.uk). Rates £202-£269 for 2 nights.
A cute one-bedroom bolthole on the edge of Hadleigh. There are books and games in the cosy living room, which you step into straight from the porch. Upstairs, the double bedroom has an unusual arched timbered ceiling.

Primrose Cottage
Church Hill, Kersey, IP7 6DZ (01787 211115, www.grove-cottages.co.uk). Rates £202-£269 for 2 nights.
Renovations to this 16th-century cottage in the middle of beautiful Kersey were finished in late 2009. There's a wood-burning stove in the sitting/dining room and all mod cons in the kitchen, while the courtyard outside is a suntrap on cloudless days. The lovely bedroom and bathroom are upstairs, but the low ceilings might challenge the very tall.

Wood Hall
Wood Hall, Little Waldingfield, CO10 0SY (01787 247362, www.thewoodhall.co.uk). Rates £85 double incl breakfast.
Georgian at the front, Tudor at the back, Wood Hall is a beautiful house with two guest rooms (one twin, one double). On sunny days, breakfast is served on the terrace in the walled garden.

LAVENHAM ★
Lavenham is a period drama producer's dream. It's the finest example of an unspoilt medieval town in England, funded entirely by Suffolk's wool and cloth trades, and then left unmodernised thanks to the lack of a significant subsequent industry to replace them (although, as with Long Melford, the town had several coconut-matting and horsehair factories in the Victorian era). These days, Lavenham calls itself a village, though there are more than 340 listed buildings in its streets. It has been much used as a set for TV and film productions (including *Lovejoy* and Stanley Kubrick's *Barry Lyndon*).

At first glance, it may look a little twee, and it's certainly always full of elderly visitors enjoying the sheer quaintness of the place, but the more time you spend in the village, the more the marvel of its survival creeps up on you. In the 16th century, Lavenham was richer than York, so it's no surprise the good burghers were able to fund a spectacular church. St Peter & St Paul is a fantastic example of the late Perpendicular style. Its 141-foot tower is one of Suffolk's tallest. Apparently, the intention was to build even higher but the architect fell off the tower at its present height and died, so it was thought unwise to provoke God's wrath by continuing. Visitors approach the church through unusually formal trimmed box bushes. Inside,

Great House

you'll find beautiful wooden ceilings, and carved wooden screens that are worth a closer look to appreciate their incredible intricacy. For the Millennium celebrations, 260 new kneelers were knitted to tell the history of the village, all framed by Lavenham blue wool. A small gift shop is located at the west end of the church.

The Guildhall – now a museum run by the National Trust (*see p272*) – is at the other end of the village, in the quiet Market Place. Nearby is Sparling & Faiers Bakery (whose bread and cakes people talk about for miles around) and Little Hall (01787 247019, www.littlehall.org.uk, open Apr-Oct), one of the oldest houses in Suffolk. But you don't have to visit a museum to experience Lavenham's unique architectural treasures. Look carefully, as you walk around, at the carvings on the buildings. Molet House on Barn Street is a fine example of a clothier's house, with a triple overhang, oriel windows and a typically wide doorway. De Vere House on Water Street is wonderfully higgledy-piggledy and named after the family who owned the house for hundreds of years; the boar and star carved around the front door are the family's heraldic symbols. Also on Water Street is Lavenham Priory (now run as an upmarket B&B; *see p283*), with intricate pargeting on its walls. Originally, all these oak-framed houses would have been open halls – only later were smaller living quarters carved out of the interior spaces.

Lavenham survives purely on tourism these days, but doesn't aim itself at the family market; this is not the place to entertain young children without being frowned at for disturbing the illusion of serenity. The chemist doesn't even sell nappies. Instead, there are plenty of gift shops and tearooms, antiques shops, art galleries and decorous hotel restaurants. To appreciate the beautiful landscape around Lavenham (among Suffolk's prettiest), you can hire bikes from the Greyhound pub (*see p283*, £10 half-day, £15 whole day) or just take one of the many footpaths that lead out of the village across meadows and past ponds.

SUFFOLK

Where to eat & drink

You can't walk far in Lavenham without tripping over a cream tea. The National Trust tearoom next to the Guildhall on the market square does a good one, but there are lots of independent cafés along the High Street too, such as Munnings (01787 249453, closed Tue) at no.29, with its lacy tablecloths, vintage chairs and nice china. Those with thicker wallets and the desire for a comfier chair should head to the Swan (*see right*), but beware the coach parties that descend late afternoon. Come the evening, Lavenham is full of well-heeled visitors looking for a good meal. Way ahead of the competition is the Great House (*see below*), but the Angel Hotel (*see below*) and the Swan are also deservedly popular. For a pubbier feel, head to the Greyhound (97 High Street, 01787 247475, www.greyhoundlavenham.co.uk), where classic pub dishes can be had for under a tenner.

Angel Hotel

Market Place, Lavenham, CO10 9QZ (01787 247388, www.maypolehotels.com). Open 11am-11pm Mon-Sat; noon-10.30pm Sun. Lunch served noon-2.15pm, dinner served 6.45-9.15pm daily.

This feels more like a gastropub than a hotel restaurant. The square bar takes up the middle of the room and around it sit scrubbed wooden tables of various shapes and sizes. Expect plenty of fish and meat on the menu, although there are vegetarian options on the daily specials board. There is a separate dining room out back, but the atmosphere in the bar is friendlier, and you get the views over Market Place. There are also eight pleasant bedrooms (£95-£105 double incl breakfast): six doubles, one twin and one family room.

Great House ★

Market Place, Lavenham, CO10 9QZ (01787 247431, www.greathouse.co.uk). Lunch served noon-2.30pm Wed-Sun. Dinner served 7-9.30pm Tue-Sat.

This is the sister restaurant of Maison Bleue (*see p287*) in Bury St Edmunds and Mariners (*see p224*) in Ipswich and every bit as good as both. The restaurant is in the two unfussily decorated rooms at the front of a Georgian-fronted house on Market Place and offers good-value set menus.

Run by Régis and Martine Crépy, the cooking style is French, but most of the ingredients are decidedly local, with game, fish and meat from nearby farms all appearing. Whatever you choose, this is one of the finest dining experiences you will have in Suffolk. Save room for the cheeseboard – although the puddings are also things of great beauty. The Great House was *Which?* magazine's East of England Restaurant of the Year 2009.

Swan

High Street, Lavenham, CO10 9QA (01787 247 477, www.theswanatlavenham.co.uk). Gallery Lunch served noon-2.30pm, dinner served 7-9pm daily. Garden Lounge Lunch served noon-2.30pm, bar snacks served 5.30-9.30pm daily. Old Bar Open noon-11pm daily.

Forged from a long line of clustered medieval houses, the Swan's interior is a bit of a labyrinth, despite being modernised relatively recently. Tourists indulge in three-tiered afternoon teas in the various cosy sitting areas, sinking into plush armchairs in front of fires that are regularly stoked in winter. The Gallery restaurant is a characterful double-height room with a mass of huge exposed timber beams, where the menu is Modern British and fairly expensive. If you want something simpler, head for the Garden Lounge, where light lunches and evening bar snacks are served.

Where to stay

The Great House (*see left*) calls itself a 'Restaurant with Rooms', but oh what rooms! All five are simply exquisite, with modern fabrics and imaginative, comfortable furnishings set off by centuries-old beams and the sheer character of the place. The fruit bowl and sherry decanter left in each room are a mark of the hotel's friendly welcome. A standard double costs a very reasonable £90-£110; breakfast is extra. The Swan (*see above*) also operates as an upmarket hotel, with 45 rooms (£170-£250 double incl breakfast) that include some extremely lavish suites with beautiful vaulted beamed ceilings, four-poster beds and little extras such as Molton Brown toiletries. The Angel Hotel (*see left*) also has accommodation.

Lavenham Priory

Water Street, Lavenham, CO10 9RW (01787 247404, www.lavenhampriory.co.uk). Rates £105-£170 double incl breakfast.

Accommodation in Lavenham is never cheap, and this B&B sets its rates high. But the six rooms are full of historic character and furnished with a decorative flounce you just wouldn't dare contemplate at home. Antique pieces, oak floorboards and exposed beams add to the atmosphere, and there's a lounge with a TV, books, an honesty bar and board games. In summer, the lovely gardens are an added bonus.

Pound Cottage

Lavenham (01787 211115, www.grove-cottages.co.uk). Rates £315-£438 for 2 nights.

This pink weavers' cottage sleeps four in two bright and airy bedrooms (one double, one twin). Downstairs, a log-burning stove keeps the place warm in winter, while a neat garden is a sheltered place to sit on summer evenings. The cottage has bikes for guests, so you can take advantage of the South Suffolk Cycle Route right on the doorstep.

Swan

Bury St Edmunds & Newmarket

This area of Suffolk isn't generally celebrated as one of the prettiest, and many of its towns were part of the post-war London Overspill plan. The landscape isn't strikingly flat like the Fens, but neither does it have the rolling countryside found further south along the Stour, or the heathland near the coast. It certainly isn't the most popular spot for holidaymakers. But Bury St Edmunds is a lovely market town, and the rest of the area has many attractions, including the open expanses of the Brecks, thoroughbred horse racing at Newmarket and plenty of pretty villages in between. There are pockets of interest and peaceful corners all around, if you know where to look.

BURY ST EDMUNDS ★

The bustling market town of Bury St Edmunds is one of Suffolk's largest urban centres. Founded around the Benedictine Abbey of Edmund (medieval England's patron saint) in the seventh century, it grew into quite a sizeable place during the industrial revolution. In the 19th century Bury made its money from textiles, but for many years sugar and beer have been the dominant industries, while its independent shops and market stalls attract shoppers from the surrounding countryside. It does pull in tourists, but not in large enough numbers to affect the day-to-day atmosphere. Charles Dickens described it as 'a handsome little town of thriving and cleanly appearance' in *The Pickwick Papers*, and not much has changed since then. It still conveys a strong sense of neatness and upright character, even when the market is in full swing.

If you're arriving by car, the best approach to Bury is from the 'sugar beet turn' off the A14 (this is the junction with the trunk road leading off to the A143/A134), so called because it takes cars past British Sugar's beet factory, where white smoke billows from the chimney and fills the air with the aroma of burnt treacle. It's not the prettiest way in, but it's easier to park.

Walk to the Butter Market on a Wednesday or Saturday and you'll find the liveliest and largest market for miles around, with numerous fruit and vegetable stalls, and others selling bread, fish, meat, clothes, sweets and miscellaneous goods. Nearby is Moyse's Hall Museum (*see p294*), which houses one of Bury's grimmest relics. Bury St Edmunds Art Gallery (01284 762081, www.burystedmundsartgallery.org, closed Mon, Sun) inside the Robert Adam Market Cross building (the entrance is between Cornhill and the Traverse) used to charge admission, but gets many more visitors now that entry is free. It presents changing contemporary art and craft exhibitions and has a good shop selling pottery, prints, jewellery and other bits and bobs, and an 'art lounge' with books for reading and art materials for children.

Plenty of other cultural activities are on offer. There are two cinemas: the Cineworld multiplex (0871 200 2000, www.cineworld.co.uk) on Parkway, and the two-screen Hollywood Film Theatre (01284 762586, www.hollywoodcinemas. net) on Hatter Street. The beautiful, Grade I-listed Theatre Royal (*see p288*), the only surviving Regency theatre in the country, is on Westgate Street. And the well-regarded Fat Cat Comedy Club (01284 754252, www.fatcatcomedyclub.com) attracts acts from the London circuit and abroad to the imposing Corn Exchange building every second Sunday of the month.

Heading south from the market square, Bury is absolutely delightful. Georgian façades give way to glimpses of unadorned medieval buildings, and the side streets are full of architectural curiosities. Fans of architect Sir John Soane will want to look at the house he designed at 81 Guildhall Street; it's owned by a firm of solicitors, so not open to the public, but you can admire the frontage.

From Abbeygate Street, you can look straight across the water meadows either side of the River Lark. These meadows are to be thanked for preventing modern development on this side of town. At the bottom of the street stands a huge 14th-century stone gatehouse, leading to the ruins of what was one of the largest and wealthiest Benedictine monasteries in Europe. (The town's motto, 'Shrine of a king, cradle of the law', is a reference to the oath sworn in the abbey by the barons who forced 'Bad' King John to sign the Magna Carta.) The flint ruins, now owned by English Heritage, compete for attention with garish flower beds in the Abbey Gardens. Audio-guides are available next door at the Tourist Information Centre (6 Angel Hill, 01284 764667, www.burystedmundstourism.co.uk, closed Sun Oct-Easter).

Bury St Edmunds Art Gallery. See p285.

Teenagers, tourists and families flock to the gardens for picnics on sunny days, and there's a playground, aviary and tennis courts too. A small hatch surrounded with picnic tables by the aviary serves coffee, tea and ice-cream; for more substantial snacks, head to the Refectory (01284 748738, closed Sun) on the other side of the wall next to the entrance of the cathedral; it's reminiscent of a National Trust café in both ambience and food.

St Edmundsbury Cathedral (01284 748720, www.stedscathedral.co.uk) – the only cathedral in Suffolk – is of moderate size. Although construction started in 1503, it wasn't completely finished until 2005, when a millennium initiative finally raised the money to build a new 150-foot gothic lantern tower. The tower (plus the new East Cloisters and Chapel of Transfiguration) is a comforting reminder that there are still masons with the skills to fashion such delicate stonework. Inside, the cathedral has a decorative painted ceiling, a very ornately carved and painted font, and lots of Victorian stained glass, depicting scenes from the Old and New Testaments. Look for the striking *Crucifixion* by world-famous sculptor Elisabeth Frink, who was born in Suffolk.

But the cathedral isn't the only interesting place of worship in the town. St Mary's, around the corner on Honey Hill, is a very grand parish church that was also once part of the abbey. The very fine medieval ceiling in the chantry is embedded with tiny mirrors, acting like enchanting stars. Mary Rose Tudor, sister of Henry VIII, is interred here, her tomb marked by a monument in the floor.

Shopping

Traditionally, Bury's many independent clothes and shoe shops have flourished in harmony alongside its chainstores. But the opening of the new ARC shopping centre in 2009 between the multistorey car park and the market square might change the shopping landscape in the old part of town. It's not that the centre is badly done – the timber-clad, Scandinavian-style units are quite tasteful, and at least it isn't covered over – but the arrival of so many popular global brands in the town centre can't help but have an impact on existing shops. Go while you can still experience the old Bury.

On St John's Street, St Andrews Bookshop (01284 769517, www.standrewsbookshop.co.uk, closed Sun) is worth a browse, as is furniture and gift shop Anything (01284 705027, www.anything burystedmunds.co.uk) and the various other independents along the street. There are several upmarket boutiques, including Anna (7 Guildhall Street, 01284 706944, www.shopatanna.com, closed Sun), which sells designer women's fashion. Cavern 4 (4 Whiting Street, 01284 700009, www.workwisesuffolk.org.uk, closed Sun) is a very unusual charity shop. It's run by Workwise, who teach skills to people who have suffered mental illness. The shop sells furniture, lamps, glasswork, pottery, textiles and accessories made by trainees; a gallery downstairs shows work by local artists. Wibbling Wools (Angel Hill, 01284 749555, www.wibblingwools.co.uk, closed Sun) has a lovely selection of hand-dyed yarns, other wools and buttons. Two rooms upstairs are used for knitting and crochet workshops, with more informal knit-and-natter mornings on Thursdays.

Where to eat & drink

Bury St Edmunds is the home of Greene King – the brewery (*see p294*) is open for tours – so you're guaranteed a good pint. The Nutshell (17 The Traverse, 01284 764867) is probably the most famous pub because of its diminutive size – at 15 by 7 feet, it's the smallest in England. Look out for the mummified cat hanging above the bar. The old-style Rose & Crown (48 Whiting Street, 01284 755934) serves good own-cooked food, and has games such as dominoes, darts and cards. The Dog & Partridge (29 Crown Street, 01284 764792) is a decent eating pub that's within barrel-rolling distance of the brewery, while gastropub fare is available at the stylish Fox Inn (*see p289*).

Bailey's
5 Whiting Street, IP33 1NX (01284 706198).
Food served 9am-4pm Mon-Sat.
Most tourists head for Harriet's Tea Room on Cornhill, but it's pricey and the staff are mainly bored teenagers trussed up in antiquated costumes. Bailey's is where locals come for a great selection of cakes and chirpy service. The building isn't as impressive, but it's quieter and more pleasant inside.

Maison Bleue ★
31 Churchgate Street, IP33 1RG (01284 760623, www.maisonbleue.co.uk). Lunch served noon-2pm, dinner served 7-9.30pm Tue-Sat.

A recent redesign (neutral colours, blond leather armchairs and banquettes) has given Maison Bleue a cooler and more streamlined look, but the food and service remain as friendly and full of love as ever. Martine and Régis Crépy have run this acclaimed French restaurant – as well as sister establishments the Great House in Lavenham (*see p283*) and Mariners in Ipswich (*see p224*) – for many years and retain the knowledgeable staff that make such a difference to a dining experience. The *Good Food Guide* rated it East of England's Restaurant of the Year 2010. The menu focuses on fish and shellfish, although there are always a couple of meat dishes. Puddings are excellent; the cheeseboard superb.

Old Cannon Brewery ★
86 Cannon Street, IP33 1JR (01284 768769, www.old cannonbrewery.co.uk). Open noon-3pm, 5-11pm Mon-Fri; noon-11pm Sat; noon-10.30pm Sun. Lunch served noon-2pm Tue-Sat; noon-3pm Sun. Dinner served 6-9.30pm Tue-Sat.
Half of this microbrewery's pub is for drinkers sampling the beers from the large shiny brewing vessels visible in the bar – try Old Cannon Best Bitter, the stronger Gunner's Daughter or various seasonal ales. The other half is given over to diners. The kitchen uses Old Cannon's own brews wherever possible in their recipes, so expect beef and ale pie, beer-battered fish and a range of beery sausages too. There's outdoor seating in the cobbled rear courtyard for warmer days. There are also five smart en suite double/twin rooms in the former brewhouse; B&B costs £85.

Race horses, Newmarket. See p291.

Things to do

BURY ST EDMUNDS

Theatre Royal ★
Westgate Street, IP33 1QR (01284 769505, www.theatreroyal.org). Box office 10am-6pm Mon-Sat. Guided tours 2pm Tue, Thur; 11am Sat, Sun. Open Doors 2-4pm Tue, Thur; 10.30am-1pm Sat, Sun. Tours £6. Open Doors £1.50.

Norwich-born architect William Wilkins, famous for designing London's National Gallery, was the man behind this elegant and gorgeous theatre, drawn up on strict classical lines. Built in 1819, it's the only surviving example of a Regency playhouse; *Charley's Aunt* premiered here in 1892. Under the stewardship of the National Trust, it underwent major renovation (nearly half the money came from enthusiastic locals), reopening in 2007. As well as theatrical productions (everything from panto to Shakespeare), there are lunchtime lectures, readings and concerts, which can be combined with a simple but excellent lunch at the Greene Room Café (the french onion soup is the best we've tasted this side of the Channel). History and theatre fans will enjoy the entertaining guided tours or just wandering around on their own on Open Doors days.

SOUTH OF THE A14

Barrow Hall Stables
Church Road, Barrow, IP29 5AX (01284 811995, www.barrowhallstables.co.uk). Open 9am-1pm, 2-8pm Tue-Thur; 9am-1pm, 2-7pm Fri; 9am-1pm, 2-5pm Sat, Sun. Rates Private lesson £31 45mins. Group hack £24 1hr.

The owners used to run stables in Culford, near West Stow, but relocated to this site a few years ago. They offer private and small group lessons in two covered riding arenas, and hacks through the surrounding countryside – check the website for the full range of options. For the more experienced rider, there's a cross-country course and a canter track.

THE BRECKS

Bike-Art
High Lodge Forest Centre, Thetford Forest, IP27 0AF (01842 810090, www.bike-art.com). Open Apr-Oct 9am-5pm Mon-Fri; 9am-6pm Sat, Sun. Nov-Mar 9am-4pm Mon-Fri; 9am-5pm Sat, Sun. Rates £7 1hr, £26 all day.

If you haven't brought your own bike, you can hire one here. Helpful staff will kit you out with whatever configuration of pedal power you'll need, including child seats and tagalongs. Then, armed with a map of the four trails – coded green, blue, red or black in terms of difficulty, like ski runs, and ranging from three to 11 miles long – you can head off into the forest.

Forest Park Riding & Livery
The Limes Avenue, Santon Downham Road, IP27 0TF (01842 815517, 07876 237946, www.forestpark-riding.i12.com). Open 8am-5pm Tue-Sun. Rates Private lesson £17 30mins. Private hack £18 1hr. No credit cards.

This riding school on the edge of Thetford Forest welcomes riders of all abilities over the age of five for private and group lessons or hacks on beautiful forest trails. Booking is essential. If you want to take your own horse on holiday, head for Little Lodge Farm (01842 813438, www.littlelodgefarm.co.uk) in Santon Downham, which has livery yard facilities, a two-mile cross-country course and access to the many bridlepaths in the forest.

Bike-Art. See p297.

Bedford Lodge Hotel. See p292.

Where to stay

The Old Cannon Brewery (*see p287*) has B&B accommodation, with free parking.

Angel Hotel

3 Angel Hill, IP33 1LT (01284 714000, www.theangel. co.uk). Rates £100-£160 double incl breakfast.

The beautiful Georgian façade of this old coaching inn faces the abbey gatehouse on picturesque Angel Hill. When Charles Dickens visited Bury, this is where he stayed, giving talks at the nearby Athenaeum (now used for private functions). If you want celebrity credentials and Dickens isn't enough, Angelina Jolie made this her base when she visited the town. The 75 bedrooms vary in style from traditional to modern; the 'prestige' rooms have more character than you'd expect from a hotel of this size. The restaurant serves food all day, including a good-value set lunch and popular afternoon teas. The sister hotel to the Angel is the Salthouse Harbour Hotel (*see p224*) next to the Marina in Ipswich.

Fox Inn

1 Eastgate Street, IP33 1XX (01284 705562, www.thefoxinnbury.co.uk). Rates £90-£95 double incl breakfast.

One of the oldest pubs in town, the Fox Inn overlooks the Abbey Gardens and St Mary's Church. In 2008, six large bedrooms were opened in the converted barn behind the pub. Much of the furniture and fittings has been made by local craftsmen and the look is an enticing mix of rustic (exposed beams, bare brick walls) and chic (chandeliers and designer wallpaper). If you're staying, breakfast is served until 11am. The restaurant makes much use of local produce – all meat comes from East Anglia, for example – and is a firm favourite with locals.

Ounce House

Northgate Street, IP33 1HP (01284 761779, www.ouncehouse.co.uk). Rates £120-£135 double incl breakfast.

A friendly B&B in a large Victorian house. The five spacious bedrooms at the Ounce House are decorated with old-fashioned chintzy elegance, and guests can make use of the drawing room and library downstairs, where there's also an honesty bar. Breakfast is served around a large table in the handsome dining room, which is stuffed with antique furniture.

NEWMARKET

Famous for being the home of the sport of kings, where monarchs kept their mistresses and avoided their responsibilities at court, Newmarket is a town of two halves. There's the town itself, and then there's everything to do with horse racing – including 5,000 thoroughbred horses, 75 trainers, 52 stud farms and two racecourses. The racing industry also gives a strong identity to nearby villages, especially those to the south, where pristine hedges, close-trimmed verges and neat-as-a-new-pin fences mark stud territory. The ruler of Dubai, Sheikh Mohammed, owns much of this land, so there's plenty of money around, although locals sometimes complain about the homogeneity of the buildings used to house stud staff. Sheikh Mohammed extended his portfolio in 2009 by purchasing Dalham Hall, a stunning red-brick house in an idyllic location in the area's prettiest village; residents hope the surrounding fields won't get swallowed up for studland as they have around Woodditton.

Dalham. See p292.

SUFFOLK

Horse racing ★

It's said that the first horse race took place here in the 12th century; nowadays, Newmarket's two racecourses (0844 579 3010, www.newmarketrace courses.co.uk) lie at the western edge of town. There's the July Course, the smaller and prettier of the two, used in summer; and the Rowley Mile for spring and autumn meets. Racing is a fun day out, a chance to dress up (jeans, T-shirts and trainers are frowned on) and have a flutter. It's also an opportunity to see the world's best thoroughbreds in action. Before each race, the horses are led around the parade ring, where race-goers can view them at close quarters.

Whether it's a race day or not, you can see the horses for free on Newmarket Heath, a chalky ridge to the east of the town between Bury Road and Moulton Road. This is the Gallops, and it's where the horses get their exercise every morning from 6.30am to 10am. Drivers beware... horses have the right of way in this town, and riders expect to walk on to roads without checking for traffic.

To learn about the history of the sport, visit the National Horseracing Museum (see p294). Tattersalls (125 High Street, 01638 665931, www.tattersalls.com), the oldest bloodstock auctioneers in the world, founded in 1766, and Europe's largest, is another experience worth seeking out. Nine annual auctions held at Park Paddocks in the centre of town offer a glimpse of a rarefied world with a strong identity and rigid codes of practice. Observers get in for free. And if you want a look at the world of horse breeding, the National Stud (see p294) runs guided tours.

The town centre

Newmarket should really be in Cambridgeshire – the county border is drawn around the town like a tight noose, with a small strip of land connecting it to the rest of Suffolk to the east. Cambridgeshire paints its rural roads with white lines, Suffolk doesn't, so travellers will notice the road markings changing frequently as the border weaves back and forth. A similar muddle is evident in the town itself, which has suffered from disjointed town planning for decades. From the 1970s Rookery development (now called the Guineas) to the 1980s multistorey car park and desultory arcade of shops, there seems to have been little focus on architectural style or holistic urban planning.

The High Street is full of pretty buildings, with a distinctive clocktower at the eastern end, but it isn't as bustling as it used to be. An out-of-town Tesco was the first blow to various family businesses, but the last straw was Waitrose moving off the High Street a few years ago; it's now difficult to access on foot and most people drive there.

The market is held on Tuesdays and Saturdays, although its site has been threatened numerous times in recent years. At least the famous 'Newmarket sausage' is not an endangered species; it's still sold by two rival family butchers, Powters (see p246) and Musk's, who guard their secret recipes fiercely.

FIVE SUFFOLK APPLE JUICES

Orchards used to be a bigger part of the Suffolk landscape. Many have been grubbed up in the last few decades, but there are still plenty of small-scale apple juice producers in the county.

Aspall
The Cyder House, Aspall Farm, Debenham, IP14 6PD (01728 860510, www.aspall.co.uk).
The Chevallier family has been producing cider for eight generations. Cider and vinegar are what most people tend to associate with the Aspall brand, but the company also produces premium apple juice using a base of cox and bramley and adding top notes with English varieties such as discovery, russet, crispin and worcester pearmain.

High House Fruit Farm
Sudbourne, Woodbridge IP12 2BL (01394 450450, www.high-house.co.uk). Open Farm shop 9am-6pm daily.
The simple, homemade-looking label belies the quality of this cloudy juice. The russet tastes very distinctively of the fruit; in fact, it's a much nicer way to enjoy this particular variety than biting into its rather clothy flesh. High House's other juices are a cox and bramley mix, and two single varieties, discovery and james grieve.

James White
White's Fruit Farm, Helmingham Road, Ashbocking, IP6 9JS (01473 890111, www.jameswhite.co.uk). Open Farm shop 9am-5pm daily.
Probably the best-known brand of Suffolk apple juice after Copella, James White makes three single-variety apple juices: bramley, cox and russet. We prefer the bramley because it has a lovely tart edge to it. There are also mixed juices, where cinnamon, elderflower or raspberries and blackberries are added to apple juice.

Suffolk Apple Juice & Cider Place
Cherry Tree Farm, Ilketshall St Lawrence, NR34 8LB (01986 781353). Open 9am-1pm, 2-5pm Mon-Fri.
The laxton, a medium-sweet apple juice, has a cidery aroma, but lacks the depth of sour and sweet tones that usually characterise top-end juice. A pity, as we've enjoyed other juices from this producer in the past. Perhaps try another variety... there are plenty to choose from.

Suffolk Apple Juice
Moat Farm, Church Lane, Kenton, IP14 6JH (01728 861227).
The ingredients are fresh apple juice and vitamin C. That's it. The charles ross variety is fruity, slightly cloudy and delicious, especially when served cold. The farm's stall operates on an honesty box basis.

SUFFOLK

For a touch of grandeur, visit the tourist information centre on Palace Street (01638 667200, www.visitforestheath.co.uk, closed Sun), which is housed in the remnant of Charles II's impressive 17th-century palace.

For a decent walk, head to Newmarket Heath to the east or Devil's Dyke to the west. The latter is an Anglo-Saxon earthwork built to keep neighbouring Mercia from attacking. A footpath runs along the top of the ridge, providing beautiful views of the surrounding countryside. Start in Woodditton village, where it's easy to park, and walk north.

Where to eat & drink

For a town that attracts so much wealth, Newmarket is curiously bereft of decent places to eat. Most people seem to end up meeting at the soulless café inside Waitrose, although you can get a decent brew, freshly made sandwiches and own-baked cakes in Coffee & Co (Palace Street, 01638 611000, www.coffeeandco.info). There's one place that everyone agrees is great, and that's the Bedford Lodge Hotel (*see below*); otherwise, discerning diners head to pubs in the surrounding villages.

Bedford Lodge Hotel ★

Bury Road, CB8 7BX (01638 663175, www.bedford lodgehotel.co.uk). Breakfast served 7-10am Mon-Sat; 8-10am Sun. Lunch served noon-2pm Mon-Fri, Sun. Dinner served 7-9.30pm Mon-Sat; 7-9pm Sun.
A former country house with its own grounds, set in a wonderful location backing on to Newmarket Heath. The Orangery restaurant offers fine dining in a sumptuous, high-ceilinged room with linen tablecloths and chandeliers. In summer, afternoon tea is served on the terrace overlooking the beautiful gardens. The top-notch rooms and suites (55 in total) are decorated in anonymous but sleek and comfortable international hotel style. The Bedford Lodge also boasts an indoor pool and a gym, plus a sauna and some steam rooms.

Where to stay

Luxurious accommodation is also available at the upmarket Bedford Lodge Hotel (*see above*) on the edge of Newmarket.

Garrads Boutique Accommodation

38-40 Old Station Road, CB8 8DN (01638 662323, www.garradsaccommodation.com). Rates £99-£120 double incl breakfast.
Minimalist chic right in the centre of town, and well placed for a morning spent watching horses on the Gallops. The front of the building looks a little unprepossessing, but inside, it's a gem, with nine stylish rooms and a smart dining room for lavish breakfasts. There's also a self-contained Coach House Mews in the garden, with two double bedrooms, living room and kitchen.

Jockey Club Rooms

101 High Street, CB8 8JL (01638 663101, www.jockeyclubestates.co.uk). Rates £160-£195 double incl breakfast.

Clay & chalk

Suffolk's landscape is not classically dramatic – but that's not to say it's without its dramas. Just ask anyone who lives in the most easterly portion of the county, the bit that meets the sea. Is there a more awesome spectacle than a coastal storm brewing along this most vulnerable of shorelines? You don't want to be in an exposed position on this strip of heathland when a big one hits: there's barely a mile of Suffolk shore that isn't vulnerable to the full weight of a North Sea tempest. This is why the coastline is eroding so rapidly – the weight of the North Sea set against a friable geology composed of soft, permeable sands and clays. Let the once-great port of Dunwich bear witness to the effects of erosion.

But there is another, far larger part of Suffolk that is composed of rather more durable stuff than Eocene sand and clay. It's the section of the county that's connected, geologically, to the Downs of Sussex and the little hills of Dorset, and which makes a firm barrier between the sandy coastline and the inland fens of Cambridgeshire. The north-eastern extremity of the Southern England Chalk Formation, it constitutes the westerly bulk of Suffolk. The county's famously intimate rolling hills are made of cretaceous chalk – and they aren't going anywhere.

For those who like their accommodation steeped in history, the Jockey Club Rooms offer olde worlde chintzy comfort in 20 bedrooms in the Jockey Club's 18th-century power base on the High Street. Guests can make use of the lovely garden.

SOUTH OF THE A14

There are some very pretty villages to the east of Newmarket. Large and thriving Moulton has a welcoming swathe of green at its centre – a patchwork of paddocks, sheep fields and common land. Along its eastern edge flows the lazy River Kennett, crossed by four bridges. The most impressive is the four-arched, late medieval Packhorse Bridge (maintained by English Heritage), which stands at the corner of the road to Gazeley. There's also a revitalised village shop with outdoor tables where customers can enjoy coffee, tea, made-to-order sandwiches and cakes. A well-trodden circular walk, mainly on footpaths and beautiful at any time of year, runs through Moulton, Dalham and Gazeley; start at Moulton church and follow signs along the river towards Dalham.

Dalham ★ has a quietly serene beauty. Because the village was controlled by Dalham Hall Estate for so long, there's very little 20th-century development. It lost its shop a few years back, but there's still a popular pub, the Affleck Arms (*see p294*). Attractive thatched cottages sit beside the river, and the footpath to St Mary's Church through an avenue of chestnut trees evokes a keen sense of history. Sitting on a ridge with spectacular views, this lovely flint church is usually open and is a perfect place for quiet contemplation.

Walkers are no longer allowed along the path in front of Dalham Hall, although many are too curious not to scoot across the unfenced boundary to take a peek. Colonial adventurer Cecil Rhodes bought the estate at the turn of the 20th century, but never moved in. The Philipps family, who lived there for many decades, recently sold the place to Sheikh Mohammed, the ruler of Dubai and a major player in the horse racing world in Newmarket; by all accounts the Philipps family will continue to live in the 18th-century mansion. A circular walk takes ramblers through Brick Kiln Wood, where you can see clusters of bluebells in springtime, past the Lawns and on to the ancient Icknield Way Path (www.icknieldwaypath.co.uk) towards Gazeley. The walk heads through a housing estate, into Gazeley churchyard and back down the hill to Moulton. There's a stile just before you descend through the woods to St Peter's Church, from where, on a clear day, you can see Ely Cathedral looking every inch its nickname, 'the Ship of the Fens'.

Three miles south of Dalham, Lidgate is pretty as a picture, full of characterful houses that date from medieval times. If you walk past Bailey Pond to St Mary's Church, you'll see the remains of the motte and bailey of a long demolished castle. The Star Inn (*see p294*) is a great spot for a pint and, unusually, classy Spanish food.

This is great cycling country. It's relatively flat and the lack of main roads means there's no through traffic. Away from the B-roads, the smaller lanes are too narrow and winding for cars to get up speed, which means cyclists (and walkers) are largely undisturbed to enjoy the views of gentle rolling fields, ancient woods and pathways.

The villages of Great Bradley and Great Thurlow, on the B1061, are full of mature trees, small greens and cute houses. The River Stour runs through both villages and on to Great Wratting, where legend has it Boudicca defeated the ninth legion of the Roman army on Red Field just behind the high street. The Icknield Way Path runs by the river. The village also offers a good lunch spot in the Adnams-run Red Lion (01440 783237). The unusual arch by the front door is actually a whale's jawbone.

Haverhill

Haverhill is one of the area's largest towns, but there's not much here for tourists seeking pastoral beauty. The High Street is full of post-modern infill, and what's left of the old town is surrounded by post-war housing and industrial estates built to cater for some of East Anglia's London Overspill quota. The accents are more Estuary English than Old Suffolk. That said, despite the discernable poverty, the town centre has undergone a significant facelift in recent years. The pedestrianised area around St Mary's Church is an improvement, and Haverhill Arts Centre (01440 714140, www.haverhillarts centre.co.uk) in the old town hall on the High Street has been running a programme of music, theatre, comedy, children's shows and independent cinema since the 1990s.

Affleck Arms. See p294.

Places to visit

BURY ST EDMUNDS

Greene King Brewery ★
Visitor Centre, Westgate Street, IP33 1QT (01284 714297, www.greeneking.co.uk). Open Visitor centre & shop 10.30am-4.30pm Mon-Fri; 10.15am-4.30pm Sat. Tours 11am Mon; 2pm Tue; 11am, 2pm Wed-Fri; 11am, 12.30pm, 2pm, 7pm Sat; 11.30am, 7pm Sun. Admission Visitor centre & shop free. Tours £8 daytime; £10 evening.
Founded in 1799, Greene King is an East Anglian success story. It's been making beer on this site for more than two centuries, and still uses water drawn from chalk beds 200ft beneath the city. You can pop into the visitor centre and shop opposite the Theatre Royal, or join a guided tour. These last an hour and a half to two hours and take visitors around the brewhouse and up to the roof for a fantastic view of Bury before – the best bit – the tasting session. A museum contains brewing facts and some history about the life of monks at the neighbouring abbey (they were allowed eight pints of beer a day, 12 if they were ill). Real Beer & Food evenings (£25 per person) add a three-course meal to the tour and tasting.

Moyse's Hall Museum
Cornhill, IP33 1DX (01284 757160, www.st edmundsbury.gov.uk). Open 10am-4pm daily. Admission £3; £2 reductions; £9 family.
At the centre of town is Moyse's Hall, which dates from 1180, and claims to be the oldest surviving residential house in England. There has been a museum of local history here since 1899 and the collection includes some fantastically eccentric exhibits. The relics from the infamous 19th-century Red Barn murder include a book about the trial of murderer William Corder, bound in the man's own skin. Also look out for the fiddle made from a horse's skull, an 1871 dolls' house and several mummified cats (often built into the fabric of a building in Suffolk for good luck).

NEWMARKET

National Horseracing Museum ★
99 High Street, Newmarket, CB8 8JH (01638 667333, www.nhrm.co.uk). Open Mar-Oct 11am-4.30pm daily. Admission £6; £3-£5 reductions; £13 family.
The history of horse racing in Newmarket is really a history of the town itself, since that's how it came into being. Exhibitions chart the characters, horses, races and scandals that have made the place what it is today. Children love the Practical Gallery, where ex-jockeys and trainers are on hand to demonstrate horsey skills such as tacking up for a race and riding a thoroughbred (on a simulator, not a real horse). The museum also mounts temporary exhibitions and runs tours to stables and studs throughout the year. Coffee, light lunches and afternoon tea are available in the café.

National Stud ★
Next to July Course, CB8 0XE (01638 663464, www.nationalstud.co.uk). Tours Feb-Sept 11.15am, 2pm. Oct 11.15am. Admission £7; £5 reductions; £20 family.
Most studs are fiercely private and will eject anyone found walking on their territory – this kind of horseflesh ain't cheap. So if you want to see multi-million-pound horses nibbling in lush paddocks, take a guided tour at the National Stud. Once owned by the government, it became part of the Jockey Club in 2008. Visitors are taken by minibus to the paddocks, stables and covering yard. You can pet the foals, admire the stallions and gasp at the sums of money involved. The café (open to all, not just those on a tour) offers excellent cream teas and own-made cakes.

SOUTH OF THE A14

Ickworth House, Park & Gardens ★
The Rotunda, Horringer, IP29 5QE (01284 735270, www.nationaltrust.org.uk/ickworth). Open House Mar-Oct 11am-5pm Mon, Tue, Fri-Sun. Park 8am-8pm daily.

Where to eat & drink

The King's Head pub (no phone) in Moulton looked doomed, until a local family stepped in; they're trying to win custom with fish and chips on Friday nights, a more varied menu on Saturday nights and roasts on Sundays. The Affleck Arms (01638 500306) in Dalham is a lovely place for a drink by the riverside in summer and by the fireside in winter. The beer's good (it's a freehouse), but the food isn't up to scratch.

Bush
The Street, Shimpling, IP29 4HU (01284 828257, www.thebushshimpling.co.uk). Open 5.30-11pm Mon; noon-3pm, 5.30-11pm Tue-Sat; noon-3pm, 7-11pm Sun. Lunch served noon-2pm Tue-Sun. Dinner served 5.30-9.15pm Mon-Sat; 7-9.15pm Sun.
The Bush's low-ceilinged bar serves a range of cask ales and has a roaring fire in winter. The large garden is a bonus, with something special for children in the summer (usually a bouncy castle), and the neat dining room serves traditional pub grub at reasonable prices.

Plough Inn
Brockley Green, CO10 8DT (01440 786789, www.the ploughhundon.co.uk). Open noon-2.30pm, 6-11.30pm Mon-Sat; noon-4pm Sun. Lunch served noon-2.30pm Mon-Sat; noon-4pm Sun. Dinner served 6-9pm Mon-Sat.
A few miles east of Haverhill, the Plough is a good destination all year round with its neat, open-plan bar area and large garden with a terrace. At lunch, expect sandwiches, deli boards and a few hot dishes. In the evenings the food gets more varied, with pub classics plus a few surprises on the menu. Adnams beer and various guest ales are served, and a beer festival takes place every April and September. There are also eight en suite rooms (£85 double incl breakfast).

Star Inn ★
The Street, Lidgate, CB8 9PP (01638 500275). Open noon-3pm, 6pm-midnight Tue-Sun. Lunch served noon-2.30pm Tue-Sun. Dinner served 7-10pm Tue-Sat.
Chef/proprietor Maria Theresa Axon comes from Catalonia, so the blackboard menu at this popular pub is full of authentic specialities from the region, along with more

Gardens Jan-Mar, Nov, Dec 11am-4pm daily. Apr-Oct 10am-5pm daily. Admission House, Park & Garden £7.90; £3.15 reductions; £18.90 family. Garden & Park only £4; £1 reductions; £9 family.

The beautiful Italianate Rotunda that stars in all pictures of Ickworth was never actually lived in. Designed by the 4th Earl of Bristol, it wasn't finished when he died in 1803, and his son thought the 30ft ceilings unsuitable for a family home, so added the East Wing (now a family-friendly boutique hotel – see p295) and the Rotunda became an incredibly elaborate guest suite. When the house was made over to the National Trust in lieu of death duties in 1956, much of the contents remained, so there are still paintings and furniture here that were designed specifically for this unusual space. The Italian-style gardens behind the house feature tall cypresses, clipped yews and formal lawns, and there's a wonderful view of the surrounding park from the raised walkway around the perimeter. The park itself is beautiful, with footpaths and cycle trails winding by the River Linnet, past idyllic thatched cottages and between fields of sheep. There's a full programme of events throughout the year (with imaginative activities for children in the school holidays) and the vineyard (01284 723399, www.ickworthvineyard.co.uk) near the walled garden runs tours and tastings by appointment.

THE BRECKS

Euston Hall
Thetford Road, Euston, IP24 2QP (01842 766366, www.eustonhall.co.uk). Open Mid June-mid Sept 2.30-5pm Thur & occasional Sun. Admission House & Garden £7; £3-£6 reductions. Garden £3. No credit cards.
Located a few miles south of Thetford, the family seat of the Dukes of Grafton is a Georgian red-brick house with an impressive art collection (including works by Sir Anthony Van Dyck and George Stubbs) and beautiful gardens that include a restored watermill. There's a gift shop and a tearoom that is run by villagers from nearby Fakenham Magna to raise funds for the local church. Note that opening hours are very limited.

Lackford Lakes
Off A1101, Lackford, IP28 6HX (01284 728706, www.suffolkwildlife.co.uk). Open Visitor centre Apr-Nov 10am-5pm Wed-Sun. Oct-Mar 10am-4pm Wed-Sun. Reserve dawn-dusk daily. Admission free.
Birdwatchers of all persuasions, from the most casual to the most avid, will enjoy the peace of Lackford Lakes. Created from former gravel pits by the Suffolk Wildlife Trust, the site has a series of bird hides from which to observe the lakes unseen. Rare species such as the black-necked grebe have been spotted here, as well as ospreys, sparrowhawks and plenty of wildfowl. It's also one of the best places in Suffolk to see a kingfisher. The visitor centre offers light refreshments, a viewing gallery and an education room that on our last visit was laid out with art materials for children.

West Stow Anglo-Saxon Village ★
Icklingham Road, West Stow, IP28 6HG (01284 728718, www.weststow.org). Open Summer 10am-4pm daily. Winter 10am-3.30pm daily. Admission £5; £4 reductions; £15 family.
This reconstructed Anglo-Saxon village features a weaver's house, a workshop, a hall, a clay weathering pit and several other buildings. Pop into the museum to see a short film about the history of the site, and view various artefacts that are a reminder of how little life has changed between the fifth century and now – the tweezers, needles, pots, knives, crockery and jewellery perform the same functions they always have. The farm area shows how animals were kept and crops tended. On special event days, volunteers dress up for re-enactments or teach visitors how to make ink, use a foot-pedal lathe, write, cook and weave the Anglo-Saxon way. There's a café, and a shop selling replica glassware and jewellery. Beyond the visitor centre is West Stow Country Park, a heathland nature reserve with walks, nature trails and two birdwatching hides.

Where to stay

Brighthouse Farm Campsite
Melford Road, Lawshall, IP29 4PX (01284 830385, www.brighthousefarm.fsnet.co.uk). Rates Camping £8-£14 for 2 people. Rooms £55-£75 double incl breakfast. No credit cards.
A secluded campsite in quiet countryside. The site is flat, well kept and you can pitch where you like (always a bonus). Basic facilities include showers, a small kitchen and a fridge. Useful footpaths lead from the site to a child- and dog-friendly pub, and a small playground. Three B&B rooms (£55-£75 double) are also available inside the farmhouse – handy for grandparents who are beyond sleeping in a tent.

Ickworth Hotel & Apartments ★
Horringer, IP29 5QE (01284 735350, www.ickworthhotel.co.uk). Rates £200-£425 double incl breakfast.
Ickworth Hotel occupies the East Wing of Ickworth House (see p294), the seat of the Hervey family for several generations but now run by the National Trust. The hotel is grand but cosy, and the location is tremendous, right in

traditional English dishes. You could try scallops santiago followed by paella, then finish with apple pie. Axon has carefully retained the atmosphere of a proper village pub – the bar billiards table and dartboard have been in residence for decades, and the Greene King beer is well looked after.

White Horse ★
Rede Road, Whepstead, IP29 4SS (01284 735760, www.whitehorsewhepstead.co.uk). Open 11am-3pm, 7-11pm Mon-Sat; 11am-3pm Sun. Lunch served 11am-2pm daily. Dinner served 7-9.30pm Mon-Sat.
For 25 years, Gary and Di Kingshott ran the much feted Beehive pub in Horringer, just a few miles away, but when the lease came up for renewal, they decided to buy the freehold of their village pub instead. They reopened the White Horse in autumn 2009 after an extensive refurb, and now serve the same excellent standard of food as before, but in prettier surroundings (the new garden is definitely a big improvement). Expect a good choice of Suffolk specialities on the daily changing menu, and fabulous roasts on Sundays. Kids will love the Tuck Shop's ice-creams and sweets; parents might prefer the local artworks for sale.

Ickworth Hotel & Apartments. See p295.

the middle of rolling Ickworth Park. Most of the 27 rooms are decorated in a modern eclectic style, which manages to combine an atmosphere of informality with a sense of special occasion. There are also 11 apartments in the separate Dower House, and the three-bedroom Butlers Lodge. It's a great place for families – there's a games room-cum-crèche, baby monitoring service, children's teas in the conservatory, and plenty of activities on hand, including a swimming pool, tennis courts, an adventure playground, and horses and bikes to ride. The attention to detail is impressive; there's even a supply of wellies and bibs for small guests. Non-parents are well catered for too, though, with pampering available in the upmarket spa and a formal, adult-only restaurant.

Old Piggery
Westley Lane, Horringer, IP29 (01728 638962, www.bestofsuffolk.co.uk/piggery.asp). Rates £495-£595 per week.
With Ickworth Park just around the corner, this is a great place for a couple who want to self-cater. It's compact, stylish and well-kitted out, with underfloor heating throughout, Wi-Fi, a small patio garden and off-road parking nearby.

THE BRECKS
The area known as the Brecks lies north of the A14, and its 370 square miles are divided fairly equally between Suffolk and Norfolk. The land is noticeably underpopulated, with vast areas of open space. It's also one of Britain's driest regions, with warm summers and cold winters, and the open heathland is home to many plants and animals not found elsewhere in the country. For hundreds of years, the area supported a series of vast rabbit warrens – the sandy soil was perfect for burrowing – managed by teams of 'warreners'. The poor soil and low rainfall meant the land had little agricultural value, and the Forestry Commission bought up huge tracts between the two world wars and planted Scots and Corsican pine in regimented lines and blocks. The wood is still felled commercially for timber, but the area has also become a vast recreation centre for outdoor pursuits. The best way to enjoy the Brecks is to get out of the car and into the fresh air.

Thetford Forest ★
The largest of the Forestry Commission areas is Thetford Forest (www.forestry.gov.uk/thetfordforest park), which straddles the county border. There's plenty to do here. Play about by the river in the pretty village of Santon Downham or walk or cycle in the forest (paths and trails of different lengths are indicated with coloured posts). There's something slightly ominous about the way each path and stand of trees looks the same, so pay attention to the signposts as it's laughably easy to get lost.

The main visitor centre is High Lodge Forest Centre (01842 815434, www.forestry.gov.uk/highlodge), off the B1107 near Brandon. Parking costs a hefty £1.60 per hour, but there's a café and picnic area, and you can hire bicycles from Bike-Art (*see p288*) or test your nerve on the high-wires, tarzan swings and zip slides at Go Ape! (0845 643 9215, www.goape.co.uk, closed Mon-Fri Mar, Nov,

all Jan, Dec), the treetop adventure park for teens and adults. Younger children get to run around a fantastic, extensive and free adventure playground. There are red squirrels and four types of deer (muntjac, roe, fallow and red) to spot. Rishbeth Wood and Lynford Arboretum lie within Thetford Forest, for those who prefer their wooded areas to have a wider variety of trees.

For the town of Thetford, in Norfolk, see p151.

Brandon
Next to the Little Ouse (the county border), Brandon used to make its money from rabbit fur and flints. As with most of the settlements around the Brecks, significant expansion after World War II to deal with the housing shortage in London, and the arrival of thousands of Americans to work at nearby US airbases have had a marked impact on the identity of the original town. It's not really a tourist destination – and is a notorious bottleneck if you're heading north on the A1065 – but you can take a walk by the river or visit the small Brandon Heritage Centre (07882 891022, www.brandonsuffolk.com/brandon-heritage-centre.asp), which tells the story of the town from the Stone Age to the present. It's open weekends and bank holidays from Easter to October. Market days are Thursday and Saturday.

Just south of town, Brandon Country Park (www.brandonsuffolk.com/brandon-country-park. asp) used to be the grounds of a country house. Parking here is free, and there's a visitor centre and tearoom. There are pretty walks by the lake from where you can see the old house (now a private nursing home), and the former vegetable garden has been turned into an ornamental walled garden.

Between Brandon and Thetford is Elveden, which is bisected by the busy A11. There's not much to see here except the large Elveden Estate Farm Shop (01842 890223, www.elveden.com) which sells meat, fish, cheese, bread, cakes, fruit and vegetables and other goods. There's also an excellent restaurant (*see p298*).

Lakenheath & Mildenhall
Visitors to the area can't fail to notice the regular boom of fighter aircraft flying overhead; nearby Mildenhall and Lakenheath have both had sizeable US Air Force bases for more than half a century. RAF Lakenheath started off as a decoy airstrip in World War II to fool German bombers into thinking they had hit RAF Mildenhall (established 1930), but it's now the biggest USAF base in the UK. Apart from a pretty church, Lakenheath itself doesn't have much else of note. Extensive postwar housing development has an American flavour, with bungalows and houses sitting in borderless grassy front yards and road designs that favour the car over the pedestrian. Both airbases used to put on occasional event days that were popular with families and aviation enthusiasts, but 9/11 put an end to all that. Tours for groups are still permitted on certain conditions, but must be planned several months in advance. Check the websites for details: www.lakenheath.af.mil and www.mildenhall.af.mil.

Mildenhall town is also heavily influenced by the nearby US airbases, and has a lot of mid 20th-century London Overspill development to boot. That said, the town centre has retained some of its identity as a medieval market town (Friday is market day), and although parts of it feel neglected and unloved, there are a few things worth visiting.

St Mary's Church is one of the largest and most impressive in Suffolk; step inside to look at the hammerbeam roof and a curious series of carved grotesques (take binoculars to see them properly). The church is open from 8.30am to 3.30pm daily, but you can get a key from Stubbings Shoe Shop in the High Street (expect to leave a deposit) if you arrive later.

The Mildenhall Museum (01638 716970, www.mildenhallmuseum.co.uk, closed Mon, Tue, Sun, all Jan, Feb) on King Street tells the story of the Mildenhall Treasure; 34 items of Roman silver found by a ploughman in 1942. He didn't realise the significance of his discovery and stored it on his mantelpiece until a visitor alerted him a few years later. The hoard is now in the British Museum, although Mildenhall Museum has some convincing replicas. In addition, there are displays about the history of the town and the nearby airbase.

West Stow

Archaeological remains have proved that the Romans were well established on the edges of the Fens. The Anglo-Saxons later settled in the area, replacing the Romans' stone buildings with their wooden ones. At West Stow, a test for possible commercial gravel and sand extraction in the 1960s led to the discovery of an Anglo-Saxon village of some size, protected for centuries by a sand dune that had formed on top of the site. Most of the original timber buildings had rotted away, but a rich variety of artefacts was found, and Dr Stanley West and his team decided to test their theories of Anglo-Saxon building methods (gleaned from studying tools and the foundations of the buildings) by reconstructing part of the village. It's now a popular tourist attraction, West Stow Anglo-Saxon Village (see p295).

If, after wallowing in the past, you're craving something more up to date, drop in at the Chimney Mill Galleries (01284 728234, http://chimney.easearch.info, closed Mon, Tue, Sun) in the village, where Hilary and Adrian Smurfitt exhibit the work of more than 40 artists.

A riverside footpath leads from the Anglo-Saxon village to Fullers Mill Trust Garden (0870 803 0248, www.fullersmillgarden.org.uk), a lovely seven-acre garden around the site of the old Fulling Mill, which once made felt cloth. It's open in the afternoon on the fourth Sunday of the month from April to September. Antiques hunters should head to Risby Barn (01284 811126, www.risbybarn.co.uk), where furniture, china, bric-a-brac, garden ornaments and all sorts of other collectable treasures are sold from a 15th-century thatched barn. There's a tearoom too.

Where to eat & drink

Elveden Estate Café Restaurant ★

Elveden, IP24 3TQ (01842 890223, www.elveden.com). Open 9.30am-5pm daily.
This eaterie beside the farm shop serves great local food at reasonable prices. Light bites include sandwiches, soups and salads, while more substantial dishes (own-made burgers, shepherd's pie, fish and chips) are given a little gourmet twist; bangers and mash is beautifully presented, with a rocket salad and fresh herbs. All main courses cost under a tenner, and there's a good children's menu too. The large courtyard terrace is always packed in the summer, and there's a little woodland trail that's perfect for kids who need to let off steam. Free Wi-Fi is offered too.

Red Lion

The Street, Icklingham, IP28 6PS (01638 711698, www.lockwoodrestaurants.co.uk). Open noon-3pm, 6-11pm Tue-Sat; noon-3pm Sun. Lunch served noon-2.30pm Tue-Sun. Dinner served 6.30-8.30pm Tue-Sat.
In an area that lacks decent restaurants, this neat, thatched country pub set well back from the road is a real treat. Chef and landlord Ed Lockwood (with front-of-house partner Aileen Towns) serve real ales in the large bar and a mix of local food and international-style dishes in the dining area. At lunch, the focus is on simple fare (own-made burgers, antipasti plates); in the evening the dishes get heartier and more varied. Prices are very reasonable for the quality.

Where to stay

Culford Farm Cottages

Culford, IP28 6DS (01284 728334, www.culfordfarmcottages.co.uk). Rates £300-£500 per week for 4 people; £500-£700 per week for 6 people. No credit cards.
There are three imaginatively converted buildings (sleeping four, four and six) on this lovely farm. Each has been kitted out to a high standard and has its own hot tub as well as access to a heated outdoor pool. There are good walks from the hamlet and, with West Stow, Lackford Lakes and the whole of Thetford Forest to explore, there's plenty to do.

Olde Bull Inn

The Street, Barton Mills, IP28 6AA (01638 711001, www.bullinn-bartonmills.com). Rates £85-£150 double incl breakfast.
This old coaching inn just outside Mildenhall has been given a modern revamp that has not destroyed its historic charm. Bright wallpaper in bold colours and statement furniture give a stylish feel to the 14 rooms.

Tuddenham Mill ★

High Street, Tuddenham, IP28 6SQ (01638 713552, www.tuddenhammill.co.uk). Rates £185-£395 double incl breakfast.
There are 15 minimalist-chic bedrooms in this beautiful 18th-century watermill set in gorgeous countryside. The huge loft suites are the most spectacular, with soaring ceilings, bespoke furniture and great views. But the other rooms, whether in the main mill or two extensions, are very striking; think luxurious bathrooms, vast beds and all mod cons. Breakfast features fresh fruit, yoghurt and own-baked cakes and a variety of imaginative cooked dishes.

SUFFOLK

Thetford Forest. See p297.

Further Reference

USEFUL ADDRESSES
www.english-heritage.org.uk
www.enjoyengland.com
www.heritageopendays.org.uk
www.metoffice.gov.uk
www.nationalrail.co.uk
www.nationaltrust.org.uk
www.ordnancesurvey.co.uk
www.sustrans.org.uk
www.thegoodpubguide.co.uk
www.thetrainline.com
www.visitbritain.com
www.ukworldheritage.org.uk

COAST & COUNTRYSIDE
www.babo.org.uk Balloon operators.
www.bbc.co.uk/coast
www.bcusurf.org.uk
www.british-trees.com Woodland Trust.
www.britsurf.co.uk
http://camping.uk-directory.com
www.classic-sailing.co.uk
www.countrysideaccess.gov.uk
www.cpre.org.uk Campaign for the
Protection of Rural England.
www.goodbeachguide.co.uk
www.lidos.org.uk Lidos in the UK.
www.nationalparks.gov.uk
www.nationaltrail.org.uk
www.naturalengland.org.uk
www.ngs.org.uk National Gardens
Scheme.
www.paddleandsail.com Cornwall
sailing school.
www.river-swimming.co.uk
www.ramblers.org.uk
www.rya.org.uk Royal Yachting
Association.
www.sas.org.uk Surfers Against
Sewage.
www.surfingwaves.com
www.ukclimbing.com
www.uk-golfguide.com
www.walkingbritain.co.uk
www.walking-routes.co.uk
www.wildaboutbritain.co.uk
www.wildswimming.com

HOLIDAY HOME COMPANIES
Best of Suffolk 01728 638962,
www.bestofsuffolk.co.uk.
The Big Domain 01326 240028,
www.thebigdomain.com. Big houses.
Boutique Boltholes 0845 094 9864,
www.boutiqueboltholes.co.uk.
Landmark Trust 01628 825925,
www.landmarktrust.org.uk.
The Little Domain 01326 240028,
www.thelittledomain.com. Small,
romantic one bedroom properties.
Suffolk Secrets www.suffolk-
secrets.co.uk Luxury holiday cottages
and accommodation.

Superior Cottages
www.superiorcottages.co.uk.
Unique Home Stays 01637 881942,
www.uniquehomestays.com.

SUFFOLK

TOURIST INFORMATION OFFICES
More details can be found at Visit
Suffolk's website: **www.visit-
suffolk.org.uk**. The main tourist
offices are listed below.
Beccles 01502 713196.
Bury St Edmunds 01284 764667.
Felixstowe 01394 276770.
Ipswich 01473 258070.
Lowestoft 01502 533600.
Newmarket 01638 667200.

USEFUL ADDRESSES
www.discoversuffolk.org.uk
Discover Suffolk.
www.eastanglianlife.org.uk
Museum of East Anglian Life.
www.golfsuffolk.org.uk
www.invitationtoview.co.uk Suffolk-
based properties of interest, open to
the public on pre-booked tours only.
www.suffolk.gov.uk
www.suffolkmuseums.org
www.suffolkonboard.com Suffolk
Public Transport Information.
www.suffolktouristguide.com
Suffolk Tourist Guide.
www.wizardballoons.co.uk Hot-air
balloon rides over Suffolk.

FICTION
Matilda Betham-Edwards Six books
set in Suffolk. Betham-Edwards was
born in Suffolk, the daughter of a
clergyman.
Ronald Blyth Akenfield A fictionalised
social history of Suffolk; also a 1974
movie.
Bernard Cornwell Richard Sharpe
novels Based on the life of John
Shipp, born in Saxmundham.
Frederick Forsyth The Fourth Protocol
A Cold War spy thriller partly set in
Suffolk, which was made into a film
starring Michael Caine and Pierce
Brosnan.
Esther Freud The Sea House A love
story set in a seaside village in Suffolk.
PD James Unnatural Causes Detective
novel set in Suffolk.
Norah Lofts (1904-1983) The 'Suffolk
Trilogy' (The Town House, The House
at Old Vine, and The House at Sunset)
spans 600 years in the history of a
house. Bless This House tells the story
of an Elizabethan house in Suffolk.

Lofts lived in Bury St Edmunds
until her death in 1983.
Alexander McCall Smith
La's Orchestra Saves the World
Unusually for a McCall Smith novel,
set in Suffolk.
Julie Myerson Something Might
Happen A macabre murder takes
place in an unnamed Suffolk
seaside town.
George Orwell A Clergyman's
Daughter. Based on his experience
as a young man in Southwold. Orwell
(an alias of Eric Blair) took his name
from the Suffolk river and lived at
Montague House in Southwold;
there is a plaque on the house
commemorating his residence.
Arthur Ransome We Didn't Mean to
Go to Sea Set on the River Orwell.
Ruth Rendall Born in Aldeburgh,
Rendall wrote the Wexford series of
novels, as well as some non-fiction
concerning her home county.
WG Sebald The Rings of Saturn A
fictional account of walking through
East Anglia, Sebald's home for more
than 20 years.

NON-FICTION
Henry Crabb Robinson A Suffolk
resident, he was the first war
correspondent, reporting the
Peninsula War for the Times.
George Ewart Evans Ask the Fellows
Who Cut the Hay A classic picture of
Suffolk's rural past revealed through
conversation dating back to Chaucer.
Charlie Haylock A Rum Owd Dew! A
guide to the Suffolk dialect; humorous
and a bit barmy.
Mark Mower Foul Deeds and
Suspicious Deaths around Suffolk;
Zeppelin Over Suffolk Mower writes
predominantly Suffolk-based murder
mysteries.
AS Neill founded his alternative school,
Summerhill, in Leiston, and wrote an
eponymous book on it.
Nikolaus Pevsner Suffolk A classic
exploration of Suffolk's architecture
Julian Tennyson Suffolk Scene
Tennyson documents his travels and
experiences through 1930s Suffolk.

POETRY
Robert Bloomfield Rural Tales, News
from the Farm Born and raised on a
farm in Honington, Suffolk, Bloomfield's
early experiences of rural life provided
inspiration for his later works.

FILM
Iris (Richard Eyre, 2001) Beach scenes
filmed in Southwold.

The Scouting Book for Boys (Tom Harper, 2009) Filmed in Suffolk.
Witchfinder General (Michael Reeves, 1968) Parts of this 1960s cult movie were filmed at Suffolk's Kentwell Hall, which also featured in *Tomb Raider* and Terry Jones's film version of *Wind in the Willows*.

TV

Grandpa in My Pocket (2009-present) A CBeebies children's show filmed in Aldeburgh and Southwold. The pre-schooler comedy is set in a fictional seaside town called Sunnysands.
Lovejoy (1986-1994) The TV drama about a British antiques dealer was filmed in various locations around Suffolk.
Space Cadets The reality-TV series was filmed in Rendlesham Forest, although the producers pretended to the participants that they were in Russia.
Whistle and I'll Come to You (1968) BBC series based on the ghost stories of MR James, set around Felixstowe.

MUSIC

Benjamin Britten Born in Suffolk, Britten found fame all over the world as an accomplished pianist, violinist, composer and conductor. In 1948 he set up the still-popular Aldeburgh Festival, an arts festival devoted mainly to classical music.

ART

John Constable A large proportion of Constable's work was inspired by, and depicts, the Suffolk countryside. He was born and raised in Dedham Vale, and his landscapes of the area are so highly regarded that the area is now known as 'Constable Country'.
Thomas Gainsborough The 18th-century Suffolk-born painter produced several landscapes of the area in his early years, before moving on to Bath and London to concentrate on portraits.

FOOTPATHS/WALKS

The Angles Way
www.discoversuffolk.org.uk An 80-mile walk along the Waveney Valley between Broads at Lowestoft and the Brecks at Thetford. One of the best waterside walks in Britain.
East Suffolk Line Walks
www.eastsuffolklinewalks.co.uk A series of linear walks that lead from each station on the Ipswich to Lowestoft line, and which take you across stunning countryside.
Stour Valley Path
www.discoversuffolk.org.uk A 60-mile route that follows the valley sides of the River Stour.
Suffolk Coast Path
www.discoversuffolk.org.uk A 50-mile walk from Felixstowe to Lowestoft,

taking you through some of the most characteristic landscapes of the Suffolk Coast and Heath Area of Outstanding Natural Beauty.

NORFOLK

TOURIST INFORMATION CENTRES

More details can be found at www.visitnorfolk.co.uk. The main tourist offices are listed below.
Aylsham *01263 733903.*
Cromer *0871 200 3071.*
Downham Market *01366 383287.*
Great Yarmouth *01493 846346.*
King's Lynn *01553 763044.*
Norwich *01603 213999.*
Wymondham *01953 604721.*

USEFUL ADDRESSES

www.bbc.co.uk/norfolk
www.epd24.co.uk Norfolk news and sport.
www.literarynorfolk.co.uk
www.norfolkbroads.com/travel Public transport information.
www.norfolkbroadscycling.co.uk
www.norfolk.gov.uk Norfolk County Council official website.
www.norfolkchurches.co.uk Fantastic round-up of Norfolk churches.

FICTION

John Betjeman *A Mind's Journey to Diss, East Anglian Bathe, Lord Cozens Hardy, Norfolk.*
Daniel Defoe *Robinson Crusoe* Defore travelled through Great Yarmouth for his *Tour Through the Whole Island of Great Britain*, and used it as the point from where Crusoe sets off.
Charles Dickens *David Copperfield* Great Yarmouth is a key location.
Charles Kingsley *Hereward the Wake* Set in the Fens.
Sir Henry Rider Haggard *Colonel Quaritch, VC* Set around Norfolk.
Edward Storey writes fiction and non-fiction based on both his personal experiences and on fenland legends and superstitions.

NON-FICTION

Benjamin Armstrong His diary details life in the Norfolk village of Dereham in the mid 19th century.
Adrian David Hoare *Standing up to Hitler: Story of Norfolk's Home Guard and Secret Army* Popular account of Norfolk's contribution to the war effort.
Nikolaus Pevsner *Norfolk 1: Norwich & North East, Norfolk 2: South & West* Classic explorations of Norfolk's architecture.
Matthew Rice *Building Norfolk* An illustrated history of Norfolk's architecture.

POETRY

John Clare *The Fens* Description of the fenland.
RN Currey *King's Lynn* Currey refers to King's Lynn as the 'town that history could have made into a city'.
Sir Walter Raleigh *Walsingham.*
Michael Rivière *On Lady Katherine Paston's Tomb at Oxnead* Contemplates the demise of Oxnead hall and the Paston Family.
John Taylor *A Very Merry-Wherry-Ferry Voyage* Recalling stopping at Cromer on a journey from London to York, and being mistaken for pirates by the townsfolk of the day.

FILM

Atonement (Joe Wright, 2007) Walpole St Andrew was used as a stand-in for Dunkirk.
Full Metal Jacket (Stanley Kubrick, 1971) The Norfolk Broads were used instead of Vietnam in many scenes.
Lara Croft: Tomb Raider (Simon West, 2003) Elveden Hall was used as a location for the Croft family home.
Shakespeare in Love (John Madden, 1998) Holkham Hall and Estate feature in the last scene.

TV

Dad's Army (1968-1977) Much of *Dad's Army* was filmed in Thetford Forest.
Kingdom (2007-2009) Various locations around Swaffham and Wells-next-the-Sea were used in filming.

MUSIC

The Darkness *Black Shuck* The name of this song is a reference to the ghostly black dog, said to roam Norfolk.
Ernest John Moeran Moeran spent the early part of his career as a composer compiling and arranging over 150 traditional Norfolk folk songs, often sitting in country pubs waiting for old men to start singing and noting them down. This work heavily influenced his later compositions.

ART

John Alfred Arnesby Brown His landscape paintings include *View of Norwich (from the Bungay Road) 1934-1935.*
John Sell Cotman Part of the Norwich school, Sell Cotman is known for his paintings of the area, such as *Norwich Market-Place 1809.*

FOOTPATHS/WALKS

Peddars Way & Norfolk Coast Path *www.nationaltrail.co.uk/peddarsway.*
Weavers Way *www.ramblers.org.uk/info/paths/name/w/weavers.htm* A 56 mile walk from Cromer to Great Yarmouth.

Norfolk Thematic Index

INDEX

Norfolk A-Z Index

INDEX

INDEX

Where to eat & drink in Norfolk

INDEX

Where to stay in Norfolk

INDEX

Suffolk Thematic Index

Suffolk A-Z Index

INDEX

INDEX

Where to eat & drink in Suffolk

INDEX

Where to stay in Suffolk

Advertisers' Index

Please refer to relevant sections for addresses and/or telephone numbers